高级商务英语系列教材

总主编：叶兴国　王光林

U0743351

国际商法教程

International Business Law:
Chinese and Comparative Perspectives

主　编：黄　洁

编　者：黄　洁　蔡建敏　李沣桦
　　　　汪　成　徐建生　叶华英

审　校：Brian M. Meyer（美）

外语教学与研究出版社
FOREIGN LANGUAGE TEACHING AND RESEARCH PRESS
北京 BEIJING

图书在版编目 (CIP) 数据

国际商法教程 / 黄洁主编；黄洁等编 . –– 北京 ：外语教学与研究出版社，2017.10
（2022.11 重印）

高级商务英语系列教材 / 叶兴国，王光林总主编
ISBN 978-7-5135-9533-9

I. ①国… II. ①黄… III. ①国际商法 – 教材 IV. ①D996.1

中国版本图书馆 CIP 数据核字 (2017) 第 256499 号

出 版 人　王　芳
项目负责　万健玲
责任编辑　万健玲
执行编辑　赵兴华
版式设计　付玉梅
封面设计　孙敬沂　高　蕾
出版发行　外语教学与研究出版社
社　　址　北京市西三环北路 19 号（100089）
网　　址　http://www.fltrp.com
印　　刷　北京虎彩文化传播有限公司
开　　本　787×1092　1/16
印　　张　25.5
版　　次　2017 年 10 月第 1 版　2022 年 11 月第 10 次印刷
书　　号　ISBN 978-7-5135-9533-9
定　　价　79.90 元

购书咨询：（010）88819926　电子邮箱：club@fltrp.com
外研书店：https://waiyants.tmall.com
凡印刷、装订质量问题，请联系我社印制部
联系电话：（010）61207896　电子邮箱：zhijian@fltrp.com
凡侵权、盗版书籍线索，请联系我社法律事务部
举报电话：（010）88817519　电子邮箱：banquan@fltrp.com
物料号：295330001

记载人类文明
沟通世界文化
www.fltrp.com

总　序

　　我国的英语教育为国家的经济社会发展作出了重要贡献。正如一位著名英语教育家所言，在经济、科技等领域的每一项重大进展背后，都活跃着一批接受过英语专业教育的人才。但是，随着经济社会的迅猛发展和变化，特别是随着英语专业教育规模的急剧扩大和教育改革的不断深入，英语专业教育在赢得喝彩的同时也招来了诟病。从20世纪90年代开始，英语教育界的有识之士开始关注英语专业人才的培养模式问题。他们关注的焦点是英语专业应该培养什么样的人、培养多少人和怎么培养人。

　　英语教育家关注的问题，就其本质而言，与经济学家关注的问题不谋而合。根据微观经济学的基本理念，在一个竞争性的市场环境中，对处于微观经济层面的企业来讲，生产什么和生产多少是一个关系到企业存亡的问题；而怎么生产则是一个事关企业得失的问题。微观经济学的这一基本理念并不是说怎么生产的问题不重要，对一个企业来说和生产什么、生产多少一样，怎么生产也是一个事关存亡的问题。但是，在一个竞争性的市场环境中，生产什么和生产多少的问题相对企业的存亡来说，是一个快变量。如果生产什么和生产多少搞错了，怎么生产的问题解决得再好，产品销不出去，企业也会即刻倒闭；而怎么生产的问题相对企业的存亡来说，是一个慢变量。如果生产什么和生产多少搞对了，就会有时间和条件去逐步解决怎么生产的问题。当然，如果怎么生产的问题长期得不到解决，企业也会在市场竞争中失败，但对企业经营者的决策来讲，解决怎么生产的问题与解决生产什么和生产多少的问题有完全不同的含义。

　　如果仅仅从在竞争性环境下发展的角度来观察英语专业管理层的决策过程，微观经济学的这一基本理念同样也适用于英语专业人才的培养。目前，全国开设英语专业的高校超过一千所，在校接受英语专业教育的学生有数十万之多。社会对英语专业人才的接受程度呈两极分化态势。一方面，2011年凤凰网和中国雅虎等媒体发布的"中国高校本科毕业生薪酬TOP24排行榜"和"高校真实就业率排行"表明，一批以外语特别是英语教育见长或英语教育特色鲜明的外语院校的毕业生在就业和薪酬方面表现出了强大的竞争力（全国外语院校协作组的 17 所外语院校仅占全国本科高校总数的 1.5%，进入上述两个榜单的外语院校协作组成员分别有 8 所和 5 所，分别占上榜院校的 33.3% 和 25%）；另一方面，社会上传言英语专业毕业生就业难，2010 年教育部阳光高考网站把英语专业列为失业量较大、就业率持续走低，且薪资较低的高失业风险型专业。

这组数据向我们昭示：在竞争日趋激烈的环境下，企业界由于没有解决好"生产什么和生产多少"问题而遭淘汰的案例也有可能在英语教育界出现；在英语专业教育规模不断扩大的形势下，千校一面的培养模式亟待改变；环境已经发生了历史性的深刻变化，英语专业人才培养模式应该随着环境的变化而变化。

举办英语专业教育的众多所高等院校尽管是在同一个专业名称下实施教育，但这些院校在国家投资力度、学科门类、隶属关系、办学形式、办学体制、科研规模、所处区域、办学水平和服务层次等方面存在巨大差异。每一所高校都可以用矩阵式的排列从两个维度来描述类与型。即使同一类型院校，其办学基础和办学特色也往往各有不同。不同的大学有不同的历史和现实条件，发展轨迹和基础条件各不相同，所处的地域也不同，在长期的办学过程中都已形成了各自的特色和优势。每个学校只要找准自己的角色定位，选择适合自己的办学模式和发展路径，办出特色，办出水平，用特色鲜明的人才培养规格去满足各种细分的市场需求，就能赢得地位和尊敬。反之，如果培养出来的英语专业人才规格千校一面，势必造成英语专业人才的积压和贬值，对国家、院系和学生个人的发展都会产生不利的影响。

为顺应各种历史性的深刻变化，各英语院系的专业人才培养模式正呈现多样化和个性化发展的趋势。改革方案虽各有特色，但就其方向而言，大致可以分为两类：有的院系主张主动为社会经济发展服务，培养复合型英语人才；有的主张正本清源，回归英语学科本质。各种主张都是各院系理性思考和选择的结果，都有其内在合理性，并没有高低优劣之分。英语专业人才培养模式的多样化和个性化发展是在英语专业培养规模急剧扩大、社会需求发生深刻变化的形势下，英语院系为求生存求发展科学定位的必然结果。

特别值得一提的是，对外经济贸易大学、广东外语外贸大学和上海对外经贸大学等院校从 20 世纪 90 年代就开始了商务英语专业建设的探索。在中国国际贸易学会商务英语研究会的指导下，已经连续举办 11 届全国高校商务英语研讨会。2006 年，教育部批准目录外试办商务英语本科专业。最近公布的《普通高等学校本科专业目录》（修订一稿）把商务英语作为"比较成熟、布点较多、稳定性好、共识度高的专业"之一列入了"基本专业"。这是教育管理高层根据变化了的形势对英语专业教育作出的适应性调整。先目录外试办，再进入基本专业的过程反映了教育管理高层积极慎重的科学态度。在一千余所高校开办英语专业本科教育，数十万在读英语专业本科生，国际贸易蓬勃开展的情况下，开办商务英语本科专业的必要性和重要性不言而喻。

目前，全国开办商务英语本科专业的院校不断壮大，开设商务英语课程的院校更是越来越多。为了给举办商务英语本科专业和开设商务英语课程的院系提供一套高质量的商务英语系列教材，我们应外研社之邀，组织编写了"高级商务英语系列教材"。在编写过程中，我们力求体现以下编写原则：

1. 与教育主管部门的战略意图相吻合。国家教育主管部门要求高校创新人才培养模式，提升人才培养质量的战略意图和《国家中长期教育改革和发展规划纲要（2010－2020年）》提出的"适应国家经济社会对外开放的要求，培养大批具有国际视野、通晓国际规则、能够参与国际事务和国际竞争的国际化人才"的要求应该在教材中有所体现。

2. 适应国际商务领域发生的深刻变化。加入世界贸易组织后，我国的商务领域已经发生了深刻变化。以国际贸易为例，贸易的运行对象已经从传统的货物贸易向包括货物贸易、服务贸易和知识贸易在内的"大贸易"拓展；贸易政策涉及的范围已经从过去单纯的贸易政策领域向与贸易有关的领域延伸；贸易的体制环境已经从封闭的国内贸易体制环境向开放的全球多边贸易体制环境转型；国家对贸易的管理方式已经从传统的内外贸分割管理向内外贸一体化管理的方向转变；贸易运行平台已经从传统的贸易运行平台转向数字化、信息化和网络化的贸易运行平台。本系列教材力求克服教材内容严重滞后于国际商务实际的通病。

3. 涵盖国际商务的方方面面。国际商务可以定义为任何为了满足个人和机构需要而进行的跨境商业交易。具体地说，国际商务包括商品、资本、服务、人员和技术的国际流通，知识产权（包括专利、商标、技术、版权等）的跨境交易，实物资产和金融资产投资，用于当地销售或出口的来料加工或组装，跨国的采购和零售，在国外设立仓储和分销系统等。商务包括贸易和投资以及与贸易和投资有关的方方面面。就所涉及的领域而言，商务涉及了营销、金融、税收、结算、跨国公司管理、对外直接投资、知识产权、电子商务、贸易法律和跨文化交际等领域。

就所涉及的行业而言，商务不仅包括贸易和投资，还包括运输、旅游、银行、广告、零售、批发、保险、电信、航空、海运、咨询、会计等行业。上述领域和行业都是商务的组成部分，上述环境下使用的英语就是商务英语。

"高级商务英语系列教材"包括《高级综合商务英语》（1-2）、《高级商务英语听说》（1-2）、《高级商务英语写作》、《新编进出口英语函电》、《高级商务笔译》、《高级商务口译》、《高级商务英语阅读》（1-2）、《国际商务导论》等。

本系列教材的编写人员都是具有长期英语教学经验的教师，主要来自上海对外经贸大学、上海交通大学、上海外国语大学、澳大利亚新南威尔士大学、香港中文大学、澳大利亚昆士兰大学等院校。

本系列教材主要供高等院校英语专业、商务英语专业和财经类专业学生使用，也可供具有相当英文水平的商界从业人员使用。

中国国际贸易学会商务英语研究会的专家学者对本系列教材的编写给予了诸多帮助。在此，向关心和帮助本系列教材编写的所有人员一并表示衷心感谢。

由于编者水平有限，书中难免有不妥甚至错误之处。我们恳切地希望大家提出宝贵意见。

叶兴国

Foreword

1

Professor Jie Huang's *International Business Law: Chinese and Comparative Perspectives* is a most welcome addition to the comparative literature on Chinese commercial and public international trade law and its counterparts in common and civil law countries, including those inspired by international organizations. The compared legal institutions are as diverse as business organizations, contracts, payment methods, transportation and insurance law (on the private law side), and sanitary and phytosanitary measures, trade remedies and dispute settlement (on the public law side).

Despite jingoistic calls for a "winner takes all trade law" (public and private), the fair and thoughtful trading world, and especially that which belongs to a "free trade" or "customs union" agreement, is experiencing a growing need for uniform or harmonized international law. In the field of contracts alone, French legislators found it necessary in 2016 to abandon (more than two centuries old) *Code Civil* contractual requisites that made a fair and cost-effective trade unaffordable in their European Union trade with partners whose legal institutions had been modernized. The same modernization is now being considered by Spain and a growing number of Central and South American, African and Asian developing countries.

Why is this comparative law book so helpful? It is true that comparative law is at its best when it is legally, culturally and socio-economically contextual. Yet, such a comparison of the many private and public legal institutions selected by Professor Huang and her contributing authors would take many thick volumes and numerous years to complete. On the other hand, a textual comparison of a legal norm (a term that includes concepts or definitions, principles and rules) and its local and foreign counterparts can contribute much to the selection of the most cost-effective and fair norm. Consider, for example, the comparison of the Chinese and United States definitions of contract discussed in Chapter 5.

The Chinese definition was found in Article 2 of its Contract Law (one of the many definitional sources possible): "[A]n agreement establishing, modifying and terminating the civil rights and obligations between the objects of equal footing, that is, between natural persons, legal persons or other organizations." In contrast, the US definition chosen was Restatement (Second) of Contracts Section1: "A contract is a promise or set of promises, for breach of which the law gives remedy, or the performance of which the law in some way recognizes as a duty." Clearly, the Chinese definition requires, as did the *Code Civil* of 1804 , Robert Pothier' Treatise on Obligations and numerous Hugo Grotius's essays, two or more common wills to bound any of the parties to the other(s). In contrast, the Restatement (Second) allows individual promises to be binding on the promisor (or offeror) from the moment of their issuance. With this datum, the task of the drafter of a modernized commercial law of contracts is to ascertain which of the two definitions better enables the most common and significant of contemporary contractual or voluntary promises, such as the firm or irrevocable promises used throughout the financial, commercial and industrial and construction sectors? And what sources of local and foreign law can best be adjusted to make that result possible? As it happens, the Restatement's rule is by far the most enabling as it also allows fully fledged contracts as well as their individual promises to bind. Yet, some local judicial, customary or doctrinal law may make that result or part of it possible. After examining the relevant texts, Professor Cai Jianmin's Chapter 4 concluded that at least one type of firm or irrevocable offer commonly in use in leading financial and commercial marketplaces is also binding in China. When a Chinese promisor/seller states: "I will hold this offer open until June 15." He cannot revoke his promises until then. This is bound to be good news for the many contemporary industries and sectors that rely on these firm or irrevocable promises, options, and derivative rights, among others, to carry on successfully their important businesses.

As a long time student of comparative commercial law, I am most grateful for Professor Huang and her contributing scholars for this pioneering, stupendous comparative law effort.

Dr. Boris Kozolchyk, Founding Director & Director of Research, at the National Law Center for Inter-American Free Trade (NLCIFT) and Evo DeConcini Professor of Law at the James E. Rogers College of Law at the University of Arizona has over 40 years of experience working in areas and issues related to international, banking and commercial law. He has extensive experience as an advisor and team leader to governments and international organizations.

2

This book fills what had been a very serious hole in materials available for students of international business law. Too often international business law books take a two-tier approach—focusing only on the relationships and interactions between just one legal system and the international business law legal order. Such an approach fails to convey the multiple approaches that any practitioner of international business law will immediately encounter in real life—that multiple legal systems are invariably involved in international business transactions. This book in contrast takes a multi-tiered approach, albeit from an initial Chinese perspective, covering more than one legal system and its relationship to the international business legal order. Critically, it does so through comparisons between two of the most important legal systems in international business—the American and Chinese legal systems. Students and other readers of this book will gain valuable insights from the book's selection of those two systems, ones with such different economic, political, cultural and legal contexts. Furthermore, not only will students gain understanding of international business law in those two systems, but the exercise of mastering the comparative challenges, provided so well through the pedagogical approaches in this book, will permit students to then apply lessons learned from the book when seeking to understand other legal systems approaches and interactions with the international business legal order. This book truly reflects a much needed approach to the field. I am sure that instructors, students and researchers will find the book of immense help as they seek to understand and develop international business law.

Professor Colin B. Picker is the Dean of School of Law at the University of Wollongong in Australia. He is also a founder of the Society of International Economic Law (the SIEL), the only global academic organization for international economic law. He served as founding executive vice president (the actual leader) of the organization from its founding in 2007 to 2014.

Preface

This book surveys important legal issues in international business transactions from Chinese and comparative perspectives. It compares Chinese law with UN conventions, WTO agreements, trade usages, and relevant US law[1] in the fields of business organizations, contracts, payment methods, transportation, insurance, tariff, technical barriers to trade, sanitary and phytosanitary measures, trade remedies, services, investment, intellectual property and dispute settlement. It also analyzes how China reforms its trade and investment law according to high-standard bilateral investment treaties or free trade agreements. Further, it provides rich quiz questions, case studies, and suggested further readings. This book is useful and essential for Chinese students who want to gain an in-depth understanding of the legal aspects of international business and for foreigners who are interested in learning Chinese law and doing business in China. This book can also be used as a textbook for junior or senior undergraduate students majoring in business English, law, economics, management, international economics and trade or other related disciplines. In sum, it features a broad scope, comparative approach, and Chinese perspective.

Broad Scope

Traditionally, Chinese international business transactions are mainly imports and exports of goods. Therefore, most of International Business Law books published in China focus on law for international sale of goods. Moreover, Chinese academics generally support the dichotomy between International Business Law and International Economic Law: the former regulates horizontal legal relationship (e.g. sale between two equal entities) while the latter governs vertical legal relationship (e.g. anti-dumping investigations initiated by a government body against an enterprise). Consequently, books

---

1   This book compares Chinese law with the US law because the US is regarded as the most important trade partner with China.

on International Business Law in China traditionally focus on the horizontal legal relationship, especially on law for international sale of goods. This scope is too narrow and should be expanded for three reasons.

First, in the 21st century, trade in services and investment has become one of the major driving forces for the world economy. For example, in value-added terms, the importance of trade in goods tumbled, from 71% of world exports in 1980 to just 57% in 2008, because of the increasing weight of services in the production of traded goods.[1] In 2014, China became the top one hosting state for foreign investment and one of the top three home states for outbound investment.[2] In 2017, China drove up investment outflows from East Asia and made it the second largest investor in the world for the first time.[3] Therefore, the scope of International Business Law should be expanded from trade in goods to trade in services and investment.

Second, international trade practitioners need to deal with both horizontal and vertical legal relationship almost in every import and export transaction. They need to negotiate contracts with sellers/buyers, shipping companies, insurance companies and banks. They also have to conduct custom clearance, comply with sanitary and phytosanitary requirements, and may request a government agency to impose trade remedies against their foreign business competitors. Not only trade in goods, trade in services and investment also involve both horizontal and vertical legal relationships. Therefore, the book needs to provide students with a complete picture of international business law at the both vertical and horizontal level.

Third, outside of China, many leading International Business Law books cover both vertical and horizontal legal relationship in international business transactions.[4] Besides subjects for international sale of goods, these books

---

1 *Emerging Economies Arrested Development*, The Economist (Oct. 4th 2014). See also generally Jeremy Rifkin, *The Third Industrial Revolution: How Lateral Power Is Transforming Energy, the Economy, and the World* (2011).

2 World Investment Report 2014, UNCTAD.

3 World Investment Report 2017, UNCTAD.

4 E.g. Ray August, Don Mayer & Michael Bixby, *International Business Law: Text, Cases, and Readings* (6th ed. 2013); John Shijian Mo, *International Commercial Law*, (5th ed, 2013); Richard Schaffer, Filiberto Agusti & Beverley Earle, *International Business Law and Its Environment* (2008); and Peter Gillies & Gabriël Moens, *International Trade and Business: Law, Policy and Ethics* (1998).

also include subjects such as trade in services, investment, and intellectual properties.

Therefore, this book discusses laws regulating both vertical and horizontal legal relationships in dispute resolution, business organizations, contracts, sale of goods, trade in goods, trade in services, investment and intellectual property. It arranges subjects in the following sequence:

International Business Law	
Chapter 1	Introduction to International Business Law
Chapter 2	Dispute Settlement (litigation and arbitration in both domestic and international tribunals)
Chapter 3	Business Organizations (sole proprietorship, partnership, corporation, limited liability company, and branch office)
Chapter 4	Contract Law (CISG, common law and Chinese law)
Chapter 5	International Sale of Goods (Incoterms®, payment and trade finance, transportation, and maritime insurance)
Chapter 6	Trade in Goods (Tariff, TBT, SPS, and Trade Remedies)
Chapter 7	Trade in Services (banking law, securities law, insurance law, and telecommunication services law)
Chapter 8	Foreign Investment Law (law for inbound and outbound investment in China)
Chapter 9	Intellectual Property (copyright, patent, trademark and unfair competition)

Moreover, different from most of other International Business Law books, this book purposefully puts Dispute Settlement right after the Introduction chapter, so as to help students better understand cases discussed in the rest of the books. This special arrangement is based upon the chief editor's years of teaching experience. International business law is to regulate merchants' day-to-day transactions, where disputes frequently occur. If Dispute Settlement is taught at the end of the course, students do not have enough opportunities to appreciate how it can play out in real-world cases. In contrast, if it is learned at the beginning of the course, students can better practice it in almost every case study in the rest of the course. Nonetheless, lecturers can choose to teach Dispute Settlement at the end of the course if they prefer.

Comparative Approach

In most chapters, this book conducts a comparative study among Chinese law, US law and international law. This approach helps students to explore the convergence and divergence of business law in the contexts of economic globalization. It assists students in evaluating common-law and civil-law (or socialist-law) approaches to regulate international business. Importantly, the comparative insights of this book also come from its formidable team of authors. All the authors contributing to this book have common-law and civil-law education background, and many have taught or practiced law in different jurisdictions. Therefore, this book benefits Chinese who want to expand business into global marketplaces and foreigners who want to do business in China.

Chinese Perspective

This book highlights Chinese law regulating international business. It helps contribute to fill the gap of the current leading English International Business Law books that do not cover Chinese law. It analyzes the most recent development of international business law concerning China, such as cases decided by WTO, ICSID and Chinese courts, new bilateral investment treaties and free trade agreements concluded by China, and China's recent reform of trade and investment law. It is written in original legal English but with an easy-to-understand approach.

Class Design

This book can be used for one semester and requires 54 teaching hours. Every chapter may take six teaching hours. Lecturers may consider using universal design for learning to select the teaching contents and determine the teaching hours to align with the various needs of their students. For example, students may be divided into groups representing lawyers from civil law or common law, or Chinese companies or US companies to analyze the differences and similarities between different legal systems. Lecturers can also require students to finish the quizzes in the book before the class so that in class students can practice what they have learned rather than just take notes and memorize those notes after class. The cases and the Suggested Further Reading in the book are generally freely available online. Therefore, lecturers may also adopt blended teaching methods to combine classroom and online teaching.

Acknowledgement

This book is made possible partly through the financial support from the Shanghai English Model Course and the Model Course for Foreign Students both supported by the Shanghai Education Commission and the Shanghai University of International Business and Economics. The final editing of this book is finished at the University of New South Wales (UNSW) Faculty of Law in Australia. We also grateful for the facilities provided by the UNSW and the Chinese International Business and Economic Law Initiative.

Author Profiles

Chief Editor:

HUANG Jie: S.J.D., Duke University School of Law (2010); Senior Lecturer at University of New South Wales Faculty of Law; Foreign Research Fellow, Max Planck Institute for Comparative and International Private Law (2009); Arbitrator at the Shanghai International Arbitration Center and Hong Kong International Arbitration Center, Member of Chartered Institute of Arbitrators Australia/UK; Qualified as a PRC lawyer.

- Authored Chapter 1 Introduction to International Business Law, Chapter 2 Dispute Settlement, Chapter 5 sections of Incoterms® and International Marine Insurance, and Chapter 8 Investment Law

Other Authors (Sorted by surname alphabet):

CAI Jianmin: LL.M., Shanghai Maritime University (1985); Associate Professor of Shanghai University of International Business and Economics School of Law; Visiting researcher at Ryukoku University Japan (1997) and Royal Melbourne Institute of Technology Australia (2000); Visiting Professor at Albany Law School and Touro Law School the US (2013); Qualified as a PRC lawyer.

- Authored Chapter 4 Contract Law

LI Fenghua: Ph.D., China University of Political Science and Law (2012) and University of Glasgow (2015); Shizi Research Fellow, Renmin University of China School of Law; Visiting Researcher, University of Copenhagen (2016-2017); Qualified as a PRC lawyer.

- Authored Chapter 5 section of Payment and Chapter 6 Trade in Goods

WANG Cheng: LL.M., the University of Michigan Law School (2004); Executive Director and Head of Legal for Greater China at Morgan Stanley; Admitted to the bar of the State of New York and qualified as a PRC lawyer.

- Authored Chapter 5 section of International Transportation and Chapter 7 Trade in Services

XU Jiansheng: LL.M., the University of Michigan Law School (2004); Partner, Sphere Logic Partners; Member, All China Lawyers Association Intellectual Property Committee; Of Counsel, Beijing Wan Hui Da Intellectual Property Law Firm and Wan Hui Da Intellectual Property Agent; Member of the Executive Committee & Asia Pacific Regional Representative, Lawyers Associated Worldwide; Admitted to the Chinese bar.

- Authored Chapter 9 Intellectual Property

YE Huaying: J.D., Case Western Reserve University School of Law (2006); Senior Legal Counsel, head of Greater China Legal Department, Dan and Bradstreet; Admitted to the bar of the State of Ohio and qualified as a PRC lawyer.

- Authored Chapter 3 Business Organizations

The authors have tried their best to present and analyze international business law from Chinese and comparative perspectives. They are very grateful for the supports from the reviewer and the editors. All errors remain to be our own. In case you have any suggestions for improvement, please contact the Chief Editor Huang Jie at humility_us@hotmail.com. All comments are highly appreciated.

Contents

Chapter 1   Introduction to International Business Law ·······························1

Chapter 2   Dispute Settlement ··· 27

Chapter 3   Business Organizations································· 75

Chapter 4   Contract Law ··· 111

Chapter 5   International Sale of Goods: Incoterms®, Payment, Transportation and

Insurance ···167

Chapter 6   Trade in Goods: Tariff, TBT, SPS, and Trade Remedies ··············215

Chapter 7   Trade in Services·································259

Chapter 8   Foreign Investment Law ···································289

Chapter 9   Intellectual Property ································325

Index of Acronym ································382

Chapter 1

Introduction to International Business Law

This chapter provides the basic concepts in International Business Law and prepares students to start the journey of learning International Business Law from the following four aspects:

Part 1 defines International Business Law.

Part 2 discusses international persons: states and their subdivisions, international organizations, business associations, and natural persons.

Part 3 presents the sources of International Business Law.

Part 4 compares the major legal systems in the world.

■ Learning Objectives

By the end of this chapter you should:

- Understand what International Business Law is.
- Know what international persons are involved and their roles in international business transactions.
- Comprehend the different sources of International Business Law.
- Know the features of the Civil Law System, the Common Law System, and the Islamic Law System.

■ Key Terms

Civil Law System	International Business Law
Code	International Trade Custom
Common Law System	Most-Favored-Nation Treatment
Economic Integration	National Treatment
Economic Union	Precedent
Free Trade Area	Source of law

Part 1   What is International Business Law?

International Business Law, also called International Commercial Law, is the body of law that regulates cross-border business transactions.

International Business Law regulates both horizontal and vertical legal relationships.

Horizontal legal relationship is the relationship between the equals, such as a seller and a buyer. Horizontal legal relationship is governed by private law. Vertical relationship refers to the relationship between an inferior and a superior, for example, the relationship between an importer and a customs or an investor and a government agency that licenses business. Vertical relationship is governed by public law. International business transactions involve both horizontal and vertical legal relationships and therefore consist of both private and public law.

For example, trade in goods involves both horizontal and vertical legal relationship if an importer wants to import goods from A country to B country:

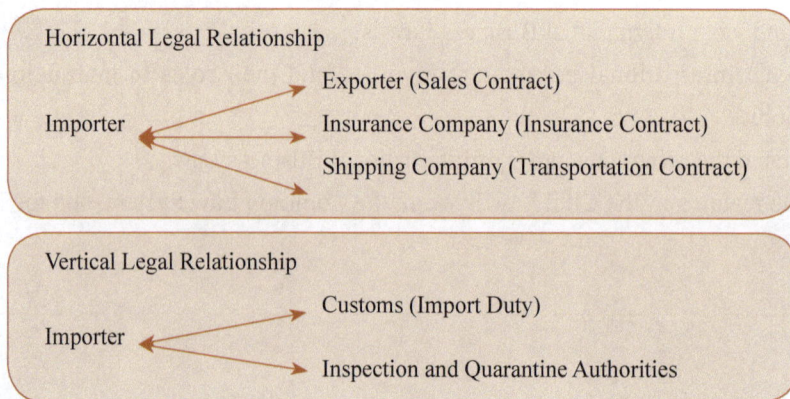

Horizontal Legal Relationship

Importer → Exporter (Sales Contract)
Importer → Insurance Company (Insurance Contract)
Importer → Shipping Company (Transportation Contract)

Vertical Legal Relationship

Importer → Customs (Import Duty)
Importer → Inspection and Quarantine Authorities

If a foreign investor plans to establish a joint venture with a Chinese company in China, the investor also needs to deal with both horizontal and vertical legal relationship:

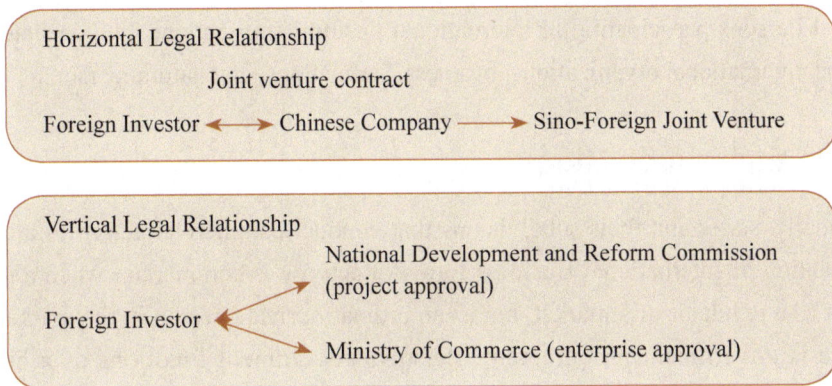

Horizontal Legal Relationship

Joint venture contract

Foreign Investor ←→ Chinese Company ——→ Sino-Foreign Joint Venture

Vertical Legal Relationship

Foreign Investor →→ National Development and Reform Commission (project approval)

Foreign Investor ←→ Ministry of Commerce (enterprise approval)

What is "international"?

A business transaction is international if the subject, the object, or the contents of the transaction is "across" national borders or involves more than two countries:

- Subject: parties have their nationalities, places of registration or places of business in different countries;
- Object: the subject matter of the transaction is located outside the country or countries of one or more parties; or
- Content: goods, services, persons, or intellectual property move across national borders.

What is "business"?

The term "business" or "commercial" should be interpreted broadly so as to cover matters arising from all relationships of a business nature, whether contractual or not. According to United Nations Commission on International Trade Law (UNCITRAL) Model Law on International Commercial Arbitration[1] and Chinese law[2], relationships of a business nature include, but not limited to, the following transactions: any trade transaction for the supply or exchange of goods or services; distribution agreement; commercial representation or agency; factoring; leasing; construction of works; consulting; engineering; licensing; investment; financing; banking; insurance; exploitation agreement or concession; joint venture and other forms of industrial or business co-operation; carriage of goods or passengers by air, sea, rail or road; environmental pollution, marine accident, and dispute over ownership.

---

1 Footnote 2 of UNCITRAL Model Law on International Commercial Arbitration.
2 Article 2 of the Notice of the Supreme People's Court on Implementing the 1958 New York Convention on Recognition and Enforcement of Foreign Arbitral Awards.

Part 2　International Persons

International Persons participating in international business transactions include states and their subdivisions, international organizations, business associations, and natural persons.

States and their subdivisions

- Traditionally, states and their subdivisions that conduct commercial activities are subject to the regulation of International Business Law. An activity is commercial when a government acts, not as a regulator of a market, but as an ordinary private person in the market. A typical example is government procurement. Because government functions as a buyer in the procurement process, its activity should be considered commercial.

- International Business Law also governs states and their subdivisions even when they exercise market regulatory authority. With the development of WTO and Free Trade Agreements (FTA), now members of WTO and FTA should follow international law established by WTO and FTAs even when regulating their own domestic markets. For example, members should provide national treatment and most-favored-nation treatment to business persons from such member countries' treaty partners. Further, such member countries' domestic legislation and judicature should satisfy the transparency and non-discrimination requirements.

International organizations

According to the United Nations Charter, there are two kinds of international organizations: (1) public or intergovernmental organizations (IGOs) and (2) private or nongovernmental organizations (NGOs).[1]

1. Public or intergovernmental organizations (IGOs)

IGOs are organizations set up by two or more countries to carry out activities of common interest. The IGOs discussed below play an influential role in developing International Business Law.

(1) The United Nations (UN)

The most important IGO is the UN. It was founded in 1945 after the Second World War by 51 countries committed to maintaining international peace and security, developing friendly relations among nations and promoting social progress, better living standards and human rights.

1　Article 71 of United Nations Charter.

(The Dumbarton Oaks Conference)

(The San Francisco Conference)

From September 21to October 7 , 1944, representatives of China, the United Kingdom, and the United States convened at Dumbarton Oaks, a mansion in Georgetown, near Washington, D.C. the US, to draft proposals for a United Nations Charter.

On April 25 , 1945, delegates of 50 nations met in San Francisco for the United Nations Conference on International Organization. The delegates drew up the 111-article Charter, which was adopted unanimously on June 25, 1945 in the San Francisco Opera House. The next day, they signed it in the Herbst Theatre auditorium of the Veterans War Memorial Building.

The United Nations Officially came into existence on October 24, 1945, when the Charter had been ratified by China, France, the Soviet Union, the United Kingdom, the United States and by a majority of the other signatories. October 24 is now celebrated each year as the United Nations Day.

Due to its unique international character and the powers vested in its founding Charter, the United Nations can take action on a wide range of issues and provide a forum for its 193 member countries[1] to express their views, through the General Assembly, the Security Council, the Economic and Social Council and other bodies and committees. The work of the United Nations reaches every corner of the globe. Although best known for peacekeeping, peacebuilding, conflict prevention and humanitarian assistance, the United Nations also regulates international business through the following organs.

a. The United Nations Commission on International Trade Law (UNCITRAL) [2]

UNCITRAL was established by the United Nations General Assembly by its Resolution 2205 (XXI) of December 17, 1966 "to promote the progressive harmonization and unification of international trade law." UNCITRAL formulates modern, fair, and harmonized rules on business transactions of a horizontal legal relationship. UNCITRAL work includes: (1) drafting

---

1   The statistics are up to July 1, 2016.

2   UNCITRAL website: http://www.uncitral.org .

conventions[1], model laws[2] and rules[3] which are acceptable worldwide; (2) providing legal and legislative guides and recommendations of great practical value[4]; (3) updating information on case law and enactments of uniform commercial law[5]; (4) offering technical assistance in law reform projects; (5) holding regional and national seminars on uniform commercial law.

b. The World Bank Group

The World Bank Group incorporates five closely associated entities that work collaboratively to regulate and enhance the world economy: the International Bank for Reconstruction and Development (IBRD), the International Development Association (IDA), the International Finance Corporation (IFC), the Multilateral Investment Guarantee Agency (MIGA), and the International Center for Settlement of Investment Disputes (ICSID).

---

1 UNCITRAL Conventions includes the United Nations Convention on the Carriage of Goods by Sea (1978), the United Nations Convention on Contracts for the International Sale of Goods (1980), the United Nations Convention on Independent Guarantees and Stand-by Letters of Credit (1995), the United Nations Convention on the Assignment of Receivables in International Trade (2001), the United Nations Convention on the Use of Electronic Communications in International Contracts (2005), the United Nations Convention on Contracts for the International Carriage of Goods Wholly or Partly by Sea (2008).

2 UNCITRAL Model Laws includes UNCITRAL Model Law on International Commercial Arbitration (1985), Model Law on International Credit Transfers (1992), UNCITRAL Model Law on Procurement of Goods, Construction and Services (1994), UNCITRAL Model Law on Electronic Commerce (1996), Model Law on Cross-border Insolvency (1997), UNCITRAL Model Law on Electronic Signatures (2001), UNCITRAL Model Law on International Commercial Conciliation (2002), and Model Legislative Provisions on Privately Financed Infrastructure Projects (2003).

3 UNCITRAL Rules includes UNCITRAL Arbitration Rules (1976, revised in 2010), UNCITRAL Conciliation Rules (1980), and UNCITRAL Notes on Organizing Arbitral Proceedings (1996).

4 A legislative guide aims to provide a detailed analysis of the legal issues in a specific area of the law, proposing efficient approaches for their resolution in the national or local context. Legislative guides do not contain articles or provisions, but rather recommendations. Legislative Guides are developed by the UNCITRAL Working Groups and subsequently finalized by the UNCITRAL Commission in its annual session. UNCITRAL has adopted the following legislative guides: UNCITRAL Legislative Guide on Privately Financed Infrastructure Projects (2000), UNCITRAL Legislative Guide on Insolvency Law (2004), UNCITRAL Legislative Guide on Secured Transactions (2007), UNCITRAL Legislative Guide on Secured Transactions: Supplement on Security Rights in Intellectual Property (2010).

5 Case Law on UNCITRAL Texts (CLOUT, http://www.uncitral.org/uncitral/en/case_law.html) includes case abstracts in the six United Nations languages on the United Nations Convention on Contracts for the International Sale of Goods (CISG) (Vienna, 1980) and the UNCITRAL Model Law on International Commercial Arbitration (1985).

Figure1: The World Bank Group[1]

WORLD BANK	The **International Bank for Reconstruction and Development (IBRD)** lends to governments of middle-income and creditworthy low-income countries.
IDA	The **International Development Association (IDA)** provides interest-free loans— called credits— and grants to governments of the poorest countries.
IFC International Finance Corporation World Bank Group	The **International Finance Corporation (IFC)** is the largest global development institution focused exclusively on the private sector. It helps developing countries achieve sustainable growth by financing investment, mobilizing capital in international financial markets, and providing advisory services to businesses and governments.
MIGA	The **Multilateral Investment Guarantee Agency (MIGA)** was created in 1988 to promote foreign direct investment into developing countries to support economic growth, reduce poverty, and improve people's lives. MIGA fulfills this mandate by offering political risk insurance (guarantees) to investors and lenders.
	The **International Centre for Settlement of Investment Disputes (ICSID)** provides international facilities for conciliation and arbitration of investor-State disputes.

c. International Monetary Fund (IMF)

IMF is a specialized agency of the United Nations but has its own charter, governing structure, and finances. It was initiated in 1944 at the Bretton Woods Conference and formally created in 1945. The IMF promotes international monetary cooperation and exchange rate stability, facilitates the balanced growth of international trade, and provides resources to help members in balance of payments difficulties or to assist with poverty reduction. The IMF supports its members by providing:

- policy advice to governments and central banks based on analysis of economic trends and cross-country experiences;
- research, statistics, forecasts, and analysis based on tracking of global, regional, and individual economies and markets;
- loans to help countries overcome economic difficulties;

---

1   http://web.worldbank.org

- concessional loans to help fight poverty in developing countries;
- technical assistance and training to help countries improve the management of their economies.

Currently, it has 188 member countries including China. Its members are represented through a quota system broadly based on their relative size in the global economy. Unlike the General Assembly of the United Nations, where each country has one vote, decision making at the IMF was designed to reflect the position of each member country in the global economy. The quota that an IMF member country has determines its voting power in the IMF. When a country joins the IMF, it is assigned an initial quota in the same range as the quotas of existing members of broadly comparable economic size and characteristics. Quotas are denominated in Special Drawing Rights (SDRs), the IMF's unit of account. The largest member of the IMF is the US, with a current quota of SDR 42.1 billion (taking 17.69% of the total SDR), and China has a current quota of SDR 9.5 billion (taking 4% of the total SDR).

d. World Intellectual Property Organization (WIPO)

WIPO is a specialized agency of the United Nations. It was created in 1967 with the adoption of the Stockholm Convention (formally the Convention Establishing the World Intellectual Property Organization). It aims "to promote the protection of intellectual property throughout the world through cooperation among states and, where appropriate, in collaboration with any other international organization."[1] WIPO currently has 189 member states including China[2] and functions as the global forum for IP services, policy, information and cooperation.

WIPO currently administers 26 international IP treaties ranging from patents, copyright, trademarks, industrial designs to geographic indications[3]. These treaties constitute the most important international IP system and have significant impact upon domestic IP laws of its member states.

WIPO helps use IP for development. WIPO Committee for Development Cooperation Related to Industrial Property and WIPO Committee for Development Cooperation Related to Copyrights and Neighboring Rights are responsible for helping countries modernize their national intellectual property laws, helping them develop administrative agencies for supervising those laws, and helping them increase, both in quantity and quality, the creation of new intellectual property by

---

1   Article 3.i of the Convention Establishing the World Intellectual Property Organization.

2   The statistics are up to June 14, 2017.

3   Such as Beijing Treaty on Audiovisual Performances; Berne Convention for the Protection of Literary and Artistic Works; Paris Convention for the Protection of Industrial Property; Patent Law Treaty; Rome Convention for the Protection of Performers, Producers of Phonograms and Broadcasting Organizations; WIPO Copyright Treaty; WIPO Performances and Phonograms Treaty; Protocol Relating to the Madrid Agreement Concerning the International Registration of Marks, and etc. For a complete list of WIPO administered treaties, see http://www.wipo.int/treaties/en/.

their own nationals. For example, WIPO significantly helped the legislation of Chinese IP laws in 1990s.

WIPO provides dispute resolution services for the protection of IP. Since 1994, the WIPO Arbitration and Mediation Center has offered Alternative Dispute Resolution options, in particular arbitration and mediation, for resolving contractual[1] or non-contractual IP disputes[2] between private parties. In 1999, WIPO's Arbitration and Medication Center was selected by the Internet Corporation for Assigned Names and Numbers to resolve bad-faith cybersquatting of trademarks.

(2) World Trade Organization (WTO)[3]

The WTO officially commenced on January 1,1995 under the Marrakesh Agreement, replacing the General Agreement on Tariffs and Trade (GATT). WTO is a global IGO that aims to supervise and liberalize international trade between states. The total membership of the WTO is 164.[4] Different from the UN, the members of the WTO comprise both sovereign states and separate customs territories that determine their own trade policies.[5] The WTO serves four basic functions[6]:

- to implement, administer, and carry out the WTO Agreement and its annexes;
- to act as a forum for ongoing multilateral trade negotiations;
- to serve as a tribunal for resolving disputes; and
- to review the trade policies and practices of member countries.

a. What is WTO's legal framework?

The WTO's legal framework includes multilateral agreements that all WTO members have ratified, such as General Agreements on Trade in Goods (GATT), Agreement on Trade-Related Investment Measures (TRIMs), General Agreement on Trade in Services (GATS), and Agreement on Trade-Related Aspects of Intellectual Property Rights (TRIPS). It also includes plurilateral agreements which are voluntarily concluded by some WTO members, and bind those members only. Plurilateral agreements are not binding on the WTO members who do not conclude them.

---

1 Eg., patent and software licenses, trademark coexistence agreements, distribution agreements for pharmaceutical products, and etc.
2 Eg., patent infringement.
3 WTO website: http://www.wto.org.
4 The statistics are up to June 9, 2017.
5 Article XII, para. 1 of Agreement Establishing the World Trade Organization (1994).
6 Article 3 of Agreement Establishing the World Trade Organization.

Figure 2: The WTO Legal Frameworks

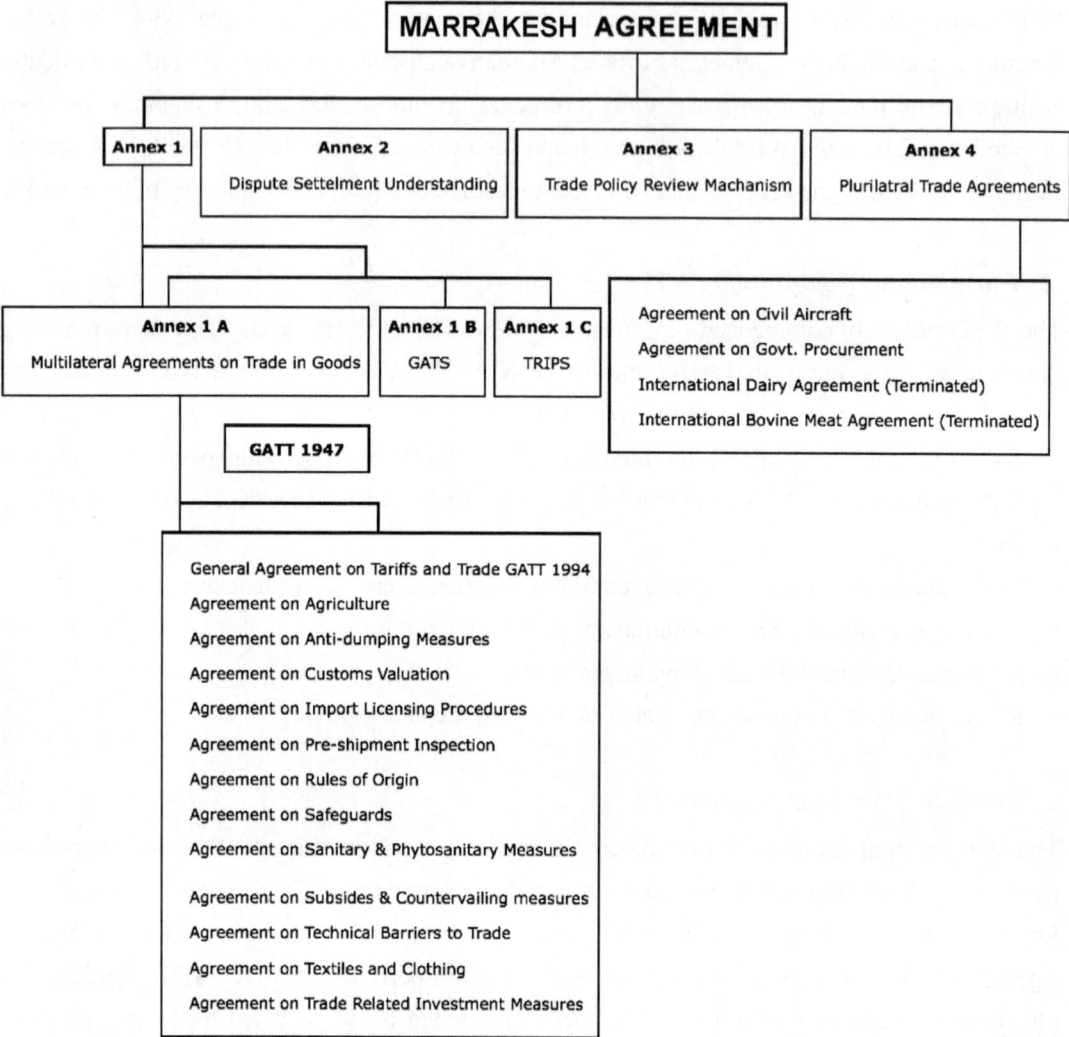

```
                          MARRAKESH AGREEMENT

   Annex 1          Annex 2                Annex 3                 Annex 4
              Dispute Settelment     Trade Policy Review      Plurilatral Trade
              Understanding          Machanism                Agreements

                                                    Agreement on Civil Aircraft
   Annex 1 A            Annex 1 B    Annex 1 C      Agreement on Govt. Procurement
   Multilateral         GATS         TRIPS         International Dairy Agreement (Terminated)
   Agreements on                                   International Bovine Meat Agreement (Terminated)
   Trade in Goods

        GATT 1947

        General Agreement on Tariffs and Trade GATT 1994
        Agreement on Agriculture
        Agreement on Anti-dumping Measures
        Agreement on Customs Valuation
        Agreement on Import Licensing Procedures
        Agreement on Pre-shipment Inspection
        Agreement on Rules of Origin
        Agreement on Safeguards
        Agreement on Sanitary & Phytosanitary Measures

        Agreement on Subsides & Countervailing measures
        Agreement on Technical Barriers to Trade
        Agreement on Textiles and Clothing
        Agreement on Trade Related Investment Measures
```

b. What is WTO's structure?

The WTO has five main organs: (1) a Ministerial Conference, (2) a General Council that also functions as the WTO's Dispute Settlement Body and Trade Policy Review Body, (3) a Council for Trade in Goods, (4) a Council for Trade in Services, and (5) a Council for Trade-Related Aspects of Intellectual Property Rights.

Figure 3: The WTO Organizational Structure

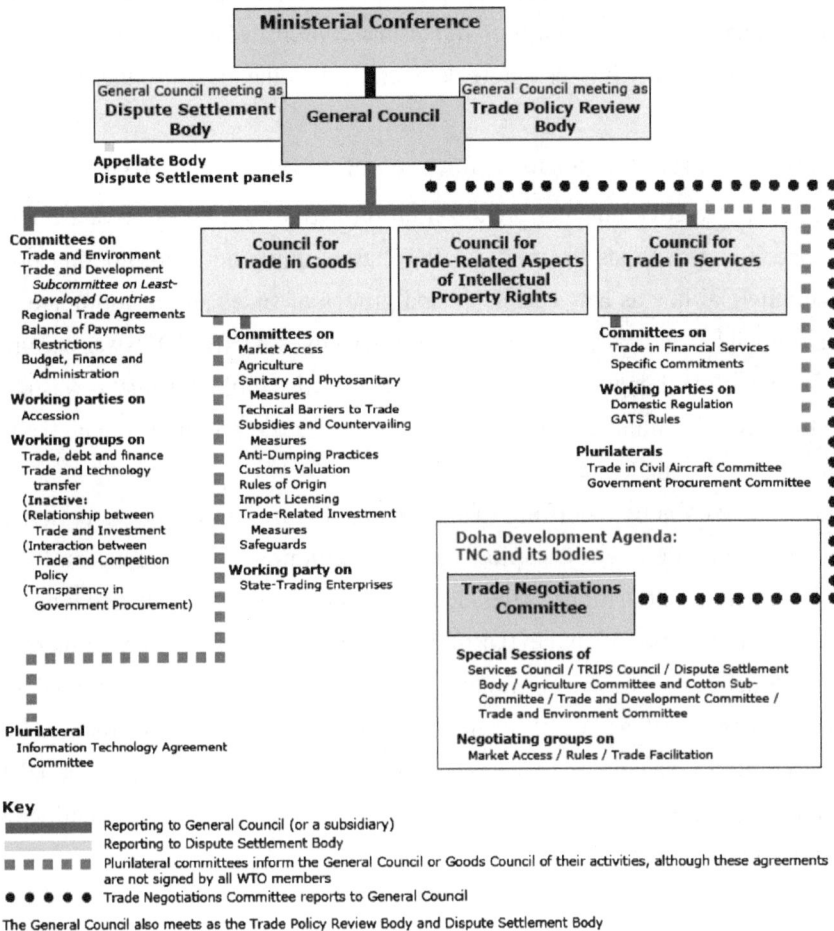

Ministerial Conference

General Council meeting as **Dispute Settlement Body**

General Council

General Council meeting as **Trade Policy Review Body**

Appellate Body
Dispute Settlement panels

Committees on
Trade and Environment
Trade and Development
Subcommittee on Least-Developed Countries
Regional Trade Agreements
Balance of Payments Restrictions
Budget, Finance and Administration

Working parties on
Accession

Working groups on
Trade, debt and finance
Trade and technology transfer
(Inactive:
(Relationship between Trade and Investment
(Interaction between Trade and Competition Policy
(Transparency in Government Procurement)

Council for Trade in Goods

Committees on
Market Access
Agriculture
Sanitary and Phytosanitary Measures
Technical Barriers to Trade
Subsidies and Countervailing Measures
Anti-Dumping Practices
Customs Valuation
Rules of Origin
Import Licensing
Trade-Related Investment Measures
Safeguards

Working party on
State-Trading Enterprises

Council for Trade-Related Aspects of Intellectual Property Rights

Council for Trade in Services

Committees on
Trade in Financial Services
Specific Commitments

Working parties on
Domestic Regulation
GATS Rules

Plurilaterals
Trade in Civil Aircraft Committee
Government Procurement Committee

Doha Development Agenda: TNC and its bodies

Trade Negotiations Committee

Special Sessions of
Services Council / TRIPS Council / Dispute Settlement Body / Agriculture Committee and Cotton Sub-Committee / Trade and Development Committee / Trade and Environment Committee

Negotiating groups on
Market Access / Rules / Trade Facilitation

Plurilateral
Information Technology Agreement Committee

Key
Reporting to General Council (or a subsidiary)
Reporting to Dispute Settlement Body
Plurilateral committees inform the General Council or Goods Council of their activities, although these agreements are not signed by all WTO members
Trade Negotiations Committee reports to General Council

The General Council also meets as the Trade Policy Review Body and Dispute Settlement Body

c. How does WTO make decisions?

The decision-making in the WTO continues GATT practices, which is based on consensus. Consensus is the making of a decision by general agreement and in absence of any voiced objection.[1] The WTO describes itself as "a rules-based, member-driven organization—all decisions are made by the member governments, and the rules are the outcome of negotiations among members".[2] The WTO Agreement foresees votes (one-member-one-vote) where consensus cannot be reached in some cases, but the practice of consensus dominates the decision-making process. This seeming well-being, nonetheless, belies the true nature of the problems and challenges the decision-making process.

- **Challenge 1:** The current decision-making process within the WTO implies the risk of deadlock, and in particular the membership's inability to respond legislatively where it

---

1   Para. 2.4., n. 1 of Understanding on Rules and Procedures Governing the Settlement of Disputes (1994).

2   See the official website of WTO.

disagrees with a panel's or the Appellate Body's legal interpretation.

- **Challenge 2:** Consensus also inherently favours the status quo and can make it extremely difficult to achieve change. There is no doubt that consensus has a number of advantages, but it is questionable whether it is also more democratic than the majority rule.[1]

(3) The International Institute for the Unification of Private Law (UNIDROIT) [2]

UNIDROIT is an intergovernmental organization on harmonization of private law. Its purpose is to study needs and methods for modernizing, harmonizing and coordinating private and in particular commercial law as between states and groups of states and to formulate uniform law instruments, principles and rules to achieve those objectives. UNIDROIT was set up in 1926 as an auxiliary organ of the League of Nations. After the demise of the League, it was re-established in 1940 on the basis of a multilateral agreement, the UNIDROIT Statute. Today, UNIDROIT has 63 member states including China.[3]

UNIDROIT's projects include drafting of international conventions[4] and production of model laws. The topics include agency, capital markets, commercial contracts, cultural property, factoring, franchising, international sales, leasing, security interests, succession, transnational civil procedure, and transportation. UNIDROIT Principles of International Commercial Contracts (UNIDROIT Principles), which were firstly published in 1994, amended in 2004 and again in 2010, have been considered as one of the most important model law of international commercial contracts. UNIDROIT Principles serve as a model for national and international legislators, help interpret and supplement existing international instruments, and also function as guide for businesspersons to draft contracts.

(4) The Hague Conference on Private International Law (HCCH) [5]

HCCH, UNIDROIT and the UNCITRAL are considered as "the three sisters" in formulating private law[6]. Different from UNIDROIT and UNCITRAL that help harmonize substantive law and procedure law, the HCCH mainly concentrates on streamlining conflict of laws. The HCCH was formed in 1893 to "work for the progressive unification of the rules of private international law." It has been pursuing this goal by creating and assisting in the implementation

---

1 Claus-Dieter Ehlermann and LotharEhring, *Decision-Making in the World Trade Organization: Is the Consensus Practice of the World Trade Organization Adequate for Making, Revising and Implementing Rules on International Trade?*, Journal of International Economic Law 8(1), 51–75.

2 UNIDROIT website: http://www.unidroit.org/.

3 The statistics are as of January 1, 2014.

4 Eg.,Convention on International Interests in Mobile Equipment (Cape Town, 2001) (including Protocols on Aircraft (2001) and Railway rolling stock (2007) and Space assets (2012); Geneva Securities Convention (Geneva, 2009); and Unidroit Convention on International Factoring (Ottawa, 1988).

5 HCCH's official website: http://www.hcch.net/index_en.php.

6 History and Overview at http://www.unidroit.org/about-unidroit/overview.

of multilateralconventions in both commercial and civil subject matters, such as product liability, road traffic accidents, maintenance, matrimonial or inheritance. As of June 2017, the HCCH has 82 members, including China.

A recent important project accomplished by the HCCH is the Convention of June 20, 2005 on Choice of Court Agreements. States ratifying this Convention agree to recognize and enforce judgments rendered by courts of another signatory state if the dispute was governed by a valid "choice of court" agreement concluded between the parties to the dispute. The goal of this Convention parallels that of the Convention on the Recognition and Enforcement of Foreign Arbitral Awards of 1958: to create the same level of predictability and enforceability for recognition and enforcement of judgments as arbitral awards worldwide[1].

2. Private or nongovernmental organizations (NGOs)

Private or nongovernmental organizations also serve as important platforms for developing International Business Law. The most important nongovernmental organization for international business transactions is International Chamber of Commerce.

(1) International Chamber of Commerce (ICC)[2]

ICC, established in 1919, champions open cross-border trade and investment, the market economy system and global economic integration as a force for sustainable growth, job creation and prosperity. ICC's global network comprises over 6 million companies, chambers of commerce and business organizations in more than 130 countries. It promotes international trade and investment in the following ways[3]:

- **Harmonizing, codifying, and standardizing international business practices**

ICC is not an intergovernmental organization, so it cannot draft or administer treaties or conventions for states. However, it has developed numerous widely-accepted voluntary rules and guidelines to facilitate business and spread good practice. Typical examples include ICC's Uniform Customs and Practice for Documentary Credits (UCP 600) that provides rules used by banks to finance billions of dollars' worth of world trade every year, and ICC Incoterms® rules that stipulates standard international trade definitions used every day in countless contracts to define the responsibilities of buyers and sellers.

- **Advocating trade and investment policy**

Through extensive consultation with member companies via the ICC global network, ICC

---

1 Originally, the HCCH planed to create a broad-scope convention covering jurisdiction and recognition of judgments. As the negotiators were not able to reach a consensus on jurisdiction, the scope of the convention was reduced to jurisdiction and recognition of judgments based on a choice of court agreement between the parties. It has come into force on October 1, 2015.

2 ICC's website is http://www.iccwbo.org.

3 International Chamber of Commerce The World Business Organization in 2013.

develops global business policy views on key issues that affect companies' ability to trade and invest across borders. These views can take the form of ICC policy statements to influence intergovernmental discussions, such as in the UN and the WTO.

- **Resolving international commercial disputes**

The ICC International Court of Arbitration is one of the world's most experienced and renowned international arbitration institutions. The Court is not a court in the judicial sense of the term. The Court's primary role is to administer ICC arbitration[1]. The ICC International Centre for ADR (Amicable Dispute Resolution) has also developed a full range of other dispute resolution rules and services for international commerce such as the ICC ADR Rules, the ICC Rules for Expertise[2], the ICC Dispute Board Rules[3], and the DOCDEX Rules for the settlement of documentary credit disputes.

3. Business organizations and natural persons

States and international organizations mainly function as regulators of international business, except when they conduct commercial activities. As a contrast, business organizations and natural persons are major players in international business. Business organizations, especially multinational enterprises, carry out more international business than natural persons. States and international organizations have adopted domestic or international laws to regulate and to promote business organizations. At the international level, the ICC, the Organization for Economic Cooperation and Development, the International Labor Organization, and the United Nations Commission on Transnational Corporations have each produced codes of conduct for multinational enterprises. However, these codes only have limited influence upon multinational enterprises because they are only suggested guidelines and not compulsory. Business organizations need to obey domestic laws when conducting international business. These laws will be discussed in detail in Chapter 3.

---

1   The ICC International Court of Arbitration does not itself resolve disputes or decide who wins or who loses an arbitration. It does not award damages or even costs. Those are all functions reserved for independent arbitral tribunals appointed in accordance with the ICC Rules of Arbitration. The Court's specific functions under the Rules include: fixing the place of arbitration; assessing whether there is a prima facie ICC Arbitration agreement; taking certain necessary decisions in complex multi-party or multi-contract arbitrations; confirming, appointing and replacing arbitrators; deciding on any challenges filed against arbitrators; monitoring the arbitral process from the filing of the request for arbitration to the notification of the final award to ensure that it proceeds in accordance with the Rules and with the required commitment to diligence and efficiency; scrutinizing and approving all arbitral awards, in the interests of improving their quality and enforceability; setting, managing and, if necessary, adjusting costs of the arbitration, including the ICC administrative expenses and the arbitrators' fees and expenses; and overseeing emergency arbitrator proceedings.

2   Expertise is a way of finding the right person to make an independent assessment on any subject relevant to business operations.

3   Dispute boards are independent bodies designed to help resolve disagreements arising during the course of a contract.

Self Quiz: Indicate whether each of the following statements is true or false.

1. International Business Law only regulates horizontal legal relationship.

2. Horizontal legal relationship is governed by private law.

3. International Business Law deals only with business between states.

4. International business mainly refers to trade in goods.

5. States and their subdivisions are never involved in horizontal legal relationship.

6. UNIDROIT is a UN organ.

7. United Nations Convention on Contracts for the International Sale of Goods (1980) is concluded under the UNCITRAL.

8. ICSID provides arbitration service for state-to-state investment disputes.

9. WIPO's Arbitration and Mediation Center can resolve disputes arising from bad-faith cybersquatting of trademarks.

10. WTO creates a plurilateral trading system.

11. "The three sisters" in formulating private law refers to UN, WTO, and WIPO.

12. The HCCH specializes in harmonizing substantive law.

13. Uniform Customs and Practice for Documentary Credits is drafted by ICC.

Part 3 Sources of International Business Law

Source of law refers to the source (such as a constitution, treaty, statute, or custom) that provides authority for legislation and for judicial decisions. The sources of international business law are foundations where judges obtain rules and use them to decide cases in international or domestic tribunals. These rules include:

- National law
- International agreements
- International custom
- The general principles of law recognized by civilized nations

National law

National law is an important source of international business law. It refers to all statutes regulating international business enacted by a state, and in common-law countries, it also includes judicial decisions in commercial cases. In China, judicial interpretations issued by the Supreme People's Court are also part of national law. Chinese national law concerning international business includes General Principles of Civil Law, Contract Law, Company Law, Law for Chinese Foreign Equity Joint Ventures, Law for Chinese Foreign Contractual Joint Ventures, Law for Wholly Owned Foreign Enterprises, Maritime Law, Insurance Law, Guarantee Law, Trademark Law, Patent Law, Copyright Law, Banking Law, Product Liability Law, Civil Procedure Law, Arbitration Law, etc. National law is limited in governing international business transactions for two reasons:

- National law of a state usually regulates only acts done by subjects who are citizens of the state or performed in its territory. Its jurisdiction upon cross-border business transactions is often limited. For example, whether a national law can govern an illegal act done by its citizens and performed outside of its territory; whether a national law can regulate acts done by a foreigner and performed abroad but harming the interests of a company registered in its territory. These are difficult questions because the extra-territoriality of jurisdiction frequently brings diplomatic and legal controversies.

- National laws in different states are often not the same. For example, national laws may have different requirements for the format of contracts and may set different thresholds for foreign businesspersons to make investment. The prosperity of international business requires harmonization and coordination between national laws.

International agreements

International agreements are the dominant source of international business law. It includes treaties and conventions at global or regional levels.[1] Treaties are legally binding agreements between two or more states. Conventions are legally binding agreements between states sponsored by international organizations, such as the UN, WTO, and UNIDROIT. Both treaties and conventions are binding upon member states because they share a sense of commitment and also because one state fears that if it does not respect its promises, other states will not respect their promises.

1. International agreements regulating horizontal legal relationship

Traditionally, international agreements for business transactions have mainly included those regulating horizontal legal relationship. Very influential conventions include United Nations Convention on Contracts for the International Sales of Goods (1980) and United Nations Convention on the Recognition and Enforcement of Foreign Arbitral Awards (1958). They significantly facilitate international business transactions.

(1) United Nations Convention on Contracts for the International Sales of Goods 1980 (CISG)

The CISG has been recognized as the most successful attempt to unify a broad range of commercial law at the international level. This self-executing convention aims to reduce obstacles

---

1 Other forms include protocol, covenant, exchange of letters and charter.

to international trade, particularly those associated with choice of law issues, by creating even-handed and modern substantive rules governing the rights and obligations of parties to international sales contracts. The CISG was developed by the UNCITRAL in the early 1970s and was signed in Vienna in 1980. Today, it has been ratified by 85 contracting states[1] that account for well over two thirds of international trade in goods, and that represent different legal traditions and diverse economic backgrounds.

The CISG governs international sales contracts if (1) both parties are located in contracting states, or (2) private international law leads to the application of the law of a contracting state (although, as permitted by the CISG, several contracting states including China have declared that they are not bound by the second ground). The autonomy of the parties to international sales contracts is a fundamental theme of the Convention: the parties can, by agreement, derogate from virtually any CISG rule, or can exclude the applicability of the CISG entirely in favor of other law. When the Convention applies, it does not govern every issue that can arise from an international sales contract: for example, issues concerning the validity of the contract or the effect of the contract on the property in (ownership of) the goods sold are, as expressly provided in the CISG, beyond the scope of the Convention, and are left to the law applicable by virtue of the rules of private international law (article 4). Questions concerning matters governed by the Convention but that are not expressly addressed therein are to be settled in conformity with the general principles of the CISG or, in the absence of such principles, by reference to the law applicable under the rules of private international law. The CISG will be further discussed in Chapter 4 of this Book.

(2) United Nations Convention on the Recognition and Enforcement of Foreign Arbitral Awards 1958 (the 1958 New York Convention)

The 1958 New York Convention has been widely recognized as the foundational instrument for international arbitration. Developed by the UNCITRAL, the Convention was adopted by a UN diplomatic conference in 1958 and entered into force in 1959. It seeks to provide common legislative standards for the recognition of arbitration agreements and court recognition and enforcement of foreign and non-domestic arbitral awards. The term "non-domestic" appears to embrace awards which, although made in the state of enforcement, are treated as "foreign" under its law because of some foreign element in the proceedings, e.g. another state's procedural laws are applied (Article 1).

The Convention's principal aim is that foreign and non-domestic arbitral awards will not be discriminated against and it obliges parties to ensure such awards are recognized and generally capable of enforcement in their jurisdiction in the same way as domestic awards are (Article 3). An ancillary aim of the Convention is to require courts of parties to give full effect to arbitration agreements by requiring courts to deny the parties access to court in contravention of their

---

1 The statistics are up to June 1, 2017.

agreement to refer the matter to an arbitral tribunal (Article 2). Recognition and enforcement of an arbitral award may be refused only in limited circumstances under the Convention, such as invalid arbitration agreement, undue process in arbitration proceedings, or the award that has not yet become binding on the parties (Article 5). The 1958 New York Convention will be further discussed in Chapter 2 of the book.

2. International agreements regulating vertical legal relationship

Since the 20th Century and especially after the World War II, the number of free trade agreements (hereinafter "FTA") and bilateral investment treaties (hereinafter "BIT") concluded by states have sharply increased. Both FTAs and BITs help to realize global or regional economic integration. Economic integration refers to trade unification between different states by the partial or full abolishing of tariffs and non-tariff barriers on trade taking place within the borders of each state. Economic integration can be divided into four stages.

Table 1: Stages of Economic Integration

Stage of integration	Reduction or elimination of tariffs and quotas among members	Establishment of common tariff and quota system	Reduction or elimination of restrictions on movements of production factors	Harmonization or unification of economic and social policies and establishment of central financial institutions
Free Trade Area	Yes	No	No	No
Customs Union	Yes	Yes	No	No
Common Market	Yes	Yes	Yes	No
Economic Union	Yes	Yes	Yes	Yes

Most of FTAs establish a free trade area. A free trade area eliminates or reduces trade barriers between its member countries but allows members to freely decide trading policies with states outside of the free trade area. Free trade areas are the first stage of economic integration and the corresponding FTAs take majority of trade agreements.

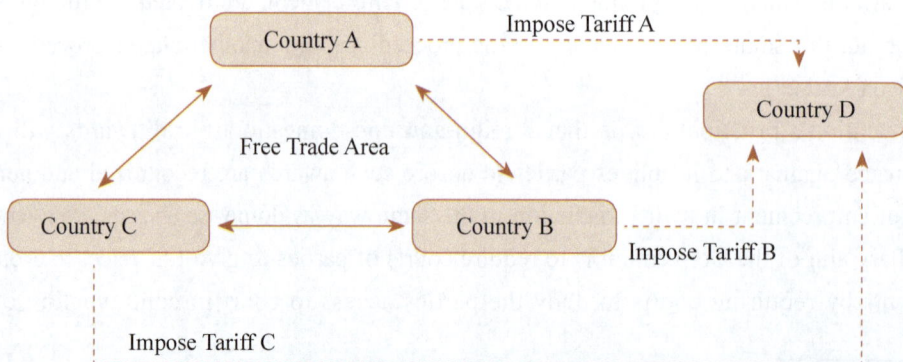

At the global level, the Marrakesh Agreement creates a free trade area (WTO) among its members. At the regional level, states also actively conclude bilateral or multilateral free trade agreements to get more favorable trade conditions than WTO.

For example, Chinese government considers FTAs as a new platform to further opening up to the outside and speeding up domestic reforms. As of June 1, 2017, China has 14 FTAs partners comprising of 23 economies and is currently negotiating 9 FTAs across the globe.[1] The US also regards FTAs as one of the best ways to open up foreign markets to US exporters. As of June 1, 2017, the US has 14 FTAs in force.[2] Cross the Atlantic, the US and the European Union launched negotiations on the Transatlantic Trade and Investment Partnership (hereinafter "TTIP") in June 2013. Although the UK decided to leave the EU by a referendum in 2016, the EU is still the most successful economic integration in the world thus far. European countries have finished the stages of free trade area, customs union, common market, and ultimately established an economic union.

The following compare the contents of FTAs concluded by China and the US.

(1) Trade in goods

FTAs concluded by China generally focus on diminishing tariff barriers in trade in goods. However, most of FTAs concluded by the US require comprehensively eliminating tariffs and emphasizing on removing non-tariff barriers in customs surveillance, inspection and quarantine to improve trade facilitation.

(2) Investment and trade in service

Compared with the FTAs concluded by the US, Chinese FTAs contain fewer commitments in investment and trade in service. The major contents in Chinese FTAs are about trade in goods. In the long run, investment and trade in service need to become an important part of Chinese future FTAs. Moreover, Chinese FTAs regulate market access with a positive list that provides which industries are open to foreign investors. However, the US adopts a negative list, which indicates industries not open to foreign investors. A negative list can provide more certainty and predictability to foreign investors than a positive list. A short negative list also demonstrates that a state is more liberal to foreign investors.

---

1   The 14 FTAs refer to the China-Australia FTA, the China-Switzerland FTA, the China-Costa Rica FTA, the China-Singapore FTA, the China-Chile FTA, the China-ASEAN FTA, the China-South Korea FTA, the China-Iceland FTA, the China-Peru FTA, the China-New Zealand FTA, the China-Pakistan FTA, the mainland of China-Hong Kong CEPA, the mainland of China-Macao CEPA, and the mainland of China-Taiwan ECFA.

2   The 15 FTAs refer to the US-Australia FTA, the US-Bahrain FTA, the US-CAFTA-DR FTA, the US-Chile FTA, the US-Colombia FTA, the US-Israel FTA, the US-Jordan FTA, the US-KORUS FTA, the US-Morocco FTA, the North American FTA, the US-Oman FTA, the US-Panama TPA, the US-Peru TPA, the US-Singapore FTA.

(3) Intellectual property protection

Most of FTAs concluded by the US require TRIPS-plus protection to intellectual property rights. Chinese FTAs still stay within the range of the TRIPS. Moreover, the US FTAs stipulate concrete rights and obligations in intellectual property provisions, while the intellectual property chapters of Chinese FTAs generally contain only declaratory provisions indicating principles and cooperation.

(4) Human rights and trade

FTAs concluded by the US generally relate labour, environmental protection and other human rights issues to trade and investment, whereas FTAs concluded by China separate these issues from trade and investment. Even if Chinese FTAs touch labor and environmental protection, the treaty provisions do not impose binding obligations upon parties.

(5) International investment dispute resolution

China was conservative about investment arbitration. Most of BITs concluded by China in 1990s or before have very restrictive investment arbitration clauses. For example, these clauses limit investment arbitration to the amount of compensation to nationalization/expropriation and only allow ad hoc arbitration. Nowadays China not only attracts inbound foreign investment but also actively encourages outbound investment. The FTAs and BITs concluded by China in recent years also become more and more liberal in investment arbitration. These agreements contain a broad scope of subject matter for arbitration and support ICSID jurisdiction. Compared with Chinese government, its US counterpart has designed more sophisticated investment arbitration procedures and gained richer experience in dealing with such disputes.

The FTAs concluded by China and the US have yet gone beyond the stage of free trade area; in contrast, 28 European countries have concluded Treaties of the European Union and reached the stage of economic union in Europe.[1] Two core functional treaties, the Treaty on European Union (originally signed in Maastricht in 1992 as the Treaty of Maastricht) and the Treaty on the Functioning of the European Union (originally signed in Rome in 1958 as the Treaty establishing the European Economic Community), lay out how the EU operates, and there are a number of satellite treaties which are interconnected with them. Within the union, the EU establishes a European Central Bank, creates the same currency (Euro), and ensures the free movement of people, goods, services, and capital. Outside of the union, the EU maintains common policies on foreign trade and investment.

---

1 The number of EU's member states is up to June 1, 2017.

Figure 4: Economic Union

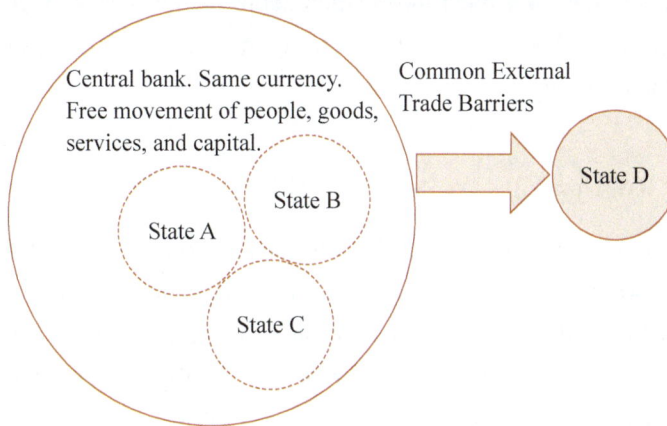

International custom

International custom is "evidence of a general practice accepted as law."[1] International trade custom means the general rules and practices in international trade activities that have become generally adopted through unvarying habit and common use. To show that a general rule or practice has become international custom, two elements must be established:

- Behavioral element: It requires consistent and recurring actions (or lack of action of the custom is one of noninvolvement) by international businesspersons. It must be accepted by a reasonably large number of businesspersons for a period long enough to be recognized by courts as establishing constant and uniform conduct.
- Psychological element: It requires that businesspersons who observe the custom must regard it as binding. That is, they voluntarily select the custom as a binding practice that they must obligatorily follow.

Lex mercatoria (Latin "mercantile law"), also called "the Law Merchant," is an example of international trade custom. It is a system of customary law that developed in Europe during the Middle Ages and regulated the dealings of mariners and merchants in all the commercial countries of the world until the 17th century.[2] It emphasized contractual freedom and alienability of property. A distinct feature of lex mercatoria is that it derives from commercial practice, responds to the needs of the merchants, and is comprehensible and acceptable to the merchants who submitted to it. Since the 20th century, international organizations, instead of merchants, have become the major force in compiling international trade customs. The ICC has published many widely recognized international trade customs, such as the International Rules for the

---

1 Article 38 (1) of the Statute of the International Court of Justice.

2 Page966 of *Black's Law Dictionary*, ninth edition.

Interpretation of Trade Terms (Incoterms®)[1], the Uniform Customs and Practice for Commercial Documentary Credits (UCP)[2]. Detailed information about Incoterms® and UCP is in Chapter 5. International trade custom does not have any legal binding effect until parties choose it as the governing law for their business transaction.

The general principles of law recognized by civilized nations

The general principles of law recognized by civilized nations are considered as a source of international law by Article 38 (1) of the Statute of the International Court of Justice. Article 53 of the 1986 Vienna Convention on the Law of Treaties also provides: "a treaty is void if, at the time of its conclusion, it conflicts with a peremptory norm of general international law. For the purposes of the present Convention, a peremptory norm of general international law is a norm accepted and recognized by the international community of states as a whole as a norm from which no derogation is permitted and which can be modified only by a subsequent norm of general international law having the same character." Although party autonomy is a fundamental norm underlying International Business Law, states and private parties cannot be absolutely free in their contractual relations and must respect certain fundamental principles deeply rooted in the international community. For example, slavery trade and piracy violate the general principles of law recognized by civilized nations.

Part 4   Major Legal Systems of the World

Most nations today follow one of the three major legal systems: civil law system, common law system, or Islamic law system. The civil law system developed in continental Europe since 450 BC. when Rome adopted its Twelve Tables. It was applied in the colonies of European imperial powers such as Spain and Portugal and was adopted by countries formerly possessing distinctive legal systems, such as Russia and Japan, which sought to reform their legal systems and gain economic and political power comparable to that of Western European countries. The common law system emerged in England during the Middle Ages (476-1453) and was applied within British colonies across the globe. Islamic law system is adopted by states in the Middle East, North Africa, and Southern Asia.

---

1   The Incoterms was first published in 1936 and have been periodically updated. The current version is the eighth version—Incoterms 2010—having been published on January 1, 2011. "Incoterms" is a registered trademark of the ICC.

2   The UCP was firstly published in 1933 and has been updated throughout the years. The current version is UCP600 and formally coming into effects on July 1st, 2007.

Civil law system

Civil law (also called "Continental Law" or "Romano-Germanic Law") system is based mainly on codes. Legislators, instead of judges, play a predominant role in developing the law. China adopts the civil law system. The civil law system has the following features:

- Countries with civil law systems have comprehensive, continuously updated legal codes (or statutes) that specify all matters capable of being brought before a court, the applicable procedure, and the appropriate punishment for each offense. Famous codes include Justinian's code (500 AD), French Civil Code (1804), German Civil Code (1900), and Swiss Civil Code (1911).

- In a civil law system, the judge's role is to establish the facts of the case and to apply the provisions of the applicable code. Though the judge investigates the matter and decides on the case, he or she works within a framework established by a comprehensive, codified set of laws. The judge's decision is consequently less crucial in shaping civil law than the decisions of legislators.

Common law system

Common law (also called "Case Law" or "Anglo-American Law") system is generally uncodified. This means no comprehensive codes. While common law does rely on some scattered statutes, it is largely based on precedents, meaning "a decided case that furnishes a basis for determining later cases involving similar facts or issues." [1] As a result, judges, not legislators, have an enormous role in shaping American and British law.

- Common Law is also called judge-made law, because the law is developed through decisions of courts and similar tribunals, rather than through legislative statues or executive action. Judges based their decisions on precedents. These precedents are maintained over time through the records of the courts as well as historically documented in collections of case law known as yearbooks and reports. Judges have wide discretion to determine which precedents should be applied in the decision of each new case. Judges can expand precedents to make them suit particular cases, and also can overrule or reject any precedents that they consider to be in error or outdated. Thus, the common law came to be made by judges.

- Compared with the UK, the US legislators have gained increasingly more important role in lawmaking since 1900s. The US Code is an example.[2] Nevertheless, case law still dominates the US legal system, and statues typically either codify judicial decisions or fill in areas of the law not covered by case law.

---

1 Page1295 of *Black's Law Dictionary*, ninth edition.

2 For more information about the US Code, see http://uscode.house.gov/.

CASE EXAMPLE: Japan v. Taxes on Alcoholic Beverages[1]

Facts: Japan and the US appealed regarding certain issues of law and legal interpretations in the Panel Report Japan-Taxes on Alcoholic Beverages (the Panel Report). That Panel (the Panel) was established to consider complaints by the European Communities, Canada and the US against Japan relating to the Japanese Liquor Tax Law (Shuzeiho), Law No. 6 of 1953 as amended (the Liquor Tax Law). The US raised the following issues in this appeal: whether the Panel erred in its characterization of panel reports adopted by the GATT CONTRACTING PARTIES and the WTO Dispute Settlement Body as "subsequent practice in a specific case by virtue of the decision to adopt them."

The WTO Appellate Body held that: Article 31 (3)(b) of the Vienna Convention on the Law of Treaties states that "any subsequent practice in the application of the treaty which establishes the agreement of the parties regarding its interpretation" is to be "taken into account together with the context" in interpreting the terms of the treaty. Adopted panel reports are often considered by subsequent panels. They create legitimate expectations among WTO Members, and, therefore, should be taken into account where they are relevant to any dispute. However, they are not binding, except with respect to resolving the particular dispute between the parties to that dispute. Therefore, we do not agree with the Panel's conclusion that panel reports adopted by the GATT CONTRACTING PARTIES and the WTO Dispute Settlement Body as "subsequent practice in a specific case" as the phrase "subsequent practice" is used in Article 31 of the Vienna Convention.

Take-away point: The "precedent system" used in the WTO is more flexible, and not as rigid as the "precedent system" in the British or American common law. That is, both the panels and the Appellate Body may rely on their own earlier legal rulings, but they are also free to deviate from those rulings as they think necessary.

Islamic law system

Different from the civil law system and the common law system, the Islamic law system is based upon religion—Islam. It is a comprehensive system covering the human being's relationship with his Creator, with his fellow human beings, and with his society and nation. It also deals with the relationship between nations in both war and peace. It is derived from the following sources in the order of their importance: (1) the Koran, (2) the Sunna or traditional teachings and practices of the Prophet Muhammad, (3) the writings of Islamic scholars who derived rules by analogy from the principles established in the Koran and the Sunna, and (4) the consensus of the legal community. Many principles in Islamic law system are different from those in the civil law system and the common law system.

---

1   World Trade Organization, Appellate Body, 1996 Appellate Body Report AB-1996-2.

Questions

1. What are the differences between the Civil Law System and Common Law System?
2. In Grant v Australian Knitting Mills Ltd [1936], is the court correct in following the precedent of Donoghue v Stevenson [1932]?

Donoghue v. Stevenson [1932]UKHL 100

Facts: While Ms. Donoghue (Plaintiff) was drinking a bottle of ginger beer, she noticed the remains of a decomposed snail. As a result she became sick and suffered shock. She did not sue the shop but manufacturer of the ginger beer, Stevenson (Defendant). Plaintiff's allegation: defendant had been careless in creating his product by allowing a snail to get into the product. Defendant's defense: plaintiff was not the direct buyer, but the shop, so even if Defendant's negligence was established, defendant had been negligent to the shop not plaintiff, so the plaintiff was not entitled to recover damages.

The court held that: The judgment should be made in favor of the plaintiff in despite of defense of privity of contract raised by the defendant. The plaintiff was entitled to recover damages against the manufacturer in negligence. This is because "all manufacturers owe a duty of care to consumers", shortly called "neighbor principle". This judgment is subsequently seen as case law.

Grant v. Australian Knitting Mills [1936]A.C. 562

Facts: Mr. Grant, a doctor, got a skin disease as a result of chemicals contained in woolen underwear he was wearing. Grant sued the manufacturer of the underwear.

The court held that: the manufacturer owed a duty of care to consumers, applying the neighbor principle established in Donoghue v. Stevenson.

Suggested Further Readings

Ray A. August, Don Mayer and Michael Bixby, *International Business Law: Text, Cases, and Readings*, International Edition, 6th edition, Pearson, 2013.

Jiang Zuoli, *International Business Law*, Law Press China, 2013.

ICC, *International Chamber of Commerce: The World Business Organization in 2013*, 2013.

UNIDROIT, *The UNIDROIT Annual Report*, 2012.

Subedi Surya P., *International Trade and Business Law*, The People's Public Security Publishing House, Hanoi, 2012.

Zhang Xuesen, *International Business Law*, Fudan University Press, 2011.

Borchardt Klaus-Dieter, *The ABC of European Union Law*, Publications Office of the EU, 2010.

Leon E. Trakman, *The Twenty-First-Century Law Merchant*, 48 AM. BUS. L. J. 775, 2011.

Chapter 2

Dispute Settlement

Cases involving foreign factors can be resolved by litigation or arbitration in municipal courts or international tribunals. This Chapter aims to help students to evaluate each international dispute settlement mechanism and to select the most favorable one for them. It overviews various international dispute settlement mechanisms from the following six aspects:

Part 1   introduces municipal courts systems.

Part 2   analyzes municipal courts' jurisdictions over cases involving foreign factors.

Part 3   discusses the choice of law rules in cases involving foreign factors.

Part 4   answers how to recognize and enforce foreign judgments.

Part 5   explores international commercial arbitration.

Part 6   presents ICSID and WTO dispute resolution mechanism.

■ Learning Objectives

By the end of this chapter you should:

- Outline the differences between municipal court systems in China and the US;
- Explain in what circumstances a court can exercise personal jurisdiction over foreign natural persons and entities;
- State how a court decides what law should be applied to a dispute;
- Know how to seek recognition and enforcement of foreign judgments;
- Understand how to use arbitration to resolve international commercial disputes; and
- Know ICSID and WTO dispute resolution mechanism.

■ Key Terms

Appellate body	Jurisdiction
Arbitration	Litigation
Choice of court	Penal
Choice of law	Reciprocity
Comity	Recognition and enforcement

Part 1   Municipal Court System

Municipal courts refer to domestic courts of various nation-states. They are often called upon to hear international civil litigations.

What is the municipal court system in China?

In China, the people's courts are judicial organs exercising judicial power on behalf of the people. China practices a system of courts characterized by "four levels and two instances of trials."

1. What is the four-level system?

- Basic people's courts: at the level of autonomous counties, towns, and municipal districts.
- Intermediate people's courts: at the level of prefectures, autonomous prefectures, and municipalities;
- Higher people's courts: at the level of the provinces, autonomous regions, and special municipalities;
- The Supreme People's Court: it is the court of last resort for the whole People's Republic of China except for Macao Special Administrative Region and Hong Kong Special Administrative Region.

Chinese court system is paralleled by a hierarchy of prosecuting offices called people's procuratorates, the highest being the Supreme People's Procuratorate. Basic people's courts, intermediate people's courts and higher people's courts are called "local people's courts." These courts have general jurisdiction upon civil, administrative and criminal cases. For military, intellectual property, and maritime disputes, China has established Courts of Special Jurisdiction.

Figure 1: Municipal Court System in China

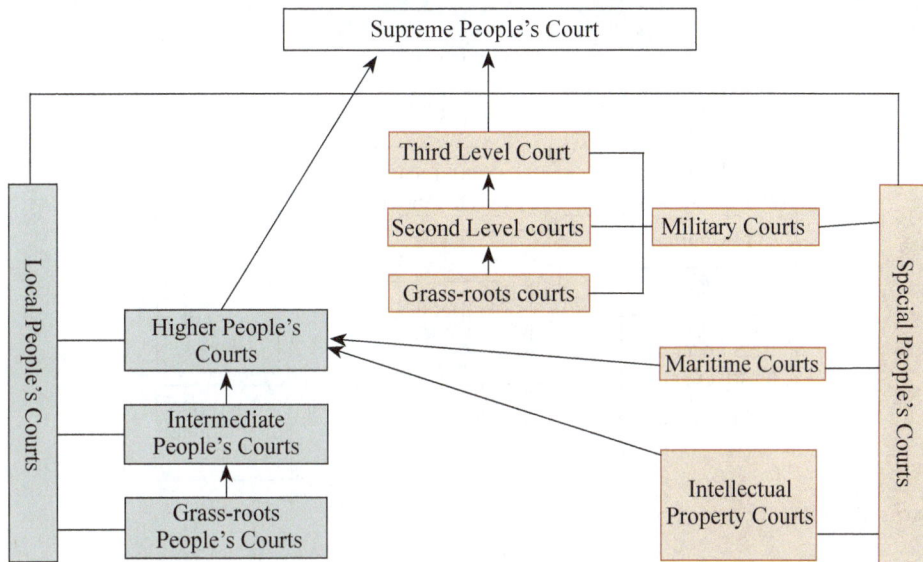

Note: the arrows point to the next superior courts, while the lines denote the components.

2. What is the two-instance-of-trial system?

In the administration of adjudication, people's courts adopt the system whereby a case should be finally decided after two trials:

- A judgment of a first instance must come from a local people's court, and a party may bring an appeal only once to the people's court at the next higher level. The people's procuratorate may present a protest to the people's court at the next higher level.
- Judgment of the first instance of the local people's courts at various levels become legally effective, namely "final" if, within the prescribed period for appeal, no party makes an appeal.
- Judgments and orders of the court of the second instance shall be seen as legally effective decisions of the case.
- Any judgments rendered by the Supreme People's Courts as the court of the first instance shall become immediately legally effective.

What is the municipal court system in the US?

The municipal court system in the US is constituted by a federal court system and a state court system. Therefore, it is more complicated than Chinese court system.

Figure 2: Municipal Court System in the US

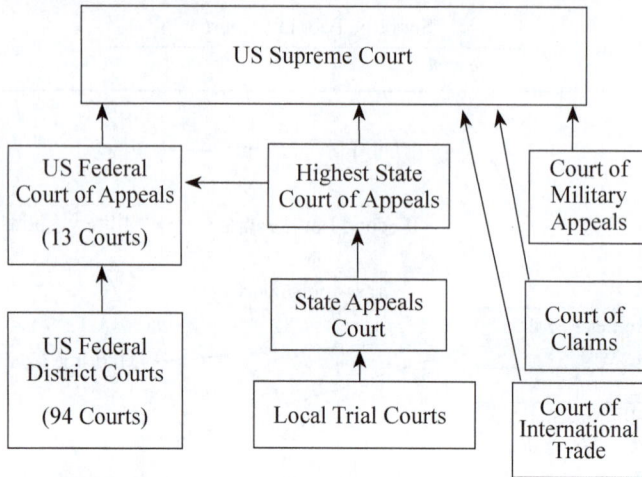

Note: the arrows point to the next superior courts.

1. US Supreme Court

The US Supreme Court is the court of last resort in the US. It has discretion to decide whether to review a case appealed from the highest court in a state or from a US federal court of appeals. The US Supreme Court will grant a writ of certiorari if it decides to review a case. Each year, about 4,500 cases are submitted to the Supreme Court. However, less than 200 cases are actually accepted for review. The justices choose the cases based on a case's implications for Americans in general or for a certain group within society, not just the impact on the parties actually involved in the lawsuit itself.

2. What is the federal court system?

The US federal court system is constituted by courts of general jurisdiction (Federal Courts of Appeal and Federal District Courts) and courts of special jurisdiction (Court of International Trade and Court of Claims).

(1) Federal District Courts

There are 94 federal district courts across the country, with at least one in every state (larger states have up to four). District courts are the only courts in the federal system in which juries hear testimonies in some cases, and most cases at this level are presented before a single judge.

(2) Federal Courts of Appeal

When cases are appealed from district courts, they go to a federal court of appeals. Courts of appeals do not use juries or witnesses. No new evidence is submitted in an appealed case; appellate courts base their decisions on a review of lower-court records.

There are 12 general appeals courts. All but one of them (which serves only the District of

Columbia) serve an area consisting of three to nine states (called "a circuit"). There is also the US Court of Appeals for the Federal Circuit, which specializes in appeals of decisions in cases involving patents, contract claims against the federal government, federal employment cases and international trade. Between 4 and 26 judges sit on each court of appeals, and each case is usually heard by a panel of three judges. Courts of appeals offer the best hope of reversal for many appellants, since the Supreme Court hears so few cases. Fewer than 1% of the cases heard by federal appeals courts are later reviewed by the Supreme Court.

(3) Court of International Trade

The Court of International Trade hears cases involving appeals of rulings of US Customs offices.

(4) Court of Claims

The Court of Claims hears cases in which the US Government is a defendant.

3. What is the state court system?

Each state has a court system that exists independently from the federal courts. Cases that originate in state courts can be appealed to the Supreme Court of the US if a federal issue is involved and usually only after all venues of appeal in the state courts have been tried. The court system in each state is constituted by courts of general jurisdiction and courts of special jurisdiction. These courts' judgments can be appealed to the state Supreme Court.

(1) State Supreme Court

Every state has a court of last resort, generally called the "supreme court." Although the state supreme court decisions are final within a state court system, sometimes they can be appealed to the US Supreme Court.

(2) Courts of general jurisdiction

State court systems have trial courts at the bottom level and one- or two-level of appellate courts. The appellate courts' judgments can be appealed to the State Supreme Court.

(3) Courts of special jurisdiction

Family courts settle such issues as divorce and child-custody disputes, and probate courts handle the settlement of the estates of deceased persons.

(4) Others

Below these specialized trial courts are less formal trial courts, such as magistrate courts and justice of the peace courts. They handle a variety of minor cases, such as traffic offenses, and usually do not use a jury.

Some basic differences between China and the US court systems

- Different from the US, China does not have a state court system.
- Unlike China, the US does not have the system of "two instances of trials"; therefore, a case may be tried by more than two instances.
- In China, the Supreme People's Court must accept a case if the first-instance court for the case is a Higher People's Court and the losing party appeals to the Supreme People's Court. However, the US Supreme Court has discretion to decide whether to accept an appealed case.

SELF QUIZ: Indicate whether each of the following statements is true or false.

1. China has a federal court system and a province court system.
2. In the US, judgments rendered by the highest court in a state cannot be appealed to the US Supreme Court.
3. Since China has four-level of courts, every case should be tried by four instances.

Part 2   Jurisdiction on Cases Involving Foreign Factors

The competence or ability of a municipal court to exercise the power to try a case is known as jurisdiction. Municipal courts can exercise jurisdiction over cases involving foreign factors[1] based on two principles: person (*in personam*) and thing (*in rem*).

What is personal jurisdiction?

Personal jurisdiction (In personam jurisdiction) is the power of a court to decide disputes relating to a natural person or entity within the forum country[2].

1. In what circumstances is a natural person subject to personal jurisdiction?

- Nationals of the forum country;
- Individuals physically present within the country;
- Individuals domiciled in the country;
- Individuals who consent to the jurisdiction of the country.

1　Cases involving foreign factors: cases involving parties, facts, or transactions from different countries. See Article 1 of Interpretations of the Supreme Peopie's Court on Several Issues Concerning Application of the Law of the Peopie's Republic of China on Choice of Law for Foreign-Related Civil Relationship(I).

2　Forum country: the country wherein a court or arbitration tribunal is located.

2. In what circumstances is an entity subject to personal jurisdiction?

If entities (including business, governmental and non-governmental entities) have sufficient existence in the eyes of the law of the forum country to function legally, sue and be sued, and make decisions through agents, they can be parties to international civil litigations. Entities are subject to the personal jurisdiction of a municipal court in much the same way that individuals are.

- Legal entities created within a country are like nationals of that country, so they are subject to the jurisdiction of that country, or
- Foreign entities who consent to the jurisdiction of the forum country.

3. How can natural persons or entities consent to the personal jurisdiction of a forum country?

Individuals and entities can consent to the personal jurisdiction of a forum country in three ways:

- Defending the substance of the case in court without disputing its jurisdiction;
- Agreeing to the jurisdiction of a particular court in a forum selection clause or agreement (namely "choice of court clause or agreement");
- Appointing an agent within a country to receive service of process on its behalf.

4. China

Chinese courts follow Chinese Civil Procedural Law to decide whether a court can exercise personal jurisdiction upon a foreign defendant. For example, Article 265 of Chinese Civil Procedure Law provides that a lawsuit brought against a defendant who has no domicile in China concerning a contract dispute or other disputes over property rights and interests, the defendant may be under the jurisdiction of the people's court located in the place where:

- The contract is signed or performed;
- The subject matter of the lawsuit is located;
- The defendant's confiscable property is located;
- The infringing act takes place;
- The representative agency, branch or business agent is located.

Article 266 of Chinese Civil Procedure Law provides that lawsuits brought for disputes arising from the performance of contracts for Chinese-foreign equity joint ventures, Chinese-foreign contractual joint ventures, or Chinese-foreign cooperative exploration and development of the natural resources in China shall be under the exclusive jurisdiction of people's courts.

Chinese Civil Procedure Law permits parties to choose foreign courts to adjudicate their disputes. In order to be valid, a choice of court clause must comply with the following requirements:

- The clause is in writing;
- The chosen court is located in the place with actual connections to the disputes, such as the place where the defendant or the plaintiff resides, where the contract is signed or performed,

or where the subject of the action is located;

- The chosen court should not violate the exclusive jurisdiction of Chinese courts.

5. The US

In the US, if there are "minimum contacts" between a natural person or entity and the forum country, US courts would infer that the natural person or entity has consented to the personal jurisdiction of the forum. The "minimum contacts" test is met if this foreign defendant:

- has direct contact with the forum country;
- has a contract with a resident of the forum country;
- have placed their product into the stream of commerce such that it reaches the forum country;
- seek to serve residents of the forum country;
- have satisfied the Calder effects test; or
- have a non-passive website viewed within the forum country.

US courts generally uphold a choice of court clause concluded by parties in an international contract, even if the chosen court has no connection with the dispute.

CASE EXAMPLE: *Calder v. Jones*[1]

Facts: Plaintiff is a California resident in the entertainment business sued the National Enquirer, located in Florida, for libel based on an allegedly defamatory article published by the magazine. The defendant argues that the court in California had no personal jurisdiction in this case.

The US Supreme Court held that: While the article was written and edited in Florida, personal jurisdiction was properly established in California because of the effects of the defendants' conduct in that state. As the article concerned a California resident with a career in California and relied on California sources, the Court found the defendants' "intentional, and allegedly tortious, actions were expressly aimed at California."

Take-away point: The Calder effects test requires (a) an intentional action, that was (b) expressly aimed at the forum state, with (c) knowledge that the brunt of the injury would be felt in the forum state. If a court finds that a defendant's actions meets the test, it may assert personal jurisdiction upon this defendant.

CASE EXAMPLE: *The Bremen v. Zapata Off-Shore Co.*[2]

Facts: A German corporation contracted with a US corporation to transport an oil rig from Louisiana to Italy. During transportation , the rig was damaged and was towed to Tampa, Florida, where the US corporation filed suit. The German corporation, however, asked the US court to enforce the choice of court clause contained in the contract placing jurisdiction in London.

---

1 Calder v. Jones, 465 US 783 (1984).

2 The Bremen v. Zapata Off-Shore Co. 407 US 1 (1972).

The US Supreme Court held that: Although London had no connection with the dispute, the choice of court clause was valid and should be enforced. The court indicated that "the expansion of American business and industry will hardly be encouraged if, notwithstanding solemn contracts, we insist on a parochial concept that all disputes must be resolved under our laws and in our courts."

Take-away point: Choice of court clauses are parties' explicit consent to a court's personal jurisdiction. They provide for orderliness and predictability. They are presumed to be valid and should be enforced unless enforcement is shown by the resisting party to be unreasonable and unjust or the clause was invalid for such reasons as fraud and overreaching.

6. Summary of differences between Chinese and the US law:

- To determine whether to exercise personal jurisdiction upon foreign defendants, US courts follow minimum contracts test and Chinese courts follow statutory provisions under the Civil Procedural Law.

- In the US, a choice of court clause in an international agreement should be enforced unless the plaintiffs can clearly show that (1) enforcement would be unreasonable and unjust, or (2) the clause was invalid for such reasons as fraud and overreaching. Choice of court clauses are presumed to be valid because they provide for orderliness and predictability. Courts do not require the chosen court has connection to the dispute. Compared with US law, Chinese law has more requirements for choice of court clauses, such as the written format and material connection between the place of the chosen court and that of the dispute.

What is *in rem* jurisdiction?

In rem jurisdiction is the power of a court to determine the ownership rights of all natural persons or entities with respect to particular property located within the territory of the forum country. For example, the ownership of real property would be determined by an *in rem* proceeding, as would the ownership of personal property physically within the forum country (such as a ship physically arrested in a port within the forum country).

Jurisdiction fine-tuning

When courts in multiple countries have jurisdiction over a case involving foreign factors, a court may refuse to exercise jurisdiction or oppose other courts to exercise jurisdiction. This is called jurisdiction fine-tuning by late American professor Von Mehrens, a famous jurist in comparative private international law.[1] Civil-law countries adopt *lis pendens,* and common law countries exercise forum non conveniens and anti-suit injunction, to fine tune jurisdictions. All these doctrines aim to avoid

---

1   A T Von Mehren, *Adjudicatory Authority in Private International Law: A Comparative Study*, Martinus Nijhoff publishers, 2007.

irreconcilable judgments, discourage forum shopping, and save judicial resources.

1. *Lis pendens*

Lis pendens is Latin for "suit pending". In civil-law countries, *lis pendens* is used as a restriction to a court to assume its jurisdiction, if another court has been seized first on the same cause of action and between the same parties. This doctrine assumes that the court first seized will render a judgment on the merits of the dispute. It is, however, applied at the stage of determining whether jurisdiction shall be exercised or stayed temporarily pending the judgment of another court. The exercise of jurisdiction may be resumed later should circumstances require.[1]

The first sentence of Article 533 of the Opinions on the Chinese Civil Procedure Law issued by the Supreme People's Court issued in 2014 is a *lis pendens* rule: if both a people's court and a foreign court have jurisdiction over a case, and a party sues in the foreign court and the other party brings an action in the people's court, the people's court can accept the case at its discretion. Therefore, in case of parallel proceedings, even if the trial in a Chinese court started after the foreign proceedings, Chinese courts still can exercise jurisdiction upon the case on the same cause of action and between the same parties.

2. *Forum non conveniens*

Forum non conveniens is a doctrine used by courts in common- law countries to refuse jurisdiction. The basic four-part test for the application of this doctrine is that the defendant will prevail if there is an alternative forum that is (1)available, and (2) adequate, and if (3) private interest factors and (4) public interest factors point toward the alternative forum and away from the US courts. Notably, plaintiffs cannot resist forum non conveniens on the basis of unfavorable substantive law in alternative forums.

China borrows *forum non conveniens* from common law countries to fine tune personal jurisdiction. Article 532 of the Opinions on the Chinese Civil Procedure Law provides that a people's court can dismiss a lawsuit and suggest the plaintiff to sue in a more convenient foreign court when the following circumstances occur. (1) The defendant alleges that this case should be heard in a more convenient foreign court or raises jurisdiction objections. (2) The parties do not reach a choice of court agreement favoring Chinese courts. (3) This case does not fall into the exclusive jurisdiction of Chinese courts. (4) This case has nothing to do with the interests of China, its citizens, legal persons or other organizations. (5) The major disputed facts do not take place in China, Chinese law is not applicable, and it is very difficult for Chinese court to ascertain the facts and applicable law in this case. (6) A foreign court has jurisdiction over this case and it is more convenient for this court to hear this case.

---

1 Lu Song, The EOS Engineering Corporation Case and the *Nemo Debet BisVexari Pro Una et Eadem Causa* Principle in China, 7 *Chinese J. Int'l L.* 143, 146(2008).

CASE EXAMPLE: *Canada Malting v. Paterson Steamships, Ltd.*[1]

Facts: Two ships of Canadian registry and ownership, each carrying cargo shipped from one Canadian port to another, collided on Lake Superior while unintentionally in United States waters, and one ship sank. While a suit was pending in a Canadian court of admiralty to determine liability as between the ships, the Canadian owners of cargo lost in the accident sued the Canadian owners of one of the vessels in a federal district court in New York. All the parties were citizens of Canada, and the officers and crew of each vessel—the material witnesses—were citizens and residents of Canada too. The cargo owners brought the suit in the US largely because US liability rules provided more favorable compensation than Canadian rules.

The US Supreme Court held that: the case should be dismissed on grounds of forum non conveniens. The appropriate forum in this case is Canada for five reasons. (1)All the parties were citizens of Canada. (2) Both the colliding vessels were registered under the laws of Canada, and each was owned by a Canadian corporation. (3) The officers and the crew of each vessel—the material witnesses—were citizens and residents of Canada, and so would not be available for compulsory attendance in a US district court. (4) The cargo was shipped under a Canadian bill of lading from one Canadian port to another. (5)The collision occurred at a point where the inland waters narrowed to a neck, and the colliding vessels proceeded in United States waters unintentionally.

Take-away point: Courts in common law countries occasionally use forum non conveniens to decline, in the interest of justice, to exercise jurisdiction, where the suit is between foreigners, or where for kindred reasons the litigation can more appropriately be conducted in a foreign court.

3. Anti-suit injunction

When a litigant sue in a foreign court, it sometimes happens that the litigant's home country is opposed to his doing so. The foreign court may dismiss the case using the doctrine of forum non conveniens; but if it does not, the court in the litigant's home country may intervene by issuing an anti-suit injunction to prevent the litigant from proceeding with the case. Two different standards are used by courts to determine whether to issue an anti-suit injunction.

- The first requires a court to consider comity when granting the injunction to protect its own jurisdiction or to prevent evasion of its public policies.

- The second allows a court to grant the injunction if the foreign proceedings are vexatious or oppressive or if they will otherwise cause inequitable hardship.

Anti-suit injunction is rarely used by courts in civil law countries. Chinese courts have never issued an anti-suit injunction.

---

1 Canada Malting v. Paterson Steamships, Ltd., 285 US 413 (1932).

Part 3　Choice of Law

In cases involving foreign factors, municipal courts are confronted with the problem of deciding which law to apply. Courts use choice of law rules to determine whether they should apply their own law or foreign law to resolve disputes. Virtually all choice of law rules follow a two-step procedure:

- First, if the parties to a dispute have concluded a choice of law clause indicating the law of a particular country should be applied, the court should apply that law.
- Second, if the parties have not agreed as to which law should apply (either expressly or impliedly) , then the court should determine for itself which law it should apply by (1) following statutory choice of law provisions, (2) determining which country has the most significant relationship with the dispute, or (3) determining which country has the greatest interest in the outcome of the case.

What are choice of law clauses?

Choice of law clause is a clause that parties agree in advance as to what law should be applied in case of disputes. In China, parties may explicitly choose the laws applicable to international business transactions in accordance with the Law of the Application of Law for Foreign -related

Civil Relations. Even if the law chosen by the parties has no factual connection with the country whose law they have chosen, their choice should be enforced by Chinese courts.

Like many other countries, in China if the law chosen by the parties violate the mandatory provisions or harm the social public interests of China, the choice of law clause is void. Mandatory provisions and relevant Chinese law will be applied. Mandatory provisions refer to laws in the following fields:

- Labors protection,
- Environment, food and public health protection,
- Foreign exchange control and financial security,
- Anti-dumping and anti-monopoly, and
- Other mandatory laws.

What are statutory choice of law provisions?

In civil law countries, if parties do not reach a choice of law agreement, a court will apply statutory choice of law provisions to their dispute. These provisions look to the subject matter of the dispute—such as real rights, creditor's rights, and intellectual properties—and provide fairly simple and straightforward guidelines.

Statutory choice of law provisions are simple and easy to apply. However, they are criticized as being too rigid. In recent years, many civil law countries have made their statutory choice of law provisions more flexible by

- Respecting party autonomy in making choice of law clauses, and
- Adopting the most significant relationship doctrine.

Most significant relationship

The most significant relationship doctrine requires a court to apply the law of the country that has the most contacts with the parties and their transaction.

1. China

The most significant relationship principle is a fundamental theory adopted by the Law of the Choice of Law for Foreign-related Civil Relationships. The Law permits parties to choose the laws applicable to contracts by agreement. If the parties do not choose, the laws that have the most significant relationship with the dispute may apply. Courts generally consider the following factors when deciding which country has the most significant relationship with the dispute:

- The place of negotiation or contracting;
- The place of tort action or injury;
- The place of performance;

- The location of the subject matter;
- The nationality, domicile, residence, or place of incorporation of the parties; and
- Other factors relevant to the dispute.

2. US

In the US, courts consider the following general factors to determine which country has the most significant relationship with a case:[1]

- The application of which country's law will best promote the needs of the international legal system for harmony in the political and commercial relations of states?
- Will the purpose of the forum country's law be furthered by applying it to the particular case?
- Will the purpose of the other country's law be furthered by applying it to the particular case?
- If a contract is involved, which country's law will best promote the underlying policies of the legal subject matter (e.g., torts, contracts, etc.) involved?
- Which country's law will best promote certainty, predictability, and uniformity of result?
- Which country's law is easiest to determine and apply?

3. Comparison between China and the US law

- Both laws adopt the most significant relationship principle.
- Courts in the two countries may interpret the principle differently. Although China is a civil-law country, Chinese courts, like the US courts, have discretion in weighing factors when deciding which country has the most significant relationship with the case.

Governmental interest analysis

US courts analyze governmental interest to determine which law should be applied when parties do not make a choice of law agreement. Governmental interest approach requires application of the law of the country with the greatest interest in resolving the particular issue that is raised in the underlying litigation. Under this approach, courts evaluate the governmental policies underlying the applicable laws and determine which jurisdiction's policy would be more advanced by the application of its law to the facts of the case under review. Analysis of governmental interest can reveal one of the following results:

- False conflict: only the forum country has an interest=>apply the forum country's law.
- True conflict: both the forum country and another country or countries have some legitimate interest=>apply the forum law, except when the other country's interest is significantly larger than the forum country.
- Unprovided conflict: no country has interests in applying its law=>apply forum law.

---

1 The Restatement (Second) of Laws: Conflicts, 1971.

Part 4   Recognition and Enforcement of Foreign Judgments

The judgments of one country's courts have no force by themselves in another country. Recognition and enforcement is a legal procedure that a country grants the same force to foreign judgments as they grant their own judgments. The court that renders a judgment is the so-called judgment-rendering court. The court where an application for recognition and enforcement of a judgment is filed is called requested court.

Recognition and enforcement are different:

- Recognition is often confined to non-monetary judgments, such as divorce decrees and other status decisions or judgments on the validity of a contract. These judgments can be recognized but do not need enforcement.
- Recognition is the precondition for enforcement. Enforcement is often related to monetary judgments in civil and commercial cases. Such judgments require the losing party to pay certain amount of money to the winning party. Notably, if a divorce decree divides property between a couple, the monetary part of the decree is enforceable.

Recognition and enforcement of foreign judgment are important not only for winning parties but also for the society at large:

- Recognition and enforcement of foreign judgments can protect winning parties' rights and interests. Winning a judgment is not the end of a lawsuit. When a losing party has no sufficient assets in the forum to fulfill the judgment, a winning party needs to seek recognition and enforcement of the judgment in a foreign forum.

- It can enhance social justice, since justice cannot be achieved unless a legally effective judgment is enforced.
- It can also help achieve judicial economy and maintain certainty between parties regarding their rights and obligations by decreasing re-litigation and consequent inconsistent judgments.

Three legal regimes exist for recognition and enforcement of foreign judgments.

Domestic law

Significant differences exist in domestic laws for recognizing and enforcing foreign judgments.

- Some countries do not recognize and enforce foreign judgments in the absence of a treaty, such as the Netherlands.
- Some countries recognize or enforce foreign judgments under the principle of reciprocity even if no treaty exists, such as China.
- Some countries recognize and enforce foreign judgments more or less to the same degree as domestic judgments, and do not require reciprocity or a treaty, such as the US.

1. China

China Civil Procedure Law provides that recognition and enforcement of foreign judgments can be conducted according to:

- treaties ratified by China, or
- the principle of reciprocity.

For judgments beyond the scope of treaties, reciprocity is the only legal basis available for recognition and enforcement of foreign judgments in China. A key issue is—what reciprocity is under Chinese law?

- **Reciprocity in practice**: Chinese courts and legislators have never defined reciprocity. Scholars generally believe "reciprocity in practice" is Chinese official view of reciprocity. This view is very restrictive: because it means that reciprocity can be established only when a foreign court has recognized and enforced a Chinese judgment in practice.
- **Reciprocity in law**: This is a liberal view of reciprocity. It means that if theoretically a Chinese judgment may be recognized and enforced according to a foreign law, reciprocity can be established between China and this foreign country. Many scholars argue that Chinese courts and legislators should adopt this view.

> **CASE EXAMPLE: Japanese Citizen *Gomi Akira* Applied for Chinese Courts to Recognize and Enforce a Japanese Judgment (1995)**
>
> In 1994, Gomi Akira, a Japanese citizen, applied for the Dalian Intermediate Court to recognize and enforce a Japanese monetary judgment concerning a loan dispute against a Japanese-Chinese joint venture.
>
> **The Dalian Intermediate Court held that:** Neither bilateral judgment recognition , enforcement treaty nor reciprocity existed between China and Japan, so the Japanese judgment should not be

recognized and enforced.

Take-away point: Reciprocity must exist between a judgment-rendering country and a requested country in the absence of a treaty.

2. US

Most of US states do not require reciprocity or a treaty on recognition and enforcement to recognize and enforce foreign judgments. Therefore, compared with China, it is much easier to recognize and enforce foreign judgments in the US.

The US law for recognize and enforce foreign judgments is state laws. These state laws are generally molded out of the following guiding uniform law documents:

- The Uniform Foreign Money Judgments Recognition Act (UFMJRA)
- The Restatement III
- The Uniform Foreign-Country Money Judgments Recognition Act (UFCMJRA)

CASE EXAMPLE: *Hubei Gezhouba Sanlian Industrial Co., Ltd. and Hubei Pinghu Cruise Co., Ltd. v. Robinson Helicopter Company, Inc. (2009)*

Facts: Plaintiffs Hubei Gezhouba Sanlian Industrial Co., Ltd. (Sanlian) and Hubei Pinghu Cruise Co., Ltd. (Pinghu) are business located in Yichang City, Hubei Province, China. Defendant Robinson Helicopter Company, Inc. (RHC) is a California corporation with its principal place of business in Torrance, California, the US. In 2009, Sanlian and Pinghu applied to the US District Court of Central District of California for recognition and enforcement of a Chinese monetary judgment[1] against RHC.

The US District Court of Central District of California held that: Plaintiffs were entitled to the issuance of a domestic judgment in this action in the amount of the Chinese Judgment, with interests calculated as set forth in the Chinese Judgment, for purposes of enforcement, because:

- Service of process in China was proper under Federal Rule 4, the 9th Circuit Direct Mail ruling, and the Hague Service Convention.
- The Chinese Judgment was final, conclusive, and enforceable under Chinese laws and involved the granting of recovery of a sum of money.
- California's UFMJRA applies to this action, seeking recognition of the Chinese Judgment, and none of the stated exceptions to recognition in the UFMJRA are applicable on the facts presented.

---

1   Early on March 14, 1995, Pinghu and the predecessor of Sanlian brought an action against the RHC for damages in the Los Angeles Superior Court (hereinafter "California State Action"). They alleged that RHC had designed and manufactured a helicopter that crashed into the Yangtze River in China in 1994 and the RHC was responsible for this accident. RHC moved to stay the California State Action on the ground of forum non conveniens. The Los Angeles Superior Court granted the motion and stayed the California State Action. Therefore, on January 14, 2001, Sanlian and Pinghu filed an action against RHC in the Higher People's Court of Hubei Province. On 10 December 2004, the Higher Court issued a judgment in favor of Sanlian and Pinghu and against RHC.

Take-away point: The US requested court applies the law of the judgment-rendering court (namely "the judgment-rendering Chinese court") to decide whether the judgment is final and conclusive. If none of the stated exceptions to recognition in the UFMJRA are applicable, a foreign judgment is recognizable and enforceable in the US. The court does not require reciprocity or a treaty for recognition or enforcement.

3. Comparison between Chinese and the US law:

- Compared with Chinese law, US law is more liberal in recognizing and enforcing foreign judgments.
- Chinese courts often use lack of reciprocity to deny recognizing and enforcing foreign judgments, but US courts generally do not require reciprocity.

Bilateral treaties

Bilateral treaties on recognition and enforcement of judgments have four benefits:
- impose international obligations to countries to recognize and enforce foreign judgments.
- provide firm rules for recognition and enforcement of foreign judgments.
- satisfy the requirement of reciprocity, and
- expand the scope of recognizable judgments.

Countries have different views towards bilateral treaties on recognition and enforcement of foreign judgments.
- Countries with more restrictive domestic laws, particularly those requiring reciprocity, tend to enter into more bilateral treaties. China has concluded bilateral treaties on judgment recognition and enforcement with more than 26 countries. France has concluded almost 40. But the US, who does not require reciprocity, has none.
- Treaties typically exist between countries with political, historical, or geographic proximities, such as between France and its former colonies, between various Arab States.
- Countries in the same legal system are easier to reach treaties, because these countries share similar legal techniques and ideologies. For example, all countries that concluded a bilateral treaty on recognition and enforcement of civil and commercial judgments with China are civil law countries.

Multilateral conventions

Multilateral conventions can help realize global free circulation of judgments. However, reaching a multilateral convention is more difficult than bilateral treaties. Therefore, there are few successful multilateral conventions on recognition and enforcement of foreign judgments in the world.

1. Brussels regime

Brussels Regime refers to Brussels Convention concerning Judicial Competence and the Execution of Decisions in Civil and Commercial Matters of 1968 and relevant regulations enacted by the European Commission.[1] It establishes a multilateral regime for recognition and enforcement of judgments among member counties of the European Union (EU). It is also the most successful multilateral Conventions for recognition and enforcement of judgments thus far. Brussels Regime is constituted by the following documents:

- Judgments in civil and commercial matters: Brussels Convention concerning Judicial Competence and the Execution of Decisions in Civil and Commercial Matters of 1968, Council Regulation (EC) No 44/2001 of 22 December 2000 on Jurisdiction and the Recognition and Enforcement of Judgments in Civil and Commercial Matters (hereinafter "Brussels I Regulation"), and Council Regulation No 1215/2012 of 12 December 2012 on Jurisdiction and the Recognition and Enforcement of Judgments in Civil and Commercial Matters (hereinafter "Brussels I a Regulation"). Brussels I a Regulation is a recast of the Brussels I Regulation and completely replaced it on January 10, 2015.

- Judgments in matrimonial matters and parental responsibility: Council Regulation (EC) 2201/2003 of 27 November 2003 concerning jurisdiction and the recognition and enforcement of judgments in matrimonial matters and the matters of parental responsibility (namely "Brussels II a Regulation or Brussels II bis Regulation").

- Uncontested claims and payment procedures: Regulation (EC) 805/2004 of the European Parliament and of the Council of 21 April 2004 Creating a European Enforcement Order for Uncontested Claims; Regulation (EC) 1896/2006 of the European Parliament and of the Council of 12 December 2006 Creating a European Order for Payment Procedure.

- Judgments concerning insolvency: judgments opening insolvency proceedings are recognized under Article 16 of the Council Regulation (EC) 1346/2000 of 29 May 2000 on Insolvency Proceedings, with the enforcing State's public policy as the only relevant defence (Article 26); other judgments of the insolvency court are enforceable under Article 25 of the Brussels I Regulation.

Brussels Regime is supplemented by the Convention on jurisdiction and the recognition and enforcement of judgments in civil and commercial matters, concluded in Lugano on October 30, 2007. It is the successor to the Lugano Convention on jurisdiction and enforcement of judgments in civil and commercial matters of September 16, 1988. Lugano Convention is largely similar to the Brussels Convention concerning Judicial Competence and the Execution of Decisions in Civil and Commercial Matters of 1968, but it is applicable among non-EU members.[2]

---

1 Regulations are enacted by the European Commission and directly applicable to EU members. European Commission has competence to enact regulations in the field of police and administration of justice according to the Treaty of Amsterdam.

2 The signatories of the 2007 Lugano Convention are the Swiss Confederation, the European Community, the Kingdom of Denmark, the Kingdom of Norway and the Republic of Iceland.

2. Hague Choice of Court Convention

The Hague Choice of Court Convention, formally the Convention of 30 June 2005 on Choice of Court Agreements is an international convention concluded under the auspices of the Hague Conference on Private International Law. It is the most recent international effort to enhance global recognition and enforcement of civil and commercial judgments. Thirty countries, including the US, Germany and China have signed this Convention.

This Convention shall apply in international cases to exclusive choice of court agreements concluded in civil or commercial matters. An exclusive choice of court agreement designates courts of one Contracting Member or one or more specific courts of one Contracting Member to have exclusive jurisdiction over the dispute. A judgment-rendering court should exercise jurisdiction based upon the exclusive choice of court agreement, and its judgments must be recognized in all Contracting Members where the Convention is applicable. Currently, the Hague Conference on Private International Law is working to expand the scope of the Convention in order to facilitate judgment recognition and enforcement worldwide.

Important requirements and exceptions for recognition and enforcement

1. Valid, final, and on the merits

According to most of domestic laws, treaties, and conventions, a foreign judgment should be valid, final, and on the merits so as to be recognizable and enforceable in other country.

- Validity means that judgments are legally effective according to the law of the rendering country.
- Finality means that judgments are not subject to ordinary appeals. Generally, finality of a judgment is determined by the law of the rendering country. However, some requested country applies its own law to decide the finality of a foreign judgment.
- Judgments must usually be on the merits. Mere procedural decisions are usually not recognizable, because each country's courts usually follow that country's own procedure law so will not be bound by another court's procedural decision.

Chinese law does not use the wordings of "validity and finality", and instead, it requires judgments should be "legally effective". Namely, a foreign judgment must be legally effective in order to be recognized and enforced in China. Chinese courts apply the law of the judgment-rendering court to determine whether a foreign judgment is legally effective.

Many treaties concluded by China requiring judgments for recognition and enforcement should be legally effective. One example is The Judicial Assistance Treaty in Civil Cases on 1 January 1995 between the PRC and Italy (hereinafter "China-Italy Bilateral Treaty").

CASE EXAMPLE: *B&T* **Insolvency Case**[1]

Facts: On December 18, 2000, B&T Ceramic Group s. r. l. (hereinafter "B&T"), domiciled at Via Calzavecchio n.23, Casalecchio d/R (Bologna), Italy, applied to the Guangdong Foshan

---

1 B&T Insolvency Case, No.633 Fozhongfajingchuzi (2000).

Intermediate People's Court for recognition and enforcement of the No. 62673 bankruptcy judgment and an adjudication order issued by Italian courts in 1997 and 1999, respectively.[1]

The Guangdong Foshan Intermediate People's Court held that: Article 21 of the China-Italy Bilateral Treaty provided that judgments should be legally effective according to the law of the judgment-rendering country. The bankruptcy judgment and the adjudication order were both legally effective according to Italian law. Therefore, the Foshan Court recognized the Italian bankruptcy judgment and the adjudication order according to China's Civil Procedural Law and Articles 20, 21 and 26 of the China-Italy Treaty.

Take-away point: A foreign judgment must be legally effective in order to be recognized and enforced in China. Chinese courts apply the law of the judgment-rendering court to determine whether a foreign judgment is legally effective.

2. Jurisdiction

Recognition and enforcement of a foreign judgment require that the rendering court had jurisdiction. A judgment-rendering court always applies its own law to determine whether it has jurisdiction over the case. The law of the judgment-rendering court does not bind the requested court. The requested court may apply the law that it thinks suitable to decide whether the judgment-rendering court has jurisdiction. There are three circumstances:

- If the requested court claims exclusive jurisdiction in an area, recognition and enforcement of a foreign judgment in that area is usually denied. For example, France had long protected the privilege of its own nationals to sue and be sued in France by not enforcing foreign judgments against French nationals who had not submitted to the foreign court's jurisdiction.

- Where no exclusive jurisdiction is claimed, some countries, such as Germany, have applied the "mirror-image principle", projecting their own rules of jurisdiction on the foreign courts and upholding the foreign courts' jurisdiction if, in the reverse situation, their own courts would have jurisdiction to hear the case.

- Some countries, such as China, have developed specific jurisdiction laws for recognition and enforcement purposes. Generally they integrate these laws into the bilateral treaties on recognition and enforcement of foreign judgments.

China has developed specific jurisdiction laws for recognition and enforcement purposes. These laws can be found in the bilateral treaties concluded by China. Generally the treaties provide that Chinese courts can deny recognition and enforcement if jurisdiction of a judgment-rendering court infringes the exclusive jurisdiction of Chinese courts. Moreover, the judgment-rendering

---

1   The No. 62673 judgment declared E.N.Groups.p.a (hereinafter "E.N.") bankrupt. The adjudication order held that overseas corporations in which E.N. hold shares, equipment, and machines, trademarks, patents and business networks were sold as a whole without exception to B&T. Therefore, B&T requested the Foshan court to transfer all property of E.N. in China to it. In China, E.N. holds 98% of share of NanhaiNassetti Pioneer Ceramic Machine Co. Ltd. (hereinafter "NanhaiNassetti") . Accordingly, B&T requested the Foshan court to confirm that B&T holds the 98% of share of HanhaiNassetti and that B&T enjoys full right of control over the corresponding assets.

court should exercise jurisdiction according to the following principles:

- The defendant has his or her domicile or habitual residence in the country where the court is located,
- The defendant has a representative office in the country where the court is located and the action is related to the activities of the office,
- The defendant accepted the jurisdiction of the judgment-rendering court by writing,
- The defendant defended the substance of the case in the judgment-rendering court without questioning its jurisdiction,
- In contractual disputes, the contract was signed, or has been or will be performed in the country where the court is located, or the subject matter is located in that country,
- In cases of tort, the conducts or results of the tort took place in the country where the court is located,
- In cases of personal status, one party has his or her domicile or habitual residence in the country where the court is located,
- In cases of maintenance, the judgment creditor has his or her domicile or habitual residence in the country where the court is located,
- In cases of inheritance, when he or she died, the inherited was domiciled or his or her main inheritance was located in the country where the court is located, or
- The subject matter is a real estate in the country where the court is located.

3. Procedure requirements

If fundamental procedural principles were violated in the judgment-rendering court, the consequent judgment is usually not recognizable and enforceable in a foreign court. Procedure defenses generally include:

- The defendant did not have adequate notice, was not properly served, and had no opportunity to be heard in court are the most important procedural defenses for recognition and enforcement.
- Judgments based upon procedural fraud or abuse of procedure are usually not recognizable and enforceable. However, a party may be precluded from invoking this defense in the enforcement proceedings if it had a chance to invoke them to void the judgment in the judgment-rendering country.
- A rarely used defense is that the judgment was rendered under a judicial system that is generally not fair. This defense not only doubts the procedure of a specific case, but also criticizes the whole judicial system of the judgment-rendering country generally.

According to most of treaties concluded by China, China courts will deny recognition and enforcement of a foreign judgment, if the defendant is not given adequate notice for the judgment-rendering proceedings or is not properly represented by a guardian if lacking legal capacity. Some treaties explicitly provide that "adequate notice" should be decided by the law of the judgment-rendering country. If treaties do not indicate which law should be applied to service, the requested courts in China will refer to the service provisions under the treaties or apply the Hague Service Convention to determine whether a defendant was given adequate notice.

CASE EXAMPLE: *Minsk Automatic Production Corporation United v. CNMTC*[1]

Facts: Minsk Automatic Production Corporation United applied to the Beijing No. 2 Intermediate Court to recognize and enforce a judgment issued by Belarus against CNMTC.

The Beijing No. 2 Intermediate People's Court held that: According to the China-Byelorussian Bilateral Treaty on Judicial Service, judgment recognition and enforcement should be denied if a defendant is not given adequate notice for the judgment-rendering proceedings. In this case, the Chinese defendant was served by way of post. The Treaty does not indicate which law should be applied to service. The Beijing Court referred to the Hague Service Convention, holding that serving Chinese defendant by "way of post" was against the reservation made by China under the Convention. Notably, Belarus also acceded to the Convention, but it did not make any reservations like China. Moreover, the service provisions of the China-Byelorussian Bilateral Treaty do not mention post as a way of service. The court concluded that, considering China's reservations under the Hague Service Convention, the recognition and enforcement of the Byelorussian judgment should be denied because the Chinese defendant was not duly served.

Take-away point: the recognition and enforcement of foreign judgments will be denied if the defendant is not duly served according to the bilateral judicial assistance treaty concluded by China or the Hague Service Convention.

---

4. *Res Judicata*

Res Judicata is the Latin term for "a matter already judged." It means that, if a final judgment has been rendered on a case, continued litigation of the same case between the same parties should be precluded and a court will use *res judicata* to deny recognition and enforcement of judgments from parallel proceedings.

Under the doctrine of *res judicata*, a court can generally deny recognition and enforcement of a foreign judgment if

- A legally effective judgment has been rendered by a court in the requested country for the same cause of action between the same parties,
- A court in the requested country has recognized and enforced a third-country judgment on the same cause of action between the same parties, or
- A court in the requested country is trying a case on the same cause of action between the same parties. Some treaties may require that the trial in the court in the requested country should begin before the commencement of foreign proceeding or the court seized the case first.

---

1   Minsk Automatic Production Corporation United v. CNMTC, the No.2 Intermediate People's Court in Beijing (2001) ErZhong Min Renzi No. 01815.

5. Public policy exception

A requested court should not review the substance of foreign judgments either under its own law or some other law. The requested court should not reject recognition simply because it would have decided the case differently. However, all legal systems and virtually all recent treaties and conventions allow countries to deny recognition to foreign judgments that violate their public policy. When recognition and enforcement of a foreign judgment would harm a strong and fundamental policy of the requested country, the recognition and enforcement can be denied for public policy exception.

Chinese courts can deny recognition and enforcement of a foreign judgment, if recognition and enforcement would cause harm to Chinese sovereignty, security, and public order. Chinese legislators have long adopted an affirmative attitude towards the application of public policy exception. But they seldom use the term, "public policy," in their legislation. Instead, they tend to use a cluster of terms together to refer to "public policy," such as "public interests," "state sovereignty," "security," "socio-economic order," and "social and public interests of the country," and etc. The focus of sovereignty and security in Chinese law results from a history of foreign invasions from 1840 to 1945. The emphasis of economic orders lies in the fact that developing economy is a predominant issue for China currently. Moreover, Chinese courts would also invoke the public policy exception to refuse recognition and enforcement of judgments tainted by fraud or involving enforcement of a foreign penal or taxation law.

SELF QUIZ: Indicate whether each of the following statements is true or false.

17. Enforcement is often confined to non-monetary judgments.

18. In China, recognition and enforcement of foreign judgments can only be conducted according to the principle of reciprocity.

19. Chinese courts have adopted the view of "reciprocity in law."

20. The US also requires reciprocity to recognize and enforce foreign judgments.

21. The Hague Choice of Court Convention does not require an exclusive choice of court agreement.

22. If a defendant was not properly served, the consequent judgment may not be recognized and enforced in a requested country.

23. China does not make a reservation of the service by post under the Hague Service Convention.

24. Chinese courts can deny recognition and enforcement of a foreign judgment, if recognition and enforcement would cause harm to Chinese sovereignty, security, and public order.

Part 5 International Commercial Arbitration

International commercial arbitration has become more and more popular in the international business community. As the President of the Singapore International Arbitration Center Court of Arbitration, Professor Gary Born, indicates "International commercial arbitration merits study because it illustrates the complexities and uncertainties of contemporary international society — legal, commercial and cultural—while providing a highly sophisticated and effective means of dealing with those complexities in a predicable and uniform manner."[1]

Overview of international commercial arbitration?

1. What is international commercial arbitration?

Arbitration is a private dispute resolution mechanism where parties agree to submit their dispute(s) to a private panel without reference to a court of law. The outcome of the proceeding is final and binding on the parties. UNCITRAL Model Law on International Commercial Arbitration (hereinafter "UNCITRAL Model Law") defines the term "commercial" broadly to cover all relations of a commercial nature, whether contractual or not.[2] An arbitration is international if:[3]

a   the parties to an arbitration agreement have, at the time of the conclusion of that agreement, their places of business in different States; or

b   one of the following places is situated outside the State in which the parties have their places of business:

  • the place of arbitration if determined in, or pursuant to, the arbitration agreement;

  • any place where a substantial part of the obligations of the commercial relationship is to be performed or the place with which the subject-matter of the dispute is most closely connected; or

c   the parties have expressly agreed that the subject matter of the arbitration agreement relates to more than one country.

2. What are types of arbitration?

There are two types of arbitration: institutional arbitration and *ad hoc* arbitration. Institutional arbitration means parties select an arbitration institution to conduct their arbitration. The institution provides arbitration rules and will administer the arbitration in accordance with its rules, and the parties will be bound to comply with them. The following are examples of famous arbitration institutions in the world.

---

1   Gary B. Born, *International Arbitration: Cases and Materials*, Preface to Second Edition (2015).

2   Footnote 2 of the UNCITRAL Model Law on International Commercial Arbitration (2006).

3   Article 3 of the UNCITRAL Model Law on International Commercial Arbitration (2006).

Figure 3: Examples of Famous Arbitration Institutions

Ad hoc arbitration is conducted without the assistance of an arbitration institution. *Ad hoc* arbitration is often conducted according to the UNCITRAL Arbitration Rules and seeks administrative supports from the Permanent Court of Arbitration at the Hague. Alternatively, parties may make up the procedural rules themselves. Chinese Arbitration Act only allows institutional arbitration. *Ad hoc* arbitration may be conducted in free trade zones in China.

Figure 4: Permanent Court of Arbitration at the Hague, the Netherlands.

3. Why arbitrate?

Compared with litigation and mediation, the most significant advantage of arbitration is that the New York Convention has established a uniformed international mechanism to recognize and enforce arbitral awards. Member states of the New York Convention shall not impose substantially more onerous conditions or higher fees or charges on the recognition or enforcement of an arbitral award under the Convention than those imposed on the recognition or enforcement of a domestic arbitral award.[1] Recognition and enforcement of the award may be refused

---

1   Id., article. 3.

according to Article V of the New York Convention. In contrast, no equivalent international mechanism exists to recognize and enforce judgments and mediation decisions internationally. Therefore, the convenience of international enforcement of arbitral awards is the best attraction for commercial parties.

A fundamental characteristic of arbitration is finality, which attracts many commercial parties who want to resolve their disputes in a timely fashion. Unlike litigation, arbitration does not provide recourse to appeal.[1] Arbitration awards can, in limited grounds, be set aside at the seat of arbitration according to lex arbitri[2] or can be rejected to recognize and enforce at the state of recognition and enforcement according to the New York Convention.

Flexibility is another advantage of arbitration. For example, parties have autonomy to determine the qualifications of arbitrators; and in disputes involving technical issues, parties can even select non legal professionals as their arbitrators. In contrast, parties cannot select judges in a litigation. Parties can also freely decide the procedure of arbitration while parties have to follow the court procedures in litigation. Arbitration institutions have emergency arbitration rules which can enable parties to get an arbitral award in a very short period of time. Litigations may be lengthy and costly. However, in recent years, arbitrations of complex commercial disputes have been judicialized. For example, arbitration institution rules become more and more complicated, the costs of arbitration are increasing, and sometimes it takes years for an arbitration panel to issue an award. Therefore, parties need to carefully evaluate the costs and benefits before entering into an arbitration.

Arbitration also has the advantage of neutrality. This partly comes from party autonomy in appointing arbitrators. The criticism is that, in order to be re-appointed, some arbitrators may have favourable bias to big companies. Neutrality of arbitration is also because parties can freely select the seat of arbitration. The most popular seats include Singapore, Paris, London and Geneva. The seat of arbitration may have no connection to the disputes and the parties, and parties select it mainly because it has pro-arbitration law and policies, it is neutral to parties, or its geographic location is convenient for parties to travel. Notably, in past decades, commercial courts have quickly emerged and flourished in London, Singapore and Dubai. These commercial courts adopt English common law, hire internationally renowned judges, and establish an international image of expertise and neutrality in commercial litigations. Parties can select these courts by a choice-of-court agreement even if their disputes have no connection with the states where the courts are located. For example, many international maritime and insurance litigations are conducted in London mainly because its courts have long history of and expertise in dealing with these disputes. Even Chinese governments have established special courts to deal with commercial disputes in its free trade zones. These courts enjoy more flexibility in applicable law compared with courts outside of the free trade zones. Therefore, parties need to notice that commercial

---

1   A notable exception is Section 69 (1) of the English Arbitration Act 1996, which provides that "unless otherwise agreed by the parties, a party to arbitral proceedings may (upon notice to the other parties and to the tribunal) appeal to the court on a question of law arising out of an award made in the proceedings".

2   *Lex arbitri* is discussed in details in the following part of "Applicable Law(s)."

courts are "competing" with arbitration in terms of neutrality.

Confidentiality has traditionally been considered as an advantage of arbitration compared with litigation, because confidentiality is an implied duty as the natural extension of the undoubted privacy of the arbitration hearing. Therefore, arbitration has the benefit to help parties to resolve their disputes while maintaining good commercial relationship and public reputation. However, the current trend is while the privacy of the hearing should be respected, confidentiality is not an essential attribute of a private arbitration. If an arbitration is involved with the affairs of public authorities, the public's genuine and legitimate interest in obtaining information about the arbitration may prevail over the parties' implied duty of confidentiality. Therefore, if parties want to ensure the confidentiality of their arbitration, they should sign a separate confidentiality agreement.

4. What is the seat of arbitration?

The "seat" of arbitration is the legal jurisdiction to which the arbitration is tied. The seat is significant because it will determine the applicable law to the arbitration and which national court may intervene during the arbitration and ultimately the extent of this intervention. The award also acquires the "nationality" of the nation where the seat is located for the purpose of enforcement under the New York Convention. For example, parties may agree that their sale of goods contract is governed by Australian Law and disputes shall be submit to an International Chamber of Commerce (hereinafter "ICC") arbitration with its seat in Singapore. In this example, issues of the interpretation of the contract shall be governed by Australian Law. The institutional rules for arbitration shall be those of the ICC. Therefore, the appointment of the arbitrators, timing for the document submissions, etc., shall follow the ICC Arbitration rules. Singapore Law will be applied to the arbitration to determine issues such as arbitrability, the extent to which Singapore court may intervene or assist the arbitral procedure, the conditions that an arbitral award may be set aside, etc. The award will be considered as an award issued in Singapore. This award can be recognized and enforced around the world according to the New York Convention because the Convention applies to Singapore.

The seat of arbitration can be different from the place of hearing. For example, the seat of arbitration can be Singapore but the place of hearing can be arranged in Paris. The place of hearing has no legal significance as the seat of arbitration.

5. What is the legal framework for international commercial arbitration?

(1) International law

The New York Convention of 1958 ensures the recognition and enforcement of arbitration agreements and awards among its member states.[1]

UNCITRAL Arbitration Rules (1976), revised in 2010, provides a comprehensive set of

---

1 Introduction to the New York Convention can be found in Chapter One.

procedural rules for the conduct of arbitral proceedings. It is not a convention and its adoption is based upon private parties' agreement.

States may refer to the UNCITRAL Model Law on International Commercial Arbitration (1985) with amendments as adopted in 2006, when enacting and reforming their domestic laws on arbitration.

(2) IBA rules

International Bar Association (hereinafter "IBA") also provides useful rules that arbitrators and parties may refer to:

- IBA Rules on the Taking of Evidence in International Arbitration (1999, amended in 2010)
- IBA Guidelines on Conflicts of Interest in International Arbitration (2004, amended in 2014)
- IBA Guidelines for Drafting International Arbitration Clauses (2010)
- IBA Guidelines on Party Representation in International Arbitration (2013)

(3) Domestic law

China develops a tri-system mechanism for arbitration:

- Disputes arising out of contract and other proprietary rights and obligations can be arbitrated according to China Arbitration Law (1995).
- Labour disputes should be arbitrated under the China Labour Dispute Mediation and Arbitration Law (2007).
- Rural Land contract disputes can be arbitrated according to the China Rural Land Contract Dispute Mediation and Arbitration Law (2009).

6. Conclusion

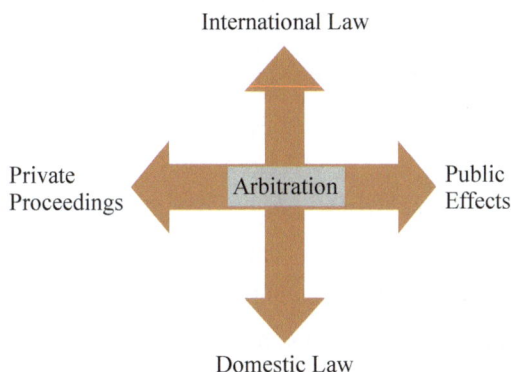

International Law

Private Proceedings — Arbitration — Public Effects

Domestic Law

International commercial arbitration is private proceedings with public effects because arbitral awards can be recognized and enforced internationally under the New York Convention. International commercial arbitration is regulated by both domestic and international laws because of its legal framework.

What are arbitration agreements?

According to the UNCITRAL Model Law, "arbitration agreement" is an agreement made by the parties to submit to arbitration all or certain disputes which have arisen or which may arise between them in respect of a defined legal relationship, whether contractual or not.[1] An arbitration agreement may be in the form of an arbitration clause in a contract or in the form of a separate agreement.[2]

1. Validity requirements

(1) Writing

Arbitration agreements must be in writing. However, writing need to have an expansive interpretation: an arbitration agreement is in writing if its content is recorded in any form, whether or not the arbitration agreement or contract has been concluded orally, by conduct, or by other means.[3] Electronic communication, such as electronic data interchange, electronic mail, telegram, telex or telecopy, are considered as writing. Furthermore, the writing requirement may be satisfied if, when negotiating a contract, parties refer to any document containing an arbitration clause and the reference is such as to make that clause part of the contract.

(2) Defined legal relationship

An arbitration agreement must submit a defined legal relationship to arbitration. The wording of the arbitration agreement is crucial because it determines the scope of the submission. For example, Article 2 of the Supreme People's Court's Interpretation of the China Arbitration Law (2006) states that if parties generally stipulate in their contract that the matter for arbitration is "contract disputes", all disputes arising out of the formation, validity, modification, assignment, performance, liabilities for breach, interpretation, rescission and so forth of the contract are subject to arbitration.

In the following case, the arbitration clause goes beyond contractual disputes and cover tort disputes.

> **CASE EXAMPLE:** *Kaverit Steel Crane Ltd v. Kone Corporation*[4]
>
> **Facts:** A license and distribution agreements contain an arbitration clause indicating all disputes "arising out of or in connection with this contract" shall be referred to arbitration. Claims concerned conspiracy and inducing breach of contract.
>
> **Alberta Queen's Bench** refused to stay the court proceeding, because the tort-based claims fell

---

1 Article 7.1 of the UNCITRAL Model Law.

2 Id.

3 Id., Article 7.3.

4 Kaverit Steel Crane Ltd v. Kone Corporation, (1994) XVII YBCA 346.

outside the scope of the arbitration clause.

Alberta Court of Appeal held that: The wording of the arbitration clause was wide enough to bring within its scope any claim that relied on the existence of a contractual relationship. Because the claim alleging conspiracy by unlawful means to harm Kaverit relied upon a breach of contract as the source of the unlawfulness, that dispute should be referred to arbitration. Claims that were not based on the existence of a contract should proceed to trial.

Take-away point: All disputes "arising out of or in connection with this contract" are often interpreted broadly to include both contractual and tort disputes.

(3) Arbitrability

Arbitrability means that a dispute is capable of settlement by arbitration. Generally, criminal matters and disputes over the grant or validity of patents and trademarks are not arbitrable. However, each state may determine arbitrability differently according to its own law. For example, antitrust issues arising out of international contracts are not arbitrable in China but are arbitrable in the US and the EU.

(4) Designate an arbitration institution

Chinese Arbitration Law recognizes institutional arbitration only. Article 16 of the China Arbitration Law provides that an arbitration agreement shall name a designated arbitration institution. The Supreme People's Courts' judicial interpretation further provides that:

- Where the arbitration institution is inaccurately designated, if the arbitration institution can nonetheless be ascertained, then the arbitration agreement is valid;
- Where parties agree to two or more arbitration institutions, they may choose any one of those arbitration institutions by a supplementary agreement, failing which the arbitration agreement is invalid;
- Where parties agree to the place of arbitration, if there is only one arbitration institution in that place, then that arbitration institution is deemed to be designated and the arbitration agreement is valid; if, however, there is more than one arbitration institution in that place, parties may choose one of the arbitration institutions by a supplementary agreement, failing which the arbitration agreement is invalid; and
- Where parties agree to the arbitration rules only, it is deemed that no arbitration institution is designated, unless the parties reach supplementary agreement on a designated arbitration institution or an arbitration institution can be ascertained according to the agreed arbitration rules.

2. Separability of an arbitration clause and an underlying contract

Separability deals with two issues:

- Whether the underlying contract is nonexistent, ineffective, or invalidity and whether this results in the non-existence, ineffectiveness, or invalidity of the arbitration clause.

- Whether a court or an arbitral tribunal, will consider on an interlocutory basis whether there is a valid arbitration clause.

Article 19 of the China Arbitration Law stipulates that an arbitration clause exists independently and is not affected by the revision, dissolution, termination or invalidity of the underlying contract. The arbitral tribunal has the power to confirm the validity of the underlying contract.[1] Both arbitration institutions and people's courts may rule on the validity of the arbitration clause. In the event that one party applies to the arbitration commission while the other party applies to the people's court, the validity of the arbitration clause shall be decided by the people's court and that any objection to the validity issue shall be raised before the first hearing of the arbitral tribunal.[2] Article 3 of the Supreme People's Court's Reply on Several Issues Concerning the Validity of Arbitration Agreements (1998) provides that, if one party applies to the arbitration institution for a confirmation of the validity of the arbitration agreement, and the other party applies to the people's court to find that the arbitration agreement is invalid, if the arbitration institution accepts the application and renders a decision before the people's court accepts the application, the people's court should not entertain the application. If the arbitration institution accepts the application but has not yet rendered a decision, the people's court should accept the application and notify the arbitration institution to terminate the arbitration.

US and English case law holds that challenges to the validity or legality of the underlying contract should be distinguished from challenges to the existence of the underlying contract. The former does not generally affect the associated arbitration clause, but the latter may. US and English courts also consider whether the challenges target the underlying contract generally or focuses on the arbitration clause specially.

- If the validity, legality, or continued effectiveness of the underlying contract is "*generally*" challenged, arbitrator decides the challenge;
- If the existence, validity, legality, or continued effectiveness of the arbitration clause is "*specifically*" challenged, the court at the seat of arbitration decides the challenge; and
- If the *existence (or formation)* of the underlying contract, as distinguished from its *validity, legality, or effectiveness*, is challenged, the court at the seat of arbitration decides the challenge.

The power of the arbitral tribunal to determine its own jurisdiction, including any objections with respect to the existence or validity of the arbitration agreement, is the so called "competence-competence" principle. In China, arbitral tribunals have no power to determine its own jurisdiction. The power is in the arbitration institutions and the court at the seat of arbitration. In the US and the UK, arbitral tribunals have more power to determine its own jurisdiction. French law even goes further and recognizes a very broad competence-competence regime: it permits arbitral tribunals to consider all jurisdictional challenges, including challenges specifically to the

---

1   Article 19 of the China Arbitration Law.
2   Id, article 20.

arbitration agreement and challenges to the existence of the underlying contract.

> **CASE EXAMPLE:** *Fiona Trust & Holding Corporation v. Yuri Privalov* **[2007] UKHL 40**
>
> **Facts:** Charter parties, which contain arbitration clauses, were procured by bribery.
>
> **Issue:** Whether the allegation of bribery targets the charter parties generally or it focuses on the arbitration clauses.
>
> **The English Court of Appeal held that:** It is not enough to say that the bribery impeaches the whole contract unless some special reason indicates that that the bribery impeaches the arbitration clause in particular. The allegation of bribery targets the charter parties generally and not focuses on the arbitration clauses specially. Therefore, the case should be arbitrated.
>
> Challenges to the "existence" of the charter parties may impeach the associated arbitration clauses when there is a claim that signatures on the charter parties were forged, because the ground of attack is not that charter parties were invalid, but is instead that the signatures to the arbitration clauses, as a "distinct agreement", were forged.
>
> **Take-away point:** If a contract is said to be invalid for reasons such as bribery, unless that bribery relates specifically to the arbitration clause, the clause survives and the validity of the contract as a whole is to be determined by the arbitrators, not the court.

3. Applicable law(s)

Lex arbitri is the law governing the existence and proceedings of the arbitral tribunal. It is often the law of the seat of arbitration. It may not be the same as the law applicable to the substantive matters in dispute.

Lex arbitri applies to the following issues:

- the definition and form of an agreement to arbitrate;
- whether a dispute is capable of being referred to arbitration (that is, whether it is "arbitrable" under the *lex arbitri*);
- the constitution of the arbitral tribunal and any grounds for challenge of that tribunal;
- the entitlement of the arbitral tribunal to rule on its own jurisdiction;
- equal treatment of the parties;
- freedom to agree upon detailed rules of procedure;
- interim measures of protection;
- statements of claim and defence;
- hearings;
- default proceedings;
- court assistance, if required;
- the powers of the arbitrators, including any powers to decide as amiable compositeurs;
- the form and validity of the arbitration award; and

- the finality of the award, including any right to challenge it in the courts of the place of arbitration.

SELF QUIZ: Indicate whether each of the following statements is true or false.

25. Arbitration proceedings should be open to the public.

26. In China, the China Arbitration Act does not apply to labour disputes.

27. Ad hoc arbitration is an arbitration conducted with the assistance of an arbitral institution.

28. The seat of arbitration is very important, because the law of the seat will apply to the arbitration, and also because the award may acquire the "nationality" of the nation where the seat is located for the purpose of enforcement under the New York Convention.

29. The seat of arbitration is the same as the place of hearing.

How to arrange international arbitral proceedings?

1. Establishment and organisation of an arbitral tribunal

According to the UNCITRAL Model Law, parties are free to determine the number of arbitrators, and failing such determination, the number of arbitrators shall be three.[1] Parties are free to agree on a procedure of appointing the arbitrator or arbitrators.[2] In China, if parties fail to agree on the method of formation of the arbitration tribunal or to select the time limit specified in the rules of arbitration, the arbitrators shall be appointed by the chairman of the arbitration commission.[3] An arbitrator can be challenged if he or she is not independent or impartial. Chinese Arbitration Act provides that the arbitrator must withdraw if [4]

- The arbitrator is a party in the case or a close relative of a party or of an agent in the case;
- The arbitrator has a personal interest in the case;
- The arbitrator has other relationship with a party or his agent in the case which may affect the impartiality of arbitration; or
- The arbitrator has privately met with a party or agent or accepted an invitation to entertainment or gift from a party or agent.

Compared with Chinese Arbitration Act, IBA Guidelines on Conflicts of Interest in International Arbitration (2014) provide more comprehensive standards to assess the impartiality and independence of arbitrators. The Guidelines provide four non-exhaustive lists:[5]

a The Non-Waivable Red List includes situations deriving from the overriding principle that no person can be his or her own judge. Therefore, the arbitrator needs to withdraw.

---

1 Article 10 of the UNCITRAL Model Law.

2 Id., Article 11.

3 Article 32 of the China Arbitration Act.

4 Id., Article 34.

5 IBA Guidelines on Conflicts of Interest in International Arbitration (2014), pages 17-27.

- For example, the arbitrator is a manager, director or member of the supervisory board, or has a controlling influence on one of the parties or an entity that has a direct economic interest in the award to be rendered in the arbitration.

b The Waivable Red List covers situations that are serious but not as severe. These situations should be considered waivable, but only if and when the parties, being aware of the conflict of interest situation, expressly state their willingness to have such a person act as arbitrator.

- For example, the arbitrator holds shares, either directly or indirectly, in one of the parties, or an affiliate of one of the parties, this party or an affiliate being privately held. Or a close family member of the arbitrator has a significant financial interest in the outcome of the dispute.

c The Orange List reflects situations that give rise to parties' doubts about the arbitrator's impartiality or independence. The arbitrator has a duty to disclose such situations. The parties are deemed to have accepted the arbitrator, if, after disclosure, no timely objection is made.

- For example, the arbitrator has, within the past three years, served as counsel for one of the parties, or an affiliate of one of the parties, or has previously advised or been consulted by the party, or an affiliate of the party, making the appointment in an unrelated matter, but the arbitrator and the party, or the affiliate of the party, have no ongoing relationship.

d The Green List includes situations where no appearance and no actual conflict of interest exists from an objective point of view. Thus, the arbitrator has no duty to disclose these situations.

- For example, the arbitrator has previously expressed a legal opinion (such as in a law review article or public lecture) concerning an issue that also arises in the arbitration (but this opinion is not focused on the case).

2. Jurisdiction of an arbitral tribunal

Jurisdiction of an arbitral tribunal has been discussed in the above section of Separability. Here we focus on how to challenge jurisdiction of an arbitral tribunal. The party who opposes the arbitral tribunal's jurisdiction may boycott the arbitration, but nonetheless, the arbitration may proceed without the presence of the opposing party and a default award may be rendered against this party.

A good practice for the opposing party is to take part in the proceedings and raise the jurisdictional matter with the arbitral tribunal at the earliest possible stage. According to the UNCITRAL Model Law, the opposing party should submit its plea that the arbitral tribunal does not have jurisdiction not later than the submission of the statement of defence. The opposing party may request the arbitral tribunal to bifurcate the disputes and issue an interim award on the jurisdiction first. If this award is against the opposing party, the party can challenge this award in the court at the seat of arbitration. Alternatively, the opposing party may continue to participate in the arbitration and expressly reserve its position in relation to the issue of jurisdiction. If the arbitral tribunal renders a final award against the opposing party, the party may challenge the award and the jurisdiction in the court at the seat of arbitration or at the place of recognition and enforcement of the award.

3. Conduct of the proceedings

UNCITAL Model Law, national arbitration laws and arbitration institution rules provide detailed guidance for conduct of the proceedings. If parties opt for *ad hoo* arbitration, they can design their own rules for conduct of the proceedings. UNCITRAL Notes on Organising Arbitral Proceedings, ICC Commission Report Controlling Time and Costs in Arbitration and ICC Commission Report—Effective Management of Arbitration are all good resources for parties and arbitrators to refer to. The fundamental principle to the proceedings is that parties shall be treated with equality and each party shall be given a full opportunity of presenting his or her case.[1]

At the stage of documentary disclosure, IBA Rules on the Taking of Evidence in International Arbitration and the Redfern Schedule are useful to help arbitrators to limit disclosure to documents that are relevant and material to the outcome of the case.

Table 1: Theoretical Example of Claimant's Redfern Schedule[2]

Document requested	Relevance and materiality of the documents requested to the outcome of the dispute	Responses and objections to the claimant's request to produce documents	Decision of the arbitral tribunal
1. Any and all documents (including documents in electronic form) consisting of information on the general structure of management and the decision-making processes of the respondent, including minutes of board meetings, shareholders' meetings, and other documentation related to the decision-making process at the top level	The claimant asserts that the way in which the management processes were organised at respondent were inadequate and/or were the cause of the delays to production and the generally poor quality of the product. To prove these assertions, the claimant needs to know the respondent's management structure and needs documents normally produced for the purposes of a company's management at the level of top management (i.e. boards, shareholders' meetings, etc.).	This request is so wide that an order for their production would impose an unreasonable burden on the respondent: see the IBA Rules on the Taking of Evidence, Art. 9.	
2. A record of all previous complaints from customers since production began	Such documents will allow the claimant to establish by the respondent, and to demonstrate that this the management methodology adopted methodology was inadequate and unprofessional.	This request is too wide. However, the respondent is prepared to produce a list of complaints received over the last 18 months, whilst keeping the names of the customers confidential.	
3. All correspondence and other documents with the respondent's legal advisers concerning complaints by other customers	Such correspondence will demonstrate the steps to which the respondent went to deny liability for obvious deficiencies in the product.	To the extent that any such correspondence exists (which is denied), it would be covered by legal professional privilege.	

---

1   Article 18 of the UNCITRAL Model Law.

2   Nigel Blackaby & Constantine Partasides, et. al., *Redfern and Hunters on International Arbitration*, 6th edition, Oxford University Press 2015.

4. Role of national courts during the arbitral proceedings

An arbitration tribunal may need a national court to issue interim/provisional/preliminary measures in situations such as an urgent interim measure is requested prior to the formation of the tribunal, the interim measure affects a third party who is not a party to the arbitration, the tribunal has difficulties in enforcing the measure, or the tribunal has no powers to issue an interim measure because of *lex arbitri*. Therefore, parties need to apply for interim measures before a court. Interim measures include measures that order attendance of witnesses, documentary disclosure, preservation of evidence, preserving the status quo, or relief in respect of parallel proceedings.

When applying for interim measures from a court, parties need to consider three questions.

- What interim measures are allowed by *lex arbitri*?
- If a party to an arbitration agreement makes an application for interim measures to the court rather than to the arbitral tribunal, will this be regarded as a breach of the agreement to arbitrate?
- If the choice between seeking interim measures from the court or from the arbitral tribunal is truly an open choice, should the application be made to the court or to the arbitral tribunal?

The answers can be generally found in *lex arbitri*. For example, Chinese Arbitration Law explicitly provides for two types of interim measures: preservation of property or assets as security for the underlying claims and preservation of evidence.[1] The law further provides that the arbitral tribunal and arbitration institution have no power to issue interim measures: the arbitration institution shall forward the parties' request for interim measures to the intermediate people's court in the place where the evidence or property is located.[2]

How to recognize and enforce arbitral awards internationally?

Recognition and enforcement of arbitral awards internationally are based on the New York Convention. The Convention applies to two kinds of awards: (1) foreign awards that are made in the territory of a state other than the state where the recognition and enforcement of such awards are sought, and (2) non-domestic awards that are not considered as domestic awards in the state where the recognition and enforcement of such awards are sought.[3] For example, awards made in the US will be non-domestic if they are made within the legal framework of another country (e.g., pronounced in accordance with foreign law or involving parties domiciled or having their principal place of business outside the state where the recognition and enforcement of such awards are sought).

Member states shall not impose substantially more onerous conditions or higher fees or charges on the recognition or enforcement of an arbitral award under the Convention than those imposed

---

1 Articles 28 and 46 of the China Arbitration Law.

2 Article 68 of the China Arbitration Law.

3 Article 1 of the New York Convention.

on the recognition of enforcement of a domestic arbitral award.[1]

Recognition and enforcement of an award may be refused according to an exhaustive list under Article V of the New York Convention.

1. Incapacity of party

Parties to an arbitration agreement must have legal capacity to conclude that agreement. Otherwise, it is invalid. Parties' capacity is determined by the law(s) applicable to the arbitration agreement according to the New York Convention and the UNCITRAL Model Law.[2] For example, a natural person's capacity may be determined by both the law of his or her place of domicile or residence or the law of the contract. More complicated scenarios regarding capacity of parties arise in non-signatory of the arbitration agreement, joinder and intervention, and class arbitration.

When determining whether an arbitration agreement between two parties may bind a non-signatory. Courts and arbitration tribunals will focus on the parties' common intention and ask questions such as:

- Whether the non-signatory actively participated in the conclusion of the contract containing the arbitration agreement,
- Whether the non-signatory has a clear interest in the outcome of the dispute, and
- Whether the non-signatory is party to a contract that is intrinsically intertwined with the contract under which the dispute has arisen

If the answers to the above questions are yes, the arbitration agreement may bind the non-signatory.

2. Lack of valid arbitration agreement

The arbitration agreement must meet any formal validity requirements imposed by the law to which the parties have subject it or, failing any indication thereon, under the law of the country where the award was made. These requirements are discussed in the part of "Arbitration Agreement".

3. Violation of "due process"

Under the New York Convention, "due process" refers to scenarios that the party against whom the award is invoked was not given proper notice of the appointment of the arbitrator or of the arbitration proceedings, or was otherwise unable to present his or her case. Arbitral tribunal should not base its decision on any evidence or argument that the parties have not had an opportunity to comment.

---

1 Id., article 3.

2 Article V (1)(a) of the New York Convention and article 36 (1)(a) of the Model Law.

CASE EXAMPLE: *CEEG (Shanghai) Solar Science & Technology Co. v. LUMOS LLC*[1]

Facts: CEEG was a Chinese solar panel manufacturer. LUMOS was a solar energy company in Colorado, the US. The parties had a co-branding agreement under which LUMOS agreed to purchase at least a minimum number of solar panels from CEEG over three years and CEEG warranted that the goods would conform to the contract specification. The agreement provided: "all documentation, notices, judicial proceedings, and dispute resolution and arbitration entered into, given, instituted pursuant to, or relating to, this Agreement be drawn up in the English language." And it provided for arbitration before China International Economic and Trade Arbitration Commission (hereinafter "CIETAC"). On the other hand, it provided that each order for goods would be subject to subsequent purchase contracts. The parties did enter into a subsequent contract, which again provided for CIETAC arbitration but did not provide for the use of English. A dispute arose regarding two shipments of solar modules that LUMOS asserted were defective and CEEG's demand for payment for those shipments. In April 2013, LUMOS received a document written in Chinese with no English translation or any explanation of its contents. All previous communications between CEEG and LUMOS (including those regarding the dispute) had been in English. LUMOS eventually learned that the document was a notice that CEEG had instituted arbitration against LUMOS under the CIETAC rules. By the time LUMOS found a translator to explain the notice and retained counsel, the deadline for selection of arbitrators had passed and the arbitration tribunal that would decide the case had been appointed.

The arbitration proceeded in Chinese, and, following a hearing, the panel issued an award in favor of CEEG. In connection with its decision, the panel determined that the dispute arose solely under the contract and that it had jurisdiction under the arbitration clause in the contract, not the agreement.

The CIETAC Rules provide that if "the parties have agreed on the language of arbitration, their agreement shall prevail. In the absence of such agreement, the language of arbitration … shall be Chinese or any other language designated by CIETAC having regard to the circumstances of the case."

CEEG tried to enforce this arbitral award in the US; LUMOS rejected the enforcement, arguing that it had not been given proper notice.

Issue: Whether the award should be recognized and enforced.

The United States Court of Appeals for the Tenth Circuit rejected the recognition and enforcement of the award. The Court ruled that, CEEG argues that CIETAC, and not CEEG, sent the arbitration notice, but this argument is undermined by the fact that the notice letter appears to have been signed by CEEG's counsel. Regardless, CIETAC's rules plainly state that absent agreement between the parties, arbitration proceedings will be held in "Chinese or any other

---

1 CEEG (Shanghai) Solar Science & Technology Co. v. LUMOS LLC (10th Circuit, the US 2016, Case No. 14-cv-03118-WYD-MEH).

language designated by CIETAC having regard to the circumstances of the case." Thus, CEEG could have moved for CIETAC to proceed in English. CEEG cannot avoid responsibility for insufficient notice by arguing that it assigned to a third party the duty to ensure that the notice was reasonably calculated to apprise LUMOS of the proceedings.

Take-away points: A party can reject recognition and enforcement of an award if it has not been given proper notice.

4. Arbitral tribunal exceeding its authority

If the award deals with a difference not contemplated by or not falling within the terms of the submission to arbitration, the arbitral tribunal exceeds its authority. The award may be set aside completely. If the award contains decisions on matters beyond the scope of the submission to arbitration, the award may be set aside to the extent of such excess of authority, except where it affects the whole award.

5. Irregular composition of the tribunal and irregular procedure

The composition of the arbitral tribunal and the arbitral procedure must comply with the parties' arbitration agreement, or, failing such agreement, with the *lex arbitri*.

6. Award not binding or set aside

If an award has not yet become binding on the parties, or the award has been set aside or nullified by the competent court at the seat of arbitration, a court may refuse to enforce it, at its discretion.

7. Non-arbitrable subject matter

The recognition and enforcement of an award may be rejected, if the subject matter of the dispute is not arbitrable according to *lex arbitri*. Arbitrability is discussed in the part of "Arbitration Agreement."

> **Case Study:** *Wu Chunying v. Zhang Guiwen*[1]
>
> **Facts:** Wu Chunying's husband and Zhang Guiwen entered into an agreement to incorporate a limited liability corporation in Mongolia. This agreement provided that any dispute arising under the contract would be submitted to arbitration with the Mongolian National Arbitration Court (MNAC). During the operation of the company the husband of Wu Chunying passed away. On November 3, 2006, Wu Chunying filed a request for arbitration with the MNAC, seeking, among other things, determination of her ability to succeed to her husband's 50% share in the corporation. The arbitral tribunal accepted her request and ruled, inter alia, that according to the Civil Code of Mongolia Wu Chunying was the legal successor to all rights and properties owed

---

1   Wu Chunying v. Zhang Guiwen, [2009] Min Si Ta Zi No. 33.

by her husband in Mongolia. Wu Chunying applied for recognition and enforcement of the award before the Binzhou Intermediate People's Court in China.

The Binzhou Intermediate People's Court held that: The award should not recognized or enforced under Article V(2)(a) of the New York Convention and Article 3 of the China Arbitration Law. In particular, the court opined that Wu Chunying's right in the corporation as her husband's successor was a matter related to succession law. The Shandong Higher People's Court affirmed this decision. The Shandong Higher People Court reported its opinion to the Supreme People's Court for review in accordance with the Notice of the Supreme People's Court on the Adjudication of the Relevant Issues About Foreign-related Arbitration and Foreign Arbitral Matters by the People's Court. The Supreme People's Court upheld this decision.

Take-away points: First, Article V(2) (a) of the New York Convention provides that recognition and enforcement of an arbitral award may also be refused if the competent authority in the country where recognition and enforcement is sought finds that the subject matter of the dispute is not capable of settlement by arbitration under the law of that country. Succession cannot be arbitrated in China. Second, refusing the recognition and enforcement of a foreign-related or foreign arbitration award in China needs the final confirmation from the Supreme People's Court.

8. Violation of public policy

Public policy generally refers to principles which are fundamental to the legal or economic system of any given state. Different states have different concepts of public policy, so an act that breaches the public policy of one state may not breach that of another state.

SELF QUIZ: Indicate whether each of the following statements is true or false.

30. The primary source of the tribunal's powers is the law of the seat.

31. The validity of an arbitration clause is separated from the validity of the contract that contains the arbitration clause.

32. In China, arbitration institutions, instead of arbitrators, are empowered to determine their own jurisdiction, with national courts having the ultimate power to adjudicate that decision on appeal.

33. Competence means that an arbitral tribunal cannot determine its own jurisdiction.

34. Parties can design arbitration procedures. Therefore, it is unnecessary for the procedure to comply with the fundamental principles of natural justice and due process.

35. A valid arbitration agreement is a prerequisite for recognition and enforcement of a consequent arbitration award.

36. A party can challenge the award either in the seat of arbitration or the place of recognition or enforcement.

37. The Washington Convention regulates the recognition and enforcement of arbitral awards.
38. An arbitrator may be challenged if his or her conducts are not impartial.
39. Incapacity of a party to the arbitration agreement can be a reason to set aside an arbitration award.
40. Arbitrators can decide issues beyond the scope of an arbitration agreement.
41. An award can be challenged for procedural and jurisdictional issues.

Part 6   Dispute Resolution in International Tribunals

Besides civil litigations and commercial arbitrations, international business disputes can also be resolved in international tribunals such as ICSID and WTO.

International Center for the Settlement of Investment Disputes (ICSID)

ICSID is a leading international arbitration institution exclusively devoted to investor-state disputes settlement. ICSID facilitates arbitration and conciliation proceedings to resolve investor-state disputes, and it has been significantly influencing the development of international investment law. It was created in 1965 by the Convention on the Settlement of Investment Disputes between States and Nationals of Other State (hereinafter "the Washington Convention"). The Convention has now been ratified by 161 countries, including China and the US.[1] The most important contribution of the Washington Convention is that it precludes the home state from intervening with the investment disputes solution between its national and the host state. This significantly departs from traditional notions of international law, which requires disputes between a state and the national of another state to be resolved only between the states alone. States that are parties to the Washington Convention are not allowed to take up disputes on behalf of their nationals unless the ICSID arbitration process fails.

In order to constitute an ICSID arbitration tribunal, two requirements must be met. First, the host state and the home state must both be parties to the Washington Convention. Second, the investor and the host state must both consent to ICSID jurisdiction. The following chart illustrates basis of consent invoked to establish ICSID jurisdiction.

---

1   The statistics is up to June 15, 2017.

Figure 6: Basis of Consent Invoked to Establish ICSID Jurisdiction in Cases Registered Under the ICSID Convention, Regulations and Rules[1]

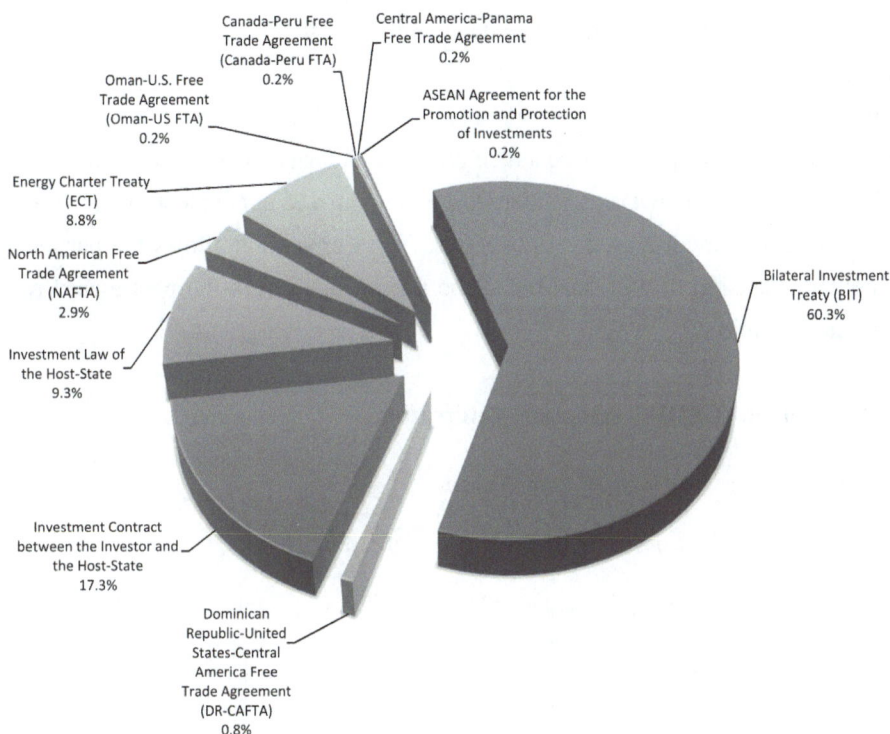

Canada-Peru Free Trade Agreement (Canada-Peru FTA) 0.2%

Central America-Panama Free Trade Agreement 0.2%

Oman-U.S. Free Trade Agreement (Oman-US FTA) 0.2%

ASEAN Agreement for the Promotion and Protection of Investments 0.2%

Energy Charter Treaty (ECT) 8.8%

North American Free Trade Agreement (NAFTA) 2.9%

Investment Law of the Host-State 9.3%

Bilateral Investment Treaty (BIT) 60.3%

Investment Contract between the Investor and the Host-State 17.3%

Dominican Republic-United States-Central America Free Trade Agreement (DR-CAFTA) 0.8%

1. How does ICSID facilitate the settlement of investment disputes?

ICSID does not conciliate or arbitrate disputes. Rather, it provides the institutional facility and procedural rules for independent conciliation commissions and arbitral tribunals constituted in each case. ICSID has two sets of procedural rules that may govern the initiation and the conduct of proceedings under its auspices. These are:

- the ICSID Convention, Regulations and Rules; and
- the ICSID Additional Facility Rules.

ICSID also administers investment cases under other rules such as the UNCITRAL Arbitration rules.

In most cases, ICSID tribunals consist of three arbitrators. ICSID maintains a list of the ICSID Panel of Arbitrators. Each ICSID Member State may designate four arbitrators to the Panel. The ICSID Panel provides a source from which the parties to ICSID arbitrations may select conciliators and arbitrators, but parties may select any person they wish.

2. What are the usual steps in an ICSID arbitration proceeding?

An ICSID Convention arbitration is initiated by submitting a Request for Arbitration to the

---

1   ICSID, The ICSID Caseload-Statistics, 2016-1, 10.

Secretary-General of ICSID. The Request outlines the facts and legal issues to be addressed. The Request will be registered unless the dispute is manifestly outside the jurisdiction of ICSID.

The next procedural step is the constitution of arbitral tribunal. Proceedings are deemed to begin once the tribunal has been constituted. The tribunal holds a first session, typically within 60 days of its constitution.

Subsequently, the proceeding usually comprises two distinct phases: a written procedure followed by in-person hearings. After the parties present their case, the tribunal deliberates and renders its award.

Once an ICSID Convention award is rendered, it is binding and not subject to any appeal or other remedy except those provided by the Convention. The Convention allows the parties to request a supplementary decision or rectification of the award, or to seek the post-award remedies of annulment, interpretation or revision.

Figure 7: Steps in an ICSID Convention Arbitration

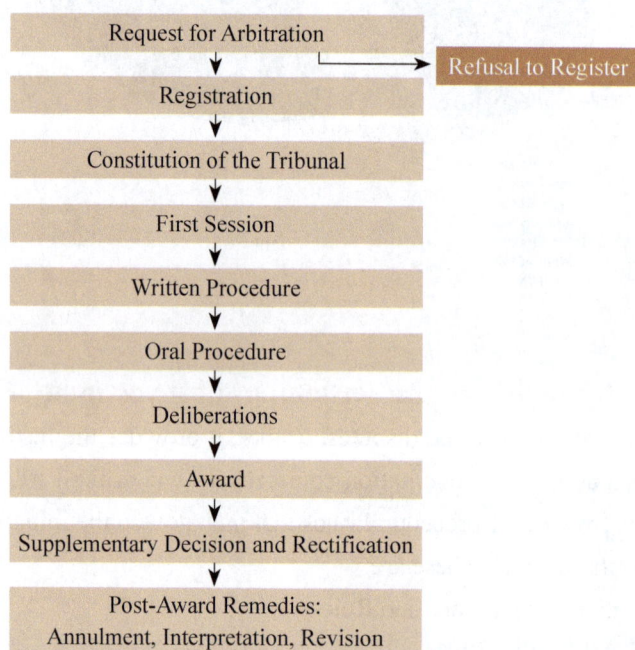

WTO

WTO is responsible for implementing and enforcing the rules of international trade between countries. The Understanding on Rules and Procedures Governing the Settlement of Disputes (hereinafter "DSU") establishes the dispute resolution mechanism of the WTO.

1. What are the organs in charge with administering and carrying out the DSU?

(1) The Dispute Settlement Body (DSB)

The DSB is responsible for establishing the panels, adopting their reports and those of the

Appellate Body, monitoring implementation of rulings and recommendations, and authorizing the suspension of concessions and other obligations in appropriate cases.

(2) The Dispute Settlement Panels

Panels are to assist the DSB by making an objective assessment of the matter referred to it , including the facts of the cases ,the applicability of and conformity with the pertinent WTO agreements, and by making findings that will help the DSB to make recommendations and rulings to resolve the dispute.

A panel is generally made up of three panelists unless the parties to the dispute agree within ten days of its establishment that it should consist of five panelists. Panelists serve in their individual capacities but not as representatives of any government or organization.

Even if a special meeting has to be convened for the purpose, a panel report is adopted automatically by the DSB within sixty days after it has been circulated, , unless (1) one of the parties to the dispute notifies the DSU that it is going to appeal or (2) the DSB decides by consensus not to adopt the report. If there is an appeal, the DSB will not consider the report until the appeal is completed.

(3) The Appellate Body

The Appellate Body only reviews the legal issues contained in the panel report and the legal interpretations developed by the panel. The Appellate Body may uphold, modify, or reverse a panel's findings and conclusions, and its report will automatically be adopted by the DSB unless the DSB decides by consensus not to do so.

The Appellate Body is made up of seven persons , three of whom will serve on any one case. The seven must be the people from recognized authorities with demonstrated expertise in law, international trade, and the subject matter of the WTO Agreement and its annexes. Their term of office is four years, and once renewable.

Table 2: The DSB Timetables

60 days	Consultation, mediation, etc.
45 days	Panel set up and panelists appointed
6 months	Final panel report to parties
3 weeks	Final panel report to WTO members
60 days	DSB adopts report (if no appeal)
Total=1 year	(without appeal)
60-90 days	Appeals report
30 days	DSB adopts appeals report
Total=1 year 3 months	With Appeal

2. Enforcement

Panel and Appellate Body reports adopted by the DSB are enforced by the DSB. The DSB is responsible for monitoring compliance and, should a state fail to comply with panel or Appellate Body decisions, the DSB may authorize either the non-complying state to pay compensation or the injured state to retaliate.

SELF QUIZ: Indicate whether each of the following statements is true or false.

42. ICSID deals with all kinds of commercial disputes.

43. One precondition for the ICSID to accept a case is that the host state and the home state must both be parties to the Washington Convention.

44. BITs and FTAs can demonstrate a host state's consent to ICSID jurisdiction.

45. WTO panel's decision is final.

46. WTO Appellate Body only reviews the legal issues contained in the panel report and the legal interpretations developed by the panel.

47. When a losing party fails to comply with panel or Appellate Body decisions, this party may have to pay compensation or the injured party may retaliate.

Questions

1. Eye Co., a shipping company headquartered and incorporated in Country I, signed a contract with Kay Co., a company headquartered and incorporated in Country K, to transport goods for Kay Co., from Country K to Country L. No provisions were made in the contract about where disputes would be settled or what law would be used to resolve them. As Eye Co.'s ship delivering the goods was entering the harbor of Country L, the ship blew up, destroying all of Kay Co.'s goods. The parties did not reach any choice of law or choice of court agreements. Kay Co. brought suit in a court in Country L. Eye Co. now argues that the court does not have jurisdiction and that Country L law should not be used to decide the dispute.

Question A

If the Country L is China, does the Chinese court in the harbor have personal jurisdiction over Eye Co.? If the Country L is the US, does the US court in the harbor have personal jurisdiction over Eye Co.?

Question B

What law should be applied?

2. During the negotiations leading to a contract, a facsimile was sent which included a statement "other terms and conditions as per…standard contract." The contract contained an arbitration clause. Some days later, the parties signed a contract in which no mention was made of any

standard contract. When the court proceedings were commenced to recover damages for breach of the contract, an application was made for a stay for arbitration.

Question: Should the court proceedings be stayed?

3. What are the problems that "Reciprocity in Practice" may create in judgment recognition and enforcement?

Suggested Further Readings

Zheng Sophia Tang, Yongping Xiao and Zhengxin Huo, *Conflict of Laws in the People's Republic of China*, Edward Elgar Publishing, 2016.

Jie Huang, *Interregional Recognition and Enforcement of Civil and Commercial Judgments: The Lessons for China form the US and EU Laws*, Hart Publishing, 2014.

Armand Mestral, *Dispute Settlement Under the WTO and RTAs: An Uneasy Relationship*, 16 J Int Economic Law 777, 2013.

Gustavo Laborde, *The Case for Host State Claims in Investment Arbitration*, 1 J Int. Disp. Settlement 97, 2010.

Franklin O. Ballard, *Turnabout Is Fair Play: Why a Reciprocity Requirement Should Be Included in the American Law Institute's Proposed Federal Statute*, 28 Hous. J. Int'l L. 199, 2006.

Susan D. Franck, *The Legitimacy Crisis in Investment Treaty Arbitration: Privatizing Public International Law Through Inconsistent Decisions*, 73 Fordham L. Rev. 1521, 2005.

Donald C. Clarke, *China's Legal System and the WTO: Prospects for Compliance*, 97 Washington University Global Studies Law Review 97, 2005.

Susan L. Stevens, *Commanding International Judicial Respect: Reciprocity and the Recognition and Enforcement of Foreign Judgments* 26 Hastings Int'l & Comp. L. Rev. 115, 2002-2003.

Sean D Murphy, *Contemporary Practice of the United States Relating to International Law,* 95 Am. J. Int'l. L. 387, 2001.

Chapter **3**

Business Organizations

Nowadays, people normally utilize some forms of business organizations to carry out business activities, so it is crucial to select the form that fits best their business situations and achieves their business goals. Business organizations have various forms, each of which has its own advantages and disadvantages. This chapter will introduce the commonly-used forms of business organizations in China and the US, analyze their characteristics, advantages, and disadvantages, and compare their similarities and differences.

This chapter consists of the following parts:

Part 1 introduces the basic forms of business organizations, identifies the key factors used to determine which form should be chosen, and lists the different forms of business organizations in China and the US.

Part 2 discusses Sole Proprietorship.

Part 3 analyzes the features of partnerships in China and the US.

Part 4 analyzes the features of corporate forms in China and the US.

Part 5 discusses a special unincorporated form of Limited Liability Company (LLC) in the US.

Part 6 explores the differences between branch offices and Subsidiaries.

▌ Learning Objectives

By the end of this chapter you should:

- Understand the common forms of business organizations.
- State the key features of sole proprietorship, partnership, corporation, limited liability company and branch office.
- Understand the characteristics of three types of partnerships: General Partnership, Limited Partnership and Limited Liability Partnership.

- Understand the differences between two corporate forms in China.
- Outline the legal requirements to establish the business organizations in China and the US.
- Identify the differences between business organizations in China and the US.

■ Key Terms

Branch office	Limited Partnership
Corporation by Share	LLC Agreement
General Partnership	Piercing the Corporate Veil
Limited Liability Company in the US (LLC)	Registered Capital (or Legal capital)
Limited Liability Corporation in China	Sole Proprietorship
Limited Liability Partnership	Subsidiary

Part 1 What Are Business Organizations?

Business organizations are the vehicles used to carry out commercial activities. Basic forms of business organizations include the following:

- Sole Proprietorship
- Partnership
- Corporation
- Limited Liability Company (LLC in the US)
- Branch office and subsidiary

Key factors in selecting forms of business organization

Imagine you want to start a business, the first question is "what kind of business organization should I use?" How to choose the best form to fit your business purpose may depend on your particular circumstances, but generally you will need to consider the following factors:

- Owner liability
- Transferability of ownership
- Number of owners
- Legal capital requirement
- Continuity requirement
- Type and size of business
- Financing
- Tax
- Other regulatory requirements

1. Owner liability

Potential liabilities (eg, debts) from operating a business organization can be either limited or unlimited for owners[1]. This means an owner risks either his or her investment into the business organization (thus "limited") or the owner's other personal assets (eg, his or her personal cars or personal bank account, thus "unlimited"). For instance, the exposure to risks for an owner in an LLC, corporation or limited partnership is limited to his or her investment, with the exception of fraud or "Piercing the Corporate Veil."[2] In contrast, the owners of a sole proprietorship, general partnership, or branch office face unlimited personal liabilities.

2. Transferability of ownership

If you want to exit your investment in a business organization, can you easily sell your share of interests to others? Do you need consent from other owners of the business organization (except for sole proprietorship)? Those questions largely depend on the factors such as shareholders and the form of business organization. Comparatively speaking, transferring shares of a corporation is easier than those of an LLC or partnership, and transferring shares to other shareholders in a corporation is easier than transferring to non-shareholders, because LLCs and partnerships are considered "closely-held" and depend mostly on the personal trust of members or partners. For instance, a shareholder of a Chinese Limited Liability Corporation can easily transfer part or all of his/her shares to other shareholders without the need to get any consent from other shareholders, while if such shareholder wants to transfer part or all of his/her shares to non-shareholders (outsiders), such shareholder will need to get the consent of more than majority of the other shareholders. In contrast, in a Chinese General Partnership, if a partner wants to exit from the partnership, such partner needs to get the consent of all other partners, or the specified situations which allows for such exit have occurred.

3. Number of owners

Different countries may have different requirements of minimum or maximum number of owners allowed in different business organization. Say, if you want to start a business by yourself, sole proprietorship may be your only option in some countries. But in China, the forms of "single-shareholder corporation" and "individual industrial and commercial household" are available, in addition to sole proprietorship. In comparison, a partnership or a LLC normally require at least two owners.

4. Registered capital requirement

The concept of "registered capital"[3] refers to the legal requirement on the minimum amount of

---

1 Owners are generally referred to as "shareholders" in a corporation, "members" in an LLC or "partners" in a partnership.

2 The principle of "Piercing the Corporate Veil" will be discussed in Part 4.

3 Registered Capital is also referred to as "Legal Capital".

capital to be invested into a business organization by owner(s). The purpose of registered capital is both to make sure a business organization has the necessary "seed money" to start business and to offer creditors some sort of protection if the business organization fails. China used to require registered capital for Limited Liability Corporations be CNY 30,000 (approximately USD 5000) and for corporations by shares be CNY 5 million (approximately USD 800,000). But these legal capital requirements have now been abolished in most industries in order to incentivize Chinese economy. In the US, registered capital requirement for corporations varies from state to state. In most states, registered capital requirement is just nominal, which means incorporating with a capital stock of USD 10 or USD 100 is possible. Partnerships or LLCs are not required on registered capital, but owners may choose to, on their own, set the minimum capital requirement in the partnership or LLC agreement.

5. Continuity requirement

A business organization can either continue perpetually or with a limited term of life, which will depend on the specification of the formation document. Generally, corporations can last forever; LLCs specify the duration in the LLC agreement; partnerships are limited to the life of a general partner.

6. Type and size of business

Type and size of business may affect the kind of business organization you can use. For instance, a sole proprietorship allows for a single owner and is more suitable for small business. If you want to engage in professional services (for instance, accounting or legal services), limited liability partnerships or general partnerships may be the appropriate forms. If you have more than 50 members, in China, you cannot use Limited Liability Corporation, but should use the Corporation by Shares.

7. Financing

Corporations are more flexible and easier to raise capital, because it is easier to attract additional investments from investors who like the easy transferability of their investment. In contrast, people may be more cautious to get into partnerships as partnerships depend more on personal trust and relationship.

8. Tax consideration

A corporation is a separate legal entity, so it faces "double taxation." This means, a corporation will be taxed for its corporate level profits, and then its shareholders will be taxed again at the personal income tax level for the dividends distributed by the corporation. In contrast, LLCs or partnerships will only have "one-layer of taxation" at the personal income tax level. Sometimes LLCs or Partnerships are called "pass-through entities," as the profits or losses of those entities will "pass through" to the owners directly.

9. Other regulatory requirements

If a business involves certain industry, additional regulatory approval or license will be required before one can start his or her own business. For instance, if it involves banking or insurance, special approval will be needed from the regulatory body, such as the banking regulatory authority or insurance regulatory authority.

Different forms of business organizations in China and the US

Now you have a general sense of what a business organization is and the key factors that affect people's decision to ultimately use which form to carry out their business. We will then take stock of different forms currently existing in China and the US in Table 1.

Table 1: Forms of Business Organization in China and the US

Forms of Business Organizations in China	Forms of Business Organizations in the US
Sole Proprietorship • Individual Industrial and Commercial Households • Single-Individual Owned Enterprise	Sole Proprietorship
Partnership • General Partnership (including Special General Partnership) • Limited Partnership	Partnership • General Partnership • Limited Partnership • Limited Liability Partnership
Corporation • Limited Liability Corporation • Corporation by Shares • Single-Shareholder Limited Liability Corporation	Corporation • C corporation • S corporation
Not Available	Limited Liabilities Companies (LLC)
Branch Office (including representative office of foreign companies)	Branch Office
Foreign Invested Enterprises • Sino-Foreign Joint Venture • Sino-Foreign Joint Cooperation Companies • Wholly Foreign Owned Entities (WFOE)	Not available

From the table above, the major forms of business organizations look similar in the US and China, but will they also have the exact same characteristics? We will examine in more details in Parts 2-6.

SELF QUIZ: Indicate whether each of the following statements is true or false

1. Owner's personal liability is not a key factor in selecting a business organization.
2. Registered Capital requirement is only to ensure that a business has enough "seed money" to start its business.
3. In China, Foreign Invested Enterprises can take the form of Sino-Foreign Joint Venture.
4. In the US, there exists the concept of Foreign Invested Enterprises.
5. In China, the minimum registered capital of RMB 30,000 is required by law.
6. In the US, all states require minimum registered capital.

Sole Proprietorship

Sole proprietorship is the oldest and simplest form of business organization. An individual may operate a sole proprietorship under his/her own name or a trade name. Due to its flexibility and simplicity, sole proprietorship is more suitable for small businesses.

Table 2: Key Features of a Sole Proprietorship

Advantages	Disadvantages
• Easy to form, and no need to file, unless necessary license or permit is required. • No registered capital required. • Sole control of ownership and operation by sole proprietor. • Flexible management and operation. • Only taxed at the personal income level.	• The sole proprietor assumes unlimited personal liability for all debts and obligations of the sole proprietorship.[1] • Difficult to get financing, as the stock of Sole proprietorship is not transferable to investors, and banks may fear the credibility of repayment if sole proprietorship fails.

Forms of sole proprietorship in China

There are two forms of sole proprietorship in China: Individual Industrial and Commercial Households and Single-Individual Owned Enterprise.

1. Individual Industrial and Commercial Households

Individual Industrial and Commercial Households (hereinafter "IICH") can be operated by an individual or by a household (family). If by an individual, the individual has the unlimited liability; if by a household, the household has the unlimited liability. No registered capital is required for IICH. To form an IICH, filing with the local Administration of Industry and Commerce (AIC)[2] is

---

1　In the US, the sole proprietor may obtain some protection through liability insurance.

2　State Administration of Industry of Commerce (hereinafter "SAIC") is a government bureau under the State Council; SAIC administers and supervises market orders and activities, including registration and supervision of business organizations. In each province and city, SAIC has the local AIC to carry out its duties.

required. The sole proprietor has to submit an application letter, copies of his or her (or the households') IDs and the address of the business operation. Once approved by the local AIC, IICH will be issued a business license listing the name of the owner, business scope and operating premises. If any item on the business license changed, the owner is required to make amendment filings at the local AIC.

CASE EXAMPLE: *ABC Gymnastics Products Corporation v. Mr. Lei*[1]

Facts: ABC Gymnastics Products Corporation (Plaintiff) was the legitimate owner of a registered trademark of "PUMA" under the trademark category No. 25 involving sports wears and clothing. Mr. Lei (Defendant) operated a booth as an IICH, selling clothes in a shopping mall located in Shapingba district, Chongqing city of China. Plaintiff sued Defendant because the Defendant sold clothing bearing the trademark of "PUMA" without proper authorization by Plaintiff. Defendant could not prove it has legitimately procured the clothes bearing "PUMA" marks and could not provide the name of the upper stream source.

The First Instance Court held that: Defendant, Mr. Lei, infringed the trademark right of Plaintiff, and was ordered to pay CNY 5,000 (USD 800) as damages to Plaintiff.

Take-away points: The owner of an IICH will need to bear personal responsibility of the debts or obligations against the IICH.

---

2. Single-Individual Owned Enterprise

A Singled-Individual Owned Enterprise, as its name indicates, can only be established by one single individual. Such individual owns and operates the business, and is responsible for the business' profits or loss, liabilities, with his or her own personal assets or family assets, and whatever he or she indicates as contributions.

It is very similar to IICH, with major differences that Single-Individual Owned Enterprise must operate with a business name and can establish branch offices.

US sole proprietorship

The US does not have special forms of sole proprietorship like China does. In the US, to form a sole proprietorship does not normally require filing nor taking other formal action. As long as you conduct business as the only owner, you have a sole proprietorship. The exception is if your business requires certain necessary permit or license. For instance, selling alcohol or firearms will require federal license, or if the sole proprietorship wants to operate under a trade name. In addition, the US sole proprietorship is run and owned by the sole proprietor, but not by the sole proprietor's household.

---

1   Chongqing City Shapingba District People's Court, Case No. (2009) Sha Fa Zhi Ming Chu Zi No.6.

Part 3   Partnership

Partnership is a type of business organization in which two or more persons[1] pool money, property, technology, or other resources and work together as partners to share profits and losses in accordance with an oral or written partnership agreement. General forms of partnership include General Partnership, Limited Partnership and Limited Liability Partnership.

Basic structure of a partnership

Unlike a corporation which is normally required by law to have the structure of shareholder's meeting, board of directors, and board of supervisors, a partnership is generally more flexible and its structure is to a very large extent shaped by its governing document—the partnership agreement. Often general partners have the general management rights; limited partners, instead, do not engage in the day-to-day management. However, the partnership agreement may delegate the management to a management team or delegate certain management rights to limited partners.

Partnerships in China

Partnership enterprises are governed by China's Partnership Enterprise Law. The law provides two forms of partnership enterprises: General Partnership and Limited Partnership. Key characteristics of a partnership enterprise include:

- Filing with government authority is required;
- Partners may include individuals or other business entities, such as corporations;
- There must be a written partnership agreement;
- General partners assume unlimited liability whereas limited partners assume limited liability only to the extent of their investment;
- General partners participate in business and management as co-owners, whereas limited

---

1   Persons can be natural persons or legal persons.

partners do not engage in the business or management.

1. Forms of partnership

(1) General partnership

General Partnership has only one type of partners: general partners who assume unlimited liabilities. Individuals, legal persons or other organizations can be general partners. However, state-owned entities, public corporations, non-for-profit enterprises and people holding special positions, such as police, prosecutors, or judges, cannot be general partners.

The method of contribution made by general partners can be flexible, including money, property, labor, skills, intellectual properties (eg, patent or trademark), and property-use right or other property rights.

A special form of general partnership ("Special General Partnership") exists in the professional areas, such as law firm or accounting firms. Due to the high specialization of those professional areas, it would be unfair, for instance, in a law firm to ask a partner who specializes in corporate law to assume unlimited liabilities for the damages caused by a partner who specializes in criminal law. As such, the liabilities of general partners in a Special General Partnership are slightly different—general partners who have caused severe damages due to their intentional conduct or gross negligence assume unlimited liability, and other general partners are liable only to the extent of their share in the General Partnership. But for all other debts/damages not caused by intentional conducts or gross negligence of general partners, the general rule of unlimited liability for all partners will apply.

(2) Limited partnership

Limited Partnership has at least one general partner and one limited partner, but no more than 50 partners in total. General partners have unlimited liabilities, whereas limited partners have only limited liabilities. Just as mentioned before, state-owned entities, public corporations, not-for-profit enterprises and people holding special positions such as police, prosecutors or judges, cannot be general partners for Limited Partnership, but they can be limited partners.

Limited partners cannot make "labor" as their contribution to Limited Partnership. But limited partners can contribute money, property, technology, or other resources, like general partners do.

2. Formation of partnership

Application with the local AIC along with an application letter, written partnership agreement and IDs of partners are required to form a Partnership Enterprise. When the application is approved, a business license is issued to the Partnership Enterprise. Like a corporation, a Partnership Enterprise can establish branches by making filing at the city where it desires to establish one.

The partnership agreement shall include the following:

    a. name of the partnership and scope of business;

b. name and address of partners;

c. contribution method, amount and deadline for contribution ;

d. profit and loss sharing plan;

e. admission and withdrawal ;

f. dispute resolution;

g. dissolution and liquidation ;and

h. liability of breach.

In addition to the above, the agreement for a Limited Partnership shall also include:

a. qualification and selection method for executive partners;

b. scope of authorization and penalty for exceeding authorization by executive partners;

c. condition for dismissal and reselection method for executive partners;

d. method used to convert Limited Partnership into General Partnership or vice versa.

3. Management of partnership

(1) General partnership

For general partnership, all partners have the same right to participate in management of partnership, but can also be flexible to choose other management styles, such as: ask one or more partners to manage, or every partner to manage a designated area. If one or more partners are designated to be executive partners, other partners will still have the right to supervise partnership matters.

The fiduciary duties prohibit partners in a general partnership from competing with the partnership by setting up another business by himself/herself or with others. Also, a general partner shall not conduct self-dealing, unless approved by all other partners.

(2) Limited partnership

For Limited Partnership, only general partners have the right to participate in management of the partnership. If a limited partner, by his/her acts, makes a third party believe such limited partner has the authority to act for the partnership, and accordingly strike a deal, this limited partner will assume unlimited liability for this particular deal.

The fiduciary duties do not prohibit limited partners from competing with the partnership or self-dealings; after all, the limited partners do not participate in partnership business and such limited involvement makes limited partners more like a shareholder in a corporation. However, the partnership agreement can provide differently.

4. Profit and loss sharing

A partnership agreement can provide specific mechanisms for the profit and loss sharing among partners. If the partnership agreement does not provide, the partners can come to a conclusion by discussion. If the discussion fails, the sharing will be according to the contribution percentage. If the contribution percentage cannot be determined, profit and loss will be allocated equally among partners.

The partnership agreement for general partnership is prohibited by law to allocate all profits or all losses to certain partners. Partners are jointly and severally liable for all obligations of General Partnership. The joint and several liability means that partnership creditors, after exhausting the partnership assets first, can go after the personal assets of any particular partner for the entire amount of remaining debts. This particular partner cannot defend that he/she is only liable for certain share according to his/her contribution. But this partner is entitled to indemnification from other partners for the portion he had paid for other partners.

In contrast, the partnership agreement for limited partnership is also prohibited by law to allocate all losses to certain partners, but is OK to allocate all profits to certain partners. The rationale behind this is to protect third party creditors who may be put into an unfair and disadvantage position by not possibly knowing the internal loss-sharing mechanism, if the agreement allocates all losses to limited partnerships. After all, limited partners are only liable to the extent of their investment

Partnership in the US

A partnership is an association of two or more persons to carry on as co-owners a business for profit. A written partnership agreement is not required to establish a partnership. Receiving a share of profits can sometimes be seen as "prima facie" evidence that a person is a partner in the business.

There are three kinds of partnerships in the US: General Partnership, Limited Partnership, and Limited Liability Partnership (for professionals).

1. General partnership

General partnership is one of the oldest forms of doing business in the US and is subject to individual state laws. Most state laws have adopted the similar definition of "an association of two or more persons to carry on as co-owners a business for profits." The US courts have also taken into consideration various factors in determining whether a general partnership is formed, especially in cases where there exists no partnership agreement. Those factors[1] include whether the parties

    a. intended to proceed as partners;

    b. shared profits or losses;

    c. had the right to participate in the control of the enterprise;

    d. jointly held real property.

As long as all factors establish that a partnership scheme exists, partners' intent to form a

---

1   In re Medallion Realty Trust, 103 B.R. 8,12-14

partnership is not required. Instead, it is possible for parties to intend no partnership or to call it something else or even expressly declare that they are not to be partners, but a factual partnership can still found to be existent. [1]Partners are jointly and severally liable for all obligations of general partnership.

> ## CASE EXAMPLE: *Lupien v. Malsbenden*[2]
>
> **Facts:** Mr. Malsbenden (Defendant) entered into a written agreement with Mr. Cragin, doing business together as "York Motor Mart" to build a car that Mr. Lupien (Plaintiff) was contracted to buy. Malsbenden and Cragin breached the purchase contract with Plaintiff, as they never delivered the car to Plaintiff. Plaintiff sued Malsbenden (Mr. Cragin was also sued, but disappeared), claiming that the Defendant should be liable as a partner to the car-building business for the breaching of that contract. The Defendant claimed that he was not a partner, and instead, he was just a creditorbecause he loaned USD 85,000 to Mr. Craig, without interest, to finance the car construction project.
>
> **The Trial Court held that:** The defendant was a partner in the car building business, because Defendant's "total involvement" in the car construction business was that of a partner. The Appellate Court confirmed and reasoned: 1) Defendant was actually involved in the day-to-day business operations of the car building business, 2) the loan made by Defendant was not in the form of fixed payments, but in the form of day-to-day purchases of parts, kits or equipment for the car construction business; also the "loan" was not paid in a fixed amount, but from the business profits.
>
> **Take-away point:** While sometimes parties may not want to form a partnership, but formation of a partnership is not solely based on the intent of the parties. If the parties pool their capital and skills, with joint control over the business and with intent to share profits and loss from the business, a partnership can be still found to exist even on the contrary to the parties' intent.

2. Limited partnership

A limited partnership has at least one general partner with unlimited liability and at least one limited partner with the liability limited to the amount invested. Characteristics of a limited partnership include:

    a. Partners may be individuals or business entities;

    b. General partners participate in the management and control of the partnership business, whereas limited partners normally don't;

    c. The limited liability of limited partners may be lost if they participate in the management of the partnership business.

Unlike general partnerships, which can be formed by partners' conducts, limited partnerships

---

1   James Bailey Co., v. Darling, 119 Me. at 328, 111A. at 411

2   Supreme Judicial Court of Maine, 477 A.2d 746; 1984 Me. Lexis 735

require partners to file documents at the Secretary of State.[1]

Unlike general partners, limited partners only have limited liabilities for the obligations of the limited partnership up to the amount they invested in the partnership. There is an exception: when limited partners participate in the control and management of limited partnership, such limited liability protection may be lost. However, whether and how this exception is applied vary from state to state. For instance, some state laws use a "substantial same control" test to apply the exception: if a limited partner is actively involved in the partnership business and exercising the substantially same powers as a general partner, the limited partner may assume unlimited liability. In contrast, the latest Revised Uniform Limited Partnership Act did not apply the exception but use the most liberal approach—offering the full-protection to limited partners regardless whether/how much they control or manage the Limited Partnership.[2]

3. Limited liability partnership (for professionals)

Limited liability partnership (LLP) is a special form of general partnership used mostly by law firms or accounting firms. LLP has similar features of general partnership except one distinct feature in terms of liability. Unlike partners of general partnership who assume unlimited liability for all of partnership obligations, partners of LLP assume unlimited liability only for certain partnership obligations. State laws vary on the extent of the liability. Some states provide that LLP partners only assume unlimited liability for certain obligations that arise from his/her own activities (i.e. negligence, wrongful acts or misconduct of the partner or of those supervised by the partner), but not from other partners' activities. Other states provide that LLP partners assume unlimited liability for contractual obligations of an LLP in addition to those arising from the partner's activities. The "limited liability" shield is intended to protect lawyers or accountants against excessive liability of wrongdoings by other partners. This makes sense because it will be unfair if a partner specializing in the corporate law be held accountable for the wrongdoing or malpractice of other partners specializing in criminal law.

To form a LLP, one needs to make filings at the local Secretary of State. If the LLP is formed before the filing, it will be deemed as a general partnership with all partners personally liable for all of partnership liability until the filing.

4. Comparison of China and the US partnership forms

- Both China and the US have similar partnership forms: general partnership and limited

---

1   Section 201, Revised Uniform Limited Partnership Act. Such document must set forth the following: name of the Limited Partnership; name and business address of each general partner; name and address of the registered agent; address of the registered office; the latest date upon which the Limited Partnership will be dissolved.

2   Section 303, Revised Uniform Limited Partnership Act. The latest RULPA offers full-protection to the limited partners from obligations of Limited Partnership, and got rid of the "control rule" exception to the limited liability in its previous versions.

partnership, which have similar features.

- A special form of general partnership used by professionals (such as attorneys and accountants) exists both in China and the US. In China, it is called "Special General Partnership", whereas in the US, it is called "Limited Liability Partnership".

- In China, filing with local government authority is required to form a general partnership, whereas in the US, no such filing is required.

- China's partnership law explicitly prohibits certain persons from acting as general partners, such as state-owned entities, public corporations, not-for-profit enterprises and people holding special positions such as police, prosecutors or judges, but the US does not.

- General partners in China and the US have similar fiduciary duty not to compete with the partnership business.

SELF QUIZ: Indicate whether each of the following statements is true or false.

11. To establish a partnership enterprise (general partnership or limited partnership) in China, one does not need to file any documentation with local government agencies.

12. In China, a state-owned entity can become a general partner in a partnership enterprise.

13. A Limited Partnership agreement can provide that all losses are borne by certain partners.

14. A limited partner in a limited partnership can contribute labor as contribution.

15. Partners in a general partnership can set up another business to compete with the general partnership.

16. In the US, partners need to file with the Secretary of State to form a general partnership.

17. Limited partners normally enjoy limited liability in a Limited Partnership.

18. Exceptions to the limited liability of limited partners exist in some US states, where such limited partners exercise the "substantially same control" as general partners do.

19. In the US, a formal written partnership agreement is required to form a general partnership.

20. In the US, the intent to form a partnership is not necessarily required to form a general partnership.

21. In the US, filing with Secretary of State is required to form a limited partnership or LLP (for professionals).

22. Partners in a US LLP (Limited Liability Partnership) have less extensive liability than partners in a general partnership do.

23. Partners in a US LLP are not liable for the misconduct or negligence of other partners.

24. In China, certain persons cannot act as general partner, such as state-owned entity and not-for-profit enterprises.

What is a corporation?

A corporation is a separate legal entity, which is incorporated through registration or filing with governmental authorities. It conducts business in its own name, has its own rights and obligations as provided by law, can own properties and can sue in its own name. Corporation is better suitable for mid-to-large business.

The key features of a corporation include the following:

- *Limited liability.* Shareholders of a corporation are not personally liable for the corporation's obligation[1]. In other words, if the corporation incurred huge losses or debts, shareholders' liability is "limited" to the amount of investment they put into the corporation, and they do not have to worry that the corporate debts or obligations will endanger their other personal assets (eg, the money sitting in their personal bank account, or their personal cars). This is one of the most critical characteristics separating corporations from other forms of business organizations, such as partnership or sole proprietorship.

- *Separate legal person.* A corporation is treated by law as a "separate legal person." A corporation has almost all the rights and liabilities of a person, including having its own legal name, owning its own properties, right to sue and to be sued. It is separate from its shareholders, directors, officers, or employees. The veil of the corporation protects those people from the corporation's debts and losses.

- *Continuous existence.* The legal existence of a corporation can be perpetual, unless the incorporation documents clearly specify the term of the corporation.

- *Centralized management.* A corporation is normally managed under the direction of a board of directors that appoints officers to manage the day-to-day operation of the corporation. Therefore, a shareholder does not normally involve in the daily operation of the corporation, unless this shareholder is also a director or an officer.

- *Transferability of ownership interest.* Transferability of ownership to non-shareholders normally will require consent from other shareholders. The details are provided in a corporation's governing document. In general, shares of a corporation are more transferable than the interest of a partnership.

Table 3: Advantages and Disadvantages of Using a Corporation

Advantages	Disadvantages
• Limited liability • Transferability of ownership • Centralized management	• Double taxation: corporate earnings are subject to corporate tax, and then shareholder dividends are subject to personal income tax.

(to be continued)

---

1   With the exception of "Piercing the Corporate Veil."

(continued)

Advantages	Disadvantages
• Easier to generate capital by either issuing or selling stocks, or getting loans from banks	• Strict requirement on corporate formality and procedures, for instance, corporations are required to hold shareholders' and board of directors' meetings and keep meeting minutes. • More costs associated with forming, operating and maintaining a corporation.

Corporation forms in China

There are two basic forms of corporation in China: Limited Liability Corporation and Corporation by Shares, both are subject to China's Corporation Law and relevant regulations. If we differentiate the nationality of shareholders, there also exist Foreign Invested Entities ("FIE"), which can be a Limited Liability Corporation or Corporation by Shares. FIEs are subject to additional sets of laws specially governing foreign invested companies.

• **Limited Liability Corporation**

Key characteristics of Limited Liability Corporation in China include the following:

  a. The number of shareholders cannot exceed 50, but can be as few as just one .
  b. A shareholder has only limited liability for the corporate debts or losses.
  c. Simplified incorporation procedures. Compared with a Corporation by Shares, a Limited Liability Corporation has a more simplified incorporation procedure.
  d. Restriction of transferability to non-shareholders. Due to the relatively small size of a Limited Liability Corporation, the close connection and trust among shareholders, transferring one's shares to non-shareholders requires consent of a majority vote of the remaining shareholders, unless the articles of association provides differently. In contrast, shareholders in a Corporation by Shares are free to transfer their shares to other shareholders.
  e. Closely-held corporation. A Limited Liability Corporation does not need to publicize its incorporation procedure nor its operation status, like a publicly-held corporation does.

Single-Shareholder Limited Liability Corporation is a special form of Limited Liability Corporation. Either an individual or an enterprise can be the single shareholder. For a single shareholder to enjoy the limited liability, this shareholder must prove clear separation of its personal assets from the corporate asset. If the shareholder fails to do so, such shareholder will bear personal liability of the Limited Liability Corporation's obligations or debts.

CASE EXAMPLE: *Mr. Ye Longying v. Suqian Yunhewan Eco-Food Limited Liability Corporation and Mr. Sun Xuezhi*

Facts: Mr. Yelongying (Plaintiff) reached an agreement with Suqian Yunhewan Eco-Food Limited Liability Corporation (Defendant) to provide sea food to Defendant and get paid at the end of each month. After Plaintiff started to provide sea food, Defendant paid only partial of the total payment due. On May 14, 2013, Defendant issued a note to Plaintiff stating "Defendant owned Plaintiff the sea food payment in the amount of CNY 239,000, which would be due on August 30, 2013". Not able to successfully get the payment, Plaintiff sued Defendant and its single shareholder Mr. Sun Xuezhi for the payment.

The First Instance Court held that: Defendant should pay to Plaintiff the amount stated on the note and Defendant's single shareholder to be jointly liable for the payment, as the single shareholder failed to provide evidence to show that his personal assets were separate and independent from the assets of Defendant.

Take-away point: In order to take advantage of the limited liability of the single-shareholder Limited Liability Corporation, the shareholder shall maintain a separate accounting system for the corporation and shall separate corporate assets from personal assets.

- **Corporation by Shares**

The key characteristics of a Corporation by Shares include the following:

   a. Registered Capital is divided into shares with equal value. This is the most important feature of a Corporation by Shares.
   b. Number of shareholders cannot be less than 2 shareholders and cannot exceed 200 shareholders.
   c. A shareholder limits his/her liability for the corporate debts or losses only to the shares it subscribed to the corporation.
   d. Free transferability of shares. Shareholders can freely transfer their shares without the prior consent of other shareholders.
   e. Publicly-held corporation. The corporation can issue more shares to the public to raise capital. It also has the disclosure obligation, such as to make public its financial numbers, in order to help the public to make investment decisions.

The table below compares the key features of Limited Liability Corporation and Corporation by Shares in China:

Table 4: Comparison of the Key Features of Limited Liability Corporation and Corporation by Shares in China

Limited Liability Corporation	Corporation by Shares
Shareholders subscribe to certain percentage/ portion of Registered Capital	Registered Capital are divided into shares with equal value
Limited liability for shareholders	Limited liability for shareholders
1 to 50 shareholders	2 to 200 initiators
Transferring shares to non-shareholders needs consent of other shareholders	Freely transfer to non-shareholders; needs NO consent of other shareholders

(to be continued)

(continued)

Limited Liability Corporation	Corporation by Shares
Closely-held corporation, depending on personal trust of shareholders; No information disclosure obligation	Publicly-held corporation. Mandatory information disclosure obligation

- **Foreign Invested Enterprises (FIE)**

There are three kinds of FIE: Chinese-Foreign Equity Joint Ventures (EJV), Chinese-Foreign Contractual Joint Ventures (CJV), and Wholly-Foreign Owned Enterprise (WFOE).

Key characteristics of EJV include the following

  a. The EJV is a Limited Liability Corporation;
  b. Both foreign and Chinese shareholders can be corporations, enterprises, other economic organizations, but foreign shareholders can also be individuals while Chinese shareholders can't;
  c. Foreign and Chinese shareholders will share profit and loss according to their contribution/investment into the EJV;
  d. Foreign shareholder(s) is/are required by law to account for minimum 25% of the total Registered Capital of EJV;
  e. EJV does not have the shareholders' meeting, instead, its highest power is the board of directors appointed by the shareholders.

Key characteristics of CJV include the following:

  a. The CJV can be a Limited Liability Corporation or a partnership;
  b. Both foreign and Chinese shareholders can be corporations, enterprises, other economic organizations, but foreign shareholders can also be individuals while Chinese shareholders can't;
  c. The contract between foreign shareholder(s) and Chinese shareholder(s) is the controlling document that govern their profit, loss sharing, and management. In other words, shareholders are not required to share profit or loss according to their contribution or investment amount;
  d. If the CJV is a Limited Liability Corporation, the 25% rule will apply, that is, the foreign shareholder(s) should contribute to at least 25% of the total registered capital;
  e. CJV has more flexibility in its management than EJV, as CJV can provide its management styles in the contract by choosing from one of the following methods: board of directors, joint management committee or authorized third-party management.

Key characteristics of WFOE include the following:

  a. WFOE is 100% owned by foreign investors;
  b. WFOE can be a limited liability corporation or a partnership, and in practice, most

WFOEs are limited liability corporations;

c. foreign investors can be corporations, enterprises, other economic organizations, or individuals.

1. What are the incorporation requirements?

In China, anyone who wants to establish a corporation needs to fill out government forms and submit supporting paperwork at the local AIC, which is the government authority in charge of company registration. The issuance of a business license indicates the formal establishment of a corporation.

- **Incorporation requirements for Limited Liability Corporation are that:**
  a. at least one but no more than 50 shareholders;
  b. the articles of association have been adopted and approved by all shareholders (or by the single shareholder);
  c. with a qualified business name and governance bodies;
  d. having the necessary company premises to conduct business.

- **Incorporation requirements for Corporation by Shares are that:**
  a. at least 2 but no more than 200 initiators. In addition, at least half of the shareholders must have residences in China, but it is not required that those shareholders have Chinese nationality;
  b. share issuance and subscription must be in compliance with the law;
  c. the articles of association have been enacted by the subscribers or at the incorporation meeting;
  d. with a qualified business name and governing bodies;
  e. having the necessary corporate premises to conduct business.

- **Incorporation requirements for FIE are that:**
  a. Any FIE needs pre-approval by relevant foreign trade bureaus before registering at the AIC;
  b. the pre-approval package of documents normally include: application letter, feasibility study, JV letter of intent (if it is a JV), contract, and articles of association, board of directors personnel etc.;
  c. within 30 days after getting the pre-approval, FIE investor(s) shall follow the normal procedure of registering a corporation at the AIC.

2. What is a business license?

In China, business licenses are issued to business organizations to indicate their legal establishment. For corporations, a legal person business license will be issued, which normally lists essential information as follows:

a. business name
b. registered address
c. name of the legal representative
d. corporation type
e. business scope
f. Registered Capital
g. date of incorporation
h. duration of the corporation

Corporations are required to display the legal person business license in public in a noticeable position at the corporation's registered address. Whenever the items on the business license are amended, the corporation has the obligation to make an amended filing at the AIC within the time period required by law.

3. The requirement of registered capital

Shareholders can contribute to the registered capital in different methods: cash, tangible property (eg. car), intellectual property (eg. patent right), land-use right, or other non-cash property.

If a shareholder contributes non-cash investment, proper evaluation needs to be made to assess the actual value of the non-cash investment. Also, the ownership of the non-cash investment should be properly and timely transferred to the corporation.

The minimum amount of registered capital is no longer required[1], but is subject to some exceptions where minimum amount of registered capital can still be required by other laws or regulations. For instance, the minimum registered capital for an insurance company should be CNY 200 million.

In addition, China also relaxes the timeline to fulfill the capital contribution, and let shareholders make the decision. For instance, the law used to require shareholders of a Limited Liability Corporation to pay contribution in full amount no later than two years from the date of the incorporation.

4. Articles of Association and its amendment procedure

The Articles of Association is the most important corporate document that specifies detailed regulations for a corporation's operations. It defines the rights and obligations of shareholders, authorities of board of directors and officers, business scope, financial or accounting rules, as well as other corporate governance matters.

The Chinese law specifies the mandatory content and the discretionary content of articles of association. The mandatory content for Limited Liability Corporations and Corporations by

---

1   This amendment is with the legislative intent to further lower incorporation thresholds for small-mid enterprise and to encourage economic development.

Shares is summarized in the table below:

Table 5: Mandatory Content for Limited Liability Corporations and Corporations by Shares

Limited Liability Corporation	Corporation by Shares
(1) Corporate name and premises (2) Business scope	
Not available	(3) Incorporation methods (to specify incorporation by initiation among initiators or by offering to the public)
(3) Registered capital amount	(4) Total number of shares, value per share, and registered capital
(4) Name of shareholders	(5) Name of shareholders (normally called as "initiators" or "promoters"), shares subscribed by each shareholder, contribution methods, and timeline for contribution
(5) Contribution method, amount of contribution, and timeline for contribution[1]	
(6) Governing bodies[2] and the rules for the formation, authorities and voting	(6) Composition, power and rules for board of directors
(7) Legal representative	
Not available	(8) Composition, power and rules for board of supervisors
Not available	(9) Profit distribution methods
Not available	(10) Reasons for winding up and liquidation methods
Not available	(11) Methods of notice and publication
(8) Other matters deemed as fit by the shareholders' meeting	(12) Other matters deemed as fit by the shareholders' meeting

If any item in the articles of association needs to be amended, the board of directors must make a motion. Then the board of directors needs to notify shareholders of such amendment. Finally, the shareholders having 2/3 voting rights shall vote for the amendment in order to pass the amendment. After this internal procedure, the corporation needs to make a filing of the articles of association amendment at the local AIC.

---

1   While the recent Amendment to Chinese Corporation Law does not require timeline for shareholders to fulfill their capital contribution in full, but the shareholders should specify their own timeline in the Articles of Association.

2   "Governing bodies" mostly refer to board of directors (or executive director) and board of supervisors (or executive supervisor).

5. Incorporation methods

There are two legally permitted incorporation methods: 1) incorporation among initiators and 2) incorporation by raising capital from the public.

(1) Incorporation among initiators

This method requires all subscriptions to the registered capital are made by initiators. A Limited Liability Corporation can only be incorporated by this method. A Corporation by Shares can either use this method or "incorporation by raising capital from the public" as below.

(2) Incorporation by raising capital from the public

This method allows all initiators to subscribe to only certain portion of the corporate shares (stocks). The remainder of the corporate shares will be subscribed by raising capital from the public (either specified/targeted public or unspecified public). A Limited Liability Corporation cannot use this method, because it is closely-held corporation where personal trust and relationship play key roles. As incorporation by raising capital from the public involves the general public's interest, laws generally require strict procedures, in order to protect such interest. For instance, in China, initiators' portion of subscription must be no less than 35% of the total corporate shares to ensure that initiators have their stake in the corporation. Please refer to the table below for the comparison.

Table 6: Incorporation methods of Limited Liability Corporations and Corporations by Shares

Incorporation methods	Limited Liability Corporations	Corporation by Shares
1) Incorporation among Initiators	✓	✓
2) Incorporation by Raising Capital from the Public	✗	✓

6. What is business scope?

Business scope is the description of business operations that a corporation is permitted by law to carry out. After being approved by the relevant authority (eg. Administration for Industry and Commerce, AIC), a corporation needs to clearly specify in its articles of association the business scope, which will also be shown in its business license. Contracts or business activities that are conducted outside the business scope may be deemed as invalid. However, there is a trend to further relax this business scope restriction.

7. Powers of shareholders' meeting

A corporation's articles of association should specify how often the regular shareholders' meetings will be held. The law also provides the situations where an emergency meeting should be held whenever one of the following situations occurs:

Table 7: Situations Where Emergency Meetings Should Be Held

Limited Liability Corporation	Corporation by Shares
1) Shareholder(s) with more than 10% voting power propose 2) Over 1/3 of directors propose 3) Supervisors' committee proposes	1) The number of directors are less than 2/3 of the number provided under the law or Articles of Association 2) Loss is more than 1/3 of the total equity 3) Shareholder(s) with more than 10% shares (individually or aggregately) propose 4) Deemed necessary by the board or supervisors' committee 5) Other situations provided by the Articles of Association.

The shareholders' meeting has the following powers by law, which are:

a. deciding on the direction of corporate operation and investment plan;

b. appointing directors and supervisors and deciding their compensation;

c. approving the reports submitted by directors and supervisors;

d. approving the financial budget and planning, and financial profit and loss plans;

e. resolving to increase or decrease registered capital;

f. resolving on matters of merger, acquisition or dissolution;

g. resolving on the amendment to the articles of association; and

h. other powers as specified in the articles of association.

8. Board of directors and corporate officers

Appointed by shareholders' meeting, Limited Liability Corporations' board of directors should consist of 3-13 directors, and for Corporations by Shares, 5 to 19 directors. For Limited Liability Corporations of a small scale or with few shareholders, one executive director is allowed. In comparison, Corporation by Shares will always have a board of directors.

The board of directors appoints management officers to run the daily operations of a corporation, including general managers, finance managers, etc.

9. Supervisors' committee

Supervisors' committee (or sometimes called "board of supervisors") is appointed by and responsible to the shareholders' meeting. As its name indicates, the main function of the supervisors' committee is to supervise the board of directors and the officers in the areas of financial and business operations. Directors or officers cannot sit in the suppervisors' committee at the same time, otherwise it will likely cause direct conflict of interest issue.

For Limited Liability Corporations and Corporations by Shares, the number of supervisors in a supervisor's committee shall be no less than 3 persons. For Limited Liability Corporation with small scale or a few shareholders, the supervisors' committee is not required, but 1 to 2 supervisors should be appointed. For corporations 100% owned by the State, the number of supervisors shall be no less than 5 persons, among whom at least 1/3 should be representatives of the employees.

10. Fiduciary duty of the board of directors, supervisors' committee and managers

The board of directors, supervisors' committee and managers have certain fiduciary duties towards the corporation to not harm the interest of the corporation and to bring optimal results for shareholders, including but not limited to:

   a. not use their positions and powers in the corporation to realize personal interest;
   b. not disclose trade secrets of the corporation;
   c. not conduct commercial bribery or other illegal conducts;
   d. not embezzle corporate assets.

In addition to the duties above, there are certain duties specific to the board of directors and the managers who are in charge of the operational decision-making and daily management, which include:

   a. not use corporate funds for their own personal benefit;
   b. not lend corporate funds to others or to use corporate funds to provide guarantee for others except with the prior approval of the board of directors or shareholders' meeting;
   c. no self dealing with the corporation alone, except with the prior approval of the shareholders' meeting;
   d. not take the business opportunities that belongs to the corporation for their own personal benefit;
   e. not engage, by themselves or together with others, in any business that competes with the corporation.

11. The doctrine of "Pierce the Corporate Veil"

If shareholders abuse "the separate legal person" status of a corporation and cause serious harm to corporate creditors, such shareholders may be personally liable for the corporate debts or liabilities. To determine "abusive" conduct, courts often take into consideration of various factors, including but not limited to:

• mingle shareholders' personal assets with a corporation's assets;
• use the corporation as a shell to conduct infringing or illegal business;
• undercapitalization of a corporation;
• fraudulent or deceived conducts by shareholders.

Corporation forms in the US

Different classifications of corporations exist in the US. We will focus on two major classifications: The first is from the aspect of federal tax treatment, S corporation and C corporation, whose names derive from the subchapter S and subchapter C of the American Internal Revenue Code; The second is from the aspect of whether shares are publicly traded, closely-held corporation and publicly-held corporation. A corporation in the US normally exists perpetually unless otherwise specified by law or by the articles of incorporation.[1]

- **S Corporation and C Corporation**

S Corporation and C Corporation are essentially similar in all aspects other than the tax treatment. A comparison table is below for easy understanding:

---

1 Section 3.02 Model Business Corporation Act. Articles of incorporation functions similarly to articles of association.

Table 8: C Corporation and S Corporation

C Corporation	S Corporation
A separate legal entity for tax purpose	A flow-through entity for tax purpose
Double taxation	Single taxation: no corporate income tax; shareholders dividends subject to personal income tax
If corporate earnings are distributed as salaries, C Corporation may deduct them as expense, which is thus not subject to tax.	Not available
Default form of corporation	Needs to elect "S" corporation as the form
No such limitation	Certain limitations: (1) no more than 75 shareholders (2) only have one class of share (3) not allow corporate shareholders (4) Non-resident alien shareholder is not allowed (5) all shareholders consent to elect S corporation

- **Closely-held Corporation and Publicly-held Corporation**

As the names indicates, a publicly-held corporation is a corporation "held by the public," meaning it has shares traded on public securities market so that the public are free to sell or buy shares; whereas a closely-held corporation is held by a close-group of people, and its shares are not traded on public securities market.

1. What are the incorporation requirements?

One or more persons may act as the incorporator(s) by delivering Articles of Incorporation to the Secretary of State for filing. Once the Articles of Incorporation are accepted by the Secretary of State, corporate existence begins, unless a delayed effective date is specified.[1] The Articles of Incorporation normally must set forth the following[2]:

    a. the corporation name;

    b. the number of shares the corporation is authorized to issue;

    c. the street address of the corporation's registered office and the name of its registered agent;

    d. name and address of each incorporator.

---

1   Sections 2.01& 2.03 Model Business Corporation Act.

2   Section 2.02 Model Business Corporation Act.

There are some other items that a corporation has the discretion to include into the Articles of Incorporation, such as the names and addresses of the directors, purpose(s) of the corporation, par value for authorized shares or classes of shares, among others.

Approval certificate is sometimes required for the companies in certain industry. For instance, for any corporation that has "bank", "trust" or "trustee" in its name, the Secretary of State shall not file the Articles of Incorporation unless a certificate of approval from Commissioner of Financial Institutions.[1]

2. What is a statutory agent?

A statutory agent, sometimes called registered agent, is the corporation's agent for service of process, notice, or other demand required or permitted by law to serve on the corporation, for instance, to receive or send legal documents on behalf of a corporation. A statutory agent can be an individual or an entity, and must reside in the same state as the state of incorporation. Appointment of a statutory agent must be filed with the Secretary of State. If a corporation wants to change its statutory agent, the corporation needs to file a statement of change to the Secretary of State. If the statutory agent needs to change its address, it shall notify the corporation and shall file a statement of change to the Secretary of State.

3. Bylaws

Bylaws are the set of rules that regulate how a corporation will be operated or managed. Bylaws are adopted by the incorporators or the board of directors. State laws normally provide for the mandatory information and optional information into the bylaws. Bylaws normally shall include the number of directors, maximum and minimum number of directors. Bylaws may include all other provisions that are not in conflict with the Articles of Incorporations and laws, including but not limited to[2]:

　　a. how shareholders' meeting, board of directors' meeting, committee meetings are conducted;

　　b. the qualifications, duties, and compensation of directors; the time of their annual election; and the requirements of a quorum for directors' and committee meetings;

　　c. the appointment and authority of committees of the board;

　　d. the appointment, duties, compensation, and tenure of officers;

　　e. the mode of determination of holders of record of its shares;

　　f. the making of annual reports and financial statements to the shareholders.

4. The doctrine of "Piercing the Corporate Veil"

One of the major advantages for corporations is the limited liability to protect the shareholders

---

1　Section 201, California Corporations Code.

2　Section 212, California Corporations Code.

against any creditors of a corporation going after the shareholders. Courts however may "Piercing the Corporate Veil" and refuse to recognize the corporation's separate existence from its shareholders in certain circumstances where shareholders will be held personally liable. The US courts may take into consideration the following factors when applying the doctrine of "Piercing the Corporate Veil":

a. commingling personal and corporate acts, for instance, paying personal bills with corporate credit cards, checks, or money;

b. undercapitalization in regards to its scale of operation and risks;

c. fraud, such as misrepresenting the corporate financials to a lender;

d. operating the corporation to always show no profit;

e. failing to observe corporate formalities and procedures.

How the doctrine of "Piercing the Corporate Veil" is applied by using what tests may vary from state to state. For instance, some states hold that merely failing to observe corporate formalities is a prima facie evidence of unfairness. Some states hold that only if common fraud is found to exist, will the "Piercing the Corporate Veil" be used. Other states take into account of "totality of the circumstances."[1]

CASE EXAMPLE: *DeWitt Truck Brokers v. W. Ray Flemming Fruit Co.*[2]

Facts: DeWitt Truck Brokers (Plaintiff) sued Mr. Flemming, the president of W. Ray Flemming Fruit Co., seeking to impose personal liability on Mr. Flemming (Defendant) of the Fruit Company's corporate debts. The Fruit Company used Plaintiff's transportation services to transport fruits to the market for sale, but did not make the payment. The trial court found various facts to support its decision of "Piercing the Corporate Veil", including 1) the Fruit Company was essentially a one-man close corporation, 90% of whose shares were owned by Defendant, 2) there was never a shareholders' meeting being held, 3) no corporate records of a real directors' meeting, although Defendant claimed the Fruit Company indeed had a director who traveled a lot, 4) neither the shareholders nor officers of the Fruit Company (except for Defendant) ever received any dividend or salary from the Fruit Company, and when Defendant withdrew funds (USD 15,000 annually) from the Fruit Company, there was never a board resolution to record those withdrawals, 5) the Fruit Company was undercapitalized and operating at no profit, 6) when Plaintiff expressed concerns of the delay in receiving the payment from Defendant, Defendant admitted his previous reply to Plaintiff "if the Fruit Company failed to make the payment, I would personally take care of it."

The Appellate Court held that: Not a single factor can serve as a sufficient ground for disregarding the corporate separate status. The court took into consideration of the various factors

---

1 Epperson & Canny, *The Capita Shareholder's Ultimate Calamity: Pierced Corporate Veils and Shareholder Liability in the District of Columbia*, Maryland and Virginia, 37 Cath. U.L. Rev. 605-626.

2 United States Court of Appeals, Fourth Circuit, 1976

which supported the corporation's separate entity status was disregarded on the grounds of equity and fairness, and confirmed the lower court's judgment of imposing personal liability on Defendant under the theory of "Piercing the Corporate Veil".

Take-away point: While the limited liability protection to a corporation's shareholders is the presumption of the corporation theory, this presumption depends on the observation of the separate and distinct status of a corporation. If the corporation is merely used as "shell" to cause unfairness and inequity, the common law doctrine of "Piercing the Corporate Veil" may rebut that presumption and impose personal liability on shareholders or officers.

5. What is the duty of care by board of directors?

As the executive body for a corporation, the board of directors is charged with the duty of care by acting in good faith for the best interest of the corporation. In practice, this means directors should be kept informed of the activities of the corporation, and be familiar with the financial status of the corporation, make sound judgments and decisions in the best interest of the corporation.

CASE EXAMPLE: *Francis v. United Jersey Bank*[1]

Facts: Two sons (also the directors) of the founder of a corporation misappropriated large sums of money from the corporation in the form of "shareholder loans," and made other improper payment using corporate money to family members. Due to this misappropriation of corporate funds, the corporation was insolvent. The bankruptcy trustee sued the other director Mrs. Pritchard (the widow of the corporation's founder) for not exercising due care in connection with the misappropriated corporate funds of more than USD 10 million. The fact revealed that Mrs. Pritchard was not active in the business of the corporation, knew virtually nothing of the corporate affairs, never read or obtained the annual financial statements. She made no effort to assure the policies and practices of the corporation, particularly regarding the withdrawal of corporate funds, complied with industry custom or relevant law. The financial statements of the corporation showed on its face the misappropriation of trust funds.

The Appellate Court held that: Mrs. Pritchard did not exercise due care as a director, was negligent in keeping a director's obligation of basic knowledge and supervision of the business of the corporation, and did not make reasonable attempts at detecting and preventing the illegal conduct of other directors. The Appellate Court upheld the trial court's decision in finding the case against Mrs. Pritchard.

Take-away point: Directors should exercise due care by acting for the best interest of the corporation.

---

1   87 N.J.15, 432 A.2d 814 (1981)

6. What is business judgment rule?

The business judgment rule is a legal principle that protects corporate directors, officers, or managers from consequences of the management decisions they made within their power. Even if those decisions may have incurred loss to the corporation, as long as those decisions are made in good faith and with reasonable skill and prudence, the US courts normally apply this business judgment rule to defer the judgment to directors or officers and not to resolve for a corporation the questions of policy and business management. The rationale behind this rule is to ensure the directors and officers to make sound but sometimes difficult decisions without the fear of personal liability.

CASE EXAMPLE: *Shlensky v. Wrigley*[1]

Facts: The Chicago National League Ball Club is a corporation owning and operating the major league professional baseball team (the Corporation). Plaintiff, a minority shareholder of the Corporation, sued the Corporation and the directors, seeking to order the Corporation and the directors to install lights in the baseball field and schedule night games. Plaintiff alleged night games served the purpose to maximize attendance, revenue and income for the Corporation. Plaintiff further claimed the directors (one director is Mr. Wrigley) refused to install lights due to some personal opinion of Mr. Wrigley who had concern for the neighborhood.

The Appellate Court held that: Unless there was fraud, illegality or conflict in the directors' decision not to install lights and not to play night games, the courts should not interfere, and concluded that Mr. Wrigley's concern for the neighborhood and the property value of the baseball field was reasonably within the decision power of the management, and beyond the court's jurisdiction.

Take-away point: The management and directors have within their authority and power to make decisions in good faith. Courts of equity will not interfere unless it is clear that the management is guilty of fraud, or misappropriation of corporate funds, conflict of interest, or other inappropriate conducts which can amount to as an abuse of discretion.

Comparison of corporate forms of China and the US

- Chinese corporations do not distinguish S Corporations from C Corporations; therefore they are subject to double taxations.
- Chinese corporations are subject to national-level laws only, such as Chinese Corporation Law. The regulations issued by AIC can only be based on those national-level laws. The US corporations are subject to various state corporate laws, which are not necessarily based on federal laws.
- Both the US and Chinese law have the similar doctrine of "Piercing the Corporate Veil."

1　Appellate Court of Illinois, 1968, 95 Ill. App. 2d 173, 237 N.E.2d 776

- Both the US and Chinese law require fiduciary duty of directors and officers.
- In China, a corporation is normally allowed to do business within the business scope stated in its business license. In contrast, there is no such limitation for US corporations, which are allowed to do any legal business.
- Chinese corporations do not require a statutory agent, while the US corporations do.

SELF QUIZ: Indicate whether each of the following statements is true or false.

35. Both China and the US have S corporation and C corporation.

36. In the US, corporate governance matters are normally governed by federal laws.

37. The doctrine of "Piercing the Corporate Veil" is to impose liability only on the parent company.

38. One of the major differences between S corporation and C corporation is the tax treatment by the US tax code.

39. S corporation limits its number of shareholders to 55.

40. One similarity between a public company and a private company is their shares can be bought or sold at public securities market.

41. The concept of "business scope" exists both in the US and China.

42. Both China and the US require incorporators to file with the relevant government agencies in order to form a corporation.

43. Both China and the US corporations have the board of supervisors.

44. The Business Judgment Rule is to protect shareholders' decisions on how the corporation should be run.

Part 5 Limited Liability Company in the US

A Limited Liability Company (LLC) is an "unincorporated" business organization operating under an LLC Agreement with the tax benefit of a partnership and limited liability of a corporation.[1] It first appeared in 1970s and gained popularity as an attractive alternative to corporations due to its characterization of the "best of the both worlds."[2] Now, most states in the US have LLC statutes.

LLC as an "unincorporated" business organization and LLC formation

As an "unincorporated" form, LLC is not subject to various corporate requirements as other

---

1   Susan Pace Hamill, *The Limited Liability Company: A Catalyst Exposing the Corporate Integration Question*, 95 Mich.L.Rev. 393,446 (1995)

2   Elf Atochem North America, Inc. v. Jaffari and Malek LLC, Supreme Court of Delaware, 1999, 727 A.2d. 286

corporations do. For instance, most state laws normally impose mandatory corporate structure and internal corporate procedures on corporations, which include the following:

a. Regular shareholders meeting and board directors meeting must be observed;
b. Notice of those meetings must be given unless expressly waived;
c. Decisions made by shareholders or board of directors must be voted upon at meetings;
d. The corporate secretary shall prepare minutes of meetings, and keep a minute book for retention purpose.

In contrast, LLC laws normally do not require those corporate formalities. The governance and operation of LLCs are mostly depending on the LLC Agreements entered by all members.

To form an LLC, filing the LLC's Articles of Organization with the local Secretary of State is required. The Articles of Organization normally include:

a. the name of the LLC, with "LLC" as part of the name;
b. the duration of the LLC's existence;
c. the statutory agent;
d. the name and address of the organizer.

LLC members and limited liability

Members are the owners of LLCs, functionally similar to partners in partnerships and shareholders in corporations. Members may be individuals or business entities (such as a corporation or another LLC). Some US states allow single-member LLC, while other states require a minimum number of two members in an LLC.

Members enjoy the limited liability as shareholders do. All LLC statutes provide that members and managers of LLCs are not liable for the LLC debts, obligations, and other liabilities. For instance, Texas Business Organization Code § 101.114 (2013) of "Liability for Obligations" provides: "Except as and to the extent the company agreement specifically provides otherwise, a member or manager is not liable for a debt, obligation, or liability of a limited liability company, including a debt, obligation, or liability under a judgment, decree, or order of a court."

> **CASE EXAMPLE:** *Phillip Alexander Hajdasz, Appellant v. Chase Merritt West Loop LLC, Appellee*[1]

Facts: A lease agreement for office space was entered into between Chase Merritt West Loop LLC (the "landlord"), and Global Funding Services LLC (the "tenant"). The tenant's operation manager (Mr. Phillip Hajdasz) signed this lease agreement. Later, the tenant could not pay its rent, so the landlord sued the operation manager to hold him personally liable for breach of lease agreement.

---

1 Court of Appeals of Texas, Fourteenth District, Houston, 2010 Tex. App. LEXIS 7129, NO. 14-09-00045-CV

The Appellate Court held that: Mr. Phillip Hajdasz was not liable based on the general rule that managers are not individually liable for the debts of an LLC unless the LLC Agreement provides differently.

Take-away point: Members or officers/managers are generally protected by the limited liability of an LLC.

Exception of "Piercing the Veil" to LLCs

As stated previously, the US courts use the common law equitable doctrine of "Piercing the Corporate Veil" to hold shareholders personally liable for the corporate debts and obligations, when the corporation is used as a "shell" to inappropriately realize shareholders' personal gains. The US courts have also applied the same doctrine to LLCs to avoid inequitable situations where members abuse limited liability protection of LLC to advance personal gains.

LLC operating agreement

An LLC operating agreement is the most important document among LLC members that provides for the governance and operation of an LLC. This agreement is functionally similar to a partnership agreement or a corporation's bylaw or articles of incorporation. The content of an operating agreement generally includes topics such as management, voting, procedures and qualification for admitting new members, transferability of member interests, procedures for amending Articles of Organization or operating agreement, or other rights and obligations. States such as Delaware, generally intend to give the maximum freedom of contract to LLC Agreement.

The operating agreement may stipulate the LLC to be managed by members (member-managed) or by appointed managers (manager-managed). For manager-managed, the operating agreement should consider matters such as the procedure to select and appoint managers, if/how to ratify managers' decision, duties of managers, and authority of managers to bind LLC.

Difference between LLC in the US and Limited Liability Corporation in China

LLC in the US is different from China's Limited Liability Corporation. LLC is essentially an "unincorporated" form, while Limited Liability Corporation is a corporate form. Therefore, LLC does not need to pay corporate level tax, whereas Limited Liability Corporation does. In addition, LLC does not necessarily have a board of directors, and LLC members can directly manage the business. In contrast, Limited Liability Corporation will have a board of directors and shareholders normally do not directly manage the business, but via the board of directors.

Part 6　Branch Office and Subsidiary

Branch office

Branch Office is not a separate entity itself. It is the extended arm of its parent company, so it has no separate legal status. Any liabilities (i.e. debts or obligations) caused by the branch office will be ultimately born by its parent company.

1. Representative office in China

In China, a special form of branch office exists solely for foreign companies coming to do business in China–the Representative Office. It is not a separate legal entity, and all obligations and liabilities will be borne by the parent non-Chinese company. A representative office does not require any registered capital.

The activities of a representative office are limited. For instance, a representative office may only engage in non-profit-generating activities related to its foreign parent company, such as market investigation, exhibition, and promotion of the parent company's products and services and liaison activities for the parent company.[1]

To form a representative office, a foreign company needs to file local AIC with various documents, such as the foreign company's incorporation documents (for instance, certificate of incorporation, articles of associations, memoranda of agreements for incorporation, a letter issued by the foreign company's bank certifying its credit), and personal information of the representatives (eg, appointment letter, detailed resume and passports of the chief representative and other representatives).[2] After the representative office is formed, it needs to make public announcement in a media designated by the local AIC.

To keep the representative office in compliance status, it needs to keep an accounting book and conduct annual inspections among others.

1　David Livdahl, Jenny Sheng, and Huiyuan Li, *Rules Further Tighten Regulation of Foreign Representative Office*, China Business Review, July 1, 2011

2　*Id.*

Subsidiary

Subsidiary is a separate legal entity (normally a corporation or LLC) that is owned or controlled (more than 50%) by another separate legal entity (corporations or LLC). The controlling entity is called the parent company. Subsidiary and the parent company are two separate and distinct entities, similar to the relationship between a corporation and its shareholder. A subsidiary is responsible for its own operation, as well as its own debts and obligations. Normally a parent company is not responsible for the subsidiary company's operation, debts and obligations. However, if the parent company uses the subsidiary as a "shell" and abuses the "limited liability", the parent company could potentially be responsible for the subsidiary's debts or obligations.

SELF QUIZ: Indicate whether each of the following statements is true or false.

52. Branch office has its own separate legal status, and thus is liable for its own debts and obligations.

53. A representative office in China is essentially a branch office.

54. A Chinese company can establish a representative office in China.

55. There is no limitation on the activities of a representative office.

56. A representative office can engage in for-profit activities.

57. A foreign company needs to file with local China agencies in order to establish a representative office.

58. A subsidiary refers to a company that is controlled by its parent company; therefore, a subsidiary does not have a separate legal status.

59. Parent company normally is not liable for the debts or obligations of its subsidiary.

60. It is possible that a parent company can be liable for its subsidiary under the "Piercing the Corporate Veil."

Questions

1. Xiaoming Tang has just quitted his job recently after working as a senior engineer for a company for more than 10 years and likes to start his own business in China. What he has in mind is to establish a high-tech business, as his engineering talents and technical skills may have their best place. He has some decent personal savings, a nice apartment and a car. While he may consider contributing some of his personal savings, he definitely does not want the potential business to risk his apartment and car. While he is perfectly OK to start his one-man shop, he also likes to consider pulling in other persons he trusts to start this exciting venture together. He hopes to open some branch offices in other cities if his business really takes off.

Question A: What form of business organization is suitable for Xiaoming Tang's case?

Question B: What if Xiaoming Tang likes to start his business in the US? Will he get different options?

2. John Dodds owns a C Corporation along with Scott Wright and Brian Oly, engaging in the sale of used cars. John owns around 75% of the business and acts as a director of the corporation. The other director is Mary Hine. The business is thriving and has the potential for expansion, as the recession has pushed people to buy used cars not new cars. The corporation rented the current space (for storing and showing cars to clients) at a very favorable price when the landlord was in need of money. The lease is about to expire in 2 months, and the landlord approached John yesterday, asking if they like to renew the same space. The landlord also said the space right next to theirs will also be available in about 2 months. John's sister Sarah Dodds recently lost her job and also wanted to get into the used car sale business. John passed the news to his sister, who immediately contacted the landlord and secured the lease with the landlord. John is recently informed that his mother was diagnosed with cancer and is in need of money to cure her disease. John takes USD 10,000 quarterly from the corporation, and luckily Mary Hine, the only other director never cares too much about the corporation and has no idea of this obvious misappropriation. The corporation is soon insolvent, and is late in payment of US$ 100,000 to the transportation company it uses to transport used cars.

Question A: What has John and Mary done inappropriately as directors?
Question B: What John has done inappropriately as shareholder?

Suggested Further Readings

2015 Annual reports on the OECD Guidelines for Multinational Enterprises - OECD.

Jiangyu Wang, *Company Law in China: Regulation of Business Organizations in a Socialist Market Economy*, 2014.

American Bar Foundation and Law and Business, Inc., Model Business Corporation Act, 2002.

Robert W. *Hamilton, Corporations Including Partnerships and Limited Liability Companies, Cases and Materials*, 8th edition, 2011.

Melvin Aron Eisenberg, *Corporations and Other Business Organizations, Cases and Materials*, 8th Edition, 2000.

National Conference of Commissioners on Uniform State Laws, Revised Uniform Partnership Act, 1997.

Susan Pace Hamill, *The Limited Liability Company, A Catalyst Exposing the Corporate Integration Question*, 95 Mich. L. Rev. 393, 446, 1995.

Michael Epperson & Joan Canny, *The Capital Shareholder's Ultimate Calamity: Pierced Corporate Veils and Shareholder Liability in the District of Columbia, Maryland and Virginia*, 37 Cath. U.L. Rev. 605-626, 1988.

Chapter 4

Contract Law

Contract law is a key issue in international business transactions. This chapter widely uses comparative studies to demonstrate the similarities and differences between civil law and common law so as to help students to better resolve contractual issues in international business. It presents contract law from the following four aspects:

Part 1   introduces the basic concepts in contract law.

Part 2   discusses how to form a contract.

Part 3   analyzes the validity of a contract.

Part 4   explores remedies for breach of contract.

■ Learning Objectives

By the end of this chapter you should:

- State the basic concepts of contract and its types, functions.
- Outline and explain the rules relating to offer and acceptance.
- Understand more elements for validity of a contract based on the formation of contract.
- Tell the differences between the rules of Chinese Contract Law and common law.
- Use the rules of contract to solve practical contractual issues and get remedies in case of breach of contract.

■ Key Terms

Acceptance	Damages
Anticipatory breach	Duress
Form	Offer
Genuine consent	Rectification
Injunction	Remedy
Legal capacity	Rescission
Legal intention	Restitution
Legality	Specific performance
Minor	Unconscionable conduct
Misrepresentation	Undue influence
Mistake	

Part 1 Introduction to Contract Law

Contracts applicable to diverse business transactions and daily lives

Business persons in all trades, regardless of whatever transactions they are involved in, have to put their work on the basis of legal regime of the contract law and other laws because

- contract law functions to stabilize the business order by imposing strict performance of the promises reflected in the contract;
- it provides business certainty by fixing the rights and duties of the parties concerned and fairly allocating the business risks;
- it could provide predictions for reasonable profits and interests after a contract has been fully performed; if the contract is not performed, contract law will be able to provide the aggrieved party legal assistance including monetary damages.

The contracts of various transactions could be either named or unnamed. Chinese Contract Law[1] has provided for 15 types of named contracts (please refer to Chinese Contract Law) with their particular rules, and there are still some named contracts acknowledged in the special law.

There are, of course, more types of contracts that are unable to be named for their complicated natures in usage. The application of those unnamed contract will be subject to the general provisions of Chinese Contract Law in general, and the rules of those named contracts may be applied mutatis mutandis. (Chinese Contract Law Article 124)

1　Chinese Contract Law: in this chapter, please do not get Chinese Contract Law mixed up with the expression of "the Chinese contract law." The former particularly refers to the Chinese Contract Law issued in 1999. The latter refers to the contractual laws of that regard, which include statuary contract law, judicial interpretations and other forms of contractual law in general.

What is contract?

1. Definition of contract under Chinese Contract Law

Contract in the Chinese contract law refers to an agreement establishing, modifying and terminating the civil rights and obligations between the objects of equal footing, that is, between natural persons, legal persons or other organizations (Chinese Contract Law Article 2).

2. Definition of contract under common law

Restatement (Second) of Contracts is one of the best-recognized and frequently-cited legal treatises in the US that provide general principles of contracts under common law.

A contract is a promise or set of promises, for breach of which the law gives remedy, or the performance of which the law in some way recognizes as a duty.

According to the *Black's Law Dictionary*, "A contract is a promise or set of promises by a party to a transaction, enforceable or otherwise recognizable at law."[1]

Different from Chinese contract law, which defines any contract as an agreement, common law does not have unanimous definition of contract. Contract, in most cases, is defined as an agreement, but at the same time, is also viewed as a promise or a set of promises. Suppose someone who promises to pay $200 for a computer, and if his promise is reasonably believed and relied upon by the computer seller, the promise must be kept legally even though there may be no "agreement through offer and acceptance."

Classifications of contract

The followings are classifications under the Chinese contract law and common law.

1. Express contract and implied contract

- Express Contract: terms of the contract expressly agreed upon in writings,orally or the combination of both.
- Implied Contract: contract reached through acts or conducts of both parties, not through writings or words, e.g., contract by conduct or performance.

2. Avoidable contract, unenforceable contract and pending contract

- Avoidable contract: It remains valid until it is repudiated by one party, either with the help of legal proceeding (lawsuit) or not. For example , if a contract is based on a serious misunderstanding, according to the Chinese law, the mistaken party may apply to the court or arbitration tribunal to declare the contract void, otherwise the contract will remain valid.
- Unenforceable contract: It is a special type of contract in common law. Although it is a valid, it cannot be enforced because of technical defect, for instance, lack of evidence.

---

1   Page 318 of *Black's Law Dictionary* (seventh edition).

- Pending contract: It is a special type of contract in Chinese contract law. The validity of this type of contract is not yet sufficiently determined unless the lacking element is made up. For instance, a contract made by a person whose contract capacity is restricted or unauthorized. The contract will not become valid unless it is ratified by the authority.

Table 1: Comparison of the Similar Contracts

Contracts compared	Effectiveness	Where it belongs	Situations where it often occurs
Avoidable contract	valid unless it is repudiated by court or arbitration authority	Chinese Contract Law; Common law	• According to Chinese Contract Law Article 54, an act of contracting in violation of fairness is as the following: fraud, coercion, serious misunderstanding, obviously unfair at the time when concluding the contract and exploitation of other party's unfavorable position.
Void Contract	invalid from the very beginning	Chinese Contract Law; Common law	• According to Chinese Contract Law Article 52, an act of contracting in violation of the interests of the state is as the following: fraud, malicious collusion, illegitimate purpose and administrative compulsory rules.
Contract with pending effectiveness	not yet determined unless ratified by authorized person	Chinese Contract Law	• contractual act carried out by a person whose legal capacity is limited; • unauthorized contracting act; • agent exceeds his authority in making contracts.
Unenforceable Contract	seems valid but unenforceable	Common law	• lack of the evidence supporting the enforceability of contract

3. Void contract and illegal contract

- Void contract: a contract that has no legal effects upon either of the party. Void contract is of civil nature relating to extreme unfairness, such as contract made under undue influence.
- Illegal contract: this type of contract has no legal effects either, furthermore, it is treated as being void not because it violates the principle of fairness, but more seriously it contravenes administrative laws. It is out of criminal nature such as the contract of robbing a bank and other public-interests-harming crimes.

4. Other classfications

- Contract with consideration: contract for sales of goods , for lease and financial leasing, for warehousing, for work, for transportation, for brokerage, for intermediation, for transfer of technology and for construction project.
- Contract without consideration: contract for guarantee, contract for donation, contract for lending, contract for storage, contract for commission, contract for loan between natural persons.
- Formal Contract

  The formation of contract is based on formalities requested by law. The formalities include written form, administrative approval or filing.

  In China, the following contracts must be in written form:
  - contract for financial leasing
  - contract for construction project
  - contract for technology transfer to foreigner, such as patent;
  - contract for Sino-foreign joint venture
- Informal Contract

  No particular form of contract is required by law, which allows conclude a contract orally or by action.
- Contract with ascertained content: the content of contract has been made certain at the time when contract is made.
- Contract with occurrence of event: The content of contract is not yet ascertained at the time when contract is made. For instance, life insurance is contract for traffic accident. Whether the beneficiary would be compensated depends on the occurrence of the insured accident. Different from contract with ascertained content that legally requests fairness in value and equal benefit, this type of contract does not require such.

Contract law as a legal system

The framework of contract law is a comprehensive one, rather than a code or statute alone. In Chinese legal system, and in its narrowest sense, Chinese contract law takes a form of:

- Codes of contract law: Chinese Contract Law, which became effective in 1999 with 23 chapters of 428 articles in total;
- Judiciary interpretations: for example Interpretations on Sales Contract by Supreme People's Court of China, which became effective in 2012 with 46 articles, covering the major issues of formation and validity of sales contract, risk allocation of subject matter, inspection, liabilities in breach of contract, reservation of ownership, special sales and miscellaneous issues;
- Case law: Judicial decisions are not laws unless it is integrated into interpretation by the Supreme Court of China;

- Other laws relevant to contracts: The General Principles of Civil Law of 1986 and the Civil Law General provisions of 2017. Both of them contain contract rules. The Civil Law General Provisions does not replace the General Principles of the Civil Law currently[1]. In conflict, the former should prevail over the latter[2].

SELF QUIZ: Indicate whether each of the following statements is true or false.

1. Contractual relation is a legal relation as it possesses rights and duties and obligations, so any relations which possesses rights and duties and obligations are contractual relations.

2. Not all contracts have names, unnamed contracts are still contracts.

3. Unenforceable contract is not a contract as contract must be enforceable.

4. Validity pending contract is not a valid contract before its validity is ratified.

5. Illegal contract is void, but cannot be seen as a void contract.

6. Oral contract must be an implied contract.

Part 2   Formation of Contract

When is a contract formulated?

To formulate a contract means to establish a contractual relation between the parties. Common law holds that the formulation of contract must, at least, have three requirements.

- Firstly, parties must have legal intention which is the foundation of a contract. No agreement could be formulated without the legal intention, even both parties have offer and acceptance.

- Parties must have an agreement through the process of offer/acceptance, which is composed by an offer made by one party and acceptance by other party.

- The agreement must have a consideration as both parties have to exchange values through offer/acceptance. Please note that consideration is only required by the common law for formation of contract, but Chinese contract law does not have consideration requirement.

Please note, even when the contract is formulated, it does not mean that the contract has been legally valid, so it is necessary to distinguish the formation of contract from the validity of contract.

- Formation of contract means parties concerned have made a consensus or an agreement on doing something or not doing something, but reaching the agreement does not necessarily

---

1   Explanation of Civil Law General Provisions (draft), presented by Mr. Jianguo Li, Vice Chairman of the National People's Congress Standing Committee at the 5th Meeting of the 12th National People's Congress on 8 March 2017.

2   Ibid.

mean the agreement is legally valid, that is, the agreement has binding force upon the parties and thus to be enforceable at law.

- Validity of contract indicates that the contract has become legally enforceable. It is based on the formation of contract and together with other requirements.

Table 2: Formation of Contract and Validity of Contract Under Common Law

Requirements for formation of contract	Requirements for validity of contract
1) Legal intention	1) Legal intention
2) Agreement (offer and acceptance)	2) Agreement (offer and acceptance)
3) Consideration	3) Consideration
	4) Legal capacity
	5) Genuine consent
	6) Legality
	7) Form

How to find contractual intention in negotiation?

Contract relation is a legal relation, therefore, parties involved in the process of contract building must have a legal intention. If not, even if the parties have reached an agreement, it does not mean a contract is legally formed.

The following statements do not absolutely demonstrate the party's intentions are legal:

- contractual statements made in a hurry or in emergency;
- contractual promising when the promisor is drunk or intoxicated;
- playing a joke with a seemingly contractual statement;
- inability in distinguishing legal and non-legal statements;
- forcing contractual statement under duress or threat or undue influence;
- by mistakes or misrepresentations; etc.

1. Test of legal intention in common law

Presumption 1 (subjective test):

It is presumed that parties coming to an agreement of domestic, social or volunteering nature do not intend to be legally bound unless it is rebutted. This is a subjective test. The law presumes people who are in non-business situation usually have no legal intention.

Presumption 2 (objective test):

It is presumed that parties coming to an agreement concerning commerce or business intend to be legally bound unless it is rebutted. This is an objective test, which presumes that people in business should have legal intention regardless of parties who are family members or relatives or friends and regardless of social or friendly agreement either, unless this presumption is otherwise rebutted.

2. Chinese contract law regarding contractual legal intention

Chinese Contract Law has no direct or specific provisions on the issue of legal intention of the parties. This issue is addressed in Articles 137-142 of the Civil Law General Provisions and relevant provisions in the General Principle of Civil Law, neither of them contain equivalent tests as those in common law. However, legal intention in the formation of contract is still a basic requirement in China.

> ## CASE EXAMPLE: *Mr. He v. Mr. Tian*[1]
>
> **Facts:** Mr. Gu promised to build a house for Mr. Tian by a construction contract, which provided that the builder Mr. Gu would be responsible for all the building material including cement. On March 1, 2009, Mr. Gu talked with Mr. He, a cement manufacturer about supply of cement for Mr. Tian's house. On April 1 and 16, Mr. He delivered the cement worth of CNY 3600 to the house worksite, and Mr. Tian signed on the delivery sheet. On August 19 Mr. He sued Mr. Tian for non-payment after several failures in requesting payment from Mr. Tian, alleging that he has delivered the cement which is evidenced by the delivery sheet with Mr. Tian's signature on it. But Mr. Tian defended that he did not make any sales contract with the plaintiff, his signing on the delivery sheet just means that he acknowledged the delivery of cement.
>
> **The Court held that:** The judgment was made in favour of the defendant Mr. Tian. This decision was made out of the following considerations:
> - the facts that the construction contract clearly stated the builder would be responsible for all the building material;
> - the fact that cement delivery matter was talked over between the builder and cement supplier, Mr. Tian was not involved;
> - the fact that Mr. Tian signed on the delivery sheet did not necessarily indicate legal intention of contract making; it may indicate to have acknowledged the reception of goods.
>
> **Take-away point:** the key issue of this case was whether the defendant had legal intention to make a contract with the plaintiff. Intention is demonstrated by not only the signature of the delivery sheet but also the whole transaction, which includes the relationship between Mr. He and Mr. Tian, and Mr. Tian and Mr. Gu.

---

1 Page43 of Understanding and Application of Interpretations on Sales Contract by the Supreme People's Court of China, compiled by the Second Court of Civil Trial of Supreme Court of China, People's Court Press 2012 edition.

Agreement

A contractual agreement occurs when one party (offeror) offers to enter into a contract and the other party (offeree) who accepts the offer. In examining a valid agreement through offer and acceptance, the following issues have to be put into consideration:

1. Agreement-offer rules

An offer is a proposal or statement or even an act made to enter into a contract with other party. But it will not become a legal offer until it meets the legal requirements.

It seems that Chinese contract law, common law and the United Nations Convention on Contracts for the International Sales of Goods (hereinafter "CISG") do have their own rules for a legally valid offer, but if compared, those rules under different laws still have much in common.

Table 3: Compare the Laws: Rules of Offer in Chinese Contract Law, Common Law and CISG

Common Law	Chinese Contract Law	CISG (rules of sales contract)
Rule 1: An offer could be made to an individual, a group of people, or the world at large.	Article 15: When the content of commercial advertisement complies with the terms of the offer, it may be regarded as an offer.	Article 14 An offer must be addressed to only one or more specific persons unless the contrary is clearly indicated by the person making the offer.
Rule 2: An offer must be communicated to the offeree to be effective.	Article 16: An offer becomes effective when it reaches the offeree.	Article 15: An offer becomes effective when it reaches the offeree.

(to be continued)

(continued)

Common Law	Chinese Contract Law	CISG (rules of sales contract)
Rule 3: An offer having an option of open time for offeree to accept must be supported by consideration.	Based on Article 20 (indirect provision): An offer shall be null and void if the offeree fails to make an acceptance when the time limit for acceptance expires.	Based on Article 18: An Offer should be kept open for some time or a reasonable time. So the acceptance should be made within the time.
Rule 4: The terms must be clear and definite.	Article 14: The offer should comply with the following stipulations: 1) Its contents shall be detailed and definite; 2) It indicates the proposal of offeror to be bound in case of acceptance. Article 12: The contents of a contract shall be agreed upon by the parties.	Article 19: An offer should be sufficiently definite , which expressly or impliedly includes the name, the quantity and the price of the goods.
Rule 5: Request for or supply of information is not an offer.	no direct or indirect provision	none
Rule 6: Invitation to treat is not an offer and could be rebutted.	Article 15: Invitation to treat (ITT) forms: mailed pricelist, public notices of auction, tender,Prospectus, and commercial advertisement, etc.	none

Explain Rule 1: An offer could be made to an individual, a group of people, or the world at large.

The key aspect of this rule lies in whether offer can be made to "the world at large," in other words, could advertisement, or ordinary means of commercial promotion, be used as a form of offer?

The answer of common law and Chinese contract law to this question is that:

- Advertisement will not become an offer until it complies with the terms of an offer;
- The advertiser does have a legal intention shown on the advertisement;

- The terms of advertisement are clear and definite.

Based on Chinese contract law, the following situations are not offers:

- an advertisement on TV show says "price to be fixed by negotiation";
- a driving taxi with top light on;
- a stock company issues prospectus to the public.

Rule 1 is also adopted by the CISG. For example, suppose that a supplier mails a catalogue (widespread communication) to 100 prospective buyers and, each envelop is addressed to a specific person. Is this valid offer under CISG? According to CISG Article 14(2), the answer is "no," because catalogue, even it is addresses to particular buyer, is still not an offer unless the catalogue clearly indicates the intent is to be bound in case of acceptance.

Explain Rule 2: An offer must be communicated to the offeree to be effective.

In order to ensure that the offer can legally reach the offeree, two aspects deserve special attention:

First: Communication must be through the legal channel;

Second: The offer should be brought to the notice of the offeree.

• Withdrawal of offer

Offer may be withdrawn before it reaches the offeree. Offer could be revoked after it reaches the offeree but before it is accepted.

CASE EXAMPLE: *Banks v. Williams* (1912)[1]

Facts: The Minster of Public Affairs has approved to purchase a piece of land, but his secretary without authorization released the information to the buyer, which was treated as an offer and then accepted by the buyer.

The court held that: The contract was invalid for the offer had not been communicated through legal channel.

Take-away point: The legal communication of offer may be either directly through offeror or indirectly through offeor's agents or other legally recognized channels,eg. Judiciary notice board open to the public.

• Revocation of offer

In order to become effective, the offer must be communicated or reaches the offeree, however, it could be withdrawn by the offeror if it has not arrived. And even, if it has reached the offeree, the offer still could be revoked, but is subject to two exceptions.

---

1   (1912) 12 SR (NSW) 382.

Table 4: Comparison of the Withdrawal and Revocation of Offer in Different Law Systems

	Withdrawal	Revocation
Common law	Offer could be withdrawn before it reaches the offeree.	The same with Article 19 of Chinese Contract Law.
Chinese Contract Law	Article 17 An offer could be withdrawn, if the withdrawal notice reaches the offeree before or at the same time when the offer arrives.	Article 19 An offer may not be revoked if (1) the offeror indicates a fixed time for acceptance or otherwise explicitly states that the offer is irrevocable; (2) the offeree has reasons to rely on the offer as being irrevocable and had made preparations for performing the contract.
CISG	Article 15 An offer, even it is irrevocable, may be withdrawn if the withdrawal reaches the offeree before or at the same time as the offer arrives.	Article 16 Until a contract is concluded, an offer may be revoked if the revocation reached the offeree before he has dispatched an acceptance. However, an offer cannot be revoked if it indicates, whether by stating a fixed time for acceptance or otherwise, that it is irrevocable; It was reasonable for the offeree to rely on the offer as being irrevocable and the offeree has acted in reliance on the offer

Explain Rule 3: An offer having an option of open time for offeree to accept must be supported by consideration (common law).

Under common law, if an offeror in his offer leaves a period of time or a reasonable time for offeree to consider before acceptance or rejection, during the time the offeror will be bound to keep the offer valid. It is called option. The option in offer is very important because offeree normally needs some time to think over the feasibility and possible profitability if he accepts the offer. But common law does not enforce offeror to provide option to offeree unless it is supported by consideration, something valuable to the offeror to keep his offer valid until the promised time or reasonable time expire (in case of sales contract, buyer's money may constitute consideration to bind the seller's promise not to revoke his offer). Without consideration, the offeror will not be bound by his promise to keep his promise open.

Consideration has been highly regarded as the corner stone for contract law under common law as it functions as a balancer for contractual regime. Consideration is briefly defined as: the price given by the promisee to pay for the promissor's promise. It means something done or promised by one party in exchange for something done or promised by the other party, highlighting the mutuality and exchanges of value for value (benefits and detriments) between contract parties. Therefore common law has consideration as one of the three conditions for formation of contract.

Under Chinese contract law, for formation of a contract there is no requirement of consideration as it is under common law. If an offer has no specified time for acceptance, reasonable time is expected (Chinese Contract Law 23).

Explain Rule 4: The offer must be clear and definite.

In Common law, the clearness and definiteness of an offer depend on the judges in particular cases and situations.

Chinese contract law explains this rule from two perspectives:

First, an offer should be so detailed that it is eligible to be accepted for certain commercial purpose.

Second, an offer should make it clear that the offeror has a legal intention to be bound. If the offer is accepted, the legal intention is separately treated as one of conditions for formation of contract.

Article 12 of the Chinese Contract Law suggests that a contract primarily includes eight elements, namely: name and domicile of parties, contract object, quantity, quality, price and remuneration, time, place and method of performance, liability for breach of contract; method of dispute settlement, which are taken as the usual standards for clearness and definiteness of an offer.

Article 14 of the CISG requires that the offer shall be sufficiently definite. For example, A had an annually-renewed contract for a number of years with B to provide technical assistance for A's computers. A opened a second office with the same type of computers and asked B to provide assistance also for the new computers. B accepted the offer but the offer did not specify any specific terms of computer.

A contract is actually concluded between A and B because the missing terms can be taken from the previous contract as constituting a practice established between the parties.

Explain Rule 5: Request for or supply of information is not an offer.

A person who asks for information is not an offeror; neither is a person who provides information that is requested during negotiation.

This rule is a rule of common law and also under the Chinese contract law. CISG has no touch of this point.

Explain Rule 6: Invitation to treat is not an offer and it could be rebutted.

Invitation to treat is a statement to other person inviting counterpart to make an offer. It is not an offer made to the counterpart, neither is it an agreement making legal intention automatically demonstrated by ITT.

According to Article 15 of Chinese Contract Law, ITT includes the following situations:

- notice of tender;
- ordinary advertisements without specific undertakings;
- price lists;
- catalogues;
- announcement for auction. Bidding in auction process is regarded as an offer, and the act that auctioneer strikes the hammer in response to the bidding is an acceptance.

2. What happens after the offer is sent?

After the offer is sent, what will happen? Various reactions may be taken by offeree even by the offeror and thus it leads to different legal results.

Table 5: What happens after the offer is sent?

Situations	Who reacts	Legal results
Acceptance	Offeree	Agreement formulated
Revocation after the arrival of offer	Offeror	The offer is terminated; no agreement reached.
Withdrawal prior to the arrival of offer	Offeror	The offer is terminated; no agreement reached.
Rejection	Offeree	The offer dies immediately; no agreement reached.
Lapse of time limit set in the offer Of lapse of reasonable time	Law	The acceptance may be invalid or remain valid depending on the situations.

An example to demonstrate how acceptance and revocation function in practice is that, supposing on June 1, a seller delivered to a buyer an offer that included a statement "I will hold this offer open until June 15". On June 2 the seller informed the buyer that "I hereby revoke my offer of June 1". On June 14 the buyer noticed the seller that he accepted the offer of June 1. The seller's revocation is not successful because he promised to hold it valid until June 15, he must keep his promise. As a general rule, offeror can revoke the offer before it is accepted. However, if the offeror in his offer has promised a period of time for acceptance, within which he can't revoke the offer, even if the time of revocation is earlier than the acceptance.

3. Agreement–acceptance rules

Article 21 of Chinese Contract Law defines the acceptance of an offer as a manifestation of intention to assent to an offer. Likewise, Common law defines acceptance as a final expression of assent to the terms of an offer, which is substantively similar to Chinese Contract Law. CISG has no much difference in the definition of acceptance.

Acceptance either in the form of express statement or in implied act will not become valid unless it meets with legal requirements.

Table 6: Rules of Acceptance in Different Law Systems

Common Law	Chinese Contract Law	CISG
Rule 1: Acceptance must be communicated by the offeree or its authorized agent.	General Principles of Civil Law Article 63: Citizens and legal persons may perform legal acts through agents.	Based on Article 18: Statement should be made by the offeree who indicates his assent to an offer.
Rule 2: Acceptance must be made within the time specified or, if not specified, within a reasonable time.	Acceptance should be dispatched within the time limit for acceptance.	Based on Article 18: Acceptance must be made within the time specified or, if not specified, within a reasonable time.
Rule 3: Acceptance must be made strictly in accordance with the conditions set in the offer.	Chinese Contract Law Article 30/31 The contents of acceptance shall comply with those of the offer. Acceptance substantially modifies the offer and constitute a new offer. Chinese Contract Law Article 28/29 Late acceptance is due to offeree and abnormal transmission.	Based on Article 19: Acceptance should conform with the offer. any material change constitute an counter offer Based on Article 21: Late acceptance is due to offeree and abnormal transmission.

(to be continued)

(continued)

Common Law	Chinese Contract Law	CISG
Rule 4: Acceptance must be communicated to the offeror to be effective except acceptance communicated by post.	Chinese Contract Law Article 26 Acceptance will not become effective until it is communicated to the offerer.	Article 18: The acceptance of an offer becomes effective at the moment the indication of assent reaches the offeror.
Rule 5: Acceptance must be in response to and in reliance of an offer.	None	None
Rule 6: Acceptance must be clear and definite.	Based on Article 30: Acceptance must be clear and definite.	Based on Article 18: Acceptance must be clear and definite. Silence or inactivity does not in itself amount to acceptance.

Explain Rule 1: Acceptance must be communicated by the offeree or its authorized agent.

This rule addresses the legal channel of communication. The channel refers to the offeree or its authorized agent. This rule is correspondent to the rule 2 for the offer (offer must be communicated to the offeree). Because an offer is communicated to an offeree, only the offeree or its authorized agent can accept his offer.

Explain Rule 2: Acceptance must be made within the time specified or, if not specified, within a reasonable time.

If time limit is not stipulated in the offer, reasonable time of acceptance is primarily decided by the mode of acceptance required by the offer.

Table 7: Reasonable Time If Offer Has no Stipulation of Time Limit for Acceptance

Form of offer	Reasonable time
In the form of dialogue	Chinese Contract Law Article 23: immediately except otherwise agreed by the parties concerned
In any form other than dialogue	Chinese Contract Law Article 23: a reasonable period of time

Explain Rule 3:

Acceptance must be made strictly in accordance with the conditions set in the offer.

After receiving the offer, the offeree has different options to handle the offer and therefore give rise to different legal results. Any option of the following relates to this rule.

Option 1: The offeree accepts the offer as requested, which is generally in the form of agreement. However, it is very rare for offeree to accept the offer without bargaining. Even though the offeree accepts the offer without bargaining, it is likely that the acceptance may be reasonably or unreasonably late which will then affect the formation of agreement.

Table 8: Late Acceptance Under Chinese Contract Law Article 28/29 and CISG Article 21

Reasons for lateness	Legal result
Dispatch beyond time limit due to offeree's subjective reasons.	not acceptance but new offer, unless the offeror accepts the late acceptance by timely notice.
Dispatch within time limit but was late due to objective reasons.	valid acceptance unless the offeror rejects the acceptance by timely notice.

Option 2: The offeree simply rejects the offer, so the offer ends and no agreement is formed. The rules for rejection of the offer are as follows:
- A rejection must be expressed clearly in spoken or written words;
- An counter-offer is a rejection of the offer;
- A request for further information or clarification is not a rejection.

Option 3: The offeree requests for further information. Offer rule says request for or supply of information is not an offer, because no legal intention is involved. Likewise, offeree requests for further information or clarification is not a rejection of offer either. But sometimes it is hard to distinguish request for further information and ask for change of the offer.

Option 4: The offeree introduces a new term or materially changes the term of the offer in the acceptance. They are not agreements any more but counteroffers.

Counteroffer is a new offer that introduces a new term or materially changes the term of the offer in the acceptance. Once an counteroffer is made, the original offer is terminated soon.

Table 9: The Offer Changed by Acceptance Materially or Immaterially in Different Law Systems

Compare the laws : acceptance has materially or immaterially changed the offer	
Chinese Contract Law Article 30: The following substantial changes make the acceptance a new offer (counteroffer). • Contract object • Quality • Quantity • Price or numeration • Time of performance • Place and method of performance • Liability for breach of contract • Settlement of dispute	CISG Article 19: Any additional or different following terms are considered to alter the terms of offer and materially make the acceptance a new offer (counteroffer). • Price • Payment • Quality of the goods • Quantity of the goods • Time of performance • Place and time of delivery • Extent of one party's liability to the other • Settlement of dispute
Chinese Contract Law Article 31: Changes in the acceptance other than the substantive terms will remain effective, unless objected by the offeror by prompt notice.	CISG Article 19: A reply to an offer which purports to be an acceptance but contains additional or different terms which do not materially alter the terms of the offer constitutes an acceptance, unless the offeror, without undue delay, objects orally to the discrepancy or dispatches a notice to the effect.

Explain Rule 4: Acceptance must be communicated to the offeror to be effective.

As to the effectiveness of acceptance, three situations need to be noticed with each situation applying different rules:

- situation 1: acceptance by letter or telegram (postal rule);
- situation 2: acceptance by silence (not acceptance unless otherwise aggreed);
- situation 3: acceptance by acts (commencement rule);
- situation 4: acceptance to be withdrawn before it reaches to the offeror (Reception rule for withdrawal of acceptance may be involved).

Situation 1: acceptance by letter or telegram (postal rule)[1]

Means of acceptance transmission may be by fax, by email, by letter and other more. But

---

1 Acceptance by post becomes effective as soon as the offeree posts a properly stamped and addressed acceptance into a mailbox before the lapse of offer and is sent through a legally authorized postal system regardless of whether the acceptance is delayed or lost in the postal system or on its way to the offeror.

historically, common law holds that acceptance by letter whose validity applies to postal rule is particularly different from other instantaneous means of dispatch.

> **CASE EXAMPLE:** *Adams V. Lindsell* (1818)[1]
>
> **Facts:** On Sept. 2 Adams posted a letter to Lindsell, offering to sell wool and requesting a response by post. Adams expected to receive a reply by Sept. 7. However, he has addressed the letter incorrectly. On Sept. 5, Lindsell received the letter and mailed his acceptance. On Sept. 8, Adams sold the wool to a third party. On Sept. 9, Adams received Lindsell's acceptance. Lindsell sued Adams for breach of contract, believing the contract had been formed on Sept. 5. But Adams defended that agreement should be formed on Sept. 9 when he received the letter of acceptance.
>
> **The court held that:** By postal rule, the acceptance took place on Sept. 5 when the letter of acceptance was posted and Adams had breached the contract although unintentionally. Therefore he was obliged to pay damages to Lindsell.
>
> **Take-away points:** According to the postal rule, the agreement was formed at the time of mailing.

Table 10: Comparison of Reception Rules and Postal Rules by Means of Communication

Means of dispatch	Acceptance	Offer
Instantaneous dispatch (Fax, E-mail, talk over telephone or face to face or electronic means eg., skype)	Reception rule: In case of instantaneous communication, the acceptance becomes valid once it reaches the offeror.	Reception rule
Postal dispatch: (Letter, telegram)	Postal rule: Once the letter /telegram is posted (mailed, shipped or presented to the front desk), the offer is accepted, unless otherwise agreed.	

Situation 2: acceptance by silence

Acceptance of offer must be expressed out orally or in writing, but silent acceptance will not be qualified as a valid acceptance.

---

1   (1818) 106 ER 250.

Case Example: *Felthouse V. Bindley* (1862)[1]

Facts: Mr. Felthouse wrote to his nephew, offering to buy a horse. In the letter it stated: "if I hear no more from you I consider the horse mine at £30 15 shillings." His nephew decided to sell the horse to his uncle but did not reply the letter. The nephew told Mr. Bindley, the auctioneer, to remove the horse away. However, Bindley sold the horse by mistake and then was sued by Felthouse on the ground that Felthouse had made a contract with his nephew before the sale of the horse, so Bindley had no right to sell his horse.

The court held that: the nephew's acceptance had not been communicated, as silence is not an acceptance. The horse did not belong to Mr. Felthouse, so he had no contractual right over the horse and then no right against Mr. Bindley, the auctioneer.

Take-away points: Silence is not an acceptance. However, according to common law there are three exceptions to this rule, if the communication of acceptance :

- is reasonably required by the offer;
- is expressly and impliedly required by custom or law;
- prior dealings and other circumstances between those particular parties has made it reasonable for the offeror to expect the offeree to give notice of rejection.

Table 11: Silent Acceptance Under Chinese Contract Law

Principle	Acceptance needs a notice to become effective.	Chinese Contract Law Article 26
Exceptions	Act of acceptance is performed in accordance with transaction practices or required in the offer if acceptance is not notified with writing notice.	Chinese Contract Law Article 26
	Implied acceptance by way of inaction will not be effective unless it is agreed by the parties or required by law.	Supreme People's Court's Opinions of General Principle of Civil Law Article 66
	The buyer to a sales transaction on trial may, during the period of trial use, buy the object or refuse to buy it. Upon the expiry of the period of trial use, if the buyer fails to express whether or not to buy the object, the purchase shall be deemed.	Chinese Contract Law Article 171

---

1   (1862) EWHC CP J 35

Situation 3: Acceptance by acts

If the offer is requested by an act of performance, commencement rule will be applied to decide the effectiveness of acceptance, while postal rule or reception rule can not. Acceptance takes effect as the acts of acceptance (tender of performance) commences and the notice of which is not required to be made to the offeror.

Table 12: Rules of Post, Reception and Commencement in Different legal Systems

Common law	Chinese contract law
Postal rule	Not recognized
Reception rule applicable to instantaneous means of acceptance	Reception rule applicable to instantaneous means of acceptance
Commencement rule applicable to acceptance by acts	Article 26 of Chinese Contract Law: Commencement rule

Situation 4: Acceptance to be withdrawn before it reaches to the offeror.

For communication of any types of acceptance form by instantaneous means, to withdraw the acceptance halfway is practically impossible, because the acceptance reaches the offeror as soon as it is sent. But the legal result of the communication of letter acceptance is a bit complicated.

Table 13: Withdrawal of Acceptance of Letter in Different Law Systems

Common law	Chinese contract law
Withdrawal is impossible for postal rule.	Reception rule has more application.
According to postal rule, acceptance of letter cannot be withdrawn as the post takes effects once dropped into the mailbox or posted .	Chinese Contract Law Article 27: acceptance can be withdrawn, but the notice of withdrawal takes effect after the notice of withdrawal reaches to the offeror.

Explain Rule 5: Acceptance must be in response to and in reliance of an offer.

The arrival of acceptance sometimes is not sufficient, so common law further requires it make the offer known to the offeree before the acceptance takes effect. In this sense, Rule 4 (Acceptance must be communicated to the offeror) and Rule 5 (Acceptance must be in response to and in reliance of an offer) are closely linked together.

To simplify, the acceptance will not become effective until it is communicated to the offeree and further, the offer is obviously known to the offeree, relying on what the offeree responds to the offer.

CASE EXAMPLE: *R v. Clarke* [1972][1]

Facts: An reward of $2000 had been offered for information of murder. Clarke then was arrested on a murder charge. To get rid of the murder charge, he gave information to police which led to a conviction of the actual offenders. But later, he tried to claim a reward to the public but got refused.

The Court held that: Clarke was not entitled to claim reward because his acceptance was not based on the reward to the public but on the desire to clear himself of the charge although he may be aware of the reward.

Take-away points: Ignorance of the offer is the same thing whether it is due to never hearing it or forgetting it after hearing.

Explain Rule 6: Acceptance must be clear and definite.

This rule should be conceived together with rule 3 (Acceptance must be made strictly in accordance with the conditions set in the offer). Although both rules require that acceptance must be clear and definite, according to rule 3, it does not mean that the offeree can amend the offer clearer and more definite, in case that an acceptance may not be clear and definite enough. In this sense, rule 3 makes this rule (Acceptance must be clear and definite) practically useless unless in the special situation where contractual relation is presumed by performance of contract. What's more, the offer rule is more important than acceptance rule in legal significance.

SELF QUIZ: Indicate whether each of the following statements is true or false.

15. Agreement could not be formed through offer in writing and acceptance in action.

16. If the offer is made by an act, neither postal rule nor reception rule will be applied to decide the effectiveness of acceptance, but commence rule will.

17. If the acceptance is communicated to offeror, the acceptance still will not take effect until the offeree knows the offer and understands the content of the offer as well.

18. Reception rule not only applies to offer and acceptance but also applies to the withdrawal or revocation of offer and acceptance.

19. According to postal rule, offer and acceptance become effective when are sent through postal system.

20. The offeree finally accepts the offer after expiry of offer, but offeror does not mind. This acceptance is legally valid.

21. Acceptance may be expressed by a third party who is able to perform the contract, but the offeree is not able to perform the contract.

---

1   (1927) 40 CLR 227.

22. The act that the auctioneer strikes the table with his hammer after bidding is an acceptance.
23. A makes an offer to B for his bike for CNY500, but B says if the price is CNY 450, he or she accepts A's offer. There is a deal between A and B.

Part 3   Validity of Contract

In addition to the requirements for the formation rules of contract (legal intention, agreement of offer/acceptance and consideration only under common law), the validity of contract also requires the following:

- Rule of capacity of parties: Parties to the contract should have capacity in making the contract;
- Rule of genuine consent: The offer and acceptance should be based on true willingness of the parties; and
- Rule of legality of the contract: The purpose of contracting must be legal.

Capacity to make a contract

1. Definition of capacity of contract making

Capacity of contract making is also called contractual capacity, defining the ability for parties to contract in fully understanding the rights, duties and obligations set forth in the contract. Different parties with different contractual capacities in making contract will bring out different legal effects.

Table 14: Parties with Different Contractual Capacities

Parties to the contract	Level of capacities	Legal effects
Minor	Full capacity	Valid contract
Mentally unsound	Limited capacity	Void contract
Intoxicated person	No capacity	Avoidable contract
Bankrupts		Unenforceable contract
Company		Illegal contract
partnership		

2. Minor's contractual capacity

Minor's contractual capacity may be at different levels, either of full capacity or limited capacity or even has no capacity depending on the contents of transactions (contract for necessary or involving continuous interest or for trade), leading to different types of contracts (valid or voidable or void contract). It is obvious that the above legal regime is designed in favor of minors as minors should have more legal protection than adults. But if the minor is negligent or fraudulent, falsely claiming his age, he will not be especially protected any more. The following chart clearly shows the characteristics and basic rules for minor's capacity in common law.

Table 15: Minor's Contractual Capacity Under Common Law

Parties	Capacities	Contracts able to make	Legal effects
Minor or Infant	Full contractual capacity	1. Contract for necessaries of daily life 2. Contract of service beneficial to the minors • Contract of apprenticeship • Contract of traineeships	Valid contract
	Limited contractual capacity	Long-term contract involves a permanent or continuous interest for minors. 1. Land transaction 2. Share transaction 3. Partnership agreement 4. Insurance policy	Avoidable contract until the minor terminating it expressly or impliedly.
	No contractual capacity	1. Trading contract 2. Contracts for non -necessary goods	Void contract
Minor is generally fully liable for his negligent and fraudulent act.			

As to the issue of minor's contractual capacity, Chinese Contract Law leaves it to the General Principles of Civil Law, which provides for the contractual capacity of natural person by three measurements—age, intelligence and mental health to test person's ability in recognizing the nature of his act.

Table 16: Contractual Capacity of Natural Person under China's General Principles of Civil Law

Capacities	Measurement		Contracts able to make	Contract effects
	Age	Intelligence & Mental Health		
Full capacity	adult of 18 years old or 16 years but able to make a living by himself/herself	fully recognize his/her act	any contract unless other requirements required by law	Valid
Limited capacity	minor between age of 10-18 years old or adult not fully able to recognize his act.		contracts proper with person's age or within person's cognitive ability	Valid
			contracts purely beneficial to the person (e.g. donation contract)	Valid
			contracts made with contracting party at the age of 10-18 years old or made by an adult who is not fully able to recognize his act.	Pending contract unless ratified by a guardian.
No Capacity	According to the General Principles of Civil Law, the age limit is below 10 years old or adult who is not able to recognize his act. According to the Civil Law General Provisions, the age limit is 8 years old.		contract purely beneficial to the person (e.g. donation contract)	valid
			daily and usual consumptive contracts (e.g., take a bus, buy a bottle of drink)	valid
			business contract	invalid

SELF QUIZ: Indicate whether each of the following statements is true or false.

24. Minor is not entitled to make a valid contract because minor has not reached the legal age.

25. Minor also could make a valid contract if the contract is for minor's daily needs.

26. The Chinese contract law treats the contractual capacity of all natural persons with both standards of age and state of mind.

27. Xiao Liu, a minor of age 9, is good at cartoon painting. He trades his creation of cartoon painting for RMB100 with a website. According to the Chinese contract law, this sale contract is valid.

3. Contractual capacity of mentally unsound or intoxicated person

Chinese law uses the general capacity measurements to judge the contracts made by people who are mentally unhealthy or intoxicated by alcohol. The legal effects of the contract made by those people may be as follows:

- Valid contract, if the mentally unhealthy or drunkard looked sober-minded at the time of contract making;
- Avoidable contract, if at the time of making contract they were mentally troubled or drunk. But they can terminate the contract later through court.

Under common law, like minors, the adults who are mentally ill or intoxicated by alcohol or drugs when they enter a contract, are also protected from being liable, if they can produce the evidences that:

- He/She was suffering from such a degree of mental instability/drunkenness that he/she was incapable of understanding the nature of contract; and at the same time, his/her lack of contractual capacity should have been known by the other party.

Table 17: Flow Chart for Contracts Made by Mentally Unsound or Intoxicated Person

Step 1	Was a defendant who entered a contract suffering from mental impairment or intoxication?
Step 2	The defendant claims that he suffered. But if he hopes to be discharged from the contractual liability, he must produce the evidence of step 3.
Step 3	Evidence 1: Was the defendant capable of understanding the nature and terms of the contract?
Step 4	If yes, contract valid. If no, one more evidence the defendant should produce of step 5
Step 5	Evidence 2: Did the plaintiff knew or should have known that the defendant was incapable?
Step 6	If no, contract becomes valid for the second time. If yes, the contract is void. But defendant still has a chance to ratify the void contract after sanity and sobriety is regained.
Step 7	If defendant ratifies the void contract, the contract becomes valid. If not, the contract remains void.

In the chart above, contracts made by mentally unsound or intoxicated person may turn out to be:

- Valid contract , if the two evidences are not able to be presented by the defendant (step 4 and 6);
- Void contract, if the two evidences are both satisfactorily presented (step 6).

But if the defendant ratifies the void contract, the contract becomes validly revitalized (step 7).

SELF QUIZ: Indicate whether each of the following statements is true or false.

28. Contract mad by a mentally unsound people is definitely void.
29. Contract made by a drug taker may be avoidable if the other party knew or should have been aware of the drug taker's abnormal mind.
30. The drug taker should not be protected in their contract making as drug taking is a crime.

4. Contractual capacity of a business organization

Like natural persons, companies, partnerships or non-business corporations are also legal entities, which have contractual capacities as well to make contracts.

- Capacity of company and non-business corporations are subject to articles of association, which are regarded as the constitution and guidance for operations.
- Capacity of partnership is confined by partnership agreement, where basic rights and duties are provided and the partners' capacity of contract making primarily depends on the partnership agreement.

Genuine consent in offer and acceptance

Agreement is reached through offer and acceptance, but the offer/acceptance must be based on genuine consent of the offer and acceptor. If not, even they are in conformity with the rules of offer/acceptance, the agreement is still not valid.

1. By mistake

(1) Mistake rules in Chinese contract law

Chinese contract code has no direct concept of "mistake," but concept of serious misunderstanding (Chinese Contract Law Article 54, and General Principle of Civil Law Article 59),which is similar to the unilateral mistake of common law in characteristics. According to China's Supreme People's Court, the serious misunderstanding refers to the understanding related to the legal nature of conduct, the identification of contractual party, the type, quality, specification and quantity of the objects. Contract led by serious misunderstanding is avoidable.

The serious misunderstanding may result from the following types of situations:

- Misunderstanding of the nature of contract. For example, to mistake lease contract for sales contract;
- Misunderstanding party A for party B;

- Misunderstanding the type of goods, for example, to mistake goods made of polyester for leather;
- Misunderstanding the quality of goods, for example, to mistake grade three for grade one.

(2) Mistake rules in Common Law

The types of mistakes could be various, either the mistake in facts or the mistake of law, or the mistake either made by one party or both parties. The following chart illustrates the general vision of mistakes under common law.

Table 18: Types of Mistakes under Common Law

Categories	Mistake made by both parties	Mistake made by one party
Mistake of fact (mistake in understanding relative facts)	• common mistake: Both parties make the same mistake. • mutual mistake: Both parties make different mistakes. Parties are at cross purposes.	• unilateral mistake: One party is mistaken about the essential fact, but the other party hopes to take advantage of the mistake. • Non est factum: The mistake is about the nature of document, and this mistake is excusable.
Mistake of law: Mistake in understanding law. generally the person making mistake will not be excused for everybody is expected to know law. Therefore, mistakes in contract law will be focused on mistake of facts.		

- **Common mistake**

Both parties are mistaken about the same fact that is essential to their agreement, which makes the contract void.

- **Mutual mistake**

Both parties misunderstand each other regarding an essential fact or each other's intention.

- **Unilateral mistake**

One party is making a mistake about essential fact (term or identity of a party to the contract) and the other party knows or ought to know the mistake but does nothing to correct it.

- *Non est factum*

There is a very special situation where the severely disabled people (blind or illiterate) signed important documents and later discovered that they had made a mistake about the nature of the document signed, which is fundamentally different from what they thought.

In such case, they could claim that the agreement was void because it was *non est factum*, meaning "not my doing" or "not my deed".

Table 19: Mistake and Serious Misunderstanding in Different Legal Systems

Points	Serious misunderstanding under Chinese contract law	Unilateral mistake under common law
Nature of the mistake	Misunderstanding must be serious, e.g., the issue of nature of contract, identity of the party, quantity and quality of goods.	Mistake in understanding essential facts.
Range of issues to be covered	Serious misunderstanding is limited to the issues above. This concept does not extend to: • misunderstanding by both parties; • motivation; • misunderstanding of laws and regulations.	Mistake has more coverage than serious misunderstanding including mistake due to third party's fault. Mistake includes common mistake. But it does not extend to mistake of motivation and of law either.
Parties involved	Serious misunderstanding is made by one party. The other party is bona fide.	Unilateral mistake was made by one party. The other party knew or should have known it , but did nothing to correct.
effect	Contract is avoidable only.	Contract is void.

SELF QUIZ: Indicate whether each of the following statements is true or false.

31. Law conditionally protects those who are mistaken about facts, not about law.

32. Common mistake and mutual mistake have same legal results.

33. Unilateral mistake is not excusable because everybody has to take care for his business.

34. Anyone who is mistaken as to fundamental documents can be excused on reliance of rule non est factum.

35. Unilateral mistake means one party makes mistake only.

2. By misrepresentation

Misrepresentation occurs when one party is induced or persuaded to have entered into a contract because he or she partly or wholly relies on a false statement of past or present facts by the other party. Misrepresentation and unilateral mistake may lead to same end, that is, a mistake finally occurs, but the two concepts are different. The distinctions between misrepresentation and mistake are that:

- Unilateral mistake occurs when one party subjectively makes a mistake;
- Misrepresentation occurs when it is induced or defrauded by the other party.

The following chart could illustrate the features and legal results.

Table 20: Types, Features, Legal Results and Conditions of Misrepresentation

Types	Fraudulent misrepresentation	Negligent misrepresentation	Innocent misrepresentation
Features	One party knowingly or carelessly makes a false statement of fact, intending to induce and actually leading to the contract and then causing damage to the other party.	One party makes a false statement due to carelessness, on which the receiver relies on the of false statement and then suffers a loss.	One party believes his statement was true, but actually wrong, which leads to a contract.
Legal results	Contract voidable. Damages available (fraud and tort action)	Contract voidable. Damages available (tortious action)	Contract voidable. No Damages
Conditions (All must be present)	1. There must be false statements of fact.		
	2. The presenter must know that his representation is false.	The presenter is recklessly careless about the truth of his representation.	The presenter believes his representation is true.
	3. The presenter intends the representee to act in reliance on it;		
	4. False statement actually deceives the innocent party and causes damage or loss.		

(1) Misrepresentation in Chinese contract law

Chinese law does not integrate misrepresentation of various reasons into one category, but treat them according to the reasons.

Table 21: Comparison Between Chinese Contract Law and Common Law

Common law	Relevant Chinese law to misrepresentations
Fraudulent misrepresentation	Chinese Criminal Law and the Section Three (tort) of the General Principles of Civil Law
Negligent misrepresentation	The Section Three (tort) of the General Principles of Civil Law
Innocent misrepresentation	Chinese Contract Law: mistake

(2) Misrepresentation in common law

Unlike Chinese law, common law divides misrepresentation into different categories:

- **Fraudulent misrepresentation**

  In case of fraudulent misrepresentation, the plaintiff can choose either action of fraud or action of tort.

> **CASE EXAMPLE:** *Derry v. Peek* (1889)[1]
>
> **Facts:** The defendants , who were the directors of tramway company, had issued a prospectus, stating that the company had a legal right to use steam to run its trams. At the time the prospectus was issued, the company had not received consent and the company never did in fact receive that consent. In reliance on the statement of prospectus, the plaintiff subscribed for shares in the company from an original allottee on the opening market. The company was subsequently wound up and the plaintiff sued the directors alleging fraudulent misrepresentation.
>
> **The court held that:** The prospectus was only issued for the purpose of obtaining members of the company on the original allotment of shares. As the plaintiff was in fact not an original allottee, there was no intention on the part of the issuers to induce the plaintiff to enter into the contract.
>
> **Take-away points:** Misrepresentation, alone, is not sufficient to prove deceit. This case is also about company laws. Importantly, the UK Companies Act 2006 overturned this case and requires full disclosure in securities markets.

---

1 [1889] UKHL 1.

- **Negligent misrepresentation**

CASE EXAMPLE: *Shaddock and Associates Pty Ltd. v. Parramatta City Council* (1981)[1]

Facts: Shaddock's solicitor contacted Parramatta City Council and asked whether an intended property would be affected by a road-widening governmental projects. The Council employees issued a form and made statements wrongly, indicating that the property would not be affected. Shaddock bought the property and suffered losses when the road was widened.

The court held that: Shaddock was entitled to compensation for negligent misrepresentation.

Take-away points: The council had a duty to exercise reasonable care that the information was correct. Therefore, the council should be liable for losses by its negligent misrepresentation.

(3) Innocent misrepresentation

CASE EXAMPLE: *Whittington v. Seal-Hayne* (1900)[2]

Facts: The plaintiff leased premises from the defendant, on the basis that the premises were in sanitary condition. The defendant genuinely believed that they were sanitary but they were found to be unsanitary after the plaintiff moved in.

The court held that: The plaintiff was entitled to rescind the lease on the basis of innocent misrepresentation and get refund of rates he had paid as well as an indemnity on repairs that he had made.

Take-away points: Innocent misrepresentation differs from negligent misrepresentation. If a party makes a statement without any grounds for knowing whether it is true or not, and an aspect of carelessness is involved, this party commits negligent misrepresentation. If a party has exhausted its reasonable effort and still fails to give a correct presentation, this party may be considered to commit innocent misrepresentation.

SELF QUIZ: Indicate whether each of the following statements is true or false.

36. Misrepresentation must be a false statement of fact, not of law.

37. Fraudulent misrepresentation is a fraud and a tort as well.

38. The difference between misrepresentation and unilateral mistake is the former induces the mistake and the latter is self-made mistake.

39. Innocent misrepresentation in common law is like serious misunderstanding in Chinese Contract Law.

---

1 [1981] ALR 385.

2 [1900] 82 LT 49.

3. By duress

Unlike misrepresentation where the representee is induced by false statement and then mistakenly enters into a contract, in situation of duress, one party (or his family) is under pressure when entering into a contract.

For duress in Chinese Contract Law (refer to Chinese Contract Law Article 54), Chinese Contract Law does not define the concept of duress, but provides that contract made under duress is voidable at the option of innocent party.

Types and legal results:

- Use violence or illegal threat to force a person to enter into a contract. (called "duress to person").
- Carry out illegal detention, seizure or damage to goods or property; (called "duress to goods or property")
- The illegitimate use of economic pressure to force a business into a contract, into which he might not otherwise have entered (called "economic duress").

CASE EXAMPLE: *Barton v. Armstrong* **(1976)**[1]

Fact: Having agreed to buy shares in several companies from Armstrong, Barton wanted to rescind the contract on the ground of duress to person. Barton claimed that he had only entered the contract because Armstrong had threatened to murder him and his family. The judge found that the threat had been made. However, that was not the sole reason why Barton had entered the contract.

The court held that: The contract could be set aside. Duress need not be the sole inducement for entering a contract. It is sufficient to prove that duress was a contributing factor.

Take-away points: Where there is duress to the person, there was no obligation to show that he would not have entered the agreement but for the threat, it simply being sufficient that the death threats were a cause.

4. By undue influence

Undue influence occurs where usually a special relationship or authoritative relationship exists between the parties. The stronger party uses his superior position of influence to persuade the weaker party to enter into a contract that benefits the stronger party. The legal result of contract made under undue influence is avoidable at the option of weaker party.

---

1   [1976] Ac 104 privy council.

Table 22: Types of Undue Influence and Onus of Proof

Special relationship	Power or position in the unequal relationship
Fiancé over fiancée (not husband over wife); Guardian over ward; Parent over child; Lawyer and client.	Those who have no or little education; Those who suffer from religious delusion; Those who are superstitious; Religious adviser and devotee.
Onus of proof: Defendant (the stronger party) is to prove that the transaction was voluntary and plaintiff understood the contract.	Onus of proof: Plaintiff (the weaker party) is to prove that he/she (the stronger party) exercise his/her power and position improperly .

Unfortunately, in Chinese Contract Law there is no any specific provision of undue influence or any similar concept. In adjudication, it is likely that the contract under undue influence would be dealt within the perspective of principle of good faith. Compared with common law, this indirect approach in China is less relevant to the legal issue.

SELF QUIZ: Indicate whether each of the following statements is true or false.

40. Threat or violence must be involved in the case of duress, but in mistake and misrepresentation, it is not necessarily.

41. Threat may be one of the reasons that contributes to legal contract.

42. Threat to family members is not duress in contractual sense.

43. Undue influence only exists when the parties are in a special relationship, like lawyer and client at the time of contracting.

44. The fair contract to both parties is valid although the parties have special relationship when making contract.

5. By unconscionable (unjust) conduct

The general rule of common law is that the courts will not interfere with a contract which appears to be the result of unconscionable conduct by one of the parties. However, in its equity jurisdiction, the court will set aside a transaction as unconscionable where there has been an abuse by the defendant of their superior bargaining position in their dealings with the weaker plaintiff.

But application of this rule must be limited according to the following table. Otherwise, the interfere will be too much to the contractual order. If we examine the conditions of unconscionable conduct carefully and then compare the similar rule of *non est factum*, it could be easily found that these two rules have a commonly interesting perspective and notion: in order to achieve fairness in particularly abnormal situation, the special disabled person should be treated specially with more favourable treatment to the disabled people.

Table 23: Conditions of Unconscionable Conduct

Conditions of unconscionable conduct	Conditions of *non est factum*
The plaintiff is specially disadvantaged.	The plaintiff is severely disabled.
The special disadvantage substantially affects plaintiff's ability to protect themselves.	The plaintiff fails to understand the document although he tries to he is not careful in reading the document.
The defendant must have known or should have been aware of plaintiff's disability and had taken advantage of it.	The defendant maybe does not know plaintiff's disability.
The adverse consequence of transaction may be not as serious as that in non est factum.	The signed document is fundamentally different from what the plaintiff thought.
The conducts of defendant are unfair to the Plaintiff.	The defendant's conduct is not so required.

> **CASE EXAMPLE:** *Commercial Bank of Australia Ltd v. Amadio* **(1983)**[1]
>
> **Facts:** Mr. & Mrs. Amadios were elderly migrants with poor business and English skills, they put up their house as security for their son's business to a bank. At the time of deal, they wrongly believed that their son's company was financially solid and their liability was only $50,000 for 6 months. The bank knew that both of their beliefs were wrong but did not disclose to Mr & Mrs. Amadios. Finally Amadios son's company got bankrupt and the bank demanded Mr & Mrs. Amadios to pay the debts of their son.
>
> **The court held that:** The contract was set aside on the ground of unconscionability. The court found that the bank was in a superior bargaining position to the Amadios as it knew the financial position of the son and also knew that the parents did not fully understand what they were entering into. The bank abused its superior bargaining position in its dealing with extremely disabled Amadios by having kept silent to the truth.
>
> **Take-away points:** "Unconscionable conduct" means the defendant abuse their superior bargaining position in their dealings with the weaker plaintiff.

The Chinese Contract Law Article 54 states that, the specially disabled person in contract-making should be treated especially favourably. This rule is deeply rooted in the value that in order to

---

1   (1983) 151 CLR 447.

realize true justice and fairness, the special unequal disparity could only be adjusted equal by unequal means (to equalize the unequal by unequal means). The rules of unconscionable conduct together with the *non est factum* all embody the value.

To solve those special legal issues, Chinese law tends to subject them to the principle of good faith, rather than to treat them with an exceptional rule, which are not in line with the main stream of rules.

Similar to the concept of unconscionable (unjust) conduct of common law, Article 54 of Chinese Contract Law has provided a rule for the contract resulting obvious unfairness. Chinese law does not allow a contract that is obviously unfair to either party at the time when the contract was concluded, but it will not interfere the contract after the conclusion of contract.

Table 24: Comparison of Unfairness Under Chinese Law and Common Law

Points	Obvious unfairness under Chinese law	Similar concepts under common law
Contract nature	The concepts under both Chinese contract law and common law are applicable only to the types of contract with consideration and bilateral contract	
Objective condition	One party's benefit gained from the contract has exceed over the limit allowed by the law. Exceptions include: • big price fluctuation; • due to ignorance of the other party; or • force majeure event	*Non est factum* is similar to obvious unfairness because the legal relation established was extremely different from what had been believed by the disabled party, so serious unfairness may be more likely to happen.
Subjective condition	one party • abuse his economic and other advantages; • failed to fulfil his legal duty to inform the other party.	Unconscionable (unjust) conduct Is similar to the situation where the stronger party abuse its economic advantages by unjustifiable approaches.

SELF QUIZ: Indicate whether each of the following statements is true or false.

45. The circumstances of special disadvantages include: the relative bargaining strengths of the parties and whether the independent legal advice was sought and could be sought.

46. The circumstances of special disadvantages also include: what normal commercial practice was and the age, health, education, literacy and mental capacity of the parties.

47. Economic ability is not the factor to consider unconscionable conduct.

48. The contract, even it is seriously unfair due to price fluctuation, is still legally valid.

What if the purpose of contracting is illegal?

If two parties have reached an agreement through offer and acceptance with other conditions (capacity, consideration, genuine consent) all in conformity with contract law except contracting purpose, the contract is still not legally valid.

1. Define the illegality of contract: illegal contract and void contract

The illegality of contract means either the subject matter or the purpose of contracting is not lawful. The unlawful subject matter includes, for example, drugs in sales contract, smuggling transportation in service contract, skills of suicide in technology transfer agreement, or price controlling monopoly right in licence agreement. The unlawful purpose is not as easy as unlawful subject matter to be found because they are hidden under an apparently lawful contract. It is intentionally felt and does not have to express out by words. Take the case above as an example, the two conspired agreements could not be found illegal if only judged from the face.

It is necessary to distinguish illegal contract from void contract, because although both contracts have no binding force in the end, they have different legal features.

Table 25: Comparison of the Illegal Contract and Void Contract

Illegal contracts	Void contracts
Illegal contracts violate the social or moral norms of the community and are prohibited as being contrary to the public interest or public policy.	Void contracts do not conform with the requirements for valid contract or are in conflict with principles of fairness.
It often subjects to administrative penalties or criminal penalization: • fine by administrative law • imprisonment by criminal law • unjust enrichment by tort law	It subjects to contractual remedies: • rescission • damages
It is totally void at the very beginning.	Void contracts do not necessarily mean void at the very beginning.

2. The circumstance of illegal contracts and void contracts

(1) Illegal contract under Chinese law

Different from the classification of illegal contract and void contract in common law, Chinese contract law does not divide the unlawful contracts into that classification. Contracts in violation of public policy are all under the heading of void contract, and some contracts may be partly void.

(2) Illegal and void contracts under common law

Common law classifies the following contracts into illegal contract:

- contracts that commit crime and fraud against a third party;
- contracts that prejudice public safety by dealing with foreign aliens during war time;
- contracts that defraud public authorities of taxes or revenue;
- contracts that promote corruption in public life;
- contracts that are prejudicial to the administration of justice.

Common law classifies the following contracts into void contracts instead of illegal contracts, as those contracts present less serious threats to the public good:

- marriage contracts, which hamper marriage status established by marriage law;
- contracts of restraint of trades, which may contravene the anti-monopoly law.

Table 26: Classification of Unlawful Contracts in Common Law and Chinese Contract Law

Common law		Chinese Contract Law	
Illegal contracts	See the above 2(2) The circumstance of illegal contracts and void contracts	Chinese Contract Law Article 52 Void contract	• By using fraud or coercion, one party damages the interest of the State; • Malicious collusion is conducted to damage the interests of the State, a collective or a third party; • An illegitimate purpose is concealed under the guise of legitimate act; • Public interests are damaged; • Compulsory provisions of laws and administrative regulations are violated.
Void contracts			
		Chinese Contract Law Article 56 Partly void contract	If part of a contract is null and void without affecting the validity of the other part of the contract, the other part shall still be valid.

What form should a contract take?

The form of a contract is the last one of seven elements for the validity of a contract. An agreement is formed through offer and acceptance, namely the meeting of minds between parties. The meeting of minds should take a form to be in existence, which comes in the form of contract. The form of contract could be either in

- Oral form: face to face talk, conversation through telephone, or skype, etc.;
- Written form: letter, fax and any other types of paper document.
- Electronic form: email, Wechat, facebook, etc;
- Actual act (performance of the contract);
- Other forms (administrative formalities or business registrations before performance).

Each of the forms must be requested to take a particular form in particular situation in conformity with the law. For example, real estate contracts must be in written form. But fortunately, in order to cater to the fast paced business and life, most types of contracts are not subject to any statutory requirements in terms of contractual form. Even the electronic form of contract tends to be allowed by majority of jurisdictions in the world.

But one point which should be kept in mind is that people in business is often advised to use a written form, which is not required by law but for the convenience of business or of probable lawsuit.

1. Precontracts under Chinese law

Precontract is generally defined as a contract prior to formulating a contract in the future. The examples of forms of precontracts in actual legal practice may be:

- subscription sheet;
- letter of intent;
- memo;
- memo of understanding;
- summary of minutes for negotiation;
- key points of agreement;
- receipt of deposit;
- agreement in general;
- some other forms.

2. The legal features of precontract

A precontract should meet the contractual validity requirements so as to be a legally binding contract. For instance, parties should have legal intention and the contents must be clear and definite, which have been already fully explained in previous sections. However, compared with requirements of formation of normal contract, precontract has its own legal features:

- The precontract is made with a purpose to make a normal contract in the future;
- Once the precontract is made, the future contract should be naturally and consequently made in the principle of good faith, and they should not be treated totally separated and independently negotiated.

Below is an illustration of precontract and its future contract about housing transaction, which demonstrates the relationship between the precontract and the contract it serves in the future.

Mr. A hopes to buy a flat so he turns to a housing developer. After negotiating with the seller, Mr. A books a suite available 6 months later by making a precontract with the seller, and then pays an advance payment accounting for 5% of total value as deposit.

Six months later, Mr. A will make a formal Sales Contract of House with the seller and then pays up the rest money in return for the flat. Three situations are included in the precontract:

- If Sales Contract of House is not made due to the buyer's fault, the deposit will not be returned to the buyer;
- If due to the seller' fault, double deposit will be returned to buyer;
- If due to reasons unconnected with either party, the deposit will still be returned to the buyer.

CASE EXAMPLE:

Facts: Company A, the buyer, made a precontract with Company B, a supplier of cotton, for 20 tons of cotton, CNY 13,000 per ton. Both agreed to make the formal contract before June 30, 2010. A paid CNY 50,000 as deposit ensuring to make the future contract. The precontract stipulated that if the future contract is not made due to the fault of either party, the defaulting party would be penalized on the basis of deposit amount. In June, 2010 the prices for cotton rose to CNY 15,000 per ton. Company B expressed its refusal to make the contract unless Company A agreed to raise the stipulated price in precontract to CNY 14,500, but Company A did not agree to change. So, Company A sued Company B for return of double deposit of CNY 100,000 and at the same time claimed for the damages CNY 40,000 because of expected benefits.

The court held that: Company A was entitled to the double deposit as agreed in the pre-contract and entitled to damages based on the breach of precontract.

Take-away point: The damages of CNY 40,000 is actually for the losses of future contract. If it had been signed and then performed, it was not the losses of expected benefits of pre-contract. So this part of damages may not seem reasonable.

SELF QUIZ: Indicate whether each of the following statements is true or false.

49. According to the Chinese law, contract of sales of goods have to be evidenced by writing at Chinese court.

50. Chinese courts may consider the sheet for goods transportation, sheet of reception, or sheet of payment as the forms of contract.

51. The correspondence for payment checkup and debit confirmation, are not written forms of contract according to Chinese law.

Part 4　Remedies for the Breach of Contract

When the contract is in the course of performance, it is likely that the contract may be breached as one party fails to perform his or her obligations as agreed. Therefore, contract law should provide legal assistance to the aggrieved party with various types of remedies, which would be rendered according to the seriousness of the breaches of contract.

The breach of contract and its consequences

When one party fails to perform his or her obligations as agreed, it is a breach of contract. The failure can occur in a number of ways as follows:
- Not comply with the term/terms of the contract;

    Eg. The quality of goods delivered by the seller is defective.
- Delay in performance where the time is very important to the contract;

    Eg. The delivery was two weeks later than the agreed time.
- The performing party announces to the other party that he will not perform his obligation before the time of performance; (anticipatory breach)

    Eg. The seller tells the buyer that he will not deliver the goods next month as agreed.

Of the three occurrences for breach of contract, the first two are actual breach, and the aggrieved party can access to the relevant remedies depending on the consequence caused by the actual breach. But the third breach is anticipatory, not actual, so the consequence of breach has to be first decided before relevant remedy is available. If the anticipatory breach has caused no damage to the innocent party, no remedy may be available.

1. Anticipatory breach under Chinese Contract Law

Article 108 of Chinese Contract Law has a provision on anticipatory breach of contract, which is similar to common law, as it has been introduced into Chinese law from common law. Chinese Contract Law recognizes both express and implied ways for occurrence of anticipatory breach and entitles the innocent party remedies for anticipatory breach of contract.

2. Anticipatory breach under Common Law

Anticipatory breach can occur expressly by words or impliedly by acts. The threatened failure to perform the contract, that is, the anticipation of breach entitles the innocent party to repudiate the contract or choose to wait for the performance until the time of performance is due.

SELF QUIZ: Indicate whether each of the following statements is true or false.

52. Anticipatory breach must occur before and during the time period of performance agreed by the contract.

53. Actual breach and anticipatory breach are all breach of contract with equal legal result.

54. If anticipatory breach occurs, the innocent party may treat it not as a breach of contract and wait the performance when the time of performance is due.

55. The defective quality of goods which has been delivered is not an anticipatory breach.

56. Anticipatory breach of contract could be shown by act, for example, the house owner resells his contracted house to a third party before delivery of the house.

Remedies available to the aggrieved party when contract is breached

Both Chinese law and common law have provided a set of remedies available to the aggrieved party.

Table 27 Contractual Remedies in Common Law and Chinese Law

Common law	Relevant Chinese law
Damages	Chinese Contract Law Article 107-119
• Ordinary damages	Chinese Contract Law Article 113
• Liquidated damages	Chinese Contract Law Article 114
• Nominal damages	None
• Exemplary damages	Chinese Contract Law Article 114
Equity:	
• Rescission	Chinese Contract Law Article 91-97

• Restitution
  - Quantum meruit
  - Quasi-contract
	General Principles of Civil Law

• Specific performance;	Chinese Contract Law Article 110
• Injunction	Civil Procedural Law
• Rectification	Chinese Contract Law Article 115 and Chinese Contract Law Article 111
• Anton Piller order	Civil Procedural Law

Contractual remedy: damages

Under the heading of damages, there are four kinds of damages, namely, the ordinary damages, the liquidated damages, the nominal damages and the examplary damages, each serving a particularly specific situation of breach of contract. However, the ordinary damages are most commonly used.

1. Types of damages

(1) Damages 1: ordinary damages

It means an award of damages, usually a monetary compensation, is to put the injured party back to the position that they would have been in if the contract had been performed as originally intended.

The legal nature of damages is not awarded to punish a wrongdoer but to compensate the innocent party, so it should not be punitive unless it is exceptionally necessary.

Ordinary damages include two types:

- general damages: damages and losses which took place from the usual or natural or normal course of things;
- special damages: special or exceptional damages and losses which will not be awarded unless they are specially made known to the defendant at the time of entering into the contract.

Ordinary damages in Chinese law

Ordinary damage at common law covers two aspects: the legal nature and types. Chinese Contract Law has the identical conception of the nature of damages that damages should be compensation of loss and normal business profit if the contract gets performed, rather than making of more profit. Chinese Contract Law does not prove a clear distinction of two types of damages as common law does. Despite this fact, the two types of common law are still accepted and well applied in Chinese courts.

(2) Damages 2: liquidated damages

It means the damages to the aggrieved party agreed in advance in case of breach of contract.

Compared with ordinary damages which is measured and set after the breach, the liquidated damages is stipulated because sometimes factual amount of damages may be difficult or impracticable to be calculated, which comes the necessity of liquidated damages.

The amount liquidated damages must be reasonable, not punitive. The functions of liquidated damages are to help to provide certainty, avoid lawsuits by providing a warning in advance, and provide an incentive to enter into contracts.

Liquidated damages in Chinese contract law

Liquidated damages are provided primarily in Article 114 of Chinese Contract Law. In order to prevent liquidated damages of punitive nature, Chinese Contract Law further provides that if the agreed liquidated damages is excessively higher than the actual loss, the request of proper deduction could be raised to judicial or arbitration authorities; and vice versa, if lower than the actual loss, the request of proper deduction could be raised.

(3) Damages 3: nominal damages

Nominal damages are awarded when the court senses that the innocent party's legal rights have been infringed, though without actual loss. Nominal damages could be as little as $1.

Nominal damages is not a legal joke or redundant. Nominal damages may become necessary when the litigants' purpose of lawsuit is not for economic benefits but for reputation; or the plaintiff's all economic claims turn out to be unreasonable and then refused by court.

The court awards nominal damages to the plaintiff just to show its legal opinion toward the dispute, rather than to solve the economic issues.

Nominal damages in Chinese contract law

In Chinese law there is no rule for normal damages, but it does not mean that the situations where nominal damages is used in common law courts do not happen in Chinese courts. The same things would take place in Chinese courts as well. But Chinese courts treat those situations with different approaches. Very often, the court would award a remedy of apologizing in public media for reputation; and the plaintiffs at court room are more likely to withdraw from the proceedings if all his claims appear to be hopeless.

(4) Damages 4: exemplary damages

Exemplary damages are awarded to punish a party that committed an intentional or excessive breach of contract.

The commitment of the breach of contract in usual sense is something unexpected, however, if the breaching party intentionally and excessively defaults in performance of contract, he/she may be punished by paying punitive damages (exemplary damages). But an exemplary damage is rarely awarded.

Exemplary damages may be awarded in the non-pecuniary losses, for example, the breach of contract has resulted in inconvenience or discomfort to the innocent party.

Exemplary damages in Chinese contract law

An exemplary damage at common law is a special damage for special breach of contract, which may be under criminal shadow. In Chinese legal system, however, if a breach of civil contract is linked with a criminal law, it would be more likely to be treated as criminal case, rather than the breach of contract where exemplary damages of contractual remedy may be awarded. When deciding a criminal case, Chinese courts would integrate the contractual claims involved into its final criminal judgement, awarding economic damages together with the criminal judgement. Notably, the guiding rules for the economic damages under the criminal case are not based on the regime of contractual remedy, so it is different from the exemplary damage at common law.

SELF QUIZ: Indicate whether each of the following statements is true or false.

57. Defendant's liability for his breach of contract is limited to the scope where he could have reasonably foreseen at the time of contracting.

58. If the loss was not reasonably foreseen by the defendant at the time of contracting, but was made noticeable by the plaintiff, the defendant is still liable for the losses.

59. Damages are a plural form for damage meaning a lot of damage.

60. Exemplary damages are alternatively called punitive damages because of punitive nature for its award.

61. Liquidated damages are different from the ordinary damages because it was agreed before the performance of contract.

2. How to remedy the aggrieved party by damages?

Supposing that an innocent party suffered losses due to breach of contract by the other party, before seeking for damages, the innocent party has to go through the following steps.

Table 28: Tests for Award of Damages

Step 1	Was there a breach of contract committed by the other party?
Step 2	Did the breach cause the damage? • Was there causation between the breach and damage? • What if the damage was due to the unexpected event or frustration, not due to breach of contract?
Step 3	Was the loss reasonably foreseeable by a third party? Or was the breaching party reasonably aware of the loss?
Step 4	What amount of money will adequately compensate the innocent party? • If the innocent party suffered no loss, could it still seek damages? • What types of loss or sufferings or detriments could be calculated into the amount of damages? • What if the volume of the innocent party's loss is beyond breaching party's expectation, could it still recover the actual volume of loss?
Step 5	Has the innocent party ever tried to mitigate the loss by taking measures to prevent the loss from being extended? • If yes, will the expenses for mitigation compensated by the breaching party? • If not, which party would be responsible for the extended loss?

(1) Step 1: Was there a breach of contract?

The innocent party (plaintiff) has to establish that the other party has breached the contract by failing to perform his obligations in the contract.

The breach may be a serious breach, a minor breach, an actual breach or an anticipatory breach.

The consequence of breaches or the timing of the contract would lead to different remedies available to the innocent party. However, in whatever breach it may be, the innocent party is entitled to the remedy of damages unless otherwise agreed in the contract or provided by law.

The breach should neither be due to unexpected events (frustration events) nor due to exclusions stipulated in the contract, which free the breaching party from paying damages.

(2) Step 2: Did the breach directly cause the damage?

This step aims at the question of causation. The injured party must prove the causation between the loss and breaching act, or in other words, that the loss is directly caused by the act of the breaching party.

> ## Case Example: *Hadley v. Baxendale* (1854)[1]
>
> **Facts:** A shaft in Hadley's mill broke, rendering the mill inoperable. Hadley hired Baxendale to transport the broken mill shaft to an engineer in Greenwich so that he could make a duplicate. Hadley told Baxendale that the shaft must be sent immediately and Baxendale promised to deliver it the next day. Baxendale did not know that the mill would be inoperable until the new shaft arrived. Baxendale was negligent and did not transport the shaft as promised, causing the mill to remain shut down for an additional five days. Hadley had paid two pounds four shillings to ship the shaft and sued for 300 pounds in damages due to lost profits and wages. The jury awarded Hadley 25 pounds beyond the amount already paid to the court and Baxendale appealed.
>
> **The court held that:** The usual rule was that the claimant is entitled to the amount he or she would have received if the breaching party had performed; i.e. the plaintiff is placed in the same position he would have been in had the breaching party performed. Under this rule, Hadley would have been entitled to recover lost profits from the five extra days when the mill was inoperable. However, in this case, Baxendale did not know that the mill was shut down and would remain closed until the new shaft arrived. Loss of profits could not be fairly or reasonably contemplated by both parties in case of a breach of this contract without Hadley having communicated the special circumstances to Baxendale. The court ruled that the jury should not have taken the loss of profits into consideration.
>
> **Take-away points:** An injured party may recover those damages which naturally occured in due course and were reasonably contemplated by the breaching party at the time of contracting.

Article 113 of The Chinese Contract Law also has the same position as to the concept of damages on basis of causation between breach and damages. And rules of causation under Chinese Contract Law coincides with common law, which says: *The amount of compensation for losses shall be equal to the losses caused by the breach of contract, including the interests receivable*

---

1   9 Exch. 341, 156 Eng. Rep. 145 (1854).

after performance of the contract, provided not exceeding the probable losses caused by the breach of contract which has been foreseen or ought to be foreseen when the party in breach concludes the contract.

(3) Step 3: Was the loss reasonably foreseeable by a third party? Or was the breaching party reasonably aware of the loss?

Sometimes an act may cause several losses. This step requires that the claimable damages should not be too remote. The loss should be reasonably foreseeable by the defendant at the time of entering into the contract.

The claimable losses are only

- those flow from the usual, normal or natural course of things;
- those special or exceptional losses, which will not be claimable because they are not reasonably foreseeable unless the defendant is especially made known to the loss at the time of entering into the contract.

The distinction between step 2 and step 3 reflects the rules of causation:

- Step 2 requests that if there are more acts of breach resulting to the loss, it is the direct breaching act, rather than the indirect ones that can help establish the causation;
- Step 3 requests that if more losses were caused by one breaching act, the loss which was reasonably foreseeable by the defendant at the time of contracting is legally claimable, while the remote losses are not acceptable.

(4) Step 4: What amount of damages will adequately compensate the innocent party?

Once the court has decided that damages are payable, in addition to ordinary losses, the following losses may be awarded according to certain circumstances:

- Expectation losses: Loss of commercial opportunity and loss of profit arising from defendant's defective performance of contract;
- Reliance losses: When it is impossible to calculate damages, but expending can be calculated as a result of relying on the defendant's promise;
- Anxiety;
- Inconvenience;
- Disappointment;
- Discomfort;
- Mental distress.

CASE EXAMPLE: *Javis v. Swan Tours* (1972)[1]

Facts: Javis arranged a two-week holiday in Switzerland through Swan Tours's office as a result of information contained in one of its brochures. However, few of the statements contained in the

---

1   [1972] EWCA8.

brochures proved to be accurate.

The Court held that: Javis was entitled to damages for disappointment, distress, upset and frustration caused by the breach. The holiday did not live up to the promise that was contained in the defendant's brochure.

Take-away Points: Discomfort, mental distress and frustration and more severe sufferings in feelings could be more acceptable by the court in claims for damages.

Damages from expectation losses and reliance losses are well accepted and practiced in China although the Chinese contract law has not gone into depth in its legislation. However, the spiritual damages in common law, for example, anxiety, disappointment, discomfort and mental distress are more likely applicable in tort cases , but are less likely in contract case.

(5) Step 5: Has the innocent party ever tried to mitigate the loss by taking measures to prevent the loss from being extended?

Whether it is actual or anticipatory breach, the person claiming damages should take all reasonable measures to reduce or minimize (mitigate) the loss.

- If he or she fails, the court would reduce the amount that can be recovered;
- If he or she is able to avoid the loss, damages would not be recoverable for potential loss that he may have suffered.

Mitigation is a question of fact, and the burden of prove is on the defendant to show that the plaintiff has failed to mitigate the loss.

Article. 119 of General Principle of Civil Law also requests the plaintiff to mitigate the loss of breach if he can, for instance, the seller has the delivered but defective goods under his control. If the plaintiff fails to perform his duty by mitigating the losses, the extended losses directly due to his failure will not be included into the claimable damages.

SELF QUIZ: Indicate whether each of the following statements is true or false.

62. Recoverable damages include both physical losses and spiritual sufferings.

63. Remedy of damages would be available unexceptionally in any situation where a breach of contract occurs.

64. Remedy of damages would be awarded together with other remedies respectively, e.g., rescission, restitution, injunction, and rectification depending on the situations.

65. The measurement of damages is based on causal relation so the loss should naturally arise from the breaching act.

66. If the loss is directly and naturally caused by the breaching act, it is claimable even it is out of defendant's expectation.

67. In calculating amount of damages the court will deduct damages for two losses: one is remote loss; the other is loss caused by non-compliance of mitigation duty imposed on plaintiff.

Contractual remedy: rescission

1. Remedy of rescission in Chinese contract law

Unlike common law that primarily focuses on rescission of contract, Chinese contract law distinguishes rescission of contract from revocation of contract. The former is similar to common law while the latter focuses more on administrative control and compulsory termination of the contract.

Table 29: Difference Between Rescission and Revocation of Contract under Chinese Contract Law

Differences	Revocation	Rescission
Nature	Administrative	Civil
situations where Contract is terminated	Article 54 Chinese Contract Law: • serious misunderstanding; • obvious unfairness; • fraud, coercion, exploitation of unfavourable position	Article 94 of Chinese Contract Law: • force majeure event; • anticipatory breach; • principal obligation delayed; • other defaulting performance
legal procedure required to terminate contract	legal procedure (court and arbitration) required	not required
effect of termination of contract	retrospective, and void ab initio	no retrospective effect and not necessary

2. Remedy of rescission under Common Law

The basic rules of rescission can be illustrated by questions and answers in the following table:

Table 30: Basic Rules about the Remedy of Rescission Under Common Law

Questions	Answers
When is it available to the innocent party?	The genuine consent is lacking to fundamental level (e.g., fraudulent misrepresentation, duress, undue influence, unconscionable conduct).
What is the innocent party's option?	This remedy is available to the innocent party who may exercise the right by rescinding the contract, or refuse to exercise the right by still affirming (continuing) the contract.

(to be continued)

(continued)

Questions	Answers
What is the legal result if the contract is rescinded?	Rescission makes contract void, which suggests that the terminated contract is deemed to have never existed before.
What to do with the performed part if rescission is exercised?	• The performed goods and money to be returned; • The performed services should be reasonably compensated. (see: quantum meruit in "5.5 Contractual remedy: restitution")
What are the situations where rescission is not available to the innocent party?	• The breach has not reached to fundamental level, or • The parties cannot return entirely or at least substantially to their pre-contract position.
What are the situations where the remedy of rescission is lost?	• If the innocent party refuses to rescind the contract by choosing to affirm the contract; • If the innocent party waits an unreasonable time before attempting to rescind; • If the subjects of contract (goods or money) have been acquired by a bona fide third party before attempted rescission.

SELF QUIZ: Indicate whether each of the following statements is true or false.

68. When a fundamental breach occurs, the innocent party should exercise his right to rescind the contract.

69. Remedy is available to the aggrieved party if a breach of contract takes place.

70. Even the innocent party has obtained the right of rescission, his right of rescission may be lost, if the goods, in case of sales contract, had been transferred to a bona fide third party.

71. Rescission discharges the liability of performance for the innocent party and the breaching party as well.

72. To the injured party, recession is more a right than a remedy because it does not require the intervention of the court.

Contractual remedy: restitution

1. Remedy of restitution under Chinese contract law

The remedy of restitution is not available in Chinese contract law; however, it does not mean Chinese legal system refuses to accept the conception of prevention of unjust enrichment.

In dealing with the situation where the contract is not completed but rescinded by an innocent party, Chinese court is more likely to refer to the rule of unjust enrichment which is expressly used in tort law to solve the problem by requesting the breaching party to return the received goods or money, if it is possible; or pay reasonable price for services received.

2. Basic rules of the remedy of restitution under common law

Restitution is defined as "return or restoration of some specific things to its rightful owner or status" or "compensation for benefits derived from a wrong done to another" in *Black's Law Dictionary*.[1] The remedy of restitution is available to a party (usually the plaintiff) who has transferred goods, money or service to the other party, but has no right to recover these benefits. For example, seller delivered goods to the buyer, but the buyer refused to pay unreasonably, so the seller chose to rescind the contract. As the contract is rescinded, the seller will have no right to request the buyer to pay any more, but he still has the right over the remedy of restitution by claiming his or her goods back which had been already delivered to the buyer. Even the sales contract is invalid, the restitution is still available to the seller. (Note: Of course, remedy of damages is also available to the seller if he claims for it). The purpose of restitution is to compensate plaintiff's loss by preventing the defendant from gaining unjust enrichment.

Concept of restitution is available in tort and criminal as in contract law as well.

Table 31: Summary of Characteristics of Restitution

Characteristics	Description
Definition	• Return or restoration of some specific thing to its rightful owner or status. Or • compensation for benefits derived from a wrong done to another.
Requirements for restitution	• Defendant received goods or money or other benefits; • the benefit was at plaintiff's expenses; • plaintiff has no contractual right to recover these benefits; • it would be unjust if the benefits are not returned to the rightful owner; • the defendant has no defenses available to him to rely on, e.g. purchase in good faith, estoppel.
Purpose of remedy	Preventing unjust enrichment
How to restitute	• return of gained goods, money or services by the defendant or • quantum meruit (for as much as he has gained)

(to be continued)

---

1   Page1315, seventh edition.

(continued)

Characteristics	Description
Situations where contract law, tort law, and criminal law are applicable	In contract law: • non-contractual and semi-contractual situations: apply quasi-contract rule; • invalid contract: restitution is still available; • part performance: apply quantum meruit rule; • mistake of law: restitution is still available .
	In tort law: prevention of aggrieving party from gaining unjust enrichment by act of tort
	In criminal law: Sometime restitution is ordered as a condition of probation in criminal law.

3. Quantum meruit under restitution

Restitution is sometimes applied to the non-contractual or semi-contractual situations, in which the non-contractual situation is treated as contractual called quasi-contract in restitution. In other words, the plaintiff is remedied as if he/she has contractual rights.

In this situation, restitution is measured by quantum meruit, (meaning "for as much as he has earned" or reasonable pay for reasonable service).The most likely situations that give rise to quantum meruit are:

• Where the parties cannot agree on the precise payment for the work done or there is a "gentleman agreement";

• Where the defendant breached the contract and prevented the plaintiff from completing the remainder of his contractual duties;

• Where the contract was void or unenforceable because the contract lacked an essential elements , such as genuine consent.

SELF QUIZ: Indicate whether each of the following statements is true or false.

73. Restitution is meant to restore or return what has been got by wrong doing to the rightful owner.

74. Restitution is a remedy of contract, but this remedy is still available to the plaintiff even he has lost his contractual right.

75. Restitution is applicable in both tort and contract law.

76. Remedy of damages is available to plaintiff under contract right while restitution not.

77. If a contract rescinded, restitution will not be available to the plaintiff any more.

78. In order to prevent unjust enrichment, quantum meruit may be applied for the work done in favour of the defendant.

Contractual remedy: specific performance and injunction

1. Definitions

Remedy of specific performance is defined as a court order to enforce a party to perform his duties in strict accordance with the contract. The remedy of injunction is defined as a court order too, but the purpose is to enforce a party stop doing something of breaching the contract.

Specific performance is not readily available as remedy of damages, and the court will be reluctant or even refuse to grant specific performance in the following circumstances:

- When damages would adequately compensate the injured party, because the remedy of monetary compensation is easier than specific performance;
- When it would cause severe hardship to the defendant, because the court is alert on avoiding unfairness to the defendant while doing justice to the plaintiff ;
- When it would require constant supervision by the court because the court is afraid of inability to implement the order.

Compared with specific performance, remedy of injunction is more ready to be available to the plaintiff unless in the situation where a contract involving personal services.

In the Judiciary, the concept of injunction is borrowed and often used in preserving evidence and assets. For example:

- Mareva Injunction: an injunction to prevent defendant from removing assets from court's jurisdiction.
- Anton Piller order: an injunction to prevent the defendant from disposing of any evidence before trial.

2. Remedy of specific performance and injunction under Chinese contract law

As to specific performance, Chinese contract law fully embodies the basic rules of common law. According to Article 110 of Chinese Contract Law, the innocent party could apply to the court to issue an order of specific performance, if the following requirements are met:

- Firstly, there must be a breach of contract. This is the precondition for applying this remedy;
- Secondly, the innocent party applies to the court to issue the order within reasonable time;
- Thirdly, the applied subject matter is specified and irreplaceable or immeasurable with money because damages prioritizes the specific performance;
- Fourthly, it must be feasible economically, that is, it will not cause unnecessary loss and waste to the defendant;
- Fifthly, it is not in violation with law. Usually it is not applicable to personal contracts.

As to injunction, Chinese Contract Law categorizes it into civil procedure law as it is seen as a proceeding right by the court, so Chinese Contract Law does not cover this remedy, as it is in common law.

79. Specific performance and injunction are both court orders.

80. The application of specific performance is more restricted than injunction.

81. Court is reluctant to grant specific performance because it requires the court to supervise the implementation of the order.

82. Specific performance is applicable in the situation where remedy of damages does not work.

83. Remedy of rescission is automatically operational once the plaintiff chooses the remedy but remedy of injunction will not be operational without the court assistance.

84. Remedy of specific performance goes well together with other remedies, e.g., with ordinary damages, liquidated damages but not with rescission.

Contractual remedy: rectification

If a contract does not reflect the true agreement or intention of the parties, it may be rectified (corrected) so that the terms conform to the true agreement.

Under common law and equity, the court cannot alter the contract to make it fairer or to correct technical defects, neither can it convert a void or avoidable contract into a valid one by rewriting or correcting, unless law allows the court to rewrite or correct the contract to make the contract valid or fairer.

The remedy of rectification is not available in Chinese contract law. In theory, this common remedy is alien to chinese law makers. Chinese courts generally would try to strike balance between the plaintiff and the defendant and would not rectify a contract in the contract dispute.

Questions

1. Case Analysis

Mr. Xie, the plaintiff, made a contract for commission with Mr. Chen, the defendant, who promised that he could get a qualification quota before the end of August 2013 for Xie's daughter for entering into the university she hopes. But Xie had to pay CNY 300,000 to fix the problem. If Chen failed, he would return all the money.

On August 9th, 2013, Xie remitted CNY 250,000 to the banking account designated by Chen, and CNY50,000 in cash to Chen who then issued a receipt for all the money.

Before the end of August 2013, Chen failed to get the qualification quota. Then, two parties made a new agreement saying: Chen was to fix the qualification problem before the end of Oct 2013. If unsuccessful, he would return the CNY 250,000 remitted and give Xie CNY50,000 more as compensation.

Since Chen did not fulfill his promise for qualification quota, and only returned CNY80,000, Xie file a lawsuit to a Chinese court against Chen for the remaining money CNY 170,000 and its interests.

The key issues of the case:

- According to Chinese contract law, is the contract valid?
- If invalid, why is it invalid? And what is the nature of the contract, avoidable or void?
- Should Xie be remedied? If yes, should he be remedied with all his claims?

2. Case Analysis

On January 6, 2013, Mr. Yuan, plaintiff, signed a sheet of confirmation with a cultural development company, the defendant. According to the confirmation, the defendant promised to display an exhibition of some cultural columns and family glory and promised to provide operational backup service after the exhibition open to the public. The total project cost and charges was CNY 200,000.

One week later, Yuan paid the half of the total, CNY100,000. Soon afterwards defendant set up a website for Yuan. But unfortunately, the project did not turn out satisfactorily.

The Plaintiff then brought a lawsuit against the defendant, among his pleadings the major ones are:

- obvious unfairness for the charge of the website the defendant setup for him. The plaintiff pledged that for the cost of setting up a website which usually cost less than CNY 2000, CNY 200,000 was 100 times as high as market price. So he requested to terminate the confirmation with the defendant and asked the defendant to return the paid CNY100,000.
- defendant should terminate the website for the plaintiff.

The defendant stated in its defense and counterclaim:

- both parties have entered contract relation through the confirmation.
- defendant, after conclusion of the contract, has completed the display of exhibition including setting up the website and endeavor to publicize the plaintiff to the well-known websites.

Relying on the above, defendant requested the plaintiff

- to continue to perform the contract by paying the remaining CNY100,000.
- to make apology to the defendant in the public, in return, defendant would agree to off line the website .

The key issues of the case:

- Whether or not there was a contract between the parties.
- Whether or not the charge was obviously unfair which in violation against Chinese law.

Suggested Further Readings

Paul Latimer, *Australian Business Law*, 35th ed. 2016.

Boris Kozolchyk, *Comparative Commercial Contracts: Law, Culture and Economic Development*, 2014.

Clive Turner & John Trone, *Australian Commercial Law*, 30th ed. 2014.

Brian A. Blum, *Contracts: Examples and Explanation*, 6th ed. 2013.

Roger Vickery & Wayne Pendleton, *Australian Business Law Principles and Application*, 5th ed. 2005.

Elliot I. Klayman, John W. Bagby & Nan S. Ellis, *Irwin's Business Law: Concept Analysis, Perspectives*, 1993.

Chapter 5

International Sale of Goods: Incoterms®, Payment, Transportation and Insurance

Chapter 1 has demonstrated that both horizontal and vertical legal relationships are involved in selling goods across borders. This chapter, "International Sale of Goods," explores the horizontal legal relationship in selling goods across borders, covering trade terms, trade finance and payment, transportation, and insurance. The vertical legal relationship will be analyzed in the next Chapter. This chapter is constituted by four parts:

Part 1 analyzes Incoterms® 2010;

Part 2 explores trade finance and payment methods in international sales of goods;

Part 3 discusses international cargo transportation;

Part 4 presents international marine insurance.

Learning Objectives

By the end of this chapter you should:

- Understand Incoterms® rules and know how to use them in international sale of goods.
- Use main trade finance tools.
- Analyze various methods for payment in international trade, in particular legal jurisprudence with respect to letter of credit.
- Tell the key differences between liner transport and charter shipment.
- Understand the legal nature of a bill of lading and its main classifications.
- Know the key international rules governing bills of lading and their different approaches towards carriers' liabilities.
- Outline the legal nature of air waybills.
- Be familiar with the concept of international multimodal transport and multimodal transport operator.

■ Key Terms

Air waybill	International multimodal transport
Assignment	Letter of credit
Bill of exchange	Liner transport
Bill of lading	Loss
Charter shipment	Multimodal transport operator
Collection	Peril
Doctrine of strict compliance	Subrogation
Endorsement	The Incoterms®
Insurable interest	

Part 1   Incoterms® 2010

The Incoterms®[1] are used worldwide in international and domestic contracts for the sale of goods. They are recognized by UNCITRAL as the global standard for the interpretation of the most common terms in sale of goods across borders. First published in 1936, Incoterms® have been periodically updated, and the eighth version—Incoterms 2010—came into effect on January 1, 2011. They provide a series of three-letter trade terms to clearly communicate the obligations, costs, and risks associated with the sale of goods. The purpose is to reduce uncertainties arising from different interpretations of the rules in different countries.

Incoterms® 2010 consists of 11 sets of trade terms (each set of terms is referred to as a "Rule"). Seven of the 11 Rules can be used when whatever mode(s) of transport are involved (including where transport is all or partially over water), and the other four Rules can only be used if the delivery of the goods is by sea or inland waterway transport. None of the Rules have been designed for transport by pipeline, because numerous other trade practices have already existed and applied to pipeline transport.

Features of Incoterms® 2010

1. Reclassification of rules

The Rules in Incoterms® 2000 were divided into four categories (departure, main carriage unpaid, main carriage paid, and arrival) but the Rules in Incoterms® 2010 are divided into two categories: (1) rules for any mode or modes of transport, which can be used when there is no maritime transport at all or if maritime transport is used for only part of the carriage; and (2) rules for sea and inland waterway transport, if the point of delivery and the place to which the goods

---

1   "Incoterms" is a registered trademark of the ICC.

are carried to the buyer are both ports.

FOB, CFR and CIF belong to the second class of rules. In respect of them, while Incoterms® 2000 refers to the "ship's rail" as the reference point for delivery, Incoterms® 2010 provides that delivery occurs when the goods are "on board" the vessel to reflect practical reality.

2. Rules apply to domestic as well as international trade

The Incoterms® have traditionally been used for international sales contracts. Incoterms® 2010 can also be used for domestic sales contracts and reference is made in a number of the Rules that export and import formalities will only need to be complied with where applicable.

3. Two new terms

Incoterms® 2000 consists of 13 rules but Incoterms® 2010 only has 11 rules. Two new rules are introduced into Incoterms® 2010: Delivered at Terminal (DAT) and Delivered at Place (DAP). Delivered at Terminal (DAT) replaces the old Delivered Ex-Quay (DEQ) and Delivered at Place (DAP) replaces the old Delivered at Frontier (DAF), Delivered Ex-Ship (DES), and Delivered Duty Unpaid (DDU). In essence, the "D" (Delivered) terms under the 2000 Incoterms® have been consolidated to reduce the number of terms that were considered to have little real difference between them.

4. String sale

String Sale refers to sell commodities several times during transit through a string of sales contracts. In string sale, there will be more than one seller and only the first seller will have been responsible for shipping the goods. The new Rules have been amended to reflect this. For example, CIF and CFR now refer to an obligation to "contract or procure a contract for the carriage of the goods..."

5. Terminal handling charges

Under the CIF or CFR of Incoterms® 2000, the buyer potentially faced paying for some freight costs twice. The reason is that the seller was often including freight costs as part of the sale price, yet the buyer was sometimes expected by the carrier or terminal operator to pay the costs of handling and moving the goods within the port or container terminal facilities. Compared with Incoterms® 2000, Incoterms® 2010 more clearly allocates such costs and better avoids this potential double exposure.

6. Electronic data interchange

Incoterms® 2000 provided for the use of Electronic Data Interchange (EDI) messages, if the parties have agreed to use them. Considering the quick development of EDI, Incoterms® 2010 gives EDI the same effect as paper communications, as long as the parties agree or the international custom requires. Therefore, if a party needs to receive hard copies (as opposed to electronic versions) of shipping documents, this party should make this point clear in the contract.

What are the Incoterms® 2010 Rules?

1. Rules for any mode or modes of transport

(1) EXW: Ex Works

"Ex Works (named place of delivery)" means that the seller delivers when it places the goods at the disposal of the buyer, at the seller's premises, or at another named places (e.g. works, factory, warehouse). The seller does not need to load the goods on any collecting vehicle, nor does it need to clear the goods for export, where such clearance is applicable. The buyer arranges and pays for loading and transportation, and is also responsible for clearing the goods through Customs. The buyer should complete all the export documentation.

Therefore, under this term, the buyer bears the maximum obligation (e.g., risks and costs) and the seller has the minimum obligations, because the buyer incurs the risks and pays for bringing the goods to their final destination. If parties wish the seller to be responsible for the loading of the goods on departure and to bear the relevant risks and costs, the sales contract must explicitly indicates so.

(2) FCA: Free Carrier

"Free Carrier (named place of delivery)" means that the seller delivers the goods to the carrier or another person nominated by the buyer at the seller's premises or another named place. Costs for transportation and risks of loss are transferred to the buyer after delivery to the carrier, so the parties are well advised to specify as clearly as possible within the named place of delivery. In the Incoterms®, the word "free" means that the seller's obligation to the goods shifts to the buyer.

(3) CPT: Carriage Paid to

"Carriage Paid To (named place of destination)" means that the seller delivers the goods to the carrier or another person nominated by the seller at an agreed place (if any such place is agreed between parties). The seller must contract for and pay the costs of carriage necessary to bring the goods to the named place of destination, but the risks are transferred to the buyer as soon as the seller hands the goods over to the first carrier at the place of shipment in the country of export. The seller is not responsible for buying insurance.

(4) CIP: Carriage and Insurance Paid to

"Carriage and Insurance Paid to (named place of destination)" means that the seller delivers the goods to the carrier or another person nominated by the seller at an agreed place (if any such place is agreed between parties) and that the seller must contract for and pay the necessary costs of carriage to bring the goods to the named place of destination. The seller also contracts for insurance cover against the buyer's risks of loss of or damage to the goods during the carriage. The buyer should note that under CIP the seller is required to obtain insurance only on minimum cover. Should the buyer wish to have more insurance protection, it will need either to agree as much expressly with the seller or to make its own extra insurance arrangements. Moreover, the risks of the goods pass from the seller to the buyer when the seller hands the goods over to the first carrier. CIP and CIF have the same meaning but CIP is used for containerized or multimodal transport while CIF is used for sea transport.

(5) DAT: Delivered At Terminal

"Delivered At Terminal (named terminal at port or place of destination)" means that the seller delivers when the goods, once unloaded from the arriving means of transport, are placed at the disposal of the buyer at a named terminal, named port, or place of destination. "Terminal" includes a place, whether covered or not, such as a quay, warehouse, container yard or road, rail or air cargo terminal. The seller bears all risks involved in bringing the goods to and unloading them at the terminal at the named port or place of destination. DAT requires the seller to clear the goods for export when applicable, but the seller has no obligation to clear the goods for import, pay any import duty or carry out any import customs formalities. After the seller delivers the goods at the terminal, the buyer is responsible for all costs and risks from this point forward including clearing the goods for import at the named country of destination. It is considered that DAT will prove to be more useful than DEQ in case that containers may be unloaded and then loaded into a container stack at the terminal, awaiting shipment. There is previously no term clearly dealing with containers that are not at the buyer's premises.

(6) DAP: Delivered At Place

"Delivered At Place (named place of destination)" which means that the seller delivers when the goods are placed at the disposal of the buyer on the arriving means of transport ready for unloading at the named place of destination, not cleared for import (buyer is responsible for effecting customs clearance and paying any customs duties). The seller bears all risks and transaction costs involved in bringing the goods to the named place of destination, excluding unloading, and the buyer bears all risks and costs from that moment onwards. If the seller incurs costs in relation to unloading the goods at the named place, the seller is not entitled to recover the costs from the buyer unless otherwise agreed by the parties.

DAP was introduced to facilitate the use in domestic and international transactions within Customs Unions where no export or import clearance obligations exist, but seller must clear the goods for export, when applicable. If the buyer wishes the seller to clear goods for import and customs formalities, then Delivered Duty Paid (DDP) should be used.

(7) DDP: Delivered Duty Paid

"Delivered Duty Paid (named place of destination)" means that the seller delivers the goods when the goods are placed at the disposal of the buyer, cleared for import on the arriving means of transport ready for unloading at the named place of destination. The seller bears all the costs and risks involved in bringing the goods to the place of destination and has an obligation to clear the goods not only for export but also for import, to pay any duty for both export and import and to carry out all customs formalities. But the seller is not responsible for unloading. All the risks are transferred to the buyer after the seller delivers at the named place of destination. Therefore, this term places the maximum obligations on the seller and minimum obligations on the buyer.

2. Rules for sea and inland waterway transport

FAS, FOB, CFR and CIF are for international sale of goods when transportation is entirely conducted by water. These terms are generally not suitable for shipments in shipping containers. This is because, under the four Rules, the risks of the loss of or damage to the goods are shifted from the seller to the buyer when the goods are loaded on board the ship, and if the goods are sealed into a shipping container, it is impossible to verify the condition of the goods at this point.

(1) FAS: Free Alongside Ship

"Free Alongside Ship (named port of shipment)" means that the seller delivers when the goods are placed alongside the vessel (e.g., on a quay or a barge) nominated by the buyer at the named port of shipment. The risks of loss of or damage to the goods are passed from the seller to the buyer when the goods are alongside the ship, and the buyer bears all costs from that moment onwards. This term requires the seller to clear the goods for export. If the parties wish the buyer to clear the goods for export, they should explicitly indicate this in the contract.

(2) FOB: Free On Board

"Free On Board (named port of shipment)" means that the seller delivers the goods on board the vessel nominated by the buyer at the named port of shipment, or the seller procures the goods to be so delivered (in the case of "string sale"). The seller is responsible for risks and costs prior to the goods placed on board the vessel. The risks of loss of or damage to the goods passes from the seller to the buyer when the goods are on board the vessel, and the buyer bears all costs from that moment onwards. That is to say, the seller pays for the transportation of goods to the port of shipment (including the loading cost) and clears the goods for export. The buyer pays the cost of marine freight transportation, insurance, unloading and transportation cost from the arrival port to destination.

The seller must physically load the cargo onto the vessel. If the goods go to a container terminal, the seller will not be able to ensure that the goods are loaded onto the vessel. Therefore, Free Carrier (FCA) should be used instead in order to limit the risk exposure between the gates of the terminal and when the goods are placed on board the vessel, if the buyer agrees. If the buyer disagrees to the use of FCA, the seller needs to insure the goods between the terminal gates and the delivery "on board" the vessel.

(3) CFR: Cost and Freight

"Cost and Freight (named port of destination)" means that the seller delivers the goods on board the vessel or procures the goods already so delivered. The risks of loss of or damage to the goods are passed from the seller to the buyer when the goods are on board the vessel at the port of shipment. The seller must contract for and pay the costs and freight necessary to bring the goods to the named port of destination.

(4) CIF: Cost, Insurance and Freight

"Cost, Insurance and Freight (named port of destination)" means that the seller delivers the goods on board the vessel or procures the goods already so delivered. The risks of loss of or damage to the goods are passed when the goods are on board the vessel. The seller must contract for and pay the costs and freight necessary to bring the goods to the named port of destination. The seller also contracts for insurance cover against the buyer's risks of loss of or damage to the goods during the carriage. The buyer should note that under CIF the seller is required to obtain the insurance only on minimum cover. Should the buyer wish to have more insurance protection, it will need either to agree as much expressly with the seller or to make its own extra insurance arrangements. The seller must obtain any required export license and pay for customs formalities and loading costs.

Figure 1: Incoterms® 2010 Quick Reference

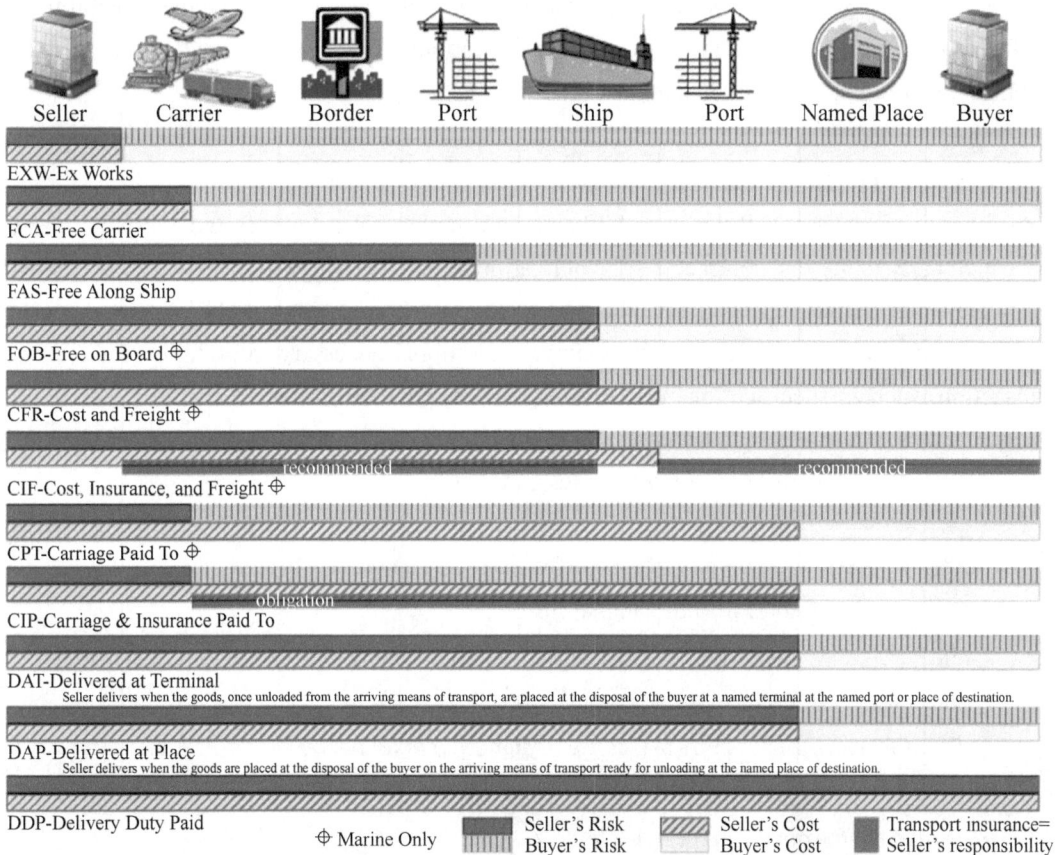

DAT-Delivered at Terminal
Seller delivers when the goods, once unloaded from the arriving means of transport, are placed at the disposal of the buyer at a named terminal at the named port or place of destination.

DAP-Delivered at Place
Seller delivers when the goods are placed at the disposal of the buyer on the arriving means of transport ready for unloading at the named place of destination.

DDP-Delivery Duty Paid

⊕ Marine Only | Seller's Risk / Buyer's Risk | Seller's Cost / Buyer's Cost | Transport insurance= Seller's responsibility

How to use the Incoterms® 2010 Rules?

1. Incorporate the Incoterms® 2010 Rules into your contract sale

If you want to apply the Incoterms® 2010 rules to your contract, please make this clear in the contract, such as, "FOB Shanghai Incoterms® 2010". If parties only indicate "Incoterms®" rather than "Incoterms® 2010" in their contract, it is not clear which set of Incoterm® Rules should be applied. If the parties wish to incorporate a specific rule from Incoterm® 2000, or all of Incoterm® 2000, they should make specific reference to this in the contract.

2. Choose the appropriate Incoterms® Rule

The parties should consider carefully which of the rules is appropriate to the type of goods being delivered, the means of their transport, and above all whether the parties intend to put additional obligations, for example, the obligation to organize carriage or insurance, on the seller or on the buyer. Whichever Incoterms® rule is chosen, the parties should be aware that the interpretation of their contract may well be influenced by customs particular to the port or place being used.

3. Specify your place or port as precisely as possible

The chosen Incoterms® rule can work only if the parties name a place or port, and will work best if the parties specify the place or port as precisely as possible. This can reduce the possibilities of confusion or disputes between the parties. A good example of such precision would be: "FCA 38 Cours Albert 1er, Paris, France Incoterms® 2010."

4. Use a formal sale contract

Remember that Incoterms® Rules do not give you a complete sales contract. Incoterms® Rules do say which party to the sale contract has the obligation to make carriage or insurance arrangements when the seller delivers the goods to the buyer, and which costs each party is responsible for. However, a formal sale contract can provide you additional necessary information for the sales transaction, such as specifications of the goods, price, payment, transfer of title to the goods, tax, warranties, consequences of breach, governing laws and dispute resolutions. Therefore, it is unwise to use the Incoterms® as a formal sales contract.

SELF QUIZ: Indicate whether each of the following statements is true or false.

1. The Incoterms® Rules are international custom.
2. EXW, FCA, CPT, CIP, DAT, DAP and DDP can be used for any mode or modes of transport including transport by pipeline.
3. FOB, CFR and CIF use "ship's rail" as the reference point for delivery.
4. Incoterms® 2010 cover string sales by adding the obligation to "procure a contract for the carriage of the goods" in several Rules.

5. Under Incoterms® 2010, if parties decide to use EDI, they need to explicitly indicate this in their contract.

6. EXW requires the seller to load the goods on the collecting vehicle sent by the buyer.

7. FCA means that costs for transportation and risks of loss of or damage to the goods transfer to the buyer after delivery to the carrier.

8. Under the CPT, the risks shift from the seller to the buyer until the buyer receives the goods at the place of destination.

9. The difference between CIP and CPT is that CIP requires the seller contracts and pays for the insurance cover against the buyer's risks during the carriage, but CPT has no such requirement.

10. CIP and CIF have the same meaning except that they are used for different modes of transport.

11. If DAT is used, the seller should clear the goods both for export and import.

12. DAT is designed for situations where no export or import clearance obligation exists.

13. DDP places the maximum obligations on the seller and minimum obligations on the buyer. EXW places the minimum obligations on the seller and maximum obligations on the buyer.

14. FOB and CIF are generally not suitable for shipments in shipping containers.

15. The buyer has the obligation to clear the goods for export when FAS is used.

16. Under the FOB, the buyer pays for transportation of goods to the port of shipment (including the loading cost) and clears the goods for export.

17. The difference between FOB and CFR is that, under CFR, the seller must contract for and pay for the transportation of the goods to the named port of destination, but the FOB has no such requirement.

18. CIF requires the seller to obtain insurance only on minimum cover.

Part 2   Tools of Payment in International Trade

Basic tools

There are two types of tool of payment in international trade, *i.e.*, currency and instruments. It is apparent that traders can choose currency which contains currency of import state, export state or a third state as the tool of payment. In general, the convertibility and stability of currency, political risk and usage of trade shall be taken into account when currency is selected as a tool of payment.

Instruments, normally negotiable instruments, also play an important role in the international trade. A negotiable instrument is a written order or unconditional promise to pay a fixed sum of money on demand or at a certain time.[1] A negotiable instrument is transferable, and the new holder obtains full legal title to the instrument.

An instrument is a "note" if it is a promise and is a "draft" if it is an order. Examples of negotiable instruments include:

- Bill of exchange/draft: a non-interest-bearing written order used primarily in international trade that binds one party to pay a fixed sum of money to another party, either immediately (a sight/demand draft) or at a specified future date (a time draft);
- Promissory note: a financial instrument that contains a written promise by one party to pay another party a definite sum of money either on demand or at a specified future date. Notwithstanding its main non-negotiable nature, a promissory note may be a negotiable instrument if it is unconditional and readily saleable;
- Certificate of deposit: a savings certificate entitling the bearer to receive interest.

Bill of exchange

(1) Content

According to the 1930 Convention Providing a Uniform Law for Bills of Exchange and Promissory Notes (Geneva Convention), a bill of exchange contains:

a. the term bill of exchange inserted in the body of the instrument and expressed in the language employed in drawing up the instrument;

b. an unconditional order to pay a determinate sum of money;

c. the name of the person who is to pay (drawee);

d. a statement of the time of payment;

e. a statement of the place where payment is to be made;

f. the name of the person to whom or to whose order payment is to be made;

g. a statement of the date and of the place where the bill is issued;

h. the signature of the person who issues the bill (drawer).

---

1 See, *e.g.*, Article 3 of US Uniform Commercial Code.

Figure 2: Bill of Exchange

Bill of Exchange

Glasgow, 23 December 2014   Amount   GBP £ 880,000

At   60 days after sight   pay against this Sole Bill of Exchange

to the order of   Ourselves

the sum of   British Pound Eight hundred and eighty thousand

for value   Received

To: For and on behalf of

Shanghai Import Banking Company   Glasgow Export Company Ltd
Bank Street
Shanghai

Drawn under Royal Bank of Scotland Plc,
Documentary Credit
N°123456, Dated 3 December 2014   Andrew Anderson, Director

Signature

(2) Endorsement

An endorsement on a negotiable instrument has the effect of transferring all the rights represented by the instrument to another individual. The ordinary manner in which an individual endorses a check is by placing his or her signature on the back of it, or if the space is insufficient, on a slip of paper annexed thereto called "allonge".

Table 1: Five Kinds of Endorsement

Blank Endorsement	If the endorser signs his name only, the endorsement is said to be in blank and it becomes payable to bearer.
Special or Full Endorsement	The endorser not only puts his signature on the instrument but also writes the name of a person to whom or to whose order the payment is to be made.
Conditional Endorsement	The endorser puts his signature under such a writing which makes the transfer of title subject to fulfillment of some conditions of the happening of some events.
Restrictive Endorsement	The endorser restricts or prohibits further negotiation. Two types of restrictive endorsements are: i) when further negotiation is prohibited, e.g. "pay X only"; and ii) when negotiation is permitted but with mere authority to deal as directed.
Partial Endorsement	Only a part of the amount of the bill is transferred or the amount of the bill is transferred to two or more endorsees severally.

(3) Acceptance and Dishonor

Acceptance is a process by which the drawee accepts the seller's bill of exchange by signing under the words "accepted" on face of the bill. By this act, the drawee becomes the acceptor and converts the bill into a post-dated check—an unconditional obligation to pay it on or before its maturity date.

Dishonor of a bill of exchange occurs when the drawee refuses to accept or make payment on the bill. A bill may be dishonored by non-acceptance or non-payment.

- Non-acceptance: The drawee refuses to accept the bill when it is presented before him for acceptance. When a bill is dishonored by non-acceptance, an immediate right of recourse against the drawer and endorser accrues to the holder. In this case, presentment for payment is not necessary.
- Non-payment: The drawer has accepted the bill but refuses to make payment of the bill on the due date. In this case, the holder has immediate right of recourse against each party to the bill.

(4) Chinese Law on negotiable instrument

The current Negotiable Instrument Law governing activities involving negotiable instruments in China was adopted in 1995 and revised in 2004. The Law is ordinarily in line with the general practice in international trade.

a. The type of negotiable instruments:

The valid negotiable instruments in China include bill of exchange, promissory note and cheque.

b. Endorsement

When a bill of exchange is negotiated by endorsement, the endorsements shall be in succession. The holder shall prove his rights on the bill by an uninterrupted series of endorsements. A person who acquires a bill of exchange by lawful means other than endorsement shall provide evidence pursuant to law to prove his rights thereon.

No condition may be attached to the endorsement. Any conditions attached to the endorsement shall have no effect of a bill.

c. Acceptance and guarantee

When accepting a bill of exchange, the drawee may not attach any conditions thereto. An acceptance to which a condition is attached is deemed non-acceptance.

The liability on a bill of exchange may be guaranteed by a guarantor. No condition may be attached to a guaranty. A guaranty with conditions attached shall not affect the liability of guaranty on the bill of exchange.

d. Dishonor and recourse

If the payment of a bill of exchange is refused at the date of maturity, the holder may exercise the right of recourse against the endorsers, the drawer and other persons liable for the bill.

Methods of payment in international trade

1. Remittance

Remittance is the process of sending money to remove an obligation. This is most usually done through a telegraphic transfer (T/T), mail transfer (M/T) and demand draft (D/D). The term also refers to the amount of money being sent to remove the obligation. Parties involved in remittance include remitter, remitting bank, paying bank and payee.

Figure 3: The Process of Remittance

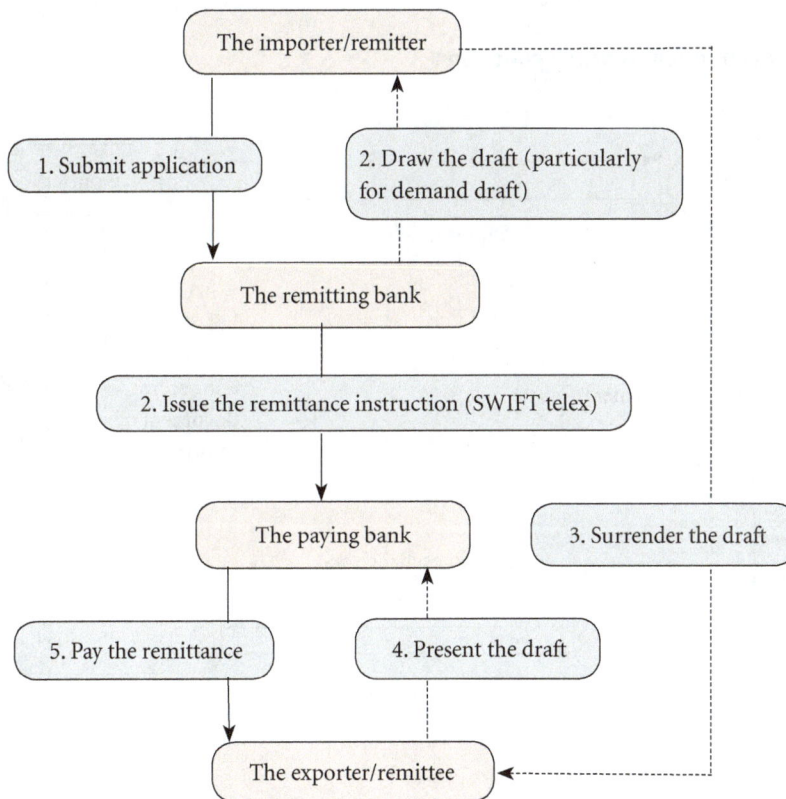

2. Collection

Collection is a trade transaction in which the exporter hands over the task of collecting payment for goods supplied to its bank, which sends the shipping documents to the importer's bank together with the payment instructions.

There are two types of collection:

- Clean collection allows a consignee to take delivery of the shipment without paying and without making a firm commitment to pay on a fixed date.
- Documentary collection (D/C) is a transaction whereby the exporter entrusts the collection of payment to the exporter's bank (remitting bank), which sends documents to the importer's bank (collecting bank), along with instructions for payment. The characteristics of

documentary collection are listed below:

a. Documentary collection can take in two forms, *i.e.*, documents against acceptance (D/A) and documents against payment (D/P);

b. Documentary collection is riskier for the exporter, though D/C terms are more convenient and cheaper than letter of credit to the importer;

c. The advantages of documentary collection are that i) Bank assistance in obtaining payment and ii) The process is simple, fast and less costly than the letter of credit;

d. The disadvantages of documentary collection are that i) Banks' role is limited and they do not guarantee payment and ii) Banks do not verify the accuracy of the documents.

Figure 4: Process of documentary collection

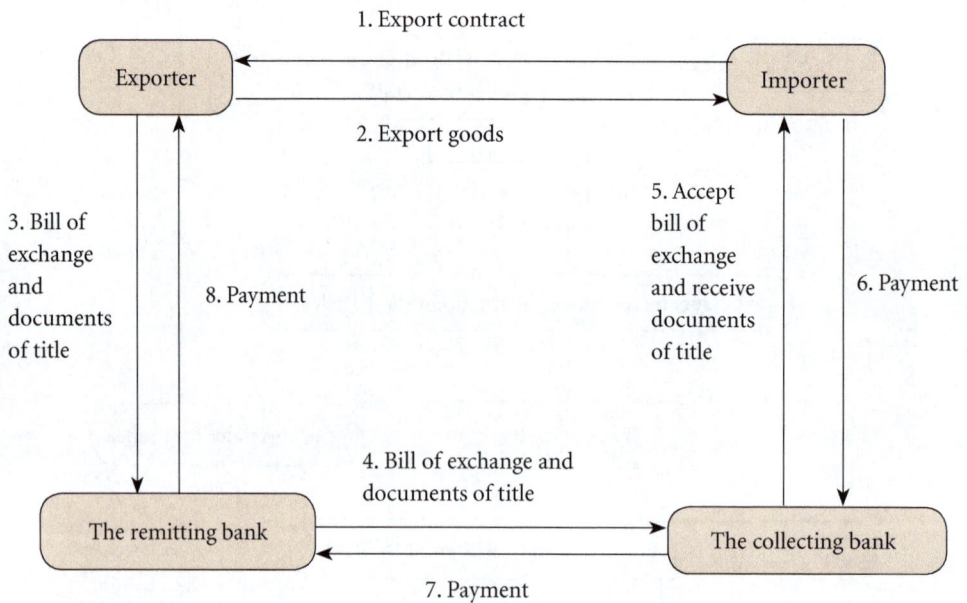

Figure 5: Legal Relationship Between Parties

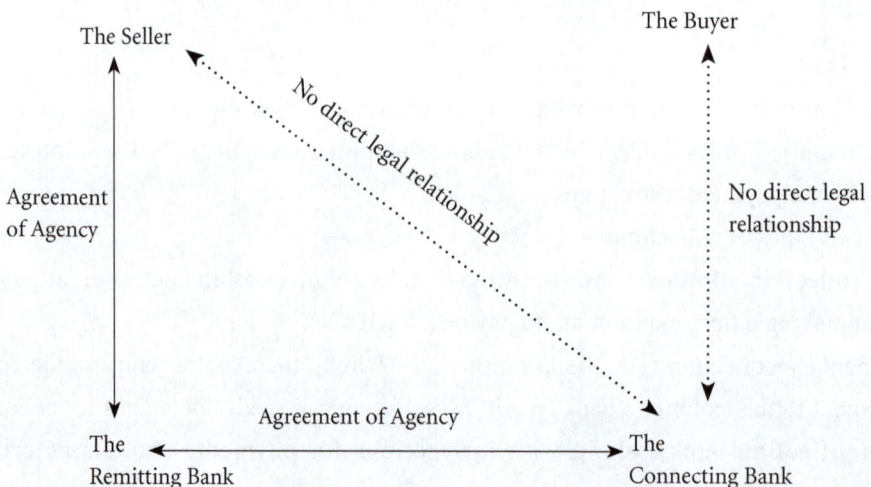

Under the ICC Uniform Rules for Collections ("URC 522"),[1] exporters may encounter three primary risks in a documentary collection transaction:

First, non-acceptance of documents risk. Under the URC 522, importers are not obligated to collect documents from their banks. Consequently, exporters have to be aware that upon arrival of the cargo to the importing country, there is a possibility that importers determine to simply leave the goods unclear at the customs without paying for the documents.

Second, non-payment risk. Non-payment risk may happen in the case that importers accept a time draft but not pay on maturity. Exporters may seek to have importer's banks aval to the time draft or bill of exchange in order to eliminate non-payment risk.

Third, risk of delivery of goods to importers without original shipment documents. Importers will be able to receive goods without the need of obtaining original shipment documents, which may give rise to a non-payment for exporters under a documentary collection payment under the following conditions: a) Importers may clear goods from the customs without having original shipment documents on road, air and rail transportation; b) Importers receive goods from transport companies under sea shipments if express bill of lading and non-negotiable bill of lading have been utilized.

3. Letter of credit

(1) Basic discipline

In simple terms, letter of credit (L/C) is a letter from a bank guaranteeing that an importer's payment to an exporter will be received on time and for the correct amount, and the bank will be required to cover the full or remaining amount of the purchase in the event that the importer is unable to make payment on the purchase. At the present time, letter of credit is one of the most secure instruments available to international traders. A letter of credit is a tool to reduce risk, in particular considering that it essentially substitutes the bank's credit for the customer's credit and helps facilitate international trade. ICC Uniform Customs and Practice for Documentary Credits (UCP)[2] and the International Standard Banking Practice (ISBP) are the most commonly used rules on letter of credit.

---

1 ICC Publication No. 522, 1995 Revision in force as of 1 January 1996.

2 As of December 2014, the UCP 600 is the most up-to-date version.

Table 2: Main Types of Letter of Credit

Irrevocable L/C	An irrevocable letter of credit cannot be cancelled or modified in any way without explicit consent by the affected parties involved.
Confirmed L/C	A confirmed letter of credit is a document issued by a bank that allows the holder of the letter to draw the funds as stated on the letter from the issuing bank. It is ordinarily used when the issuing bank of the letter of credit may have questionable credit worthiness and the seller seeks to get a second guarantee to assure payment.
Transferable L/C	A Transferable L/C is used in cases where there are three parties in a transaction: an importer (buyer), an exporter (supplier), and an intermediary party such as a broker who is responsible for arranging the sale.
Revolving L/C	A revolving letter of credit is a single letter of credit that covers multiple-shipments over a long period. Instead of arranging a new L/C for each separate shipment, the buyer establishes a L/C that revolves either in value (a fixed amount is available which is replenished when exhausted) or in time (an amount is available in fixed installments over a period).
Sight L/C	A sight letter of credit is payable once it is presented along with the necessary documents. An organization offering a sight letter of credit commits itself to paying the agreed amount of funds, provided that the provisions of the letter of credit are met.
Back to back L/C	A back to back letter of credit refers to a special arrangement in which one irrevocable letter of credit serves as the collateral for another; the advising bank of the first letter of credit becomes the issuing bank of the second letter of credit.
Stand-by L/C	A stand-by letter of credit is issued by a bank on behalf of the buyer and guarantees that the seller (beneficiary) will receive payment upon the presentation of specified documents in the event that the buyer fails to pay the beneficiary according to the terms of the contract. Stand-by letter of credit is usually employed to guarantee performance or to strengthen the credit worthiness of a customer.

Figure 6: The Process of the Letter of Credit

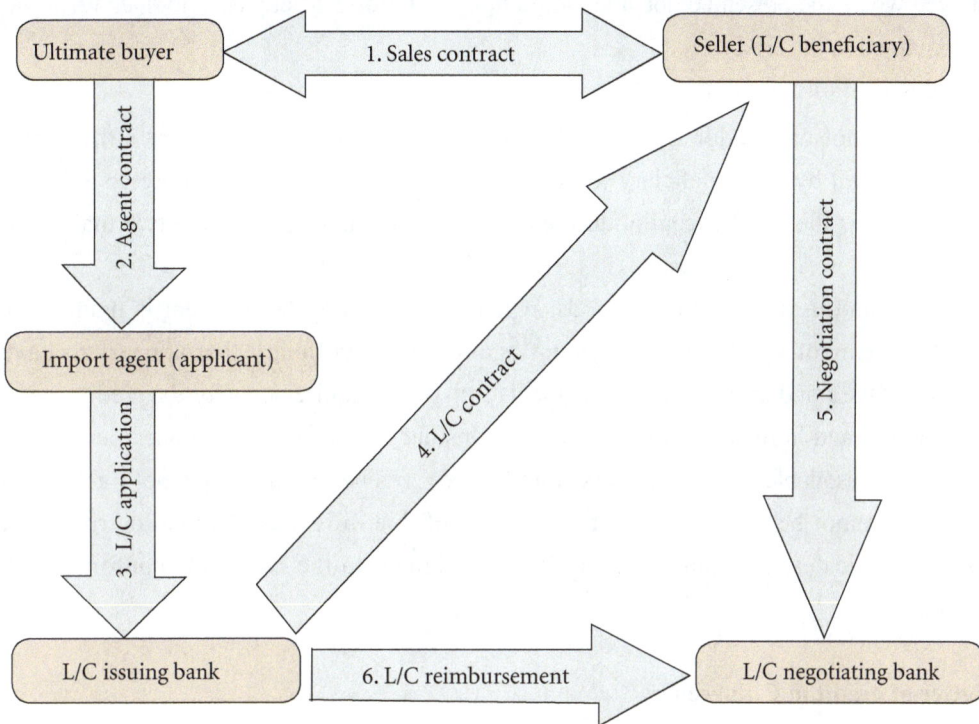

(2) Legal principles

a. Autonomy

Autonomy or "self-governing" is the essence in a letter of credit transaction, which means that a letter of credit is separate from or independent of the underlying sale contract.

The autonomy principle establishes that credits, by their very nature, are autonomous from the transactions to which they are related. Therefore, even if the underlying transaction is not performed, the bank must honor if there is a complying presentation of documents under the credit.

b. Standards for examining documents

A nominated bank acting on its nomination, a confirming bank, if any, and the issuing bank must examine the presentation to determine, on the basis of the documents alone, whether or not the documents appear on their face to constitute a complying presentation.

c. Doctrine of strict compliance

Every single party under a letter of credit transaction is required to tender strictly complying documents in order to be entitled to receive payment. These usually include a particular time and place to present the original letter of credit and the exact documents that must accompany the letter. The underlying ground for this doctrine is that the letter of credit is established on an agent-collaborated transaction, and thus the principal should be entitled to disown the act of its agent.

d. Doctrine of substantial compliance

Minor typographical or syntax errors in the presenting documents will not justify non-payment.

The effect of applying "substantial compliance" is to compel issuing banks to honor the letter of credit even where the presented documentation fails to conform strictly (i.e., in *haec verba*) to the terms contained in the credit.[1]

e. Fraud exception

A bank needs not pay under a credit when it knows a tendered document either contains statements known by the beneficiary to be false or contains a forged signature or a fraudulent alteration. This is the fraud exception to the doctrine of autonomy. There are two main types of fraud:

The first is fraud in relation to the goods, which arises before the payment is made, and the issuing bank cannot withhold the payment against the beneficiary that appears to have no knowledge of the fraud as long as the documents satisfy the requirements for the credit.

The second is fraud in relation to the documents. Insofar as documents are concerned, the banks must act in a reasonable manner to prevent and detect possible fraud, but are not liable to losses if the fraud cannot be revealed after the exercise of due diligence. As the doctrine of strict compliance indicates, the bank's responsibility is limited to the ostensible conformity of the documents.

(3) Letter of credit in Chinese law

The General Principles of the Civil Law, Contract Law and Security Law are applied to the rights and responsibilities stemming from remittance, collection and L/C. Ordinarily, Chinese courts take into account the applicable Uniform Rules for Collections (URC) and Uniform Customs and Practice for Documentary Credits (UCP) when adjudicating disputes arising out of collection and L/C.

In addition, the Chinese Supreme Court in 2005 issued the Rules on Hearing Letter of Credit Dispute Cases which would be applied to disputes arising from the issuance, notification, amendments, revocation, confirmation, negotiation and reimbursement in a letter of credit transaction.

a. Applicable law

Chinese courts apply the relevant international practices or other rules that the parties thereto agreed upon. In the absence of such agreement, Chinese courts shall apply UCP and other international practices.

b. Examination of documents

After issuing the bank's commitment to pay, accept or perform its other obligations under a credit, it shall perform its payment obligation within the time limit as specified by the credit, if the documents which appear on their face are in compliance with the terms and conditions of the credit and documents which appear on their face to be consistent with one another.

---

1   Fairfax Leary, Jr. & Michael R. Ippoliti, *Letters Of Credit: Have We Fully Recovered from Three Insolvency Shocks?*, University of Pennsylvania Journal of Business Law 595, 605 (1987).

The issuing bank has rights and obligations to examine the documents independently and is entitled to determine in its own judgment whether the documents are in compliance with the terms and conditions under the credits and decides based on its own judgment whether to accept or reject the discrepancy between the documents and the terms and conditions of the credit and the inconsistence between one document and another.

The issuing bank may decide based on its own judgment whether to approach the applicant for a waiver of the discrepancies. Unless otherwise agreed by the applicant and the issuing bank, whether the applicant will waive the discrepancies or not will have no impact on the issuing bank's decision on acceptance or rejection of the discrepancy.

c. Credit fraud

In case of the occurrence of any of the following circumstances, credit fraud shall be ascertained:

First, the beneficiary forges document(s) or the beneficiary presents document(s) containing false information;

Second, the beneficiary refuses to deliver goods in bad faith or the beneficiary delivers goods with no value;

Third, the beneficiary and the applicant or any other third party in collusion presents false document(s) without true underlying transactions;

Fourth, other circumstances involving credit fraud.

CASE EXAMPLE: *Zhongbao Commodity Import & Export Co., Ltd. v. Billiongold Int'l Ltd., Winwick Shipping Ltd. and Rishelle Navigation Inc*[1]

Facts: The plaintiff entered into a sales contract with the beneficiary, pursuant to which the plaintiff opened an irrevocable L/C in favor of the beneficiary. The beneficiary, in conjunction with the second defendant (the carrier), presented a set of forged documents to the issuer. The bill of lading stated that it was issued by the second defendant, on behalf of the third defendant (a charter party). In fact, the third defendant never authorized the second defendant to issue the bill of lading on its behalf. The plaintiff then obtained all documents from the issuer. After the issuer accepted the draft drawn by the beneficiary, the beneficiary discounted the accepted draft to a bank in London. Upon the arrival of the vessel at the designated port, the plaintiff discovered that the expected goods were not on board. The applicant then sued the beneficiary, requesting that the court declare the sales contract invalid, void the L/C and stop payment, and hold the defendants jointly liable for its losses.

The Court held that: i) the sales contract signed between the plaintiff and the beneficiary is invalid. The B/L and related documents issued by the second defendant are also invalid. The payment under the L/C should be stopped; ii) the beneficiary and the second defendant are jointly liable to cover the losses of the applicant incurred in issuing and amending the L/C; and iii) charges against the third defendant are dismissed.

---

1 Xiamen Maritime Court, (1996) Xia Hai Fa Shang Chu Zi No. 074 [PRC].

Take-away point: The underlying sales contract and relevant documents should be held invalid due to the fraud committed by the seller, and therefore the L/C opened pursuant to the sales contract should be voided and the payment under the L/C should also be stopped. The decision, however, remains controversial. In this case, it is also essential to take into account the issue of the payment finality of an accepted draft and further examine whether the holder of the accepted draft is in due course or not. Besides, it is not ambiguous that the rights and interests of the holder in due course have been deprived, since the holder was not given the opportunity to participate in the case and defend its interests.

SELF QUIZ: Indicate whether each of the following statements is true or false.

19. A bill of exchange is essentially an order made by one person to another to pay money to a third person.

20. On delivery of a bill of exchange to the drawee, the drawee has to pay immediately. The bill cannot be paid on some future date.

21. Although banks do act as facilitators (agents) for their clients under collections, documentary collection offers no verification process and limited recourse in the event of non-payment.

22. A standby letter of credit is issued as a back-up or form of insurance for the seller if the buyer defaults on the agreed-upon payment terms.

23. Under Chinese law, conditions may be attached to the endorsement of negotiable instruments.

24. Autonomy underpins the character of the letter of credit in international trade as an independent and separate undertaking by the bank to pay the beneficiary.

25. The documents which are tendered by the beneficiary must be in strict conformity with the terms and conditions of the letter of credit under the doctrine of strict compliance.

26. UCP regulates the standards for examination of the documents, which should be ordinarily taken into consideration together with ISBP.

Part 3　International Cargo Transportation

International carriage of goods by sea

Despite the vast development in the means of transportation in the past century, the majority of goods in international trade are transported by sea, typically from one port to another. The primary legal relationships in international maritime transportation normally involve those between the shipper (who typically is also the seller of the goods), the carrier (who typically is the operator of vessels) and the consignee (who typically is also the buyer of the goods). Given the cross-jurisdictional nature of international transportation by sea, the legal rules governing the foregoing relationships encompass international treaties, international practices, domestic legislation and case laws, as well as legal documents concluded or used between the parties involved.

1. Liner transport and charter shipment

International cargo transportation by sea can be classified into two main types: liner transport and charter shipment.

Similar to the concept of shuttle bus, liner transport is shipment of goods by liner carriers on fixed routes in accordance with fixed schedules. Because the schedule and timing of this method of maritime transportation are fixed, its freight is calculated with reference to freight rates issued by the liner operator. In contrast, charter shipment resembles more like a car rental or taxi service, where the charterer hires the entire vessel for a single voyage or a specific period of time. Charter shipment can be further classified into the following three types:

- Voyage charter: the charterer hires a vessel for a specified voyage (e.g., from port A to port B), while the vessel's owner i) provides the crew, bunkers and supplies, and ii) manages the vessel along with the crew;
- Time charter: the charterer hires a vessel for a specific period of time. While the owner of the vessel still manages the vessel and provides crew, the charterer gives orders for the deployment of the vessel (i.e., the charterer orders the ports of destination);
- Demise or bareboat charter: this arrangement enables the charterer to take complete control over the vessel along with the legal and financial responsibilities for the vessel. The charterer would also need to provide crew and supplies for the vessel.

2. Bill of lading (B/L)

(1) What is a bill of lading?

A bill of lading, commonly abbreviated as a B/L, is a document issued by a carrier to a shipper upon receipt of goods from the shipper. A bill of lading serves three purposes in international cargo transportation: it evidences a carrier's receipt of goods; it evidences a contract of shipment; and it serves as a document of title (in other words, the due holder of a bill of lading is presumed to be the owner of the goods represented by the bill).

The use of a bill of lading alleviates some of the risks of the buyer and seller in international sale of goods, because, thanks to its nature of a document of title, the seller may deliver to the buyer a bill of lading acceptable to the buyer as a constructive delivery of goods, against which the buyer makes payment for the goods. By the same token, the buyer, via its receipt of a bill of lading, ensures that it holds the title to the goods in question before physical possession and such goods are purported to be in acceptable condition when shipped.

(2) Main contents of a bill of lading

For illustrative purposes, below is a sample front page of a form of bill of lading of a Chinese carrier.

Figure 7: One Sample Front Page of a Chinese Bill of Lading

Shipper	B/L NO.

Consignee

山东省烟台国际海运公司
SHANDONG YANTAI INTERNATIONAL MARINE SHIPPING CO.

Notify Party

BILL OF LADING

Shipped on board the vessel named above in apparent good order and condition (unless otherwise indicated) the goods or packages specified herein and to be discharged at the above mentioned port of discharge or as near thereto as the vessel may safely get and be always afloat. The weight, measure, marks, numbers, quality, contents and value, being particulars furnished by the Shipper, are not checked by the Carrier on loading. The Shipper, Consignee and the Holder of this Bill of Lading hereby expressly accept and agree to all printed, written or stamped provisions, exceptions and conditions of this Bill of Lading, including those on the back hereof. One of the Bills of Lading duly endorsed must be surrendered in exchange for the goods or delivery order. In witness whereof, the Carrier or his Agents has signed Bills of Lading all of this tenor and date, one of which being accomplished, the others to stand void.

Pre-carriage by		Place of Receipt	
Ocean Vessel	Voy, No.	Port of Loading	
Port of Discharge		Place of Delivery	Final Destination (of the goods-not the ship) See Article 7 paragraph (2)

Particulars Furnished by Merchants

Marks & Nos Container. Seal No.	No. of Containers or P'kgs	Kind of Packages: Description of Goods	Gross Weight kgs	Measurement

TOTAL NO. OF CONTAINERS OR PACKAGES (IN WORDS)

FREIGHT & CHARGES	Revenue Tone	Rate	Per	Prepaid	Collect

SHIPPED ON BOARD

Ex. Rage:	Prepaid at	Payable at	Place and date of Issue
	Total Prepaid	Np. of Original B(s)/L	Signed for the Carrier

LADEN ON BOARD THE VESSEL
DATE   BY - - - - - - - - -

(TERMS PLEASE FIND ON BACK OF ORIGINAL B/L)

As Agent for the Carrier of
SHANDONG YANTAI INTERNATIONAL MARINE SHIPPING CO.

As is shown above, the main contents of a bill of lading are as follows:[1]

a. description of goods, mark, number of packages or pieces, weight or quantity and a statement, if applicable, for the dangerous nature of the goods;

b. name and principle place of business of the carrier;

c. name of the vessel;

d. name of the shipper;

e. name of the consignee;

f. port of loading and the date on which the goods were taken over by the carrier at the port of loading;

g. port of discharge;

h. place where goods were taken over and place where the goods are to be delivered in case of a multimodal transport bill of landing;

i. date and place of issuance of the bill of lading and the number of originals issued;

j. payment of freight;

k. signature of the carrier or of a person acting on his/her behalf.

(3) Types of bills of lading

a. Straight bill of lading and order bill of lading

A straight bill of lading, also known as a non-negotiable bill of lading, is issued to a named person (the consignee) and serves as a receipt for the goods and a contract with the carrier stating the terms and conditions of carriage. Due to its non-negotiable nature, a straight bill of lading cannot serve as a document of title. As such, possession of the actual straight bill of lading does not confer rights over the goods to a person in possession of the document, unless such person is the consignee named in the straight bill of lading.

An order bill of lading, also known as a negotiable bill of lading, is issued to a named person or order, thus allowing the named person (the consignee) to endorse the bill of lading to order delivery of the goods to others. It serves as a contract with the carrier, a receipt for the goods and a document of title for the goods. If possession of an order bill of lading is transferred to a third party that it is endorsed to, then such third party becomes a prima facial owner of the title over the goods covered by the bill of lading. The original consignees may endorse the order bill of lading either in blank by a bare signature or by a special "endorsement" with a remark that specifies the name of the intended holder (e.g., "Deliver to John Smith, or order").

b. Clean bill of lading and unclean bill of lading

A clean bill of lading is a bill of lading issued by a carrier declaring that the goods have been received in an appropriate condition and without the presence of defects in respect of packaging or quantity. Typically, the carrier marks a statement that the goods are "in apparent good order and condition" on a clean bill of lading. If there is no modification to this statement, the bill of

---

1   See Article 73 of the Maritime Law of the People's Republic of China.

lading is presumed to be clean. For the purpose of payment against documents, the payment bank usually requires a clean bill of lading.

An unclean bill of lading is issued when the goods received by the carrier are damaged or do not meet specifications. Typical remarks on unclean bills of lading including "inadequate packaging," "wet/stained cartons," and "damaged crates," etc. A payment bank in payment against documents transactions typically does not accept an unclean bill of lading.

c. Shipped on board bill of lading and received for shipment bill of lading

A shipped on board bill of lading (certifies that the goods specified on the bill of lading have been received in apparent good order and condition from the named shipper and have taken aboard the named vessel on the stated date. The buyer and the buyer's bank often require receiving a shipped on board bill of lading, against which the payment will be made to the seller or seller's bank, so that the buyer can ensure that the goods purchased are being shipped.

A received for shipment bill of lading indicates that the goods have merely been received by the carrier but have not yet been loaded onto the vessel. It is typically used when the goods arrive at the port of departure before the vessel arrives. Usually this is not a sufficient document to which the buyer's bank can make payment, because there is no guaranty as to when the goods will be shipped. After the goods have been loaded onto the vessel, the received for shipment bill of lading may be replaced by the carrier with a shipped on board bill of lading (or remarked by the carrier to such effect), against which payment can be made.

CASE EXAMPLE: *Zhejiang Textile Import & Export Group Co., Ltd. v. Evergreen International Storage & Transport Corp.*

Facts: On July 31 and August 7, 2000, respectively, Zhejiang Textile Import & Export Group Co., Ltd. ("Zhejiang Textile") entered into sales confirmation letters to sell a batch of uniforms to a buyer outside the PRC. Subsequently, through a number of freight forwarding agents, the uniforms in question were accepted by Evergreen International Storage & Transport Corp. ("Evergreen") for shipment to the buyer. The shipping fee was also ultimately paid to Evergreen. In connection with such shipment, Evergreen, through its agent, issued 21 sets of bill of lading. While Zhejiang Textile received the original copies of all of the bills of lading, the named shippers on those bills of lading were three overseas shipping agents instead of Zhejiang Textile. After shipment, Zhejiang Textile sought for payment collection from the buyer against, among others, the original bills of lading. The buyer refused to pay and the bills of lading were returned to Zhejiang Textile through collection banks. However, the buyer managed to took possession of the uniforms from Evergreen without ever presenting the original bills of lading. As such, Zhejiang Textile sued Evergreen for releasing goods without bills of lading before the Shanghai Maritime Court.

The court held that: Although Zhejiang Textile was neither named as a shipper nor a consignee on the bills of lading, an international shipment contract existed between Zhejiang Textile and Evergreen. This contract could be proved by those bills of lading. As bearer of the original copies of the bills of lading, Zhejiang Textile had the right to claim for the title over the goods shipped under the bills of lading. Given that Evergreen had released the goods to the buyer without being presented with the original bills of lading, it was liable for compensating Zhejiang Textile for all of the losses of such goods. The appellate court, the Shanghai People's High Court, withheld the above ruling of the Shanghai Maritime Court.

Take-away points: (1) Under Chinese law, a legitimate holder of a bill of lading is presumed as the holder of the title over the goods covered by such bill of lading, regardless of whether it is a named shipper or endorsee on such bill of lading; (2) A carrier's release of goods without a bill of lading is a breach of the shipping contract evidenced by the bill of lading, as well of an impeachment of the title over the goods enjoyed by the legitimate holder of the bill of lading.

3. International conventions on bills of lading

Regulation of the terms of a bill of lading, or the relationship between the carrier and its customers, is subject to three international conventions: the Hague Rules, the Hague-Visby Rules and the Hamburg Rules. More recently, the international maritime law community adopted the Rotterdam Rules, which haven't taken legal effect yet, in order to unify the international law in this respect.

(1) The Hague Rules

The Hague Rules[1] were adopted in 1924 and set forth rules governing ship owners' liabilities to shippers for cargo loss and damage. The Hague Rules contain 16 articles in total and 10 of them deal with legal issues relating to bill of lading and the rest are concerning procedural issues relating to the operation of the Rules. The purpose of the Hague Rules is to unify the rules governing the liability of carriers in international transportation by sea. Under the Hague Rules, a carrier in international cargo transportation by sea has a general liability to provide a seaworthy ship and handle the goods with care. However, the Hague Rules also enumerated a total of 17 exemptions from carriers' liabilities, which include fault of master of the ship or pilot in the navigation or management of the ship, act of God, act of war, riots, strikes, saving life or property at sea, etc. Through these 17 mandatory exemptions, the Hague Rules preclude additional contractual exculpatory clauses in bills of lading. In addition, the Hague Rules limit the liability of a carrier to 100 British sterling per package or unit, unless the parties have agreed to a higher value.

---

1   The full name of the Hague Rules is International Convention for the Unification of Certain Rules of Law Relating to Bills of Lading. It was initially proposed by the International Law Association at a meeting at The Hague in 1921 and recommended for adoption at a diplomatic conference held in Brussels in 1924.

(2) The Visby Rules

Since the Hague Rules has long been perceived to be more pro-carriers and without balancing the interests of shippers, a protocol amending the Hague Rules, commonly referred as the Visby Rules[1], was adopted in Brussels in 1968 and entered into force in the same year. Given its nature as an amendment to the Hague Rules, the Visby Rules are commonly referred together with the Hague Rules as the Hague-Visby Rules. The Visby Rules addressed certain issues that had arisen under the Hague Rules, such as the broadness of the carrier's liability exemptions and the inadequacy of carriers' liability limit. Most notably, the Visby Rules increased carriers' liability limit to 666.67 SDRs[2] per package or 2 SDRs per kilogram of gross weight of the goods lost or damaged, whichever is higher, unless the parties have agreed to a higher value. In addition, the Visby Rules restrict a carrier's limitations of liability for the damage caused by its own intentional or reckless actions.

(3) The Hamburg Rules

Despite the improvements, the Hague-Visby Rules have still been complained by many countries as being too favourable to the carriers, especially those developing countries that are often shippers exporting goods to developed countries. In 1978, at a United Nations diplomatic conference held in Hamburg, Germany, a new convention was adopted (thus named the Hamburg Rules) and later took in force in 1992.[3] The Hamburg Rules are a major departure from the Hague Rules and the Hague-Visby Rules by substantially decreasing carrier's liability exemptions and increasing the amount of carrier's liability limits to 835 SDRs per package or 2.5 SDRs per kilogram of gross weight of goods lost or damaged. Under the Hamburg Rules, the carrier is liable for losses resulting from the loss of or damage to the goods, as well as from delay in delivery, as long as the occurrence which caused the loss, damage or delay took place while the goods were in the carrier's charge. More significantly, instead of availing a list of carrier's liability exemptions, the Hamburg Rules provide that unless the carrier can prove that its employees and agents have taken all necessary measures that could reasonably be required to avoid the occurrence and its consequences, the carrier should be presumed to be liable for the loss or damage to the goods in its charge.

Although the Hamburg Rules is the international convention that favours shippers most, they have not been widely adopted. Most of the countries adopting the Hamburg Rules are developing and landlocked countries that are short of advanced shipping industry.[4]

---

1 The full name of the Visby Rules is Protocol to Amend the International Convention for the Unification of Certain Rules of Law Relating to Bills of Lading.

2 SDRs stand for Special Drawing Rights, an international currency unit established by the International Monetary Fund (IMF). See discussion on the IMF in Chapter 1 of this book.

3 The full name of the Hamburg Rules is United Nations Convention on the Carriage of Goods by Sea.

4 As of August 2016 there were 34 countries being the parties to the Hamburg Rules.

(4) The Rotterdam Rules

In December 2008, the United Nations General Assembly adopted the Convention of Contracts for the International Carrying of Goods Wholly or Partly by Sea and authorized a signing ceremony for the convention to be held in Rotterdam, recommending the new Convention known as the "Rotterdam Rules" which extend and modernize the existing international rules relating to the contract of maritime carriage of goods and the laws governing bills of lading. The Rotterdam Rules aim at replacing the Hague Rules, the Hague-Visby Rules and the Hamburg Rules, thus achieving uniformity of law in the field of carriage of goods by sea. The Rotterdam Rules will come into force one year after ratification by the 20th UN member state. By far, although 24 countries have signed the Rotterdam Rules, Spain has become the first nation to ratify this convention. Therefore, there is still a long way to go for the Rotterdam Rules to become an international convention with full force and effect.

Compared to the Hague-Visby Rules and the Hamburg Rules, significant changes in the Rotterdam Rules can be summarized as follows:

a. Article 12 of the Rotterdam Rules states that the period of responsibility of the carrier of the goods under the convention "begins when the carrier or a performing party receives the goods for carriage and ends when the goods are delivered." In other words, the Rotterdam Rules provide for a door-to-door carriage while the Hague-Visby rules provide for a period of responsibility to govern the carriage of goods from loading on board to the discharge;

b. The Rotterdam Rules maintain a fault-based regime when it comes to the carrier's liability. The carrier is liable if the cargo interests prove that the loss, damage or delay took place during the period of the carrier's responsibility. However, the carrier may be exempted from liability if it can prove that the cause is not attributable to its fault or falls within the scope of the enumerated exemptions, such as fire and perils of the sea. If the shipper can prove that the conduct of the carrier contributed to the loss, notwithstanding any applicable liability exemptions, the carrier remains liable. This significantly limits the scope of the exemptions as presently applied under the Hague-Visby Rules;

c. The error of navigation exemption availed under the Hague-Visby Rules has been excluded, which from a practical point of view, significantly weakens the defenses available to the carrier, as it concerns an exemption which is frequently relied upon by carriers in practice;

d. The limits of liability have been increased. Compared to the Hague-Visby Rules, the limit per package has been increased up to 875 SDR and the limits per kilogram have been increased from 2 up to 3 SDR;

e. The obligation for the carrier to exercise due diligence to make the ship seaworthy before and at the beginning of the voyage has been extended to also cover the voyage by the wording "during the voyage by sea."

4. Carrier's liabilities under international conventions and the approach adopted by the PRC Maritime Law

As discussed above, one of the most intensely debated issues relating to the laws governing bills of lading is the allocation of liability between the shipper and carrier in international carriage of goods by sea. Among the international conventions, the Hague-Visby Rules are the most favourable to carriers while the Hamburg Rules are the most favourable to shippers; the Rotterdam Rules, while not in effect yet, endeavour to strike a balance between the interests of the carriers and the shippers.

In respect of Chinese law, the primary source of legislation defining the allocation of liabilities between carriers and shippers is the PRC Maritime Law which was effective as of July 1, 1993. Given China's global status as both a major goods exporter and a country with strong shipping industry, the relevant provisions in the PRC Maritime Law strive to take care of the interests of both carriers and shippers by absorbing the rules in both the Hague-Visby Rules and the Hamburg Rules. The table below summarizes the comparison of carrier's liabilities provisions in the Hague-Visby Rules, the Hamburg Rules, the Rotterdam Rules and the PRC Maritime Law.

Table 3: Comparison of Carrier's Liabilities Provisions in Hague-Visby Rules, Hamburg Rules, the Rotterdam Rules and the PRC Maritime Law

	Hague-Visby Rules	Hamburg Rules	Rotterdam Rules	PRC Maritime Law
Period of responsibility of carrier	From when the goods are loaded onto the vessel to the time they are discharged from the vessel.	The period during which the carrier is in charge of the goods at the port of loading, during the carriage and at the port of discharge.	Begins when the carrier or a performing party receives the goods for carriage and ends when the goods are delivered.	- As to goods carried in containers: the entire period during which the carrier is in charge of the goods, starting from the time the carrier has taken over the goods at the port of loading, until the goods have been delivered at the port of discharge. - As to non-containerized goods: the period, during which the carrier is in charge of the goods, starting from the time of loading of the goods onto the ship until the time the goods are discharged therefrom.

(to be continued)

	Hague-Visby Rules	Hamburg Rules	Rotterdam Rules	PRC Maritime Law
Basic obligations of the carrier	- Make the ship seaworthy. - Properly man, equip and supply the ship. - Properly load, handle, stow, carry, keep, care for and discharge the goods.	Not provided.	- Subject to the convention and contract, carry the goods to the place of destination and deliver them to the consignee. - Make and keep the ship seaworthy. - Properly and carefully receive, load, handle, stow, carry, keep, care for, unload and deliver the goods. - Properly crew, equip and supply the ship and keep the ship so crewed, equipped and supplied throughout the voyage.	- Before and at the beginning of the voyage, exercise due diligence to make the ship seaworthy. - Properly man, equip and supply the ship. - Properly and carefully load, handle, stow, carry, keep, care for and discharge the goods carried. - Carry the goods to the port of discharge on the agreed or customary or geographically direct route (unless deviation is necessary to save life or property). - Deliver the goods at the designated port of discharge within the time expressly agreed upon.

(to be continued)

	Hague-Visby Rules	Hamburg Rules	Rotterdam Rules	PRC Maritime Law
Exoneration	Carrier is not responsible if it can prove the occurrence the following 17 events: (a) act, neglect of the master, mariner, pilot or servants of the carrier in the navigation or management of the ship; (b) fire, unless caused by the actual fault or privity of the carrier; (c) perils, dangers and accidents of the sea or other navigable waters; (d) act of God; (e) act of war; (f) act of public enemies; (g) arrest restraint or seizure; (h) quarantine restrictions; (i) act of omission of the shipper or owner of the goods, his agent or representative; (j) strikes or lockouts or stoppage or restraint of labor; (k) riots and civil commotions; (l) saving or attempting to save life or property at sea; (m) wastage in bulk of weight or any other loss or damage arising from inherent defect of goods; (n) insufficient packaging; (o) insufficient marks; (p) latent defects not discoverable by due diligence; (q) any other cause arising without the actual fault or privity of the carrier, its servants and agents.	Carrier is presumed liable unless it can prove that: (a) it, its servants or agents has taken all measures that could reasonably be required to avoid the occurrence and its consequences; or (b) except in general average, the loss, damage or delay in delivery resulted from measures to save life or from reasonable measures to save property at sea.	Similar to the Hague-Visby Rules, except the following: (a) error in navigation and in management is no longer a valid defense; (b) while the "fire defense" still exists, the carrier cannot rely on the defense if any performing party (i.e., the carrier, its servants, agents, employees etc.) caused the fire.	Same approach as adopted in the Hague-Visby Rules.

(to be continued)

	Hague-Visby Rules	Hamburg Rules	Rotterdam Rules	PRC Maritime Law
Limitation of liability	Unless the nature and value of such goods have been declared by the shipper before shipment and inserted in the bill of lading, neither the carrier nor the ship shall in any event be or become liable for any loss or damage to or in connection with the goods in an amount exceeding 666.67 SDRs per package or unit or 2 SDRs per kilogram of gross weight of the goods lost or damaged, whichever is higher.	The liability of the carrier for loss resulting from loss of or damage to goods according to the provisions of article 5 is limited to an amount equivalent to 835 SDRs per package or other shipping unit or 2.5 units of account per kilogram of gross weight of the goods lost or damaged, whichever is higher.	The carrier's liability for breaches of its obligations under the convention is limited to 875 SDRs per package or other shipping unit, or 3 SDRs per kilogram of the gross weight of the goods that are the subject of the claim or dispute, whichever amount is higher, except when the value of the goods has been declared by the shipper and included in the contract particulars, or when a higher amount than the amount of limitation of liability set out in this article has been agreed upon between the carrier and the shipper.	The carrier's liability for the loss of or damage to the goods shall be limited to an amount equivalent to 666.67 SDRs per package or other shipping unit, or 2 SDRs per kilogram of the gross weight of the goods lost or damaged, whichever is the higher, except where the nature and value of the goods had been declared by the shipper before shipment and inserted in the bill of lading, or where a higher amount than the amount of limitation of liability set out in this Article had been agreed upon between the carrier and the shipper.

International carriage of goods by air

1. Conventions governing international carriage by air

(1) The Warsaw Convention

The first international air transportation convention, the Convention for the Unification of Certain Rules relating to International Carriage by Air (commonly referred to as the Warsaw Convention), was entered into in Warsaw in 1929. This convention aims at unifying the rules on international carriage by air. It applies to all international carriage of persons, luggage or goods performed by aircraft for reward, as well as gratuitous carriage by aircraft performed by an air transport undertaking. The Warsaw Convention provides a comprehensive framework of a unified liability regime applicable to claims arising out of international air transport, irrespective of the domicile of the parties, the place of loss or injury, or the venue of the trial.

The Warsaw Convention creates a presumption of fault on the part of the carrier. In other words, the claimant does not need to adduce evidence to prove that the carrier was at fault. The burden is upon the carrier to prove that it was not at fault by using one of the limited defenses available to it. Under certain specific circumstances, the conduct of the carrier is considered so reprehensible that the claimant may "break" the monetary cap limiting the carrier's liability, with the result that the carrier loses the right to the limitation and is liable in full. However, such circumstances are strictly limited.

In addition, a notable rule in the Warsaw Convention is in respect of a monetary cap limiting the carrier's liability in relation to both passengers and their luggage and cargo. The monetary cap is 125,000 gold francs[1] for passenger injury or death, 250 gold francs per kilogram for loss or damage to cargo or registered baggage and 5,000 gold francs per passenger for unregistered baggage.

(2) The Hague Protocol

After the World War II, there had been growing dissatisfaction in some countries with the level of the monetary limitation of the air carrier's liability in the Warsaw Convention, especially for passengers, along with the erosion of the value of the gold franc. In 1955, a protocol amending the Warsaw Convention, commonly known as the Hague Protocol,[2] was adopted in the Hague at a diplomatic conference.

The Hague Protocol doubled the monetary cap on the carrier's liability in respect of passenger injury or death from 125,000 to 250,000 gold francs. However, it did not change the financial limitation of the carrier's liability in respect of cargo and registered baggage (which remains at 250 gold francs), or in respect of unregistered baggage (which remains at 5,000 gold francs per passenger). Other notable improvements vis-à-vis the Warsaw Convention contained in the Hague Protocol include:

    a. It simplified the particulars to be included in the documents of carriage;

---

1   Gold franc is a French monetary unit at the time of signing of the Warsaw Convention and consisted of a specified quantity of gold. At the rates of exchange prevailing in 1929, one gold franc equals to US$0.04.

2   The full name of the Hague Protocol is Protocol to Amend the Convention for the Unification of Certain Rules Relating to International Carriage by Air.

b. It clarified that legal costs are excluded from a claimant's award of damages;

c. Introduced an incentive for out-of-court settlements.

(3) The Montreal Additional Protocol Number 4 (the "MAP 4")

The most significant changes in relation to the liability regime for the international carriage of cargo by air were introduced by a further amendment to the Warsaw Convention, which was drawn up in Montreal and known as the Montreal Additional Protocol Number 4 of 1975, commonly referred as the MAP 4 1975, which includes the following significant changes to the Warsaw Convention and the Hague Protocol:

a. It simplified and modernized the particulars to be included in the document of carriage and removed the penalty for non-compliance with the documentary requirements;

b. It introduced the concept of an electronic air waybill;

c. It introduced four specific defenses for the carriage of cargo;

d. The monetary cap limiting the carrier's liability for cargo remained the same, but the monetary unit of 250 gold francs per kilogram was replaced by 17 SDR per kilogram;

e. The monetary cap limiting the carrier's liability became unbreakable for the carriage of cargo.

(4) The Montreal Convention

Given that the Warsaw Convention has been amended for a number of times over years and the international calls for a unified convention system for claims arising out of contracts of international carriage of goods by air, the Convention for the Unification of Certain Rules Relating to International Carriage by Air (commonly referred as the Montreal Convention) was adopted in May 1999. The Montreal Convention provides that it "shall prevail over any rules which apply to international carriage by air" among its signatory states that are also signatory states of the Warsaw-system Conventions.

The cardinal achievement of the Montreal Convention is that it consolidates all the various Warsaw-system Conventions in one single text. It therefore provides certainty as the applicable international air convention and contracts the parties' corresponding rights and obligations. As a result, it creates greater international uniformity of legislation and reduces the need for costly litigation as to the applicable legal regime. The Montreal Convention reflects changes to the Warsaw-Hague Convention which had been affected by MAP 4, in relation to the carriage of cargo. In addition, the Montreal Convention introduces some substantive changes in relation to the carriage of passengers and their luggage.

2. Air waybill

The air waybill (sometimes abbreviated as "AWB") is by far the most essential document issued in respect of the international carriage of cargo. It evidences the contract or agreement of the international carriage between the parties and plays a central role in the liability regime. Modern air waybills are usually not negotiable. This is explained by the speed of air transport, which means that there is normally no need for a document which enables sale of goods in transit.

The airline members of the International Air Transportation Association (the "IATA") agreed in 2004 to introduce a standard form of air waybill for international carriage by air of cargo.[1] For illustration purpose, the front side of the form[2] is reprinted as below.

Figure 8: The Front Side of an Air Waybill

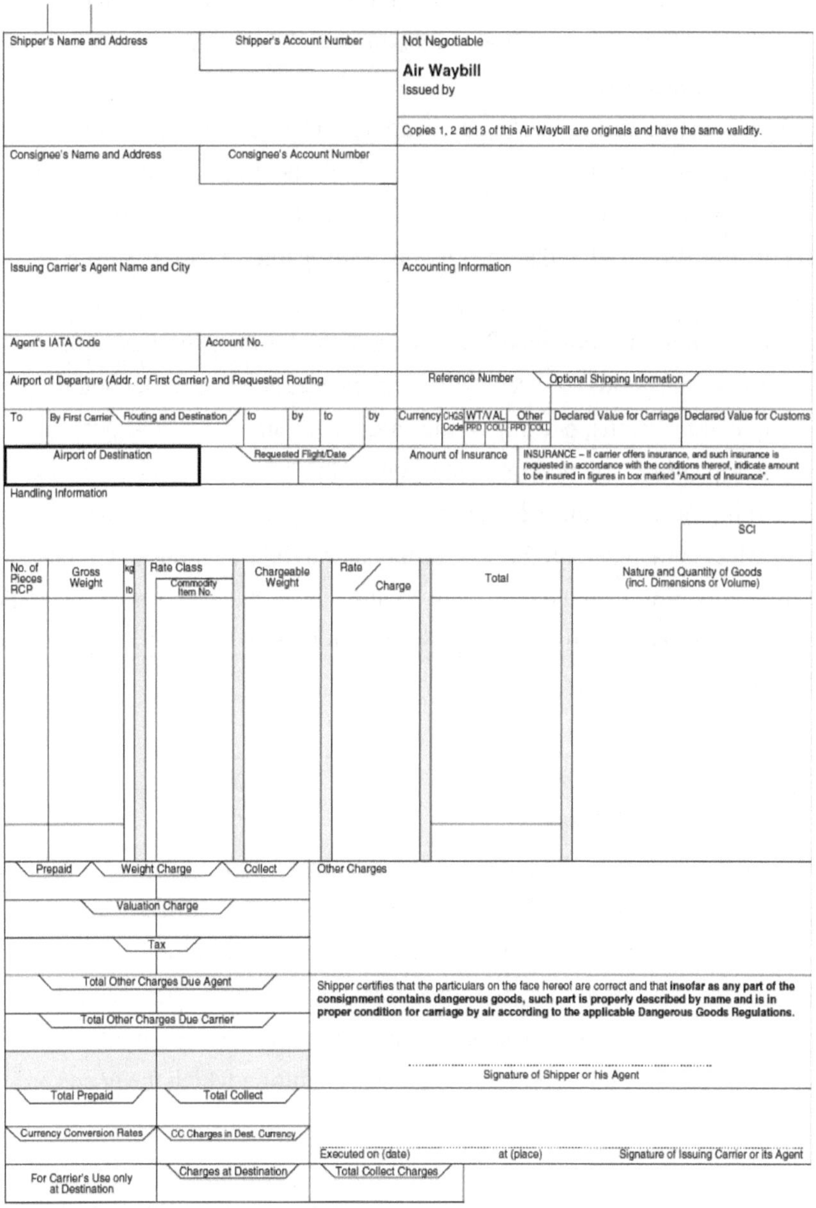
Shipper's Name and Address
Shipper's Account Number
Not Negotiable
Air Waybill
Issued by
Copies 1, 2 and 3 of this Air Waybill are originals and have the same validity.
Consignee's Name and Address
Consignee's Account Number
Issuing Carrier's Agent Name and City
Accounting Information
Agent's IATA Code
Account No.
Airport of Departure (Addr. of First Carrier) and Requested Routing
Reference Number
Optional Shipping Information
To | By First Carrier | Routing and Destination | to | by | to | by
Currency | CHGS Code | WT/VAL PPD COLL | Other PPD COLL | Declared Value for Carriage | Declared Value for Customs
Airport of Destination
Requested Flight/Date
Amount of Insurance
INSURANCE – If carrier offers insurance, and such insurance is requested in accordance with the conditions thereof, indicate amount to be insured in figures in box marked "Amount of Insurance".
Handling Information
SCI
No. of Pieces RCP | Gross Weight | kg lb | Rate Class | Commodity Item No. | Chargeable Weight | Rate / Charge | Total | Nature and Quantity of Goods (incl. Dimensions or Volume)
Prepaid | Weight Charge | Collect
Other Charges
Valuation Charge
Tax
Total Other Charges Due Agent
Total Other Charges Due Carrier
Shipper certifies that the particulars on the face hereof are correct and that **insofar as any part of the consignment contains dangerous goods, such part is properly described by name and is in proper condition for carriage by air according to the applicable Dangerous Goods Regulations.**
Signature of Shipper or his Agent
Total Prepaid
Total Collect
Currency Conversion Rates
CC Charges in Dest. Currency
Executed on (date)
at (place)
Signature of Issuing Carrier or its Agent
For Carrier's Use only at Destination
Charges at Destination
Total Collect Charges

1 Air Waybills Specifications–Reso.600a/Conditions of Contract–Reso.600b (II), adopted by the IATA and effective as of October 1, 2004.

2 This form contains three duplicative parts: the first part is for the carrier, the second part is for the consignee and the third part is for the consignor. The sample below is only one part of the air waybill.

This form has been adopted as the international norm because its layout and wording enable the incorporation of all the particulars required by the various international air conventions. The airline members of IATA have also agreed on the alternative form of Conditions of Contract, printed on the reverse of the standard form of air waybill. The Conditions of Contract include the provisions required under the international air law conventions, as well as other terms, applicable in cases where none of the conventions applies or deals with matters not regulated in the conventions. Terms cover issues such as limitation of the air carrier's liability, the liability of servants and agents of the carrier, written notice of complaint within a specified number of days, time limitation and related matters.

The air waybill is the most important cargo document issued by the carrier or its authorized cargo agent and serves several purposes, among which the most important one is its evidentiary function. The Warsaw-system Conventions and the Montreal Convention (with minor changes indicated in parentheses) provide that the air waybill or cargo receipt has prima facie evidence of the following:

   a. the conclusion of the contract of carriage and conditions of carriage;
   b. the receipt of the goods (or acceptance of the cargo) by the carrier and the statements as to the weight, dimensions, packing of the cargo and number of packages;
   c. the stated quantity, volume and condition of the cargo (as against the carrier); however, only if i) the carrier, in the presence of the consignor, has checked these and ii) a statement to this effect is included on the face of the air waybill, or if the stated fact is related to the apparent condition of the cargo. This means that in the absence of any indication on the face of the air waybill, there is no presumption that the carrier received the cargo in good condition.

3. Air carrier's liability for loss, damage or delay

(1) Carriers' presumed liabilities

Under the Warsaw Convention, as amended, an air cargo carrier is liable for damage sustained in the event of destruction or loss of or damage to cargo, as long as the occurrence which caused the damage took place during the transportation by air. The Montreal Convention tweaked the conditionality of the presumption to the effect that the "event" which caused the damage took place "during the carriage by air." The terms "transportation by air" and "carriage by air" have been specified in both conventions to refer to the period during which the goods are "in the charge of the carrier."

Additionally, if the goods are delayed for an unreasonable amount of time, or if the delay (even if not unreasonable in its duration) causes the destruction or loss of the cargo, the cargo owner does not need to prove that the carrier was at fault. Subject to giving written notice of complaint within the prescribed time-limits, both Warsaw Convention and the Montreal Convention provide that the air carrier is liable for damage occasioned by delay in the carriage of goods or cargo. It should be noted that there are no special rules on the monetary limitation of liability in case of delay and the rules applicable to the loss of or the damage to cargo apply equally to the damage caused by delay.

(2) Defenses available to the carrier

To rebut the presumed liability discussed above, a carrier must prove the existence of a defense to its liability under the conventions. The Warsaw Convention and the Montreal Convention avail the carriers the following choices of defense to liability:

a. It has taken all necessary measures (or all measures that could reasonably be required) to avoid the damage, or it was impossible to take such measures;

b. The damage of goods was caused by negligent pilotage[1] or negligence in the handling of the aircraft or in navigation, and that in all other respects the carrier and its agents have taken all necessary measures to avoid the damage;

c. The negligence on the part of the claimant caused or contributed to the loss, damage or delay in question;

d. The damage or loss of cargo was caused by one or more of the following circumstances: inherent defect, quality or vice of the cargo, defective packing of the cargo performed by a person other than the carrier or its agent, an act of war or an armed conflict, and an act of public authority carried out in connection with the entry, exit or transit of the cargo.

(3) Limitation of liability

Under the Warsaw Convention, as amended, and the Montreal Convention, the liability of the carrier is limited to a sum of 250 gold francs or 17 SDR per kilogram, unless the consignor has made, at the time when the package was handed over to the carrier, a special declaration of the value and has paid a supplementary sum, if so required. If a special declaration of the value has been made, the carrier's liability may not exceed the declared sum, except if the carrier proves that the consignor has declared a value which is greater than the actual value of the package at delivery. In practice, carriers commonly provide in their conditions of contract for an acknowledgment by the consignor that he (i.e., the consignor) has had the opportunity to make a special declaration of the value of the goods at delivery and identify such special declaration in the entry on the air waybill of "declared value for carriage."

International multimodal transport

International multimodal transport means the carriage of goods by at least two different modes of transport on the basis of a multimodal transport contract from a place in one country, at which the

---

1   In light of the technological progress in air navigation equipment since the adoption of the Warsaw Convention in 1929, the defence of "negligent pilotage" subsequently became unnecessary and difficult to justify. Thus, the defence of "negligent pilotage" has not been reproduced in the other Warsaw-system Conventions or the Montreal Convention.

goods are taken in charge by the multimodal transport operator to a place designated for delivery situated in a different country.

The key features of a multimodal transport are: the carriage of goods by two or more modes of transport, under one contract, one document and one responsible party (i.e., a multimodal transport operator) for the entire carriage, who might subcontract the performance of some, or all modes, of the carriage to other carriers.

1. What is multimodal transport operator (the "MTO")?

Multimodal transport operator means any person who on his own behalf or through another person acting on his behalf concludes a multimodal transport contract and who acts as a principal, not as an agent or on behalf of the consignor or of the carriers participating in the multimodal transport operations, and who assumes responsibility for the performance of the contract.

2. International conventions governing international multimodal transport

(1) The United Nations MT Convention

In May 1980, under the efforts of a number of developing countries, the United Nations adopted the Convention on International Multimodal Transport of Goods, commonly referred to as the United Nations MT Convention. However, due to an insufficient number of countries that has ratified the convention, it has not yet entered into force.

In respect of the liability of an MTO for loss of or damage to goods, as well as delay in delivery is based on the principle of "presumed fault or neglect." In other words, the MTO is liable if the occurrence which caused the loss, damage or delay in delivery took place while the goods were in its charge, unless the MTO can prove that it or its agents or any other person of whose services it makes use for the performance of the contract, took all measures that could reasonably be required to avoid the occurrence and its consequences. The period of responsibility of the MTO includes the entire period during which it is in charge of the goods, which is from the time it takes the goods in its charge to the time of delivery.

Under the United Nations MT Convention, a MTO's liability for loss of or damage to goods is to be limited to an amount not exceeding 920 SDRs per package or other shipping unit, or 2.75 SDRs per kilogram of gross weight of the goods lost or damaged, whichever is higher. If, however, the multimodal transport does not, according to the contract, include carriage by sea or by inland waterway, the limitation amount is raised to a higher level of 8.33 SDRs per kilogram of gross weight of the goods lost or damaged, without alternative package limitation. The limitation of liability of the MTO for loss resulting from delay in delivery is calculated by reference to the threat of freight, that is, an amount equivalent to two and a half times the freight payable for the goods delayed, but without exceeding the total freight payable under the multimodal transport contract. The MTO, however, is not entitled to limit its liability if it is proved that the loss, damage or delay in delivery is resulted from an act or omission of the MTO done with the intent to cause such loss, damage or delay or is reckless with knowledge that such loss, damage or delay would probably result.

(2) UNCTAD/ICC Rules for multimodal transport documents

Pending the entry into force of the United Nations MT Convention, in 1991, the UNCTAD and the International Chamber of Commerce (ICC) jointly prepared the UNCTAD/ICC Rules for Multimodal Transport Documents (the "UNCTAD/ICC MT Rules"), which came into force in January 1992. Similar to the Incoterms®, the UNCTAD/ICC MT Rules do not have the force of law but are of purely contractual nature and apply only if they are incorporated into a contract of carriage, without any formal requirement for "writing" and irrespective of whether it is a contract for unimodal or multimodal transport involving one or several modes of transport, or whether or not a document has been issued. Once they are incorporated into a contract, they override any conflicting contractual provisions, except that so far as they increase the responsibility or obligations of the multimodal transport operator. These rules, however, can only take effect to some extent that they are not contrary to the mandatory provisions of international conventions or national law applicable to the multimodal transport contract.

Similar to the United Nations MT Convention, the liability of the MTO under the UNCTAD/ICC MT Rules is based on the principle of presumed fault or neglect. As such, an MTO is liable for loss of or damage to the goods as well as delay in delivery, if the occurrence which caused the loss, damage or delay in delivery took place while the goods were in its charge, unless it can prove that no fault or neglect of its own, its servants or agents or any other person of whose services he made use of for the performance of the contract, caused or contributed to the loss or delay in delivery. Despite the similar presumption, the UNCTAD/ICC MT Rules provide for exceptions that are not available under the United Nations MT Convention. These exceptions are:

    a. The MTO is not liable for the loss following delay in delivery unless the consignor has made a declaration of interest in timely delivery which has been accepted by the MTO;

    b. If the multimodal transport involves carriage by sea or inland waterways, the MTO will not be liable for loss, damage or delay in delivery with respect to goods carried by sea or inland waterways when such loss, damage or delay during such carriage has been caused by: act, neglect, or default of the master, mariner, pilot or the servants of the carrier in the navigation or in the management of the ship; or fire, unless caused by the actual fault or privity of the carrier.

The limitation amounts established by the UNCTAD/ICC MT Rules for loss of or damage to goods are primarily modeled after the limits set by the Hague/Visby Rules for international maritime transportation. Thus, unless the nature and the value of the goods have been declared by the consignor and inserted in the multimodal transport document, the MTO shall not be liable for any loss of or any damage to the goods in an amount exceeding the equivalent of 666.67 SDRs per package or unit, or 2 SDRs per kilogram of gross weight of the goods lost or damaged, whichever is the higher. Similar to the United Nations MT Convention, a higher limit is provided for cases where the multimodal transport does not, in accordance with the contract, include carriage by sea or inland navigation. In such a case the liability of the MTO is limited to an amount not exceeding 8.33SDRs per kilogram of gross weight of the goods lost or damaged.

3. Chinese laws governing multimodal transport

Section 8 of Chapter Four of the PRC Maritime Law is devoted to multimodal transport contract, under which the MTO undertakes, against the payment of freight for the entire transport, to transport the goods from the place where the goods were received in its charge to destination and deliver them to the consignee by two or more different modes of transport, one of which is sea carriage. As such, the provisions in connection with multimodal transport in the PRC Maritime Law are only applicable to multimodal transport activities with at least one sea leg.

Under Article 104 of the PRC Maritime Law, the MTO is responsible for the performance or the procurement of the performance of the multimodal transport contract and is therefore responsible for the entire transport. While the MTO may enter into separate contracts with unimodal carriers with different sections of the transport under the multimodal transport contract, its responsibility with respect to the entire transport will remain unaffected. Furthermore, if the loss of or the damage to the goods has occurred in a certain section of the transport, the provisions of the relevant laws and regulations governing that specific section of the multimodal transport shall be applicable to the matters concerning the liability of the MTO and the limitations thereof. Thus, if it can be determined at which stage of the transport the loss or damage occurred, the rules and regulations applicable to that branch of the transport will be applied. If, however, the section of transport in which the loss of or damage to the goods occurred could not be ascertained, the MTO shall be liable for compensation in accordance with the stipulations regarding the carrier's liability and the limitation thereof as set out in the relevant provisions in the PRC Maritime Law.

SELF QUIZ: Indicate whether each of the following statements is true or false.

27. In charter shipment arrangements, the owners of the vessel provide the crew to manage the vessel and the charter orders the destination of the transport.

28. The consignee named on the bill of lading is the holder of title over the goods covered by the bill of lading.

29. In order to be paid by the bank issuing a letter of credit, the seller typically needs to present a clean bill of lading instead of an unclean bill of lading.

30. Among the key international conventions governing the legal relationship between carriers and shippers in international maritime cargo transportation, the Hague-Visby Rules are more pro-shippers' interests, while the Hamburg Rules are more pro-carriers' interests.

31. The PRC Maritime Law takes the same approach as the Hague-Visby Rules in respect of exoneration of liabilities of carriers.

32. Like a bill of lading, an air waybill is negotiable and can be endorsed for multiple times during shipment.

33. In China, provisions in respect of multimodal transport contracts in the PRC Maritime Law are applicable to all multimodal transport activities involving China.

Part 4 International Marine Insurance

Carriage of goods by sea cannot develop without marine insurance. Marine insurance contract, also referred to as waterborne insurance contract, is an agreement where the insured undertakes the payment of premium and the insurer issues an insurance policy or a certificate and undertakes to indemnify the insured to the extent of all losses, damages and costs that arise from maritime perils, unless specified otherwise in the contract.

The subject matter of marine insurance contract may include:
- Ship;
- Cargo;
- Income from the operation of the ship including freight, charter hire and passenger's fare;
- Expected profit on cargo;
- Crew's wages and other remuneration;
- Liabilities to a third person;
- Other property that may sustain loss from a maritime peril and the liability and expenses arising therefrom.

The insured must have insurable interest in the insured subject matter at the time of the loss; otherwise, the insurer is not liable. "Insurable interest" refers to the legally recognized interest that an insurer has in the insured subject matter. For example, an insured cargo you own suffers from fumigation damage during the transportation. You have the insurable interest in the damaged cargo because you are the owner. Therefore, you can claim indemnification according to the marine insurance contract.

Perils and losses

1. Perils
Carriage of goods by sea may be confronted with the following perils:
- Loss or damage from the sea (e.g., weather, collision, stranding, sinking);
- Fire;
- Jettison (i.e., the dumping of cargo in order to protect other property);
- Forcible taking of the ship;

- Barratry (i.e., the fraudulent, criminal, or wrongful conduct of the captain or crew);
- Explosion;
- Fumigation damage;
- Damage from loading, discharging, or transshipping cargo.

2. Losses

Perils may cause losses, which include total loss and partial loss.

Total loss can be further classified into two types: actual total loss and constructive total loss.

- Actual total loss: Where after a peril, the subject matter insured is lost or is so seriously damaged that it is completely deprived of its original structure and usage or the insured is deprived of the possession thereof.
- Constructive total loss: Where an actual total loss is considered to be unavoidable after the cargo has suffered a peril, or the incurred expenses for avoiding the total actual loss plus that for forwarding the cargo to its destination would exceed its insured value, it shall constitute a constructive total loss.

Partial loss means any loss other than an actual total loss or a constructive total loss. Partial loss can be further divided into general average and particular average. Here "average" means the loss.

- General average means the average resulting from an intentional partial sacrifice of ship or cargo to avoid total loss. The liability is proportionately shared by all parties who had an interest in the voyage.[1] Loss or damage sustained by the ship or goods through delay, whether on the voyage or subsequently, such as demurrage and loss of market as well as other indirect losses, shall not be admitted as general average. In order to prove a general average claim, the claimant must show that (1) the ship, cargo, and crew were threatened by a common danger; (2) the danger was real and substantial; and (3) the cargo or ship was voluntarily sacrificed for the benefit of both, or extraordinary expenses were incurred to avert a common peril.
- Particular average is the average resulting from an accidental partial loss or damage. Any average that is not general is termed particular. The liability is borne solely by the person who suffered the loss.[2]

CASE EXAMPLE:

Facts: A ship carried paper and cotton cloth. In its voyage, one of its cabins caught fire. The captain ordered his crew to douse the fire with water. After the fire was extinguished, they found out half of the paper had been burned out. Although the other part of the paper has not caught fire, they cannot be used because of damping. As a result of that, this part of paper has to be used as pulp, losing 80% of its original value. Besides, the cotton cloth, although has not been burned, also suffered from water stains. Consequently, the cotton cargo has to be sold at a reduced price,

---

1 Page155 of *Black Law Dictionary*, 11th edition.

2 Page 155-56 of *Black Law Dictionary*, 11th edition.

losing 20% of its original value. Are the 80% loss of the value of the paper and the 20% loss of the value of the cloth partial losses? Why?

The Court held that: The 80% loss of the original value of the paper cargo should be considered as total loss, and the 20% loss of the value of the cotton cargo as partial loss. This is because the total loss in the insurance service can be divided into actual total loss and constructive total loss. The actual total loss can be further divided into three types: all loss; losing usable value (such as cement changing into hard lumps); having secondary use value, but the goods loses its original usable value. In the first circumstance (paper losing 80% value), originally, paper should be used to print books, newspapers or processing into other products; but now, it has to be used as pulp to making paper. Thus, it belongs to the third type of the total loss. Although the cotton cloth has been waterlogged, it can still be sold as cloth after processing; and the original purpose does not change, therefore, it is partial loss.

Take-away points: Actual total loss includes three circumstances: all loss, losing usable value, and losing original use value but having secondary use value. All loss refers to the complete destruction of insured property so that it no longer exists in their original form and has no secondary use value as well. This type of loss is easy to understand. In practice, more attention should be put on the other two types of actual total loss.

Formation of marine insurance contracts

Conclusion of a marine insurance contract requires mutual consent between the insured and the insurer. The consent is based on the utmost good faith of the parities. The insurer should truthfully indicate the contents of the insurance contract to the insurer; and the insured should clearly disclose the condition of the insured subject matter to the insurer.

1. The insured's disclosure

Before a contract is concluded, the insured shall voluntarily inform the insurer of material circumstances that (1) the insured has knowledge or ought to have knowledge of the ordinary course of business and (2) may influence the insurer in fixing the premium or determining whether to provide insurance or not. The insured need not to inform the insurer of the facts that the insurer has knowledge or the insurer ought to have knowledge of his or her ordinary business practice if about which the insurer made no inquiry.

If due to its intentional act the insured fails to voluntarily inform the insurer of the material circumstances, the insurer has the right to terminate the contract without refunding the premium. The insurer shall not be liable for any loss arising from the perils insured against before the contract is terminated.

Where, not due to the insured's intentional act, the insured fails to voluntarily inform the insurer of the above material circumstances, the insurer has the right to terminate the contract or to demand a corresponding increase in the premium. In case the contract is terminated by the insurer, the insurer shall be liable for the loss arising from the perils occurring prior to the termination, except where the material circumstances uninformed or wrongly informed of have an impact on the occurrence of such perils.

If the insured is aware that the subject matter insured has suffered a loss due to the incidence of a peril insured against when the contract is concluded, the insurer shall not be liable for the indemnification but shall have the right to the premium. If the insurer is aware that the occurrence of a loss to the subject matter insured due to a peril insured against is impossible, the insured shall have the right to recover the premium paid.

2. The insurer's disclosure

If parties reach mutual consent upon the contents of a marine insurance contract, the insurer shall issue to the insured an insurance policy or other certificate of insurance in time, and the contents of the contract shall be contained therein.

Termination of marine insurance contracts

Prior to the commencement of the insurance liability, the insured may terminate the marine insurance contract but shall pay the handling fees to the insurer, and the insurer shall refund the premium.

After the commencement of the insurance liability, neither the insurer nor the insured may terminate the contract, unless otherwise agreed in the contract[1]. If the insurance contract provides that the contract may be terminated after the commencement of the liability, and the insured demands the termination of the contract, the insurer shall have the right to the premium payable from the day of the commencement of the insurance liability to the day of termination of the contract and refund the remaining portion. If it is the insurer who demands the termination of the contract, the unexpired premium from the day of the termination of the contract to the day of the expiration of the period of insurance shall be refunded to the insured.

Assignment of marine insurance contracts

Assignment is an established insurance principle that the assignor transfers the benefits of the insurance policy to a third party. An assignee can only avail itself of the benefits of the insurance to the extent that the assignor has agreed to assign.

A marine insurance contract for the carriage of goods by sea may be assigned by the insured by endorsement or otherwise, and the rights and obligations under the contract are assigned accordingly. The insured and the assignee shall be jointly and severally liable for the payment of the premium if such premium remains unpaid up to the time of the assignment of the contract.

---

1   Notably, according to Chinese Maritime Law, the insured may not terminate the contract for cargo insurance and voyage insurance on ship after the commencement of the insurance liability.

Subrogation

Subrogation means that the insurer shall, from the date of payment of indemnity to the insured, be subrogated to the rights of the insured to claim compensation from a third party who caused the loss. The compensation is limited to the amount of indemnity that the insurer has already paid to the insured. Subrogation aims at preventing the insured from double compensation from the insurer and damages from the third party who caused the loss. The rule of subrogation has two basic factors:

- It is a condition precedent to the exercise of the right of subrogation that the insurer has paid indemnity to the insured pursuant to the insurance contract in question;
- The third party is liable for the loss of, or damage to, the insured subject matter in respect of which the insurer has paid the assured.

PICC Ocean Marine Cargo Clauses

Ocean Marine Cargo Clause of the People's Insurance Company of China (hereinafter "PICC Ocean Marine Cargo Clauses") is a typical marine cargo insurance clause widely used in China. It mainly provides two types of coverage: basic coverage and additional coverage. Additional coverage includes risk of clash and breakage by vibration, clash or pressing, and etc. Basic coverage can be classified into three categories: Free from Particular Average (FPA), With Particular Average (WPA) and All Risks.

1. Free from Particular Average (FPA)

FPA refers to the non-liability of indemnification to particular average. It is the most limited form of cargo insurance coverage. Its coverage includes:

- Total or constructive total loss of the whole consignment insured caused in the course of transit by natural calamities, such as heavy weather, lightning, tsunami, earthquake and flood;
- Total or partial loss caused by accidents, such as the carrying conveyance being grounded, stranded, sunk or in collision with floating ice or other objects as fire or explosion;
- Partial loss of the insured goods attributable to heavy weather, lightning and/or tsunami, where the conveyance has been grounded, stranded, sunk or burnt, irrespective of whether the event or events took place before or after such accidents;
- Partial or total loss consequent on falling of entire package or packages into sea during loading transshipment or discharge;
- Reasonable cost incurred by the insured in salvaging the goods or averting or minimizing a loss recoverable under the policy provided that such cost shall not exceed the sum insured of the consignment so saved;
- Losses attributable to the discharge of the insured goods at a port of distress following a sea peril as well as special charges arising from loading, warehousing and forwarding of the goods

at an intermediate port of call or refuge;

- Sacrifice in and contribution to general average and salvage charges;
- Proportion of losses sustained by the ship owners is to be reimbursed by the cargo owner under the Contract of Affreightment "Both to Blame Collision" Clause.

2. With Particular Average (WPA)

Aside from the risks covered by FPA, WPA also covers the partial losses of the insured cargo caused by bad weather, lightning, tsunami, earthquake and/or flood. In other words, WPA provides a more extensive coverage than FPA against all loss or damage due to marine perils throughout the duration of the policy.

3. All Risks

All Risks is the most comprehensive one among the three basic coverage. It is also adopted by most cargo insurance policies. All Risks means that the insurer shall undertake, in addition to the liabilities under FPA and WPA, the liabilities to indemnify the insured the total or partial loss on the insured cargo either arising from perils of the sea or general extraneous risks during the course of transit. It does not cover loss, damage or expense caused by delay or inherent vice or nature of the subject matter insured, or special extraneous risks of war, strike, etc.

4. Exclusions

Basic coverage excludes the following loss or damage:

- Loss or damage caused by the intentional act or fault of the insured;
- Loss or damage falling under the liability of the consignor;
- Loss or damage arising from the inferior quality or shortage of the insured goods prior to the attachment of this insurance;
- Loss or damage arising from normal loss, inherent vice or nature of the insured goods, loss of market and/or delay in transit and any expenses arising therefrom;
- Risks and liabilities covered and excluded by the Ocean Marine Cargo War Risks Clauses and Strike, Riot and Civil Commotion Clauses of the People's Insurance Company of China.

SELF QUIZ: Indicate whether each of the following statements is true or false.

34. Expected profit on cargo can be the subject matter of marine insurance contract as long as parties agree.

35. The insured must have insurable interest in the insured subject matter at the conclusion of the contract.

36. If a ship's total loss is considered to be unavoidable after a peril, or the expenses necessary for avoiding the occurrence of an actual total loss would exceed the insured value, it shall constitute a constructive total loss.

37. Total loss can be further divided into general average and particular average.

38. General average is proportionately shared by all parties who had an interest in the voyage.

39. If due to its negligence, the insured fails to voluntarily inform the insurer of the material circumstances, the insurer has the right to terminate the contract without refunding the premium.

40. As long as a marine insurance contract takes effect and the insurance liability commences, neither the insurer nor the insured may terminate the contract, unless otherwise agreed in the contract.

41. An assignee can enjoy all the rights as the assignor under a marine insurance contract.

42. After the insurer has paid indemnity to the insured, the insurer can subrogate the insured and directly claim compensation from the third party who causes damages to the insured subject matter.

43. The insurance coverage of With Particular Average is smaller than Free from Particular Average and All risks.

Questions

1. A foreign company A sells a batch of equipment to company B in China, and the two companies have reached an agreement on "FOB (Incoterms®2010)." Then, the batch of equipment is shipped to China. According to the Incoterms®2010 and United Nations Convention on Contracts of International Sales of Goods, which of the following choice is correct?

   A. Company A is responsible for concluding the transportation contract and paying freight.

   B. The risk to the goods is shifted from the seller to the buyer when the goods passes the ship's rail at the port of shipment.

   C. Suppose that the sales contract is silent about package requirement, if the batch of equipment is damaged because its package does not meet the general packaging requirement for the same kind of goods, the company A should shoulder the liability.

   D. If the batch of equipment infringes the third party's patent right in China, company A is not liable for company B.

2. Company A in China signed a contract with Company B from a foreign country to purchase 2,500 tons of chemical fertilizer on CFR (Incoterms® 2010). The letter of credit (L/C) opened by Company A stipulated the time of shipment was from January 1 to 10, 2014. However, the ship "Leone" charted by Company B suffered from a hurricane on its way to the port of loading. As a result, the loading was delayed and finally finished on January 20. After obtaining a letter of guarantee issued by Company B, the carrier issued a bill of lading in accordance with the terms of the L/C. Then "Leone" departed away from the port of loading

on January 21. Company A has insured WPA. On January 30, 2014, "Leone" caught a fire when passing through the Dardanelles Straits. Consequently, part of the chemical fertilizer was burned, and in the process of extinguishing fire, part of the chemical fertilizer was damaged by damp. Due to the delay in the port of loading, when "Leone" arrived at the destination, the market price for the chemical fertilizer declined. Therefore, when selling the rest of the chemical fertilizer, Company A had to cut the price significantly; thus Company A suffered great loss. According to the case above, please answer the following questions:

(1) According to Chinese Maritime Insurance Law, what kind of loss should the chemical fertilizer burned on voyage belong to? Who should be liable for that? Why?

(2) What kind of loss is the damp-damaged chemical fertilizer on voyage? Who should be liable for that? Why?

(3) Could Company A recover from losses caused by the declined market price because of late arriving of "Leone"? Why?

(4) Could the carrier recover losses from the shipper (Company B)? Why?

Suggested Further Readings

Robin Warner & Stuart Kaye (ed.), *Routledge Handbook of Maritime Regulation and Enforcement*, 2016.

Ling Zhu, *Probing Compulsory Insurance for Maritime Liability*, 45 Journal of Maritime Law and Commerce 63, 2014.

Juana Coetzee, *The Interplay Between INCOTERMS® and the CISG*, 32 Journal of Law and Commerce 1, 2013.

William P Johnson, *Analysis of INCOTERMS as Usage Under Article 9 of the CISG*, 35 University of Pennsylvania Journal of International Law 379, 2013.

John D. Kimball, *The Central Role of P&I Insurance in Maritime Law*, 87 Tulane Law Review 1147, 2013.

Edward G. Hinkelman, *A Short Course in International Payments*, World Trade Press, 2011.

John F. Wilson, *Carriage of Goods by Sea*, Longman, 2011.

Bernard Eder, David Foxton QC, Andrew Burrows, Stewart C. Boyd, *Scrutton on Charterparties and Bills of Lading*, Sweet & Maxwell, 2011.

Charles Proctor, *The Law and Practice of International Banking*, Oxford University Press, 2010.

Chapter 6

Trade in Goods: Tariff, TBT, SPS, and Trade Remedies

This chapter analyzes the establishment and operation of GATT and WTO, in particular the regulations concerning trade in goods. It begins with a conversion from GATT to WTO, then probes into the fundamental principles of treatments and regulations under the WTO law, and finally examines trade remedies. The chapter consists of seven parts:

Part 1 introduces the basis of international trade regulation framework, the most essential principles in trade in goods and the relevant Chinese law;

Part 2 looks into the mechanisms with respect to tariffs protection;

Part 3 sheds light on the rules of origin;

Part 4 enumerates the technical barriers to trade and its importance;

Part 5 discusses the sanitary and phytosanitary measures;

Part 6 focuses on the trade remedies, i.e., anti-dumping, anti-subsidy and safeguard;

Part 7 elucidates government procurement in trade in goods.

▌ Learning Objectives

By the end of this chapter you should:

- Have a firm understanding of the trade in goods within the WTO framework, and be able to analyze and advise on legal issues relating to trade in goods by multinational corporations;
- Be capable of outlining recent development of trade in goods, in particular changes regarding technical barriers and trade remedies;
- Be able to examine the evolution of the GATT, to identify current trends in trade in goods, and to further understand the emergence of new laws and rules from the perspective of developing countries' interests.

■ Key Terms

Agreement on Government Procurement

Agreement on Technical Barriers to Trade

Agreement on the Application of Sanitary and Phytosanitary Measures

Agreement on Trade-Related Investment Measures

Dumping

Preferential Trade Agreements

Safeguard

Subsidy

The General Agreement on Tariffs and Trade

Transparency

World Trade Organization

Part 1　Introduction: from GATT to WTO

The GATT in the WTO era

The General Agreement on Tariffs and Trade was a multilateral agreement regulating international trade. The GATT was conceived as reciprocal and mutually advantageous arrangements direct to the substantial reduction of tariffs and other barriers to trade and to the elimination of discriminatory treatment in international commerce.[1]

In order to keep GATT 1947 up-to-date, multilateral trade negotiations (informally called "rounds") were regularly convened by the contracting parties. The creation of the WTO took place in the Uruguay Round. According to the Agreement, the WTO is meant to provide a common institutional framework for the conduct of trade relations among its members in matters related to the agreements and associated legal instruments included in the Annexes to this Agreement.[2] The WTO is headed by ministerial conferences of all members that convene at least once every two years.

The relationship between GATT and WTO: First, in terms of organization, the WTO replaces the GATT as an international organization. Second, in terms of rules, the GATT has been incorporated into the WTO and meanwhile, the WTO has developed the GATT. Such a development is embodied in two aspects. As to the content, in addition to trade in goods covered by the GATT, the WTO also regulates trade in services and trade-related intellectual property rights. As to the binding force, while the GATT gives priority to the application of national law, the WTO underlines its dominance.

1　See the Preamble of the GATT.

2　Agreement Establishing the World Trade Organization, article II, para.1.

Table 1: Key Differences Between GATT and WTO

	GATT	WTO
Foundation	Protocol of Provisional Application of the General Agreement on Tariffs and Trade (Geneva, 1947)	Vienna Convention on the law of treaties (Vienna, 1969)
Purpose	To strengthen international trade	To govern GATT and international trade practices
Framework/Function	An *ad hoc* and provisional organization without privileges and immunities	A permanent institution with its own secretariat. The institution and its staff shall be accorded by its members with privileges and immunities on functional basis.
Scope	Trade in goods	Trade in goods; trade in services and trade-related aspects of intellectual property rights
Application	Allows existing domestic legislation to continue even if it violates GATT agreement	Does not permit the incompatibility of domestic legislation and WTO agreement
Dispute Resolution	Has a permanent appellate body to review findings and settle disputes, but the dispute resolution system is slow and less effective	Disputes are resolved faster as the settlement system has a select time frame. Although the WTO simply recommends its rulings and allows for tariff retaliation, WTO members commonly implement promptly the recommendations and rulings of the DSB.

Essential principles

1. National treatment

Under the national treatment, if a state provides its own citizens with certain rights and privileges, equivalent rights and privileges should be also accorded to foreigners who are currently in the state. The principle offers foreigners the same treatment as one's own nationals. More thoroughly, national treatment is a form of non-discrimination with deepest impact on national regulatory autonomy, requiring sovereign states to adopt regulations in a way so as not to treat its citizens more favorably than foreigners.[1]

Article III of GATT requires that imports be treated no less favorably than the same or similar domestically-produced goods once they have passed customs. Nonetheless, the article does not specify which measures come under its purview. In general, it has been acknowledged that the normative elements of the article consist of the followings:[2]

- Imported products should not be subject to internal taxes or other internal charges in excess of those applied to like domestics;
- Imported products should not be accorded treatment less favorable than that accorded to like domestic products with regard to laws, regulations and requirements affecting their sale, purchase, transportation, distribution or use;
- Members cannot have any quantitative regulation requiring compulsory utilization of a product from a domestic source in preference to using a like imported product;
- A member cannot apply internal taxes or other internal charges or quantitative regulations in a manner so as to provide protection to domestic production.

2. Most-Favored-Nation treatment

(1) Basic discipline

Most-Favored-Nation Treatment (MFN Treatment) is a principle that requires contracting parties accord the most favorable tariff and regulatory treatment given to the product of any contracting party at the time of import or export to "like products" of all other contracting parties. In accordance with the WTO agreement, countries cannot discriminate, as a general rule, between their trading partners by virtue of, for example, granting the other parties a lower customs duty rate for one of their productions. The first article of the GATT provides contracting parties with most-favored-national treatment.

(2) Scope and coverage

Article I of the GATT stipulates that the MFN treatment encompasses:

- customs duties and charges of any kind imposed on or in connection with importation or exportation or imposed on the international transfer of payments for imports or exports;
- the methods of levying such duties and charges;
- all rules and formalities related to importation and exportation;
- internal taxation and regulation of the type covered by article III:2 and article III:4;
- any advantage, favor, privilege or immunity granted by any contracting party to any

---

1 Nicolas F. Diebold, *Non-Discrimination in International Trade in Services: "Likeness" in WTO/GATS*, Cambridge University Press, 2010, p.17.

2 Bhagirath Lal Da, *The World Trade Organization: Guide to the New Framework for International Trade*, Zed Books Ltd., 1999, p.30-31.

product originating in or destined for any other country shall be accorded immediately and unconditionally to the like product originating in or destined for the territories of all other contracting parties.

(3) MFN treatment test

It is submitted that article I of the GATT set out a three-tier test of consistency[1] which indicates that three inquiries have to be conducted to determine whether there is a violation of the MFN treatment obligation.

- Whether the measure at issue confers a trade "advantage" of the kind covered by article I;
- Whether the products concerned are "like products";
- Whether the advantage at issue is granted "immediately and unconditionally" to all like products concerned.

3. Exceptions

National treatment and most-favored-nation treatment should be applied with the exception.

(1) Preferential trade agreement

Preferential trade agreement (PTA) is an agreement among a group of countries to extend special trading advantages, usually in the form of tariff rates, which are lower than most-favored nation rates. PTA can be accordingly regarded as a trading bloc providing preferential access to certain products from the participating countries. Under article XXIV of the GATT, countries may enter into preferential trade agreements by fully liberalizing "substantially" all trade between them while not raising trade barriers on outsiders. They are thereby sanctioned to form

(a) Free Trade Areas (FTAs), in which participating countries simply eliminate barriers to internal trade while maintaining independent external trade policies; or

(b) Customs Unions (CUs), participating countries additionally agree on a common external tariff against imports from non-members.

(2) Special and differential treatment for developing countries

The WTO Agreements contain special provisions which give developing countries special rights and which give developed countries the possibility to treat developing countries more favorably than other WTO members. These special provisions include:

(a) longer time periods for implementing the Agreements and commitments;

(b) measures to increase trading opportunities for developing countries;

(c) provisions requiring all WTO members to safeguard the trade interests of developing countries;

---

1   Peter Van den Bossche, *The Law and Policy of the World Trade Organization*, Cambridge University Press, 2008, p.325.

(d) support to help developing countries build the capacity to carry out WTO work, handle disputes, and implement technical standards;

(e) provisions related to least-developed country (LDC) members.

One example of derogation to the non-discrimination is the Enabling Clause, which allows tariff preferences to be granted to developing countries in line with the Generalized System of Preferences (GSP).

(3) Intellectual property exception

Article 66 of the TRIPS Agreement provides least-developed countries with a longer time-frame to implement all the provisions of the TRIPS Agreement and encourages technology transfer. Article 67 refers to the provisions of technical assistance.

(4) Trade in service exception

Article IV of the GATS aims at increasing the participation of developing countries in world trade. Article XII allows developing countries and countries in transition to restrict trade in services for reasons of balance-of-payment difficulties.

4. Transparency

(1) The general transparency obligation in the GATT

Transparency is a principle that requires trade regulations of GATT members be published and available to all other GATT nations and their nationals. As a cornerstone of the multilateral system, transparency takes an essential part in trade in goods, without which other fundamental principles of non-discrimination, proportionality, and special and differential treatment are of less practical use. Article X of GATT imposes a general transparency obligation, and the other Annex 1A agreements contain various specific transparency obligations, such as the obligation to notify safeguard measures.

Normally, transparency as a means aims to promote a rules-based approach to trade policy at the national level, facilitate the surveillance of compliance with WTO obligations, and further facilitate future multilateral trade negotiation. The obligations of transparency can be demonstrated in three aspects:

• First, obligation to publish promptly or make publicly available domestic measures of general application affecting trade, usually before their application or enforcement;

• Second, obligation to notify various forms of governmental actions or possible changes;

• Third, obligation for consistent, impartial, uniform and reasonable administration of those measures.

CASE EXAMPLE: *US-Underwear*[1]

Fact: On 22 December 1995, Costa Rica requested consultations with the US concerning US restrictions on textile imports from Costa Rica. Costa Rica alleged that these restrictions were in violation of the Agreement on Textiles and Clothing (ATC). Further to Costa Rica's request, the DSB established a panel at its meeting on 5 March 1996. India reserved its third-party rights. The Panel found that the US restraints were not valid. On 11 November 1996, Costa Rica notified its decision to appeal against one aspect of the Panel report. The Appellate Body upheld the appeal by Costa Rica on that particular point. Transparency was one of key findings of the Appellate Body where the Appellate Body elucidated the policy underlying article X:2 as pertaining to transparency and due process.

The WTO Appellate Body held that: Article X:2 might be seen to embody a principle of fundamental importance—promoting full disclosure of governmental acts affecting members and private persons and enterprises, whether of domestic or foreign nationality. The relevant policy principle was widely known as the principle of transparency and had obviously due process dimensions. The essential implication was that members and other persons affected, or likely to be affected, by governmental measures imposing restraints, requirements and other burdens, should have a reasonable opportunity to acquire authentic information about such measures and accordingly to protect and adjust their activities or alternatively to seek modification of such measures.

Take-away point: The Appellate Body disagreed with the Panel's finding that article 6.10 of the ATC was "silent" as to whether a transitional safeguard measure could be backdated or not and found that article 6.10 prohibited such backdating. The Appellate Body determined that prior publication of a measure, as required under article X of GATT, could not, in and of itself, justify the retroactive effect of a restrictive governmental measure.

(2) The trade policy review mechanism

a. Objectives

The General Council meets as the Trade Policy Review Body to undertake trade policy reviews of members under the Trade Policy Review Mechanism (TPRM) and to consider the Director-Generals' regular reports on trade policy development. Surveillance of national trade policies is a fundamentally crucial activity running throughout the work of the WTO. The TPRM is at the centre of this work. In principle, the purpose of the review process is to strengthen members' observance of WTO provisions and to contribute to the smoother functioning of the multilateral trading system. The review mechanism further serves as a valuable resource for improving the transparency of members' trade and investment regimes. Accordingly, the review mechanism enables the regular collective appreciation and evaluation of the full range of individual members' trade policies and practices and their impact on the functioning of the multilateral trading system. It does not, nonetheless, intend

---

1   Appellate Body Report, *United States—Restrictions on Imports of Cotton and Man—Made Fibre Underwear*, WT/DS24/AB/R, 10 February 1997.

to serve as a basis for the enforcement of specific obligations under the Agreements or for dispute settlement procedures, or to impose new policy commitments on members.

Furthermore, the assessment carried out under the review mechanism takes place, to the extent relevant, against the background of the wider economic and developmental needs, policies and objectives of the member concerned, as well as of its external environment. Be that as it may, the function of the review mechanism is to examine the impact of a member's trade policies and practices on the multilateral trading system. All WTO members are reviewed, and the frequency of each country's review varies in accordance with its share of world trade.

In practice, notwithstanding the divergence of each review that highlights the specific issues and measures concerning the individual member, it can be noted that certain common themes emerge during the course of the reviews. These include:

- transparency in policy-making and implementation;
- economic environment and trade liberalization;
- regional trade agreements and their relationship with the multilateral trading system;
- tariff issues, including peaks, escalation, preferences, rationalization and the gap between applied and bound rates;
- import and export restrictions and licensing procedures;
- the use of contingency measures such as anti-dumping and countervailing duties;
- technical and sanitary measures and market access;
- state involvement in the economy and privatization programmes;
- trade-related competition and investment policy issues;
- incentive measures such as subsidies and tax forgone;
- technical assistance in implementing the WTO Agreements and the experience with the Integrated Framework.[1]

b. How are the reviews organized?

The trade policies and practices of all members shall be subject to periodic review. The procedures of reviews consist of the following steps:

- To begin with, reviews are conducted by the Trade Policy Review Body on the basis of a policy statement by the member under review and a report prepared by economists in the Secretariat's Trade Policy Review Division;
- Secondly, the TPRB's debate is stimulated by two discussants that are selected beforehand for this purpose;
- Thirdly, the Secretariat in preparing its report seeks the cooperation of the member, but has the sole responsibility for the facts presented and views expressed;
- Last but not least, the reports consist of detailed chapters examining the trade policies and practices of the member and describing trade policymaking institutions and the

---

1 See WTO Doc WT/TPR/134 of 27 June 2003.

macroeconomic situation; these chapters are preceded by the Secretariat's Summary Observations, which summarize the report and present the Secretariat's perspective on the member's trade policies. The Secretariat report and the member's policy statement are published after the review meeting, along with the minutes of the meeting and the text of the TPRB Chairperson's Concluding Remarks delivered at the conclusion of the meeting.

c. Transparency and participation

The WTO is deficient with respect to its openness, since WTO business is criticized for being conducted by committees and panels that meet behind closed doors in Geneva, Switzerland. Questions as to how to improve WTO transparency and participation have been raised but a further question of whether individuals and NGOs should be able to observe and participate in the WTO is highly contested. Some commentators has presented their observations on future steps for the WTO, including both procedural and substantive dimensions of national transparency, improvements inside the WTO by virtue of negotiations, rulemaking, dispute settlement and parliamentary input.[1]

Foreign trade in China

1. Trade law and regulations

As China entered the new period of reform and opening up, foreign trade became an essential approach to accelerating modernization, promoting the growth of economy, and improving comprehensive national strength. Since 1978, in the process of economic restructuring, China has opened wider to the outside world, and has reformed its foreign trade system continuously with the purpose to establish a new system suitable to the market economy and international trade standards. During the negotiations over the restoration of its GATT membership and entry into the WTO, and after it became a WTO member, China gradually adopted international trade practices, and established a unified, open foreign trade system compatible with multilateral trade rules.

China enacted the Foreign Trade Law in 1994 and the new version of the Foreign Trade Law took effect in 2004. The Law governs all cross-border transactions involving goods, addressing the issues concerning:

- foreign trade dealer;
- import and export of goods;
- foreign trade order;
- foreign trade investigation;
- foreign trade remedies;
- promotion of foreign trade.

In principle, the Law deregulates access to foreign trading rights, and clarifies the roles of

---

1   Steve Charnovitz, *Transparency and Participation in the World Trade Organization*, 56 Rutgers L. Rev. 927 (2003-2004).

governmental authorities, foreign and domestic corporations, state-operated trading entities and trade associations.

In the meantime, the State Council of China promulgated the Anti-Dumping and Anti-Subsidy Regulations in 1997 so as to elaborate rules on the trade remedies. Due to organizational change, the Anti-Dumping and Anti-Subsidy Regulations were revised in 2004.

Table 2: Current Regulations and Policies

Import licensing administration	China maintains an import licensing system applicable to some AV laser discs and electronics products, chemicals that are used for military weapons, toxicant or drugs as well as ozone depleting materials.
	China imposes restrictions or prohibitions on imported waste materials of plastic and metal, used machinery and electrical products except special approval from relevant authority.
Automatic import licensing	All quantitative restrictions on imported goods were removed and transferred to the category of free import or automatic import licensing for monitoring. For products under automatic import licensing, so long as the content and format of the application are correct, the issuing entity should grant the license immediately or within a few days.
Import duties and taxes	China has fulfilled its tariff reduction commitment since its WTO accession.
Customs requirements	Before clearing customs and lodging declaration, most goods are subject to mandatory inspection and quarantine under the Catalogue of Import-Export Commodities Subject to Compulsory Inspection and Quarantine.
	Pre-shipment inspection is required for importing wastes.
Product standards	Import commodity inspection is required for all goods in the published Inspection List, or subject to inspection pursuant to other laws and regulations.
Goods Export System	MOFCOM and GAC jointly release a catalogue of export goods requiring licenses on an annual basis.
	For goods subject to export restrictions, China implements an export licensing administration system.
	Three types of export license are: export quota license (*e.g.*, corn, cotton, crude oil, wheat); export quota tender (*e.g.*, magnesia); export license (*e.g.*, beef, chicken, pork).

2. National treatment, most-favored-nation treatment and transparency in China

(1) National treatment and most-favored-nation treatment

In general, the Protocol on China's accession to the WTO provides a non-discrimination clause, which stipulates that foreign individuals and enterprises and foreign-funded enterprises shall ordinarily be accorded treatment no less favorable than that accorded to other individuals and enterprises in respect of: (a) the procurement of inputs and goods and services necessary for production and the conditions under which their goods are produced, marketed or sold, in the domestic market and for export; and (b) the prices and the availability of goods and services supplied by national and subnational authorities and public or state enterprises, in areas including transportation, energy, basic telecommunications, other utilities and factors of production.[1]

In addition, national treatment is also required under the Constitutional Law and the Foreign Trade Law. In particular, under the Foreign Trade Law, China shall, in accordance with the international treaties and the agreements to which it is a contracting party or a participating party, grant the other contracting parties, or participating parties, or on the principle of reciprocity grant the other party most-favored-nation treatment or national treatment in the field of foreign trade.[2]

(2) Transparency

Under the Protocol on China's accession to the WTO, China undertakes that only those laws, regulations and other measures pertaining to or affecting trade in goods or the control of foreign exchange that are published, and readily available to other WTO members, individuals and enterprises, shall be enforced. In addition, China shall make available to WTO members, upon request, all laws, regulations and other measures pertaining to or affecting trade in goods or the control of foreign exchange before such measures are implemented or enforced. In emergency situations, laws, regulations and other measures shall be made available at the latest when they are implemented or enforced.

China designates *China Foreign Trade and Economic Cooperation Gazette* as the official journal dedicated to the publication of all laws, regulations and other measures pertaining to or affecting trade in goods or the control of foreign exchange and, after publication of its laws, regulations or other measures in such journal.

China shall establish or designate an enquiry point where, upon request of any individual, enterprise or WTO member, all information related to the measures required to be published under paragraph 2(C)1 of this Protocol, may be obtained.[3]

The Foreign Trade Law underpins the transparency, requiring the authority responsible

---

1 Article 3 of the Protocol on the Accession of China.

2 Article 6 of the Foreign Trade Law.

3 Article 2 of the Protocol on the Accession of China.

for foreign trade shall give a notice in case of initiating foreign trade investigations. The investigation may take the form of questionnaires in writing, hearings, on-the-spot investigations, entrusted investigations and otherwise, and the authority shall, on the basis of the findings, submit investigation reports or make determinations and give public notices.[1] Furthermore, the state establishes the foreign trade public information service system, providing foreign trade dealers and the public with information services.[2]

Finally, the Legislation Law, the Administrative License Law and the Ordinance on Governmental Information Disclosure also provide clauses concerning transparency related to foreign trade in China.

3. Relationship between WTO law and Chinese law

There is currently a lack of settled law concerning the direct effect of WTO treaties within the Chinese domestic legal system. China has a monist approach that an international treaty becomes part of domestic law automatically upon ratification and will immediately be valid under the Chinese legal system once that treaty enters into force under international law.[3]

The Constitutional Law is silent on the hierarchy between the WTO Law and the Chinese Law. However, the General Principles of the Civil Law stipulates that if any international treaty concluded or acceded to by China contains provisions differing from those in the General Principles of civil laws, the provisions of the international treaty shall apply, unless the provisions are ones on which China has announced reservations. Moreover, international practice may be applied on matters for which neither the Chinese law nor any international treaty concluded or acceded to by China has any relevant provisions.[4]

4. Agency system in foreign trade

The foreign trade agency system, also known as "import and export agency system", is an essential system that China has long established in which foreign trade enterprises offer services to domestic commodity suppliers and recipients by representing them in handling import and export issues. The foreign trade agency system was introduced in Chinese practice in 1984 and was regulated within the China's regulation framework when the Ministry of Foreign Trade and Economic Relations[5] issued the Provisional Rules on Foreign Trade Agency System in 1991. In accordance with the Foreign Trade Law which provides that foreign trade dealers may accept the

---

1 Article 38 of the Foreign Trade Law.

2 Article 54 of the Foreign Trade Law.

3 Simon Lester, Bryan Mercurio, *et al.*, *World Trade Law: Text, Materials and Commentary*, Hart Publishing, 2008, p.147.

4 Article 142 of the General Principles of the Civil Law.

5 It was superseded in 2003 by the Ministry of Foreign Trade and Economic Cooperation.

authorization of others and conduct foreign trade as an agent within its scope of business,[1] there are two forms of foreign trade agency in China, i.e., direct agency and indirect agency.

• Direct Agency: the agent acts as an import or export business agent for another corporation or enterprise (principal), and signs contracts with the foreign party in the name of this principal. The General Principles of the Civil Law and the Contract Law are applied to the rights and responsibilities of both parties in the case of direct agency.

• Indirect Agency: the agent enters into the contracts with foreign parties in his own name where the Foreign Trade Law is applicable to the rights and responsibilities of both parties.

Figure 1: Direct Agency

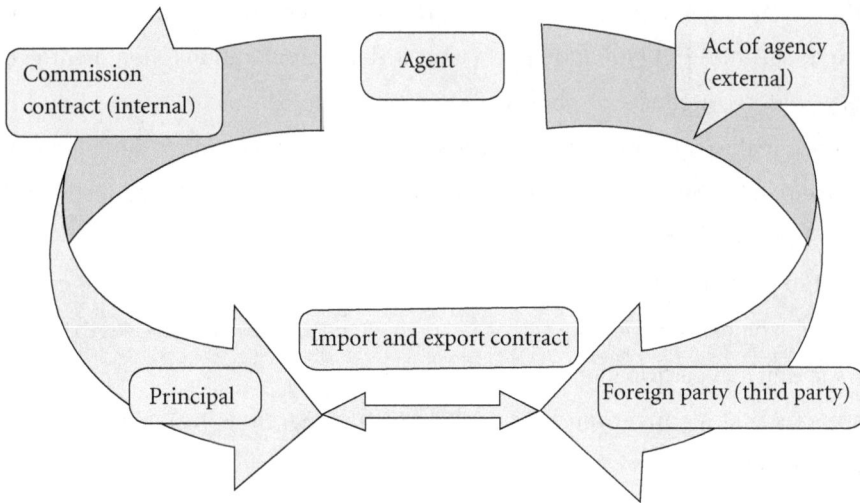

Figure 2: Indirect Agency

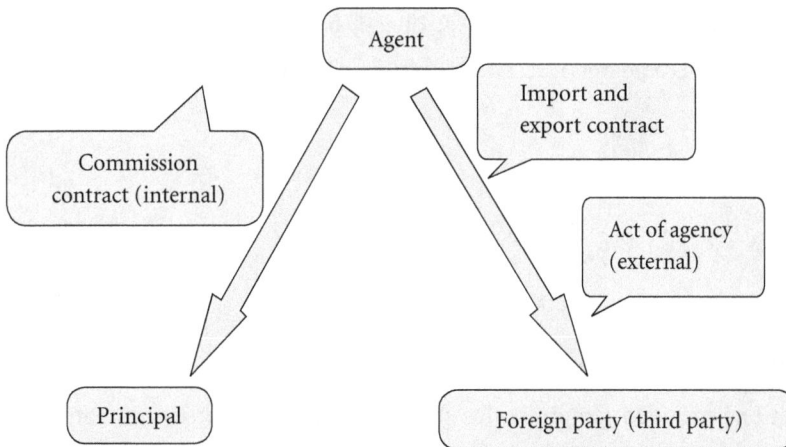

---

1 Article 12 of the Foreign Trade Law (2004).

Part 2　Tariffs Protection

Basic discipline

WTO negotiations produce general rules that apply to all members; meanwhile, individual member governments may also make specific commitments. The specific commitments are listed in documents called "schedules of concessions," which reflect specific tariff concessions and other commitments that they have given in the context of trade negotiations, such as the Uruguay Round.

For trade in goods in a general context, schedules of concessions usually consist of maximum tariff levels which are often referred to as "bound tariffs" or "bindings." In the case of agricultural products, these concessions and commitments are also related to tariff rate quotas, limits on export subsidies, and some kinds of domestic support.

Under normal situations, all WTO members have a schedule of concessions, which is either annexed to the Marrakesh Protocol to the GATT 1994 or to a Protocol of Accession. The content of the schedules changes over time to take account of different modifications.[1] This is the reason why determining a member's concession for a specific tariff line could involve, in some cases, examining several different legal instruments.

In a nutshell, WTO members are authorized to impose a tariff on an imported product at the time of import, but the tariff must be applied in accordance with the MFN principle under the WTO law. In addition, members may commit to binding certain customs duties that may usually be understood as committing to maximum duties for particular products.

In general, a WTO member's goods schedule consists of four elements.

Table 3: Member's Goods Schedule

	Most Favored Nation tariffs: *i.e.*, records the maximum tariff levels that can be imposed on goods originating from other WTO members.
Elements I	Elements I is further divided into: section I: A - agricultural products–tariffs; section I: B - agricultural products–tariff quotas; section II - other products (which are referred to as "non-agricultural" products in the context of the Doha negotiations)
Elements II	Preferential Tariffs: records (historical) preferential tariff arrangements listed in Article I of the GATT 1994.
Elements III	Non-Tariff Concessions: enumerates concessions made related to non-tariff measures.
Elements IV	Agricultural Products-Commitments Limiting Subsidization: records specific commitments on domestic support and export subsidies on agricultural products.

WTO members' basic obligations under their schedules may be found in Article II of the GATT. In brief, this article sets forth the following rules depicted in the following Table.

---

1   E.g., GATT article XXVIII negotiations or rectification procedures.

Table 4: Tariffs Obligation Under GATT

Article II: 1(a)	Requires members to accord to the commerce of the other members treatment no less favorable than that provided for in their Schedules.
	This means that the treatment can in practice be more favorable if the member so decides.
Article II: 1 (b) first sentence	Provides the basic disciplines on tariffs/ordinary customs duties. This is the legal foundation for the "bound tariffs" in the GATT 1994.
	Please note that this treatment is to be granted in an unconditional manner, unless there are "terms, conditions or qualifications" in the Schedule limiting such concession.
Article II: 1 (b) second sentence	Sets forth the basic disciplines on "other duties or charges" (ODCs).
Article II: 1 (c)	Sets forth the rules applicable to products entitled to preferential treatment as provided in members' Schedules.
Article II: 2	Lists the charges and duties that are not covered by the disciplines in Article II and which may be applied to products in excess of those provided in the Schedules (as long as the relevant provisions are respected).
Article II: 3	Prohibits members from altering their methods of determining dutiable value or methods of converting currencies so as to impair the value of tariff concessions.
	Please note that the determination of value for customs purposes is regulated by Article VII of GATT and the Agreement on Customs Valuation.
Article II: 4	Establishes disciplines for those cases in which imports into a certain members are to take place under a monopoly.
Article II: 5	Lays down procedures to address a situation in which a member believes that the treatment contemplated in a concession by another member is not being provided.
Article II: 6	Provides that currency revaluations should not undermine the value of tariff concessions expressed in terms of specific duties, for which it makes reference to the rules of the International Monetary Fund, which at the time were based on the "gold standard".
Article II: 7	Specifies the legal status of a Schedule as an integral part of the GATT 1994. Since the GATT 1994 is an integral part of the WTO Agreement, Schedules of concessions are also an integral part of the WTO Agreement.

The Mechanics of binding the duties

1. The harmonized system

In order to bind duties, WTO negotiators first had to agree on a common language to describe goods, and then exchange concessions based on this common language. The Harmonized System supplies the common language. The tariff schedules follow the format called the Harmonized Commodity Description and Coding System (Harmonized System), established by the World Customs Organization (WCO). This system for classifying goods trade internationally entered into force in 1988 for those countries which were members of WCO. It contains more than 5,000 six-digit subheadings, which may be subdivided further to reflect national administrative and statistical requirements.

Under the system, the broadest categories of products are identified by two-digit "chapters" (e.g., 04 is for dairy products, eggs and other edible animal products). These are then sub-divided by adding more digits: the higher the number of digits, the more detailed the categories. The codes are standardized up to six digits, the most detailed level that can be compared internationally.

Based on the Harmonized System classification, trading nations will exchange, on a reciprocal basis, tariff concessions on various goods. Article II of GATT explains the legal obligations assumed in this context.

2. Typology, multilateral trade negotiations and certification of schedules

As for the typology of ordinary customs duties, consolidated concessions (that is, bound import duties) are, in practice, expressed in:[1]

- *Ad valorem* duties

An *ad valorem* duty is a tariff that is expressed as a percentage of the value of the imported product. Duties are *ad valorem* when they are based on the value of an import.

- **Specific duties**[2]

Specific duties require importers to pay amounts based on imported goods' characteristics such as units, weight or surface area.

- **Compound duties**

Duties are compound when they are based on both the value and characteristic of imported goods.

- **Alternative duties (or mixed duties)**

Duties are alternative or mixed when they are valued at the minimum or maximum resulted from

---

1   See Michael Trebilcock, Robert Howse and Antonia Eliason, *The Regulation of International Trade*, Routledge, 2013, p.268.

2   Customs duties can be designated in either specific or *ad valorem* terms or as a mix of the two. In case of a specific duty, a concrete sum is charged for a quantitative description of the good.E.g., a tax of 20 cents per kilogramme of a product would be a specific tariff. The customs value of the good does not need to be determined, as the duty is not based on the value of the good but on other criteria. In this case, no rules on customs valuation are needed and the Valuation Agreement does not apply. In contrast, an *ad valorem* duty depends on the value of a good. E.g., a 20 per cent tariff on the value of an imported airplane is an *ad valorem* tariff.

alternative forms of duty calculation methods such as *ad valorem* and specific.

- **Technical duties**

Technical duties are based on particular factors that are quite product-specific such as alcohol and sugar content.

Concessions will be exchanged in multilateral trade negotiations, the so-called trade rounds. Article XXVIII of the GATT provides that there is not a pre-determined kick off for any round; and it is the WTO membership that will decide, when warranted, to open up multilateral talks. At the end of a round, schedules will be certified (validated) through a multilateral process. Clarifications might be sought and, eventually, the Protocol shall be registered under the provisions of article 102 of the UN Charter.[1] As long as tariffs have been consolidated (bound),WTO members cannot impose duties above their level (tariff ceilings that they have negotiated). Lower duties are applicable. It is also worth mentioning that the schedule may be subject to changes, such as switching between different types of duties (within the tariff ceiling), withdrawing concessions from members leaving the WTO, renegotiating the tariff protection, rectifying and modifying the schedule.

From customs valuation to trade facilitation

1. Customs valuation

Once duties are shipped from one country to the other, they will form the object of customs valuation which is a customs procedure applied by customs authorities to determine the customs value of imported goods. Customs authorities engage, by and large, in this procedure as a means of protecting tariff concessions, collecting revenue for the governing authorities, implementing trade policy, protecting public health and safety.

Article VII of the GATT outlines the requirements for Customs Valuation purposes, and is applicable to all WTO members. The Agreement on Implementation of Article VII, known as the WTO Agreement on Customs Valuation or the "Valuation Agreement", ensures that determinations of the customs value for the application of duty rates to imported goods are conducted in a fair, neutral and uniform manner, precluding the use of arbitrary or fictitious customs values.[2]

The primary basis for customs valuation under the agreement is the "transaction value" which is the price actually paid or payable for the goods when sold for export to the country of importation.[3] The methods of customs valuation, in descending order of precedence, are:

- Transaction value of merchandise in question—price actually paid or payable for the goods sold (Article I);

---

1 See Petros C. Mavroidis, *Trade in Goods: The GATT and the Other Agreements Regulating Trade in Goods,* Oxford University Press, 2008, pp.78-86.

2 See preamble of the Agreement on Implementation of Article VII of the GATT 1994.

3 Article I of the Agreement on Implementation of Article VII of the GATT 1994.

- Transaction value of identical merchandise (article 2);
- Transaction value of similar merchandise (article 3);
- Deductive value (article 5);
- Computed value (article 6);
- Derivative method (article 7).

2. Trade facilitation

Trade facilitation is the simplification and harmonization of international trade procedures, including both import and export procedures. To be precise, trade facilitation aims at examining how procedures and controls governing the movement of goods across national borders can be improved to reduce associated cost burdens and maximize efficiency without prejudice to safeguarding legitimate regulatory objectives. Procedures in this context largely refer to the activities (both practices and formalities) involved in collecting, presenting, communicating and processing the data required for movement of goods in international trade.

Trade Facilitation became a topic of discussion at the WTO at the Singapore Ministerial Conference in December 1996, when members directed the Council for Trade in Goods "to undertake exploratory and analytical work…on the simplification of trade procedures in order to assess the scope for WTO rules in this area."[1] In line with the "Bali Package" adopted in December 2013, WTO members adopted on 27 November 2014 a Protocol of Amendment to insert the new Agreement into Annex 1A of the WTO Agreement. The Trade Facilitation Agreement will enter into force once two-thirds of members have completed their domestic ratification process. In February 2017, Chad and Rwanda—along with Oman and Jordan—ratified the Trade Facilitation Agreement, pushing the Agreement past its necessary two-thirds threshold among WTO members to enter into force. The agreement is the first major agreement to have been reached by WTO members since the conclusion of the Uruguay Round 20 years ago.

The Trade Facilitation Agreement creates binding commitments across its WTO members to expedite movement, release and clear goods, and improve cooperation among WTO members on customs matters, and help developing countries fully implement the obligations.[2] The agreement will increase customs efficiency and effective collection of revenue, and help small businesses access new export opportunities through measures like transparency in customs practices, reduction of documentary requirements, and processing of documents before goods' arrival.

---

1   Singapore Ministerial Declaration, para.21.

2   Technical assistance for trade facilitation is provided by the WTO, WTO members and other intergovernmental organizations (including the World Bank, the World Customs Organization and the United Nations Conference on Trade and Development). In July 2014, the WTO announced the launch of the Trade Facilitation Agreement Facility, which would assist developing and least-developed countries in implementing the WTO's Trade Facilitation Agreement. The Facility becomes operational with the adoption of the Trade Facilitation Protocol.

In general, the Trade Facilitation Agreement

- contains provisions for expediting the movement, release and clearance of goods, including goods in transit;
- sets out measures for effective cooperation between customs and other appropriate authorities on trade facilitation and customs compliance issues;
- contains provisions for technical assistance and capacity building in this area.

The key disciplines of the Trade Facilitation Agreement include

- publication of laws, regulations and procedures;
- internet publication of practical steps to import, export and transit goods;
- enquiry point for trade information;
- information on new laws and regulations before their implementation;
- provision of advance rulings;
- enhanced right of appeal;
- notification of detained goods;
- disciplines on fees and charges;
- penalty disciplines to prevent conflicts of interest;
- pre-arrival processing of goods;
- use of electronic payment;
- use of guarantees to allow rapid release;
- promoting risk management;
- creation of authorized operator schemes;
- procedures for expedited shipments;
- quick release of perishable goods;
- reduced documents and formalities;
- utilizing common customs standards;
- promoting use of single window;
- uniformity in border procedures and documents;
- temporary admission of goods;
- simplified transit procedures;
- customs cooperation; and
- facilitate developing country implementation.

Chinese law

The Regulations on Import and Export Duties (2004) and the Notice of the Customs Tariff Commission of the State Council on Issues Concerning the Power to Interpret the Regulation on Import and Export Duties (2004) shall be applied, in general terms, to the goods that are allowed to be imported into or exported from China. On balance, the following points highlight the

Chinese law on tariffs protection.

1. Tariff commission

The Tariff Commission is established by the State Council, which is responsible for:

- handling the adjustment and interpretation of tariff headings, tariff lines and tariff rates of the Customs Tariffs and the Table of Tariff Rates of Import Duties of Entry Articles;
- making decisions on goods on which temporary tariff rates are to be applied, the tariff rates to be applied, and period of application of the temporary tariff rates;
- determining tariff rate quota; determining whether or not to levy anti-dumping duties, countervailing duties, safeguard duties, retaliatory duties, and other measures with regard to duties.

2. Tariff rates

Import duties are categorized as the Most-Favored-Nation tariff rate, contractual tariff rate, preferential tariff rate, normal tariff rate, tariff-rate quota (TRQ) rate, retaliatory tariff rate and others. Temporary tariff rate may be applied to imported goods within a specified period of time.

3. Determination of customs value

Customs value of imported goods is determined by the customs according to the transaction value conforming to the terms and conditions in article 3 of the Regulations and on the basis of the transportation and related fees and insurance of the goods up to the point they are to be unloaded at the destination in China.

SELF QUIZ: Indicate whether each of the following statements is true or false.

11. The extent of bindings of customs duties varies from one WTO member to another, and is the outcome of trade negotiations.

12. An *ad valorem* tariff is based on a fixed percentage of the value of the good that is being imported, while a specific tariff relies on a designated amount of money that does not vary with the price of the product.

13. The WTO defined trade facilitation as "the simplification and harmonization of international trade procedures" while trade procedures are the "activities, practices and formalities involved in collecting, presenting, communicating and processing data required for the movement of goods in international trade."

14. Trade facilitation aims at simplifying not only the documentation required to clear goods, but also the procedures employed by border agencies.

Part 3　Non-tariff Barriers to Trade: Rules of Origin

Basic discipline

A number of WTO agreements deal with a variety of bureaucratic or legal issues that could involve hindrances to trade.[1] In particular, "rules of origin" are the criteria used to define where a product was made. Rules of origin are used:

- to implement measures and instruments of commercial policy such as anti-dumping duties and safeguard measures;
- to determine whether imported products shall receive most-favored-nation treatment or preferential treatment;
- for the purpose of trade statistics;
- for the application of labeling and marking requirements;
- for government procurement.

There are two common types of rules of origin depending upon application, namely, the preferential and non-preferential rules of origin. The Agreement on Rules of Origin provides a useful definition for the harmonized non-preferential rules of origin and for the preferential rules of origin.

- Non-preferential rules of origin shall be defined as those laws, regulations and administrative determinations of general application applied by any member to determine the country of origin of goods.
- Preferential rules of origin shall be defined as those laws, regulations and administrative determinations of general application applied by any member to determine whether goods qualify for preferential treatment under contractual or autonomous trade regimes leading to the granting of tariff preferences going beyond the application of paragraph a of Article 1 of GATT 1994.

Origin criteria

In general, two basic criteria are applied in determining the country of origin of goods, namely, wholly-obtained criterion and substantial transformation criterion[2].

Wholly-obtained goods refer to goods that naturally occurr, live animals born and raised in a given country, plants harvested in a given country, and minerals extracted or taken in a single country.

The definition of wholly-obtained also covers goods produced from wholly-obtained goods alone or scrap and waste derived from manufacturing or processing operations or from consumption.

For a product which has been produced in more than one country, the product shall be determined to have origin in the country where the last substantial transformation took place. To determine exactly what the last substantial transformation was, three general rules are applied:

1　E.g., the Agreement on Import Licensing Procedures and the Preshipment Inspection Agreement.

2　The World Customs Organization, Rule of Origin-Handbook.

- a criterion of a change of tariff classification

  A good is considered substantially transformed when the good is classified in a heading or subheading (depending on the exact rule) different from all non-originating materials used.

- a criterion of value added (*ad valorem* percentages)

  Regardless a change in its classification, a good is considered substantially transformed when the value added of a good increases up to a specified level expressed by *ad valorem* percentage. The value added criterion can be expressed in two ways, namely a maximum allowance for non-originating materials or a minimum requirement of domestic content.

- a criterion of manufacturing or processing operations

  Regardless a change in its classification, a good is considered substantially transformed when the good has undergone specified manufacturing or processing operations.

Chinese law on rules of origin

The rules on the origin of export goods and their implementation provisions primarily govern the origin of export goods in China. In general terms, the origin of export goods is in China if the export goods meet one of the following criteria:

- products made or manufactured fully in China, including
  - mineral products extracted from the territory and the continental shelves of China;
  - plants and their products harvested or collected within the territory of China;
  - animals and their products multiplied or bred within the territory of China;
  - products obtained from hunting or fishing within the territory of China;
  - the aquatic and other products or their processed products obtained from the sea by ships or other means of China;
  - wastes and waste materials recycled in the course of production and processing within the territory of China and other discarded and waste materials collected within the territory of China;
  - products made or processed fully from the aforementioned products and other non-import raw materials within the territory of China.
- products containing imported materials or spare parts finished or processed mainly within the territory of China, thus making substantial alterations in the appearance, nature, state or purposes of the imported materials or spare parts.

Part 4   Technical Barriers to Trade

Basic discipline

Technical barriers to trade are a category of non-tariff barriers to trade under the WTO framework.

They are the broadly different measures that states use to regulate markets, protect their consumers, or preserve their natural resources or other objectives on the one hand, while the measures can also be used, or at least perceived by foreign states to discriminate against imports with the intention of protecting domestic industries on the other.

The Agreement on Technical Barriers to Trade (TBT Agreement) establishes rules governing the way WTO members use technical barriers and is to make certain, as a preventive instrument, that measures taken by members do not result in discrimination or arbitrary restrictions on international trade. More specifically, the TBT Agreement is an agreement which ensures that regulations, standards, testing and certification procedures do not create unnecessary obstacles, while also providing members with the right to implement measures to achieve legitimate policy objectives, such as the protection of human health and safety, and environment.

There are six principles at the core of the WTO TBT Agreement:

1. Non-discrimination and national treatment

The principle requires that a measure taken by a WTO member should not discriminate among different importing members, and should apply in the same way to both imports and similar domestic goods.

The non-discrimination obligation has two elements: "most-favored-nation treatment" which is an obligation not to discriminate between "like products" imported from different WTO members and "national treatment" which is an obligation not to discriminate between domestic and imported "like products".

2. Transparency

The principle requires that a WTO member planning to introduce a measure that might have an important impact on trade should notify this plan to the WTO, and take into account comments submitted by other countries on the draft legislation.

The TBT Committee has emphasized that transparency is a "fundamental pillar" in the implementation of the TBT Agreement and a key element of good regulatory practice.[1]

An OECD study concludes that "transparency mechanisms applied at different stages of the design, finalization and implementation of domestic regulation significantly contribute in identifying and addressing potential barriers to domestic economic activity and international trade and investment".[2]

3. Harmonization

The principle requires that members are encouraged to participate in the international

---

1   G/TBT/26, 12 November 2009, para 29.

2   Evdokia Möisé, *Transparency Mechanisms and Non-Tariff Measures: Case Studies*, OECD Trade Policy Working Paper No. 111, TAD/TC/WP(2010)4/FINAL, 18 March, 2011, para 78.

harmonization of standards, and to use agreed international standards as a basis for domestic technical regulations and standards.

The emphasis on harmonization is based on the view that (i) trade is disrupted less if members use internationally agreed standards as a basis for domestic regulations and standards, and(ii) producers and consumers benefit from a degree of harmonization (because of economies of scale and questions of technical compatibility respectively).

4. Proportionality

The principle requires that a measure should not be more trade restrictive than necessary to achieve the legitimate goal pursued.

Technical regulations, standards and conformity assessment procedures must not be prepared, adopted or applied to create unnecessary obstacles to international trade.

5. Use of relevant international standards

The principle requires that whenever possible, international standards should be used as a basis for technical regulations. Article 2.4 of the TBT Agreement provides that where technical regulations are required and relevant international standards exist or their completion is imminent, members shall use them, or the relevant parts of them, as a basis for their technical regulations except when such international standards or relevant parts would be an ineffective or inappropriate means for the fulfillment of the legitimate objectives pursued, for instance because of fundamental climatic or geographical factors or fundamental technological problems.

6. Equivalence and mutual recognition

The principle requires that WTO members should consider accepting technical regulations of other members as equivalent to their own, provided that these measures are an effective way of addressing the objectives pursued. Members are encouraged to enter into negotiations for the mutual recognition of the results of conformity assessment procedures.

The Coverage

The TBT Agreement is applicable to "technical regulations", "standards" and "conformity assessment procedures" and aims to ensure that these regulations, standards and procedures are non-discriminatory and do not create unnecessary obstacles to international trade.

As to the definition of "technical regulations", it is defined by the Annex 1.1 of the TBT Agreement as document which lays down product characteristics or their related processes and production methods, including the applicable administrative provisions, with which compliance is mandatory. It may also include or deal exclusively with terminology, symbols, packaging, marking or labelling requirements as they apply to a product, process or production method.

The Appellate Body in *EC–Sardines* held that if a measure is a technical regulation:

i. the document applies to an identifiable product or group of products;

ii. the document must lay down one or more product characteristics;

iii. compliance with these characteristics must be mandatory.[1]

A "standard" is defined in Annex 1.2 of the TBT Agreement:

Document approved by a recognized body, that provides, for common and repeated use, rules, guidelines or characteristics for products or related processes and production methods, with which compliance is not mandatory. It may also include or deal exclusively with terminology, symbols, packaging, marking or labeling requirements as they apply to a product, process or production method.

A "conformity assessment" procedure is set forth in Annex 1.3 of the TBT Agreement:

Any procedure used, directly or indirectly, to determine that relevant requirements in technical regulations or standards are fulfilled.

CASE EXAMPLE: *European Communities—Asbestos*[2]

Facts: French Government which had previously been an importer of large quantities of chrysotile asbestos imposed a ban on the substance as well as on products that contained asbestos and asbestos fibres, so as to control the health risks associated with asbestos. Therefore, Canada brought the case in the WTO against the EU. Brazil, Zimbabwe and the US participated in the case as third parties. One of the most essential issues analyzed by the Appellate Body was the criteria for determining if the EU measure constituted a technical regulation.

The Appellate Body held that: the EU Decree should have been examined as a whole. Accordingly, the Appellate Body proposes the following criteria to identify if the measure in question is a technical regulation:[3]

- The document must apply to an identifiable product or group of products: It is important to note that a product does not necessarily have to be mentioned explicitly in a document for that product to be an identifiable product, as "identifiable" does not mean "expressly identified."

---

1 Appellate Body Report, *EC—Sardines*, WT/DS231/AB/R, 16 September 2002, paras. 175–176. The AB stated that:

   "As we explained in EC—Asbestos [at paragraph 59], whether a measure is a "technical regulation" is a threshold issue because the outcome of this issue determines whether the TBT Agreement is applicable. If the measure before us is not a "technical regulation", then it does not fall within the scope of the TBT Agreement.

   We interpreted this definition in EC—Asbestos [at paragraphs 66–70]. In doing so, we set out three criteria that a document must meet to fall within the definition of "technical regulation" in the TBT Agreement. First, the document must apply to an identifiable product or group of products. The identifiable product or group of products need not, however, be expressly identified in the document. Second, the document must lay down one or more characteristics of the product. These product characteristics may be intrinsic, or they may be related to the product. They may be prescribed or imposed in either a positive or a negative form. Third, compliance with the product characteristics must be mandatory. "

2 Appellate Body Report, European Communities—Measures Affecting Asbestos and Products Containing Asbestos, WT/DS135, 12 March., 2001.

3 Ibid, paras. 67-69, 180.

- The document lay down one or more characteristics of the product: paragraph 1 of Annex 1 gives certain examples of "product characteristics" which may be prescribed or imposed in either a positive or a negative form, and which include not only features and qualities intrinsic to the product itself but also related "characteristics," such as the means of identification, the presentation and the appearance of a product;
- Compliance with the product characteristics must be mandatory: A technical regulation must regulate the "characteristics" of products in a binding or compulsory fashion. It follows that, with respect to products, a "technical regulation" has the effect of prescribing or imposing one or more "characteristics."

Take-away points: a ban as an "integrated whole" is a "technical regulation" as defined in Annex 1.1 and thus covered by the TBT Agreement, if (i) the products subject to the ban are identifiable (i.e., any products containing asbestos in this case); (ii) the measure was a whole laid down product; and (iii) compliance with the measure is mandatory.

Chinese law on TBT

Compared to EU's comprehensive policy related to standards, testing and certification requirements and a widespread set of instruments to combat the market-segmenting effect of technical trade barriers, there is still a scarcity of a uniform regulation system specifying standards and technical instructions assessment applicable to a variety of industry sectors and regions in China. Ordinarily, laws and regulations concerning technical trade barriers can be identified dispersedly in the Foreign Trade Law, the Law on Product Quality, Standardization Law, the Food Sanitation Law, the Drug administration law and other laws. Among these laws, the Law on Import and Export Commodity Inspection spells out the general requirements as to the inspection of commodity in China.

1. Inspection authorities
- The State Administration of Commodity Inspection is in charge of the inspection work of import and export commodities for the whole country. The local import and export commodity inspection authorities set up by the State Administration of Commodity Inspection shall be responsible for the inspection work of import and export commodities in regions under their jurisdiction.
- The State Administration of Commodity Inspection shall adjust and publish the List of Import and Export Commodities Subject to Inspection Enforced by the Commodity Inspection Authorities.

2. Inspection
- Inspection on import and export commodities performed by the commodity inspection authorities shall cover: quality, specifications, quantity, weight, packing and requirements for

safety and sanitation/hygiene.

- Import and export commodities governed by the compulsory standards or the inspection standards which must be complied with as provided by the laws or administrative rules/regulations shall be inspected in accordance with such compulsory standards or the inspection standards.
- In the absence of such stipulations, import and export commodities shall be inspected in accordance with the inspection standards agreed upon the foreign trade contract stipulations.

Part 5   Sanitary and Phytosanitary Measures

Basic discipline

The Agreement on the Application of Sanitary and Phytosanitary Measures (SPS Agreement) is an agreement on how governments can apply food safety and animal and plant health measures (sanitary and phytosanitary measures). The Agreement sets out the basic rules concerning the application of sanitary and phytosanitary measures. It was negotiated during the Uruguay Round, and entered into force with the establishment of the WTO at the beginning of 1995.

The objectives of the SPS Agreement set forth in the preamble of the agreement stipulate that:

- No member should be prevented from adopting or enforcing measures necessary to protect human, animal or plant life or health;
- Members are not required to change their appropriate level of protection of human, animal or plant life or health;

At the same time sanitary and phytosanitary measures are not applied in a manner that constitutes:

- a means of arbitrary or unjustifiable discrimination between members where the same conditions prevail;
- a disguised restriction on international trade.

The coverage

The SPS Agreement applies to all measures which have the purpose to protect, within the territory of a member:

- animal and plant life or health from the entry, establishment or spread of pests, disease-carrying or disease-causing organisms;
- human or animal life or health from food-borne risks (risks arising from additives, contaminants, toxins or disease-causing organisms in foods, beverages or feedstuffs);
- human life or health from diseases carried by animals, plants or products thereof;
- a member's territory from other damage arising from the entry, establishment or spread of pests.

Measures taken to protect the health of fish and wild fauna, as well as of forests and wild flora, from the risks stated above are also within its scope of application. It is noteworthy that pests include weeds, while contaminants include pesticide and veterinary drug residues and extraneous matter.[1] Meanwhile, SPS measures taken by members are subject to the following conditions and limitations:

The Panel in *EC-Hormones* identified two requirements that must be met for a measure to fall within the realm of the SPS Agreement: "According to Article 1.1 of the SPS Agreement, two requirements need to be fulfilled for the SPS Agreement to apply: (i) the measure in dispute is a sanitary or phytosanitary measure; and (ii) the measure in dispute may, directly or indirectly, affect international trade."[2]

TBT or SPS?

There is no doubt that quarantine policies play a key role in ensuring the protection of human, animal and plant health. Yet under the SPS agreement, quarantine barriers can be, however, a "technical trade barrier" used to keep out foreign competitors.[3]

Taking international trade of apples for example:

Figure 3: TBT and SPS Measures Relating to the International Trade of Apples

ENGLISH COX

TBT
Minimum size of apple
Colour of pericarp
Packaging

SPS
Use of anti-pest sprays

Special provisions for developing countries

Normally, the general disciplines of the SPS Agreement apply equally to developed and developing countries. Nevertheless, given that developing countries may find implementation challenging due to resource constraints and limited expertise, the SPS Agreement does reflect a special recognition of the financial and technical resource constraints that developing states face.

---

1   Footnote 4 to Annex A.

2   Panel Reports, *Canada-Continued Suspension of Obligation in the EC-Hormones Dispute,* WT/DS321/R, 31 March 2008, paras.8.36, 8.39.

3   See Pradip Kumar Sinha, Sanchari Sinha, *International Business Management: A Global Perspective,* Excel Books, 2012, p.276.

Table 5: Technical Assistance and Special Treatment

Technical assistance	WTO members agree to facilitate the provision of technical assistance to other members, especially developing states, either bilaterally or through international organizations such as the Three Sisters[1]. The form of this technical assistance and how it can be provided is broadly defined.[2]	
	As a broad term, technical assistance encompasses:	• the provision of information to enhance member's understanding of their rights and obligations under the SPS Agreement;
		• the provision of practical and detailed training on the operation of the SPS Agreement; the provision of "soft" infrastructure (training and formation of technical and scientific personnel and the development of national regulatory frameworks);
		• "hard" infrastructure (laboratories, equipment, veterinary services, establishment of disease free areas).[3]
Special and differential treatment	Preparation and application of SPS measures	
	Phased-in introduction of measures	
	Reasonable adaptation period	
	Time-limited exemptions	
	Facilitation of participation in international organizations	
	Special provisions on notification	
	Transitional periods	

Chinese law on SPS

The Law on the Entry and Exit Animal and Plant Quarantine and its implementation regulations, the Law on the Frontier Health and Quarantine and its implementation regulations and the Customs Law are the primary laws concerning the Sanitary and Phytosanitary Measures in China. These laws have provided specific provisions relating to the quarantine authorities, prohibited items and frontier health and quarantine offices in China.

---

1 Codex (Joint FAO/WHO Codex Alimentarius Commission) responsible for food safety issues, IPPC (International Plant Protection Convention) responsible for plant health issues and OIE (World Organization for Animal Health) responsible for animal health and zoonoses, known as SPS's "three sisters," are the three international standard-setting bodies referenced in the SPS Agreement.

2 Article 9 of the SPS Agreement.

3 G/SPS/GEN/206, dated 18 October 2000.

1. Quarantine authorities

- An animal and plant quarantine department instituted under the State Council conducts a unified administration of the entry and exit animal and plant quarantine in China.
- The department in charge of the quarantine of animal products leaving the country for trade purposes shall be designated by the State Council as it deems appropriate.

2. Prohibited items

- Pathogenic micro-organisms (including seed cultures of bacteria and viruses) of animals and plants, insect pests and other harmful organisms;
- Relevant animals and plants, their products and other quarantine objects from countries or regions with prevalent epidemic animal or plant diseases;
- Animal carcasses;
- Soil.

3. Frontier health and quarantine offices

- Setting up at international seaports, airports and ports of entry at land frontiers and boundary rivers of China;
- Carrying out the quarantining and monitoring of infectious disease and health inspection.

SELF QUIZ: Indicate whether each of the following statements is true or false.

15. Rules of origin are the criteria needed to determine the national source of a product. Their importance is derived from the fact that duties and restrictions in several cases depend upon the source of imports.

16. Like many other WTO agreements, the TBT Agreement includes the GATT's national treatment and the most-favored-nation treatment obligations.

17. Members should not take into account the special needs of developing and particularly least-developed country members in the preparation and application of SPS measures.

18. The TBT Agreement covers three kinds of measures: technical regulations, standards and procedures taken by a government related to the assessment of conformity with technical regulations and standards ("conformity assessment procedures").

19. Negotiators introduced in the TBT Agreement a complementary approach to technical harmonization, known as "equivalence". Technical barriers to international trade could be eliminated if members accept that technical regulations different from their own fulfill the same policy objectives even if through different means.

20. The SPS Agreement requires that sanitary and phytosanitary measures be applied for no other purpose than that of ensuring food safety and animal and plant health.

21. China has developed a uniform regulation system specifying standards and technical instructions assessment applicable to a variety of industry sectors and regions.

Anti-dumping

1. Basic discipline

Dumping is not a concept defined in the Anti-dumping Agreement (AD Agreement), but it can be said, in general terms, that dumping is a kind of predatory pricing that occurs when the export by a country or company of a product at a price that is lower in the foreign market than the price charged in the domestic market. Article VI of the GATT 1994 and the AD Agreement explicitly authorize a member to impose specific anti-dumping measures on imports from a particular source, in addition to ordinary customs tariffs.

In general, a product is to be considered as being dumped when it is introduced into the commerce of another country at less than its "normal value", normally the comparable price at which the product is sold in the domestic market of the exporting country, or if there is in the absence of such domestic price, the highest comparable price for the like product for export to any third country in the ordinary course of trade, or the cost of production of the product in the country of origin plus a reasonable addition for selling cost and profit.

In brief, dumping would exist where the export price is lower than the domestic price.

From the definition of dumping as set forth in article VI of the GATT 1994, the following three elements are crucial to a proper determination of dumping:

- Normal value;
- Export price;
- Adjustments for factors affecting price comparability.

WTO members can impose anti-dumping measures only if the following three elements are demonstrated under article VI of the GATT 1994 and the AD Agreement:

- that dumping is occurring;
- that the domestic industry producing the like product in the importing country is suffering material injury or threat thereof, or that the establishment of a domestic industry is being materially retarded;
- that there is a causal link between the two.

2. Determination of dumping

The demonstration of foregoing elements should be done through an investigation. The investigation also needs to determine the margin or amount of dumping, which is indispensable for setting the permissible level of the eventual anti-dumping duty.

(1)   Determination of normal value

- The normal value is generally the price of the product at issue, in the ordinary course of trade, when destined for consumption in the exporting country market. In certain circumstances, for instance, when there are no sales in the domestic market, it may not be possible to determine the normal value on this basis. The Agreement provides alternative methods for the determination of normal value in such cases.

- The preferred method of establishing normal value in Australia, Canada, the EU and the US is the use of prices of sales transactions in the domestic market of the foreign producer provided that such sales (i) are in the ordinary course of trade; and (ii) permit a proper comparison with the export sales.[1]

(2) Determination of export price

- The export price will normally be based on the transaction price at which the foreign producer sells the product to an importer in the importing country.
- As is the case with normal value, the Agreement recognizes that this transaction price may not be appropriate for purposes of comparison.

(3) Fair comparison of normal value and export price

- The Agreement requires that a fair comparison of the export price and the normal value should be made. The basic requirements for a fair comparison are that the prices being compared are those of sales made at the same level of trade, generally the ex-factory level, and of sales made at as nearly as possible the same time.
- As part of the Agreement's requirements concerning transparency and participation, the investigating authorities are required to inform parties of the information needed to ensure a fair comparison, for instance, the information with respect to adjustments, allowances, and currency conversion, and may not impose an "unreasonable burden of proof" on parties.

(4) Calculation of dumping margins and duty assessment

- The Agreement contains rules governing the calculation of dumping margins. In the usual case, the Agreement requires either the comparison of the weighted average normal value to the weighted average of all comparable export prices, or a transaction-to-transaction comparison of normal value and export price (article 2.4.2).
- A different basis of comparison can be used provided that there is "targeted dumping", that is, a pattern which exists of export prices differing significantly among different purchasers, regions or time periods. In this case, if the investigating authorities provide an explanation to why such differences cannot be taken into account in weighted average-to-weighted average or transaction-to-transaction comparisons, the weighted average normal value can be compared to the export prices on individual transactions.

---

1   Edwin A. Vermulst, *The Antidumping Systems of Australia, Canada, the EEC and the USA: Have Anti Dumping Laws Become A Problem in International Trade?*,10 Mich. J. Int'l L. 765, 793 (1989).

- A broad formula for the calculation of the dumping margin is: Dumping Margin = Normal Value – Export Price

(5) Determination of injury and casual link

- An important decision must be made early in each investigation to determine the domestic "like product." "Like product" is defined in the Agreement as "a product which is identical, alike in all respects to the product under consideration or, in the absence of such a product, another product which, though not alike in all respects, has characteristics closely resembling those of the product under consideration."
- The determination involves first examining the imported product or products that are alleged to be dumped, and then establishing what domestically produced product or products are the appropriate "like product." The decision regarding the like product is of importance for the reasons that it is the basis of determining which companies constitute the domestic industry, and that determination in turn governs the scope of the investigation and determination of injury and causal link.

Figure 4: Dumping and Anti-Dumping

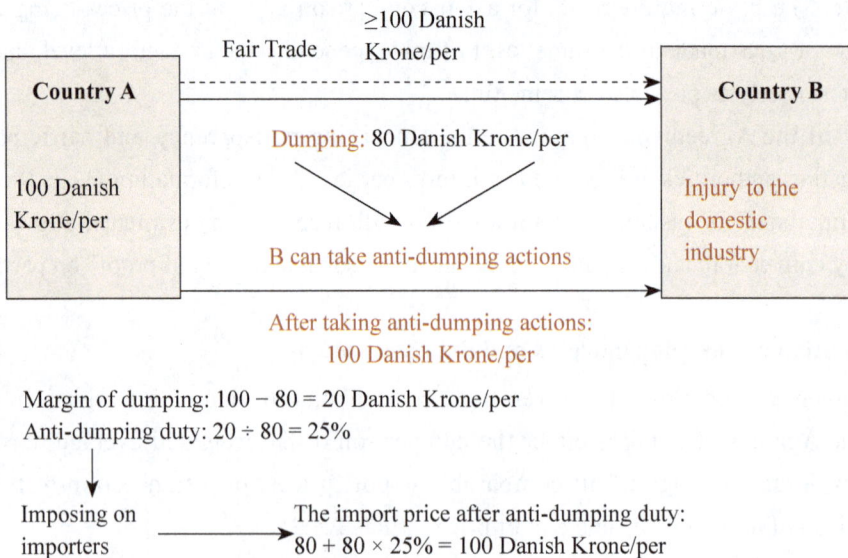

Margin of dumping: 100 − 80 = 20 Danish Krone/per
Anti-dumping duty: 20 ÷ 80 = 25%

Imposing on importers → The import price after anti-dumping duty: 80 + 80 × 25% = 100 Danish Krone/per

Subsidies and countervailing measures

1. Basic discipline

A subsidy is a grant or other financial contribution made by (or on behalf of) a government or public body which confers a benefit to the recipient.

Examples of subsidies are as follows:[1]

---

1   Article 1 of the Agreement of Subsidies and Countervailing Measures.

- a direct or potential transfer of funds (e.g., grants, loans, equity injection or loan guarantees);
- government revenues (which are otherwise due) are foregone or not collected (e.g., tax credits);
- government provision of goods and services (other than general infrastructure);
- government purchase of goods;
- any of the functions above performed by a private body (e.g., a bank) on the instruction of the government.

The Agreement on Subsidies and Countervailing Measures disciplines the use of subsidies, and it regulates the actions countries can take to counter the effects of subsidies. In accordance with the agreement, a country can use the WTO's dispute-settlement procedure to seek the withdrawal of the subsidy or the removal of its adverse effects. A country is also entitled to launch its own investigation and ultimately charge extra duty ("countervailing duty") on subsidized imports that are found to be hurting domestic producers.

2. Categories of specific subsidies

The agreement defines two categories of subsidies: prohibited and actionable.

(1) Prohibited subsidies

- Subsidies that require recipients to meet certain export targets, or to use domestic goods instead of imported goods.
- They are prohibited because they are specifically designed to distort international trade, and are therefore likely to hurt other countries' trade.
- They can be challenged in the WTO dispute settlement procedure where they are handled under an accelerated timetable.
- If the dispute settlement procedure confirms that the subsidy is prohibited, it must be withdrawn immediately. Otherwise, the complaining country can take counter measures. If domestic producers are hurt by imports of subsidized products, countervailing duty can be imposed.

(2) Actionable subsidies

- In this category the complaining country has to show that the subsidy has an adverse effect on its interests. Otherwise, the subsidy is permitted. The agreement defines three types of damage they can cause.
- One country's subsidies can hurt a domestic industry in an importing country. They can hurt rival exporters from another country when the two compete in a third market. Domestic subsidies in one country can hurt exporters trying to compete in the subsidizing country's domestic market.
- If the Dispute Settlement Body rules that the subsidy does have an adverse effect, the subsidy

must be withdrawn or its adverse effect must be removed. Again, if the domestic producers are hurt by the imports of subsidized products, countervailing duty can be imposed.

3. Countervailing measures

The Agreement on Subsidies and Countervailing Measures provides for two primary requirements that could be fulfilled for any imposition of countervailing measure. First, the agreement sets out the following substantive requirements:

- A member may not impose a countervailing measure unless it determines that there are subsidized imports, injury to a domestic industry, and a causal link between the subsidized imports and the injury.
- The existence of a specific subsidy must be determined in accordance with the criteria in part I of the agreement. However, the criteria regarding injury and causation are found in Part V.
- One significant development of the SCM Agreement in this area is the explicit authorization of the accumulation of the effects of subsidized imports from more than one member where specified criteria are fulfilled.
- In addition, Part V contains rules regarding the determination of the existence and amount of a benefit.

Second, the agreement contains detailed rules concerning the initiation and conduct of countervailing investigations, the imposition of preliminary and final measures, the use of undertakings, and the duration of measures. A few of the more significant innovations in the Agreement are identified below:

- Standing. The Agreement defines in numeric terms the circumstances, under which there is sufficient support from a domestic industry to justify initiation of an investigation.
- Preliminary investigation. The Agreement ensures the conduct of a preliminary investigation before a preliminary measure can be imposed.
- Undertakings. The Agreement places limitations on the use of undertakings to settle contervailing duty investigations, in order to avoid Voluntary Restraint Agreements or similar measures masquerading as undertakings.
- Sunset. The Agreement requires that a countervailing measure be terminated after five years unless it is determined that continuation of the measure is necessary to avoid the continuation or the recurrence of subsidization and injury.
- Judicial review. The Agreement requires that members create an independent tribunal to review the consistency of determinations of the investigating authority with domestic law.

Safeguard

1. Basic discipline

A WTO member may take a "safeguard" action (e.g., restricting imports of a product temporarily) to protect a specific domestic industry from an increase in imports of any product which is causing, or which is threatening to cause, serious injury to the industry.

The Agreement on Safeguards establishes rules for the application of safeguard measures by members, as provided in Article XIX of the GATT 1994. Effective safeguard rules are essential to the viability and integrity of the multilateral trading system. Among its key provisions, the Safeguards Agreement:

- requires a transparent, public process for making serious injury determinations;
- sets out clearer definitions of the criteria for serious injury determinations;
- requires that safeguard measures be steadily liberalized over their duration;
- establishes maximum periods for safeguard actions;
- requires a review no later than the mid-term of any measure with a duration exceeding three years;
- allows safeguard actions to be taken for three years, without the requirement of compensation or the possibility of retaliation.

It is noteworthy that safeguards were infrequently used, and some governments preferred to protect their industries through "grey area" measures ("voluntary" export restraint arrangements on products or orderly marketing agreements such as cars, steel and semiconductors). The Agreement on Safeguards broke new ground in prohibiting "grey area" measures, setting time limits ("sunset clause")[1] on all safeguard actions.

2. Conditions for the application of a safeguard measure

In brief, the conditions for the application of a safeguard measure are:

- The increased imports are sharp[2];
- Due to unforeseen developments;
- Causing (or threatening) serious injury to domestic industry (a higher level of injury than the material injury required for anti-dumping and anti-subsidy)[3].

To be precise, article 2 sets forth the conditions under which safeguard measures may be applied. These conditions are:

---

1   The agreement provides that safeguards should only be undertaken when WTO members with substantial interests have been consulted and agree to the restraint or receive appropriate compensation in the form of offsetting trade concessions. "Sunset" is a metaphor to describe that safeguard measures are temporary. See Kyle W. Bagwell, George A. Bermann, Petros C. Mavroidis (eds), *Law and Economics of Contingent Protection in International Trade* (Cambridge University Press, 2010) 402.

2   The "increase in imports must have been recent enough, sudden enough, sharp enough and significant enough ... to cause or threaten to cause serious injury". See the Appellate Body Report, *US-Steel Safeguards*, WT/DS248/AB/R; WT/DS249/AB/R; WT/DS251/AB/R; WT/DS252/AB/R; WT/DS253/AB/R; WT/DS254/AB/R; WT/DS258/AB/R; WT/DS259/AB/R, 10 November 2003, para 346.

3   "Article XIX and the Agreement on Safeguards confirm the right of WTO Members to apply safeguard measures when, as a result of unforeseen developments and of the effect of obligations incurred, including tariff concessions, a product is being imported in such increased quantities and under such conditions as to cause or threaten to cause serious injury to the domestic industry that produces like or directly competitive products. However, as Article 2.1 of the Agreement on Safeguards makes clear, the right to apply such measures arises "only" if these prerequisites are shown to exist". See ibid, para 264.

(1) Increased quantity of imports

The determination of increased quantity of imports that a member must make before it may apply a safeguard measure can be of either an absolute increase or an increase relative to domestic production.

(2) Injury: two possibilities

- Serious injury

  The Agreement defines "serious injury" as a significant overall impairment in the position of a domestic industry. In determining whether serious injury is present, investigating authorities are to evaluate all relevant factors having a bearing on the condition of the industry.

- Threat of serious injury

  "Threat of serious injury" is threat that is clearly imminent as shown by facts, and not based on mere allegation, conjecture or remote possibility. If present serious injury is not found, a safeguard measure nevertheless can be applied if a threat of serious injury is found.

The factors that may make influences on the determination of safeguard measure include:

• Domestic industry

A "domestic industry" is defined as the producers as a whole of the like or directly competitive products operating within the territory of a member, or producers who collectively account for a major proportion of the total domestic production of those products.

• Causation

A determination of serious injury cannot be made unless there is objective evidence of the existence of a causal link between increased imports of the product concerned and serious injury.

• Need for investigation

New safeguard measures may be applied only following an investigation conducted by competent authorities in accordance with established procedures. Under article XIX of GATT 1947, there is no explicit requirement for an investigation.

• Procedural transparency

Investigation procedures must be established and published prior to being used. Although the Agreement does not contain detailed procedural requirements, it does require reasonable public notice of the investigation.

• Participation by interested parties

Investigating authorities are required to hold public hearings or provide other appropriate means for interested parties (importers, exporters, producers, etc.) to present their views and to respond to the views of others with respect to the matters being investigated.

• Confidential information

As a general rule, information for which confidential treatment is requested must be accompanied by a public summary thereof, or an explanation why no such summary is possible.

3. Definitive safeguard measures

Safeguard measures can take a wide range of forms. The most common forms include tariff increases above bound rates, quotas, and tariff-rate quotas.

(1) Tariff measures

Other than the general requirement that safeguard measures be applied only to the extent necessary to remedy or prevent serious injury and to facilitate adjustment, the Agreement provides no guidance as to how the level of a safeguard measure in the form of an increase in the tariff above the bound rate should be set.

(2) Level of quotas and quota modulation

If the measure takes the form of a quantitative restriction, the level must not be below the actual import level of the most recent three representative years, unless there is clear justification for setting a different, lower level.

Rules also govern how quota shares are to be allocated among supplier countries based on past market shares. These levels may be departed from (i.e., the quota levels may be modulated) if

- The percentage increase in imports from certain members has been disproportionate to the overall increase in imports;
- The reasons for the departure from the general rule are justified;
- The conditions of such a departure are equitable to all suppliers of the product concerned.

(3) Duration and review of measures

The maximum duration of any safeguard measure is four years, unless it is extended consistent with the Agreement's provisions. In particular, a measure may be extended only if it is found, through a new investigation, that its continuation is necessary to prevent or remedy serious injury, and only if evidence shows that the industry is adjusting. The initial period of application plus any extension generally cannot exceed eight years.

(4) Level of concessions and other obligations

Members applying safeguard measures generally must "pay" for them through payment of compensation. A member applying a safeguard measure must maintain a substantially equivalent level of concessions and other obligations with respect to affected exporting members.

(5) Reapplication of measures to a product

Special rules limit reapplication of safeguard measures to a given product. Normally, a safeguard may not be applied again to a product until a period equal to the duration of the original safeguard measure has elapsed provided that such period of non-application must generally be at least two years.

Nonetheless, if a new safeguard measure has a duration of 180 days or less, it may be applied so long as one year has elapsed since the date the original safeguard measure was introduced, and so long as no more than two safeguard measures have been applied on the product during the five years immediately preceding the date of introduction of the new safeguard measure.

Chinese law

In order to elaborate rules on the trade remedies, the State Council of China promulgated the Anti-dumping and Anti-Subsidy Regulations in 1997, and revised them in 2004. The Anti-dumping Regulations, the Anti-subsidy Regulations and the Safeguards Measures Regulations are, in general terms, in accord with the WTO Agreements.

1. The latest version of anti-dumping regulations

- The latest version covers a number of provisions on investigations and applications of anti-dumping measures, including dumping and injury, anti-dumping investigation, and anti-dumping measures (temporary anti-dumping measures, price undertakings and anti-dumping duties).
- An investigation of a foreign competitor is initiated by complaint of a Chinese domestic entity alleging dumping. The complaint must be made to the Ministry of Commerce, and must include sufficient evidence to persuade the Ministry of Commerce to initiate an investigation.
- In addition to the obvious responses of no dumping or no damages or risk of damages to the local industry, there are other grounds for response, which include: the quantity of alleged under-priced products is minimal; the alleged subsidized products are imported for industrial research or development, or for environmental protection, or promoting development of "backward areas"; the dumping margin is minimal; although the alleged products are in fact below "normal" price and the domestic industry has faced obstacles or suffered damages, there is no causal relation between the two facts.

2. The current anti-subsidy regulations

- Covering several provisions as regards subsidy and injury, anti-subsidy investigation, anti-subsidy measures (temporary measures, promise and anti-subsidy tax), anti-subsidy tax and promised time limit and review.
- Imposing anti-subsidy tariffs should be in compliance with the public interest: the Ministry of Commerce may decide on suspending or terminating anti-subsidy investigations and not impose temporary anti-subsidy measures or tariffs if it deems that the undertaking (offered by the party involved) is acceptable and in the public interest.

3. Main contents of the safeguards measures regulations

- Containing investigation, safeguards measures, duration and review of safeguards measures.
- When a product is imported in increased quantities and such increase has caused or threatens to cause serious injury to a domestic industry that produces like or directly competitive products, an investigation shall be initiated and safeguard measures applied in accordance with the provisions hereof.

SELF QUIZ: Indicate whether each of the following statements is true or false.

22. "Threat of serious injury" can be based on mere allegation, conjecture or remote possibility.

23. Prohibited subsidies are prohibited because they are specifically designed to distort international trade, and are therefore likely to hurt other countries' trade.

24. WTO members are entitled to apply measures against imports of a product at an export price below its "normal value" (ordinarily the price of the product in the domestic market of the exporting country) if such dumped imports cause injury to a domestic industry in the territory of the importing contracting party.

25. The export price is the transaction price at which the product is sold by a producer/exporter in the exporting country to an importer in the importing country.

26. Countervailing duty can only be charged after the importing country has conducted a detailed investigation similar to that required for anti-dumping action.

27. WTO members may restrict imports of a product temporarily if their domestic industry is injured or threatened with injury caused by a surge in imports.

28. Tariff increases above bound rates, quotas, and tariff-rate quotas are typical forms for safeguard measures.

Part 7 Government Procurement

Basic discipline

The Agreement on Government Procurement (GPA) is a plurilateral agreement that regulates the government's procurement of goods and services by the public authorities of the parties to the agreement, based on the principles of openness, transparency and non-discrimination. Apparently, the procurement of goods by government agencies for their own purposes is a crucial element of the operation of governments in that it secures the inputs that enable governments to fulfill their tasks, and further has a major impact on key stakeholders in society. Aside from its domestic consideration, government procurement is also an essential aspect of international trade.

In view of the fact that public resources are scarce, the efficiency of the procurement process is a primary consideration of every procurement regime. Open, transparent and non-discriminatory procurement is generally considered to be the best tool to achieve "value for money" as it optimizes competition among suppliers. In addition, a number of WTO members still use their purchasing decisions to achieve domestic policy goals, e.g. the promotion of specific local industry sectors or social groups.

Three areas of WTO work on government procurement

There are three main aspects of the WTO's work on government procurement:
- The plurilateral Agreement on Government Procurement (GPA) signed by some WTO members, and administered by a plurilateral committee;
- Work on transparency in government procurement carried out by a Working Group comprising all WTO members (this work is currently on hold pursuant to a decision of the WTO General Council adopted on 1 August 2004);
- Multilateral negotiations on services procurement pursuant to article XIII:2 of GATS, handled by the Working Party on GATS Rules.

Chinese government procurement law and policy

Government procurement in China is principally under the regulation of two national statutes, namely, the Government Procurement Law and the Tender Law, and may be also subject to certain local government procurement measures.

1. Governing laws
- The Government Procurement Law: One of the objectives of the Government Procurement Law is to bring fairness, transparency and integrity to the government procurement in China.
- The Tender Law: The Tender Law applies to the procurement of construction projects that require tenders under the Government Procurement Law.
- The Implementation Regulations of the Government Procurement Law.
- Local Government Procurement Measures: Local governments at the provincial and municipal levels also publish the government procurement measures applicable within their jurisdictions.

2. Methods of government procurement
- Public tender;
- Private tender or tender by invitation;
- Competitive negotiation;
- Single-source procurement;
- Inquiry;
- Other methods approved by the State Council regulatory authority for government procurement

3. Exemptions

- Military Procurement;
- Emergency Procurement due to serious natural disasters or other force;
- Majeure situations;
- National Security Procurement;
- Procurement with International Loans

SELF QUIZ: Indicate whether each of the following statements is true or false.

29. Openness, transparency and non-discrimination are very important principles for the Agreement on Government Procurement.

30. All government procurements in China are subject to the regulation of the Government Procurement Law.

Questions

1. What types of technical assistance are available under the SPS Agreement? Do you think they are satisfactory? Why or why not?
2. What are the possible bases for determining normal value of dumping?
3. How to identify whether a measure is TBT or SPS?

Suggested Further Readings

Petros C. Mavroidis, *The Regulation of International Trade: The WTO Agreements on Trade in Goods*, Massachusetts Institute of Technology Press, 2016.

Gregory Messenger, *The Development of World Trade Organization Law: Examining Change in International Law*, Oxford University Press, 2016.

Michael Trebilcock, *Advanced Introduction to International Trade Law*, Edward Elgar, 2015.

Michael Trebilcock, Robert Howse and Antonia Eliason, *The Regulation of International Trade*, Routledge, 2013.

Pradip Kumar Sinha, Sanchari Sinha, *International Business Management: A Global Perspective*, Excel Books, 2012.

Petros C. Mavroidis, *Trade in Goods: The GATT and the Other Agreements Regulating Trade in Goods*, Oxford University Press, 2008.

Bernard Hoekman and Michel Kostecki, *The Political Economy of the World Trading System: WTO and Beyond*, Oxford University Press, 2008.

WTO Institute for Training and Technical Cooperation, WTO E-Learning.

Simon Lester, Bryan Mercurio, *et al.*, *World Trade Law: Text, Materials and Commentary*, Hart Publishing, 2008.

Chapter **7**

Trade in Services

This chapter provides an overview on international and Chinese domestic laws in the field of trade in services. It contains the following parts:

Part 1   introduces the concept of trade in services, the General Agreement on Trade in Services and China's domestic legal framework on trade in services.

Part 2   overviews China's financial services laws, which primarily consist of banking law, securities law and insurance law.

Part 3   explores the basics of China's telecommunication services law.

▌ Learning Objectives

By the end of this chapter you should:

- Understand what is trade in services and its four modes of supply.
- Know the background and key principles of GATS.
- Be familiar with how the schedules of specific commitments made by WTO members under GATS are structured.
- Outline the basics of China's Commercial Banking Law, Securities Law and Insurance Law.
- Comprehend the roles and responsibilities of the PBOC, CBRC, CSRC and CIRC, respectively.
- Analyze the key market access restrictions in respect of China's commercial banking, securities and insurance sectors, respectively.
- Know the key market access restrictions in respect of China's value-added telecommunications sectors.

Key Terms

Telecommunication services	Schedule of specific commitments
Commercial banks	Sector-specific Commitments
Horizontal commitments	Securities exchange
Initial Public Offerings	Trade in services
Insider information	Value-added telecommunication services

Part 1　Introduction

What is service?

Traditionally, service is defined as an economic activity carried out by individuals and/or entities for customers with the assistance of tools, facilities, equipment and media. It is intangible in nature and inseparable from the recipient of the service. In recent years, with the development of information technology, the definition of service has evolved with a broader scope. As such, service is generally re-defined as a process, through necessary means and ways, to meet the demands of its recipients. Under this definition, the necessary means and ways include the tangible ones, such as tools, machinery, equipment and products, as well as the intangible ones, such as labor, intelligence, technology and software. The following flow chart illustrates the modern definition of service:

Figure 1: Illustration of the Modern Definition of Service

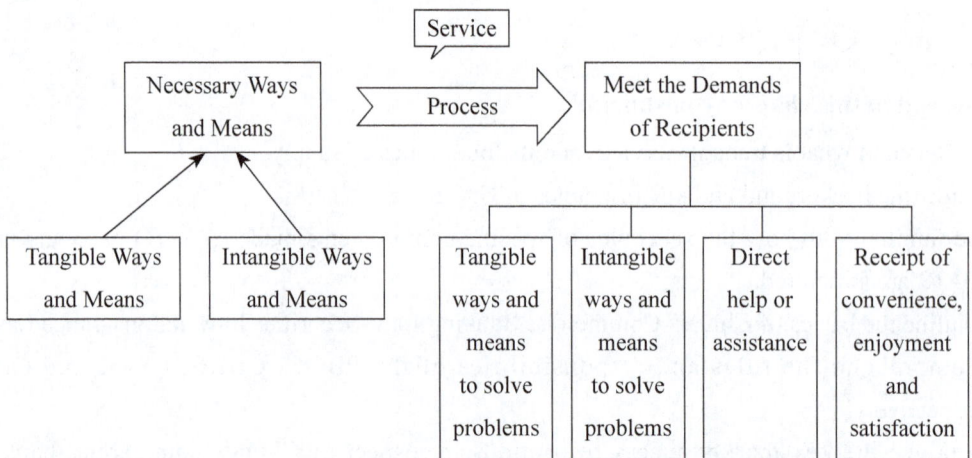

What is trade in services?

Traditionally, because services are mostly intangible, perishable and inseparable between its provision and its consumption, it is difficult to carry out trade in services, especially internationally. However, with the globalization of international economies and the expansion of international trade in goods, together with the vast development of technologies, which enable and facilitate the delivery of services, trade in services has become a vital part of international trade.

Generally speaking, trade in services refers to the sale and delivery of an intangible product, called service, between the service provider and the service recipient. In the event that the service provider and the service recipient are located in different countries or economies, such type of trade in services is called international trade in services.

In accordance with the General Agreement on Trade in Services ("GATS"), international trade in services is further defined by the following four modes of supply:

• **Cross-border supply (mode 1):**

This mode of international trade in services is defined to cover services that flow from the territory of one country/economy into the territory of another country/economy. A typical example of cross-border supply would be an Internet company located in the US providing Internet services to Internet users located in China. In recent years, with the rapid development of e-commerce and the flow of information and payment increasingly relying on the Internet, more and more services can be delivered across borders without the movement of people or establishing a local entity. As such, cross-border supply has become a more popular method of international trade in services.

• **Consumption abroad (mode 2):**

This mode of international trade in services refers to a situation where a service recipient moves into another country/economy's territory to receive services (an example of consumption abroad would be a patient residing in China visiting a hospital located in Switzerland).

• **Commercial presence (mode 3):**

This mode of international trade in services implies that a service provider of one country/economy establishes a territorial presence, including through ownership or lease of premises, in another country/economy's territory to provide services (an example of commercial presence would be a British bank opens a branch in China to serve customers in China).

• **Presence of natural persons (mode 4):**

This mode of international trade in services involves persons of one country/economy entering the territory of another country/economy to supply services (an example of presence of natural persons would be an accountant residing in the United States traveling to China to provide accountancy services to a company located in China).

General Agreement on Trade in Services (GATS)

1. Background of GATS

GATS was formally signed by all members of the WTO in April 1994 and became effective in

January 1995, which is the same time of the creation of the WTO. It is the first multilateral treaty among nations regulating trade in services.

GATS was essentially inspired by the same objectives as its counterpart in trade in goods, namely the General Agreement on Tariffs and Trade, which include creating credible and reliable system of international trade rules, ensuring fair and equitable treatment of all participants, stimulating economic activity through guaranteed policy bindings and promoting trade and development through progressive liberalization. As a framework of a legal document to regulate international trade in services under the WTO multilateral trade system, GATS is an important milestone in liberalizing trade in services through binding international treaties. Given the continued globalization of the international economy and the momentum of international trade in services, the need for internationally coordinated and recognized rules has become increasingly strong.

2. Basic purpose of GATS

As stated in its preamble, GATS is intended to contribute to trade expansion "under conditions of transparency and progressive liberalization and as a means of promoting the economic growth of all trading partners and the development of developing countries." In addition, the preamble of GATS sets out the following aspirations of the WTO members when entering into the treaty:

- Achieving progressively higher levels of liberalization of trade in services through successive rounds of multilateral negotiations aimed at promoting the interests of all participants on a mutually advantageous basis and securing an overall balance of rights and obligations, while giving due respect to national policy objectives;
- Balancing the right of WTO members to regulate, and to introduce new regulations, on the supply of services within their territories in order to meet national policy objectives, as well as the asymmetries existing with respect to the degree of development of services regulations in different countries and the particular need of developing countries to exercise this right;
- Facilitating the increasing participation of developing countries in trade in services and the expansion of their service exports including, *inter alia*, through the strengthening of their domestic services capacity and its efficiency and competitiveness.

3. Scope and application of GATS

According to Article I:1 of GATS, the treaty applies to measures by WTO members affecting trade in services. The term "measures" in the foregoing provision includes measures taken by central, regional or local governments and authorities, as well as non-governmental bodies in the exercise of powers delegated by central, regional or local governments or authorities. This scope covers any measure, whether in the form of a law, regulation, rule, procedure, decision, administrative action or any other form in respect of the following:

- the purchase, payment or use of a service;
- the access to and use of, in connection with the supply of a service, services which are required by those WTO members to be offered to the public generally;

- the presence, including commercial presence, of persons of a WTO member for the supply of a service in the territory of another WTO member.

In determining the applicability of GATS, under Clauses (b) and (c) of Article I:1 of GATS, the term "services" includes any service in any sector except services supplied in the exercise of governmental authority, which means any service which is supplied neither on a commercial basis, nor in competition with one or more service suppliers. Examples of the foregoing exception include police services, fire protection services, social security services, customs administration services and tax collection services.

Another exception in respect of the applicability of GATS is related to air transportation services. Under GATS' Annex on Air Transportation Services, only measures affecting aircraft repair and maintenance services, the selling and marketing of air transportation services and computer reservation system services have been included under the scope of GATS. Other air transportation services, such as air traffic rights, are excluded. Such exclusion, however, is subject to periodic review under the Annex on Air Transportation Services.

4. Classification of services under GATS

As is described above, GATS has defined international services in trade with four modes of supply: cross-border supply, consumption abroad, commercial presence and movement of natural persons.

For the purposes of structuring the market access and national treatment commitments made by WTO members, the WTO has developed a classification system for services that is comprised of the following 12 core services sectors:

- business services;[1]
- communication services;
- constriction and related engineering services;
- distribution services;
- educational services;
- environmental services;
- financial services;
- health-related and social services;
- tourism and travel-related services;
- recreational, cultural and sporting services;
- transportation services;
- other services not included elsewhere.

The above 12 service sectors are further subdivided into a total of approximately 160 subsectors. Under this classification system, any service sector, or segments of any service sector, may be included in a WTO member's schedule of specific commitments with specific market access and national treatment obligations. According to Article XX:1 of the GATS, each WTO member has

---

1   Including professional services and computer services.

submitted a schedule to the WTO detailing their commitments in opening the relevant service sectors to other WTO members.

5. General principles of GATS

Similar to the approach as provided in the General Agreement on Tariffs and Trade (GATT),[1] each member of the WTO (who is also a signatory to GATS) must comply with some general principles of GATS regardless its specific commitments made to other members. Key principles of GATS include the most-favored-nation treatment (the "MFN treatment"), market access, transparency and national treatment. As is discussed in greater detail below, while these principles reflect the same spirits of their counterpart in GATT, the provisions related to GATS regulations (a) focus more on the ways and means governmental authorities regulate services sectors; and (b) are more accommodating for signatories to make specific exceptions to the principles.

(1) Most-favored-nation Treatment

MFN treatment means that every WTO member, immediately and without any condition, must provide the other WTO members with the same treatments in service, or service provider as the treatments as once providing to one WTO member. In other words, in respect to the opening up of domestic markets to foreign service providers, the MFN treatment principle requests the best access conditions that have been granted to one WTO member be automatically extended to all other WTO members. Despite the general applicability of the MFN treatment principle, under the Annex on Article II Exemptions of GATS, there is a possibility for WTO members, at the time of entry into force of the GATS or the date of its accession into the WTO, to seek exemptions in general not exceeding a period of ten years.

(2) Transparency

Under the principle of transparency, each WTO member must publish promptly and, except in emergency situations, at the latest by the time of its entry into the WTO, all relevant measures of general application which pertain to or affect the operation of GATS. International agreements pertaining to or affecting trade in services to which a WTO member is a signatory should also be published. In addition, each member must promptly and at least annually inform the Council for Trade in Services of the WTO of the introduction of any new, or any changes to existing, laws, regulations or administrative guidelines which significantly affect trade in services covered by its specific commitments under GATS and respond promptly to all requests by any other member for specific information on any of its measures of general application or international agreements that may affect the operation of GATS.

---

1   See Chapter 5 for a more detailed discussion of some of these principles in the context of GATT.

(3) Market access

According to Article XVI of GATS, WTO members shall not maintain the following six types of restrictions unless specifically set out in its schedule of specific commitments: (a) restriction on the number of service suppliers; (b) restriction on the value of service transactions or assets; (c) restriction on the number of operations or quantity of output; (d) restriction on the natural persons supplying a service; (e) restriction on the type of legal entity or joint venture; and (f) restriction on the participation of foreign capital.

(4) National treatment

Article XVII of GATS requires that, unless otherwise set forth in its schedule of specific commitments, each WTO member must accord to services and service suppliers of any other member, in respect of all measures affecting the supply of services, treatment no less favorable than that it accords to its own like services and service suppliers.

6. Other key rules of GATS

Other than the general principles as described above, GATS has set out the following key rules for the WTO members:

(1) Legal procedures

Under Article VI:2 of GATS, WTO members are committed to operating domestic mechanisms (i.e., judicial, arbitral or administrative tribunals or procedures) where individual service suppliers may seek legal redress. At the request of an affected supplier, these mechanisms should provide for the "prompt review of, and where justified, appropriate remedies for, administrative decisions affecting trade in service."

(2) Monopolies

Article VIII: 1 of GATS requires WTO members to ensure that monopolies or exclusive service providers do not act in a manner inconsistent with the MFN obligation and commitments. The GATS defines a "monopoly supplier" as an entity that has been established by the member concerned, formally or in effect, as the sole supplier of a service.

(3) Business practices

Under Article IX:1 of GATS, it is acknowledged that certain business practices (other than monopoly-related practices which are covered by Article VIII) may restrain competition and thereby restrict trade in services. Article IX requires each WTO member to, at the request of any other member, enter into consultations with a view to eliminating such business practices.

(4) International payments and transfers

GATS Article XI requires that members allow international transfers and payments for current transactions relating to specific commitments. It also provides that the rights and obligations of members of the International Monetary Fund (IMF) shall not be affected, but if such rights and obligations are inconsistent with the member's specific commitment under GATS, the specific commitment should prevail.

(5) Exceptions

Regardless of relevant GATS obligations, WTO members are allowed in specified circumstances to restrict trade in services (a) in the event of serious balance-of-payments difficulties and external financial difficulties (or threat of such difficulties), (b) due to healthy and other public concerns (e.g., to protect public morals, to maintain public order, to prevent fraud and to protect individual privacy), or (c) to pursue essential security interests (e.g., restrictions for the purpose of provisioning a military establishment, relating to fissionable and fusionable materials or taken in time of war).

7. Specific commitments under GATS

In addition to observing the general obligations as set out in the main body of GATS, each WTO member is required to assume specific commitments relating to market access and national treatment. Those specific commitments are provided in each member's schedule of specific commitments submitted to the WTO upon the entry into force of GATS or, if the member joined the WTO after the entry into force of GATS, upon its accession into the WTO.

The rationale of allowing WTO members to qualify their national treatment and market access obligations in the schedule of specific commitments lies in the particular nature of trade in services – it is impossible to operate tariff-type measures across large segments of trade in services, so if members are not allowed to qualify their national treatment and market access obligations, it would essentially mean the trade in services of WTO members are completely liberalized, which was not a goal of GATS at the time of its inception (as is discussed above, one of the goals of GATS as listed in the preamble of this treaty is the progressive liberalization of international trade in services).

According to Article XX:1 of GATS, the schedule of specific commitments submitted by each member should contain at least the following:

- terms, limitations and conditions on market access;
- conditions and qualifications on national treatment;
- undertakings related to additional commitments;
- where appropriate the time-frame for implementation of such commitments; and
- the date of entry into force of such commitments.

A typical schedule of specific commitments takes the form of a chart containing four columns. The first column specifies the sector or sub-sector of services concerned; the second column sets out any limitations on market access; the third column contains any limitation on national treatment and the final column provides the additional commitments related to the sector or sub-sector. Any of the entries under market access or national treatment may vary within the following range: full commitment without limitation (sometimes noted as "none") and full discretion to apply any measure falling under the relevant article of GATS (sometimes noted as "unbound"). Additionally, the schedule is divided into two parts: horizontal commitments, which stand for qualifications/restrictions that apply across all service sectors, and sector-specific commitments.

By way of illustration, the following is an excerpt of China's Schedule of Specific Commitments on Services, which is a result of numerous rounds of negotiations between the Chinese government and other WTO members in respect of China's accession into the WTO.[1]

Table 1: An Excerpt of China's Schedule of Specific Commitments on Services

Modes of supply: (1) Cross-border supply; (2) Consumption abroad; (3) Commercial presence; (4) Presence of natural persons.

Sector or sub-sector	Limitations on market access	Limitation on national treatment	Additional comments
II. SPECIFIC COMMITMENTS			
A. Professional Services a. Legal Services (CPC 861, excluding Chinese law practice)	(1) None (2) None (3) Foreign law firms can provide legal services only in the form of representative offices in Beijing, Shanghai, Guangzhou, Shenzhen, Haikou, Dalian, Qingdao, Ningbo, Yantai, Tianjin, Suzhou, Xiamen, Zhuhai, Hangzhou, Fuzhou, Wuhan, Chengdu, Shenyang and Kunming only. Representative offices can engage in profit-making activities. Representative offices in China shall be no less than the number established upon the date of accession. A foreign law firm can only establish one representative office in China. The above-mentioned geographic and quantitative limitations will be eliminated within one year after China's accession to the WTO. … (4) Unbound except as indicated in Horizontal Commitments.	(1) None (2) None (3) All representatives shall be resident in China no less than six months each year. The representative office shall not employ Chinese national registered lawyers outside of China. (4) Unbound except as indicated in Horizontal Commitments.	

8. Trade in services agreement–a (possible) new chapter of GATS

The Trade in Services Agreement ("TiSA") is a trade agreement currently being negotiated by 23 members of the WTO, including key countries and regions in international trade in services

---

1   The entire Schedule of Specific Commitments of China is a document with over 50 pages (see, WTO Official Document No.: WT/ACC/CHN/49/Add.2). Some of China's commitments made under such schedule will be discussed in greater detail below in this chapter.

such as the US, the EU, Australia, Canada, Japan, Republic of Korea, New Zealand, Norway, Switzerland and Turkey. Together, these countries account for over 70% of international trade in services. The negotiations are based on trade liberalization proposals made by the participants. TiSA aims at opening up markets and improving rules in areas such as licensing, financial services, telecommunications, e-commerce, maritime transport, and professionals moving abroad temporarily to provide services. TiSA is open to all WTO members who want to open up trade in services beyond their respective existing commitments under GATS. China is currently seeking to join the TiSA negotiation, which is supported by the US and the EU.

TiSA is based on the framework of GATS and the key provisions of the GATS (e.g., scope, definitions, market access, national treatment and exemptions) are also found in TiSA. By doing so, the participants make it possible at a later stage to integrate the plurilateral agreement into the GATS. Beyond the current GATS provisions, it is intended that TiSA should contain additional provisions to govern how each participant could take commitments. In this respect, it was agreed that commitments on national treatment would in principle be applied on a horizontal basis to all services sectors and modes of supply, i.e., the understanding on national treatment would be closer to the GATT model. Exemptions to this horizontal application should be listed in the participant's schedule of specific commitments. Participants in the negotiations might also agree that commitments would in principle reflect actual practice and that future elimination of discriminatory measures would be automatically locked in unless an exemption were listed.

The advancement of the TiSA negotiations is largely an effort by a subset of WTO members to overcome the stalemate of the WTO Doha Round of Multilateral Trade Negotiations, particularly the talk on further opening the services sectors. However, it is widely expected that TiSA will ultimately be mutilateralized and brought into the WTO treaty system and incorporated into GATS, particularly when the number of TiSA participants has reached a critical mass.

Overview on China's legal system on trade in services

1. Legal framework

China does not have a national law that is dedicated to services or trade in services. The general rules and principles governing trade in services are provided in the Foreign Trade Law of the People's Republic of China (amended in 2004). As is defined in Article 2 of the Foreign Trade Law, "foreign trade" includes the import and export of goods, technology and the international trade of services. On the market access and national treatment with respect to international trade of services, Article 24 of the Foreign Trade Law provides that China only grants such treatments to services and services providers from other countries in accordance with its commitments made in international treaties and agreements. Largely consistent with the relevant exceptions set forth in GATS, Articles 26 and 27 of the Foreign Trade Law list the following grounds on which the Chinese government may impose restrictions on international trade in services:

- to maintain state security, social public good or public morality;

- to protect human health or security, the life or health of any animal or plant, or the environment;
- to establish or accelerate the establishment of a certain domestic service industry;
- to ensure the balance of international payments of the state;
- for any military reasons, relating to fissionable and fusionable materials or at the time of war; or
- any other reason provided in any law, administrative regulation or international treaty signed by China.

In addition to the general provisions in the Foreign Trade Law and the development plans as set forth in the Twelfth Five-Year Plan for Trade in Services, China's legal system for trade in services is comprised of numerous laws and administrative regulations issued in each sector of service. For example, China has adopted its Commercial Banking Law, Securities Law, Insurance Law, Lawyers Law, Tourism Law and Civil Aviation Law. The State Council and various ministerial-level government agencies have also issued a number of administrative regulations and rules governing the provision of different services in different sectors. These sector-specific laws and regulations will be discussed in greater details in the remaining parts of this chapter.

2. Development plans

As to national-level government policies dedicated to trade in services, in July 2016, the Ministry of Commerce of the PRC issued a Thirteenth Five-Year Plan on Commerce, which contains, among others, China's plans and priorities with respect to the development of its trade in services up to 2020. Under this plan, it is envisaged that the annual import and export volume of trade in services will exceed US$1trillion, with an annual growth rate of 10%.

In addition, on January 28, 2015, the State Council of the PRC issued the Several Opinions on Accelerating the Development of Trade in Services. These opinions set out the following main steps the Chinese government seeks to take to develop China's trade in services;
- scaling up the volume of trade in services by focusing on cultivation of the following key sectors: transportation, telecommunications, finance, insurance, computer and information services, consulting, research, development and design, energy conservation and environmental protection, environmental services;
- optimizing the structure of trade in services by increasing the composition of capital-and technology-intensive services and services with high value-add in the overall volume of trade in services;
- establishing a number of functional zones dedicated to trade in service as export bases;
- innovating the development mode of trade in services by leveraging new technologies, such as big data, Internet of things, mobile Internet and cloud computing;
- fostering the providers of trade in services by supporting the growth of large-scale multinational companies in services sector and guiding the mid-and small-sized services providers to be more integrated into the international supply chain;

- further opening up the services sectors and exploring a "national treatment plus negative list approach" in administering foreign market access into China's services sectors;
- supporting China's outbound investments in services sectors through the means of greenfield projects, acquisitions and cooperation.

SELF QUIZ: Indicate whether each of the following statements is true or false.

1. International trade in services is a type of international trade.

2. Members of the WTO are automatically signatories to the GATS.

3. Establishment of a Sino-foreign joint venture securities company falls into the cross-border supply mode of international trade in services.

4. An example of the consumption-abroad mode of international trade in services is a customer located in China purchases an e-book on the US site of Amazon.com.

5. The term "services" under GATS encompasses services provided by both private enterprises and governmental authorities.

6. Horizontal commitments in specific commitments by parties of GATS are those qualifications/restrictions that apply across all service sectors.

7. TiSA is a new international agreement on trade in services that all members of WTO can enter into.

8. The Foreign Trade Law of the PRC only covers trade in goods.

Part 2　Financial Services Law

Banking laws

The legal system for banking services can be divided into two key layers: central bank legal system and commercial bank legal system. The People's Bank of China (the "PBOC") is China's central bank and it is responsible for enacting and enforcing the nation's monetary policies. Its functions are similar to those of the Federal Reserve of the United States and the European Central Bank. Commercial banks, while most of which are owned and controlled by the state, generally do not perform governmental functions. They are commercial enterprises carrying out, among others, deposit and lending businesses. Commercial banks in China are highly regulated by the government and are primarily under the regulatory supervision of the China Banking Supervisory Commission (the "CBRC").

1. Central bank law and the role of the PBOC

The centerpiece of China's central bank law is the Law on the People's Bank of China, which is initially adopted by the Standing Committee of the National People's Congress (the "NPC") in 1995 and subsequently amended in 2003. Under this law, the PBOC is officially designated as China's central bank with the following missions: (1) formulate and implement monetary policies; (2) prevent and dissolve financial risks; and (3) maintain the stability of the nation's banking industry. The PBOC is a ministerial government institution under the direct leadership of the State Council. As such, the PBOC and its local branches are independent from other ministries at the central level and all of the governmental agencies at local levels, effectively preventing them from undue influence in discharging their duties.

Specifically, Article 4 of the Law on the People's Bank of China enumerates the following powers and functions of the PBOC:

- issue and implement decrees and regulations in relation to its functions;
- formulate and implement monetary policies in accordance with the law;
- issue Renminbi (RMB) and control its circulation;
- supervise the interbank lending and bonds markets;
- administer foreign exchange and supervise interbank foreign exchange market;
- supervise gold market;
- hold, control and manage the state foreign exchange reserve and gold reserve;
- manage the state treasury;
- maintain the normal operation of the systems for payments and settlements of accounts;
- supervise, enforce and monitor anti-money-laundering work of the financial industry;
- responsible for the statistics, investigation, analysis and forecasting of the financial industry;
- undertake the relevant international banking operations as the central bank of the state; and
- other functions as assigned to it by the State Council.

In discharging its functions, the PBOC may extend loans to commercial banks with terms of up to one year. However, under the Law on the People's Bank of China, it may not lend any capital to any government agency, non-bank institution or individual. Neither is it allowed to provide any guarantee to any entity or individual.

Since the stock market rout took place in the summer of 2015, the Chinese government has been weighing various options in reforming the financial regulatory systems to avoid the fragmented and uncoordinated decision-making by different financial regulators, particularly in light of the increasing level of integration among financial sectors and consolidation of China's financial institutions. In July 2017, at the National Financial Work Conference, it was announced that a new Financial Stability and Development Committee will be set up under the State Council. According to the announcement, this committee is expected to help strengthen and coordinate the oversight of the financial system to contain risks. It has also been reported that PBOC will be in charge of coordinating the formation of this new committee, whose responsibilities will include formulating plans for the development of the financial sector, ensuring regulatory cohesion, formulating rules and regulations to fill in regulatory gaps, and holding regulators accountable when supervision is lacking.[1]

2. Commercial banking law and the role of the CBRC

The Commercial Banking Law of the PRC (the "Commercial Banking Law") was initially adopted by the Standing Committee of the NPC in 1995 and was subsequently amended in 2003. Under the Commercial Banking Law, commercial banks are defined as enterprise legal persons established in accordance with this law and the Company Law of the PRC to accept public deposits, make loans, arrange settlement of accounts and engage in other businesses. As such, commercial banks in China can only take the form of corporations, which include limited liability companies and joint stock companies.

Under Article 3 of the Commercial Banking Law, the specific businesses that commercial banks in China may engage in are enumerated as follows:

* accept deposits publicly;
* make short-term, medium-term and long-term loans;
* arrange settlements for domestic and overseas accounts;
* handle acceptance and discount of negotiable instruments;
* issue financial bonds;
* issue cash and undertake the sale of government bonds as agents;
* trade government bonds and financial bonds;
* conduct interbank borrowings;
* trade foreign exchange proprietarily or as agents;
* engage in bank card businesses;
* provide letter of credit services and guarantee;
* handle receipts and payments and insurance business agency;
* provide safe services; and
* other businesses as approved by the CBRC.

It should be noted that a commercial bank in China does not automatically have the power to conduct all the businesses as listed above. For commercial banks that are newly established, small in scale or foreign-invested, CBRC typically allows them to conduct only a few lines of businesses in the list above.

Establishment of any bank in the PRC is subject to the approval of the CBRC. According to Chapter 2 of the Commercial Banking Law, to establish a commercial bank in China, the following conditions, among others, must be satisfied to secure the CBRC's approval:

* Articles of association: The shareholders of the bank must adopt a set of articles of association of the commercial bank that meet the requirements of the CBRC. In particular, in July 2013, the CBRC issued the Guidelines on Corporate Governance for Commercial Banks, detailing the specific corporate governance requirements commercial banks in the PRC must follow and

---

1 See, Reuters News: *China Central Bank to Coordinate Work of New Financial Oversight Body.*

stipulate in their respectively articles.

- Feasibility study report: In this report, the applicant must detail the motivation of establishing the commercial bank, its main businesses and the feasibility thereof, internal organization structure and other plans for the business of the bank.

- Minimum registered capital requirement: The minimum amount of registered capital for establishing a national-level commercial bank is RMB1 billion. The minimum amount of registered capital for establishing a municipal commercial bank is RMB100 million. The minimum registered capital for a rural commercial bank is RMB50 million. Although the Company Law of the PRC allows the partial payment of registered capital during the initial stages of a company, the Commercial Banking Law of the PRC requires that the registered capital of commercial banks must all be paid-in capital. In addition, the CBRC may, pursuant to the principal of prudent supervision, require higher amounts of registered capital.

- Personnel qualification requirement: Directors and senior management personnel of commercial banks must possess certain amount of special knowledge and related experience, which are examined and approved by the CBRC on an individual basis. In addition, the legal representative and the principal personnel in charge of business should work full-time for the bank and should not hold positions elsewhere.

- Organizational structure and management system requirements: Commercial banks must have sound organizational structures that follow the Company Law of the PRC and the Corporate Governance Guidelines issued by the CBRC. They should also adopt a series of internal rules and procedures to ensure the smooth operations of the bank.

- Facilities requirements: Commercial banks must have their places of business equipped with safeguard measures meeting the requirements and other facilities in relation to their businesses.

In connection with the amendment of the Commercial Banking Law of the PRC in 2003, the Standing Committee of the NPC also adopted a Banking Sector Supervision Law of the PRC, which was subsequently amended in 2006. The Banking Sector Supervision Law has defined the goals and principles of banking regulation and the roles and responsibilities of the CBRC, China's primary regulator for the banking sector. Pursuant to Chapter 3 of the Banking Sector Supervision Law, the key responsibilities of the CBRC can be classified into the following aspects:

- Make and enforce rules and policies for the banking sector: The CBRC has the power to issue rules and regulations for the purpose of supervising banking financial institutions and their prudent operations. It is also empowered to conduct on-site examination and off-site surveillance over banking institutions, and take enforcement actions against entities and individuals that violate the rules;

- Approve banking financial institutions and their key shareholders: The establishment and dissolution of any bank, as well as any change to the articles of association, key personnel, organizational structure, shareholding structure and branching structure are all subject to the approval of the CBRC or its local branches. The CBRC also reviews and approves the qualifications of the key shareholders (holding 5% or more of the outstanding share capital) to ensure that they are not harmful to the operations of banks.

- Approve products of banking financial institutions: The business scope of each commercial bank is subject to the approval by the CBRC. Additionally, certain financial products offered by commercial banks also need to be approved by or filed with the CBRC.

- Regulate the market access of the banking sector: Under the Banking Sector Supervision Law, CBRC's prior approval is required for the establishment of any banking financial institution and for any entity or person to carry out banking activity.

- Risk management and control: When a risk event (such as a liquidity crisis) takes place that may hurt the depositors' interests, the CBRC may take actions to take over the banking institution that is in trouble or cause a restructuring of such institution.

3. Foreign access to China's banking sector

The first administrative regulation that specifically targets the foreign access to China's banking sector was the Administrative Regulations on Foreign-Investment Financial Institutions, issued by the State Council in February of 1994. In 2006, the State Council issued the Administrative Regulations on Foreign-Invested Banks of the PRC (the "FIB Regulations") to replace the Administrative Regulations on Foreign-Investment Financial Institutions. The FIB Regulations was amended in December 2014 with a goal to relax the requirements on foreign banks seeking to open new subsidiaries (including joint ventures) or branches or to expand their existing networks in China.

Under the newly amended FIB Regulations, foreign-invested banks include the following types of institutions: (a) wholly foreign-owned banks; (b) joint venture banks formed by foreign financial institutions and domestic companies; (c) branches of foreign banks; and (d) representative offices of foreign banks.

The minimum amount of registered capital of a wholly foreign-owned bank or a Sino-foreign joint venture bank is RMB1 billion. If a wholly foreign-owned bank or a Sino-foreign equity joint venture bank establishes a branch in China, its headquarters must allocate to it an operating capital of at least RMB100 million.

For a foreign financial institution to establish a foreign-invested bank, it must meet the following qualification requirements:

- It is a profit-making bank with good credit standing and does not have any record of material violation of any law or regulation;

- It has sufficient international financial experience;

- It has an effective anti-money laundering system;

- It is under the effective supervision of the financial regulatory authority of the country or region where it is located, and its application shall have been approved by it; and

- Other prudentialregulatory conditions as prescribed by the CBRC.

If such foreign financial institution applies to be a controlling shareholder of a foreign-invested bank, it must meet the following additional qualification requirements:

- It is a commercial bank;
- Its total assets is more than US$10 billion; and
- Its capital adequacy ratio[1] meets the requirements of the financial regulatory authority of the country or region where it is located and those of the CBRC.

CASE EXAMPLE: Local Incorporation of HSBC in China

The Hong Kong and Shanghai Banking Corporation Limited, which is based in Hong Kong, is the founding member of the HSBC Group, one of the largest banking and financial services organizations in the world. Established in Hong Kong and Shanghai in 1865, The Hong Kong and Shanghai Banking Corporation Limited had a continuous presence in the mainland of China. When the Chinese government reopened the country's economy to the world in 1979, The Hong Kong and Shanghai Banking Corporation Limited was the first foreign bank that opened a representative office in Guangzhou. The bank built up expertise in working with the mainland of China, especially as many of its customers began to relocate their operations from Hong Kong to Shanghai, or Beijing. In 1984, HSBC became the first foreign bank since 1949, to be granted a foreign bank branching license in China for its branch in Shenzhen, followed by branches in Shanghai, Beijing and other key Chinese cities.

Following China's accession into the WTO and the State Council's promulgation of the FIB Regulations, The Hong Kong and Shanghai Banking Corporation Limited applied in 2006 to convert all of its then-existing branches into a domestically incorporated bank headquartered in Shanghai. In April 2007, after receiving approval from the CBRC, HSBC Bank (China) Company Limited, a banking limited liability company incorporated in the PRC and wholly-owned by its foreign parent, The Hong Kong and Shanghai Banking Corporation Limited, started its operations. This wholly foreign-owned bank incorporated the previous mainland branches of its parent, which retains only one branch in Shanghai that conducts foreign currency wholesale banking.

With local incorporation completed, HSBC Bank (China) Company Limited successfully secured the licenses from the CBRC to provide a full range of banking services to Chinese citizens, including a full range of RMB retail and corporate banking services. In contrast, foreign banks that do not incorporate locally continue to be restricted in the range of services they can offer.

Take-away points:

- Local incorporation of foreign banks is generally viewed as a positive development for the foreign banks in the Chinese banking market.

---

1 Capital adequacy ratio, sometimes referred to as capital to risk (weighted) assets ratio, is the ratio which determines a bank's capacity to meet the time liabilities and other risks such as credit risk, operational risk In the simplest formulation, a bank's capital is the "cushion" for potential losses, and protects the bank's depositors and other lenders. Banking regulators in most countries define and monitor capital adequacy ratio to protect depositors, thereby maintaining confidence in the banking system.

- Local incorporation has enabled a number of foreign banks to further expand their networks and services, in particular RMB products and services.

Securities laws

1. Overview of the PRC securities law

China's securities markets were initially formed in early 1990s, as evidenced by the establishment of the Shanghai Stock Exchange and Shenzhen Stock Exchange. However, it was until December of 1998 that the Standing Committee of the NPC adopted the nation's first Securities Law of the PRC (the "Securities Law"), which came into effect in July of 1999. In 2004, 2005, 2013 and 2014, respectively, the Securities Law was amended to adapt to market-oriented developments in the securities market. In April 2015, the Standing Committee of the NPC conducted its first round of review of the draft amended Securities Law.

Below is a brief overview of the key provisions in the Securities Law, as amended in 2014:

(1) Scope of securities

Although the Securities Law does not provide for a definition on the term "securities", Article 2 of the law provides that the issuance and trading of the following are subject to the law: stock, corporate bonds, government bonds, shares in securities investment funds and other securities as designated by the State Council. The same Article 2 also empowers the State Council to issue regulations on the issuance and trading of derivatives of securities with reference to the Securities Law. It is worth noting that Article 2 of the Securities Law expressly states that anything that is "not provided under this law" shall be governed by the PRC Company Law and other laws regulations – this exclusion provision has effectively made equity interests in limited liabilities companies not a type of "security" regulated by the Securities Law.

In defining the scope of securities, it is worth contrasting the different approaches as provided in the Securities Act of 1933 of the United States (the "Securities Act") vis-à-vis the scope of securities in the Securities Law. Section 2(1) of the Securities Act defines three basic categories of "securities" that are subject to the registration requirements: (a) interests of instruments specifically mentioned in the Securities Act (including stock, promissory notes, pre-organization subscriptions for securities, factional, undivided interests in oil, gas or other mineral rights, collateral trust certificates, certain types of receipts for securities and equipment trust certificates); (b) investment contracts; and (c) any interest or instrument commonly known as a security.

(2) Issuance of securities

Issuance of securities can be classified into public issuance and private issuance (also referred to as private placement). If an issuance meets any of the following criteria, it is a public issuance under the Securities Law: (a) issuance to unspecified targets; (b) issuance to over 200 specified targets; and (c) other issuance activities that are provided in other laws and regulations as public issuances.

Private issuances or placements of securities in generally are not heavily regulated by the Securities Law and generally do not require the approval by the China Securities Regulatory Commission (the "CSRC"), which is the government watchdog of securities issuance and trading activities. However, under Article 10 of the Securities Law, any private issuance or placement of securities cannot be conducted through advertisement, public solicitation or other de facto public methods.

Public issuance of securities is under much higher scrutiny under the Securities Law. According to Article 10 of the Securities Law, any public issuance of securities must meet the criteria set forth in laws and regulations and be approved by the securities regulatory and supervision authority of the State Council (i.e., the CSRC) or other departments authorized by the State Council[1]. In addition, for certain types of public issuance of securities, such as stock, corporate bonds and convertible bonds, the issuer must engage a financial institution (typically a securities firm that is also one of the lead underwriters of the issuance) to act as a sponsor, which should submit a sponsorship opinion to the CSRC together with the public issuance application materials.

(3) Securities listing and trading

Any listing and trading of securities may only be conducted at an exchange or market system legally established and approved by the State Council. Listing of securities on securities exchanges are approved by those exchanges and a listing agreement must be entered into between the issuer and the exchange.

In accordance with Article 50 of the Securities Law, the following conditions must be satisfied in order for a joint stock company to qualify for a listing of its stock on a stock exchange:

- The stock must have been publicly issued upon the approval of the securities regulatory authority of the State Council (i.e., the CSRC);
- The total amount of capital stock of the company must be no less than RMB30 million;
- The shares publicly issued must be more than 25% of the total shares outstanding, provided that, if the total amount of capital stock of the company exceeds RMB400 million, the shares publicly issued must be more than 10% of the total shares outstanding; and
- The company must have no record of material violation of law or false financial reporting in the past three years.

The securities that are publicly traded must be legally issued and free from trading or transfer

---

1 In China, the approval authority in respect of securities issuance to a large extent is dependent on the nature of the issuer. For example, public issuance of stock and corporate bonds by listed companies is approved by the CSRC, while public issuance of financial bonds by commercial banks is approved by the CBRC and PBOC. In contrast, the United States federal law adopts a unified securities regulatory regime whereby any issuance of securities is regulated by the SEC.

restriction. Chapter 3 of the Securities Law sets forth the following scenarios in which trading of certain securities are either prohibited or restrained:

- Any personnel working in securities exchanges, securities firms, securities settlement agencies and securities regulatory authorities may not trade publicly listed stock;
- Any institution or personnel who issues audit reports, appraisal reports or legal opinions may not trade the stock that is the subject of such reports/opinions during the underwriting period of such stock and six months thereafter;
- Any director, supervisor, senior management personnel or shareholder holding more than 5% of total shares of a listed company must disgorge the profit from its short-swing trading of the stock (e.g., a purchase and sale, or a sale and purchase of the same stock within any six-month period) of such company to the company;
- Any person with the knowledge of insider information may not trade the securities with the advantage of such information–under Article 75 of the Securities Law, insider information refers to non-public information concerning the business or finance of a company or may have a major effect on the market price of the securities thereof; examples of insider information include: a major merger or acquisition event of a company, plan of a company concerning any distribution of dividends or increase of capital, any major change in a company's equity structure, any major change in the guaranty of the company's debt;
- Any trading of securities that constitutes securities market manipulation is prohibited– examples of securities market manipulation include jointly or consecutively buying and selling securities by taking advantage of pooled capital, shareholding or information, collaboration with other persons to trade securities on agreed-upon time, price and method, and self-trading of securities using different accounts controlled by one person, in all cases the price and trading volume are manipulated and would not reflect true market conditions.

(4) Securities exchanges and securities firms

According to Article 102 of the Securities Law, a securities exchange is a legal person that provides places and facilities for concentrated securities trading, organizes and supervises securities trading, and implements self-regulated administration. The establishment and dissolution of any securities exchange is subject to the approval by the State Council. In addition, the articles of association and the appointment of the general manager of any securities exchange are also subject to the approval by the State Council. Under Article 118 of the Securities Law, a securities exchange may, pursuant to the laws and regulations, formulate rules on, among others, listing, trading and membership management, which shall be approved by the CSRC. Therefore, although the securities exchanges are not governmental agencies, they have the power to make rules that are binding to their members and other market participants, such as companies listed on and securities firms that trade in such exchanges.

Chapter 6 of the Securities Law set forth the basic rules governing securities firms, the establishment of which is subject to the approval of the CSRC. Under Article 123 of the

Securities Law, securities firms in China must be formed pursuant to the PRC Company Law and can only take one of the two forms: limited liability company or joint stock company. Article 124 of the Securities Law enumerates the following conditions for the approval of the establishment of a securities firm:

- It must have a set of articles of association that is compliant with laws and regulations;
- Its major shareholders must be able to be profitable continuously, enjoy good credit standing, with no record of material violation of laws and regulations in the past three years, and with a net asset of no less than RMB200 million.
- It must have a registered capital that meets the legal requirements[1];
- Its directors, supervisors and senior management personnel must obtain qualification for assuming such posts and to practice in securities business;
- It must have sound risk management and internal control systems;
- Its business place and facilities for operations must meet legal requirements; and
- Other condition set forth in laws and regulations or issued by the CSRC.

(5)　Roles and responsibilities of the CSRC

According to Article 178 of the Securities Law, the CSRC shall carry out supervision and administration of the securities market pursuant to laws in order to preserve the order of the securities market and ensure its legitimate operations. Specifically, Article 179 of the Securities Law listed the following responsibilities of the CSRC:

- formulate relevant rules and regulations on the supervision and administration of the securities market and exercising the approval and examination powers;
- carry out the supervision and administration of the issuance, listing, trading, registration, custody and settlement of securities;
- carry out supervision and administration of the securities activities of the securities issuers, listed companies, stock exchanges, securities firms, securities registration and clearing institutions, securities investment fund management companies and securities trading service institutions;
- formulate the standards for securities practice qualification and code of conduct and carry out supervision and implementation thereof;
- carry out supervision and examination of information disclosure concerning issuance, listing and trading of securities;
- guide and supervising the activities of the securities industry associations;
- investigate into and punish any violation of any law or administrative regulation on the supervision and administration of the securities market; and
- perform any other functions and duties as prescribed by any law or regulation.

2. Overview of the initial public offering process in China

1　According to Article 127 of the Securities Law, the minimum registered capital of securities firms ranges from CNY50 million to CNY500 million, depending on the types of business it proposes to engage in.

As discussed above, with an attempt to imitate the initial public offering process in England and China's Hong Kong, the public offering of stock in China is based on a sponsorship system, under which a lead underwriter takes on specific statutory responsibilities to oversee the integrity of the offering. The CSRC has issued quite stringent requirements and procedures and administers a rigorous IPO application process.

In general, the IPO process in China can be summarized into the following six major steps: (a) preparing for offering and submission of application materials to the CSRC by the issuer, the sponsor and lead underwriter(s) (in most cases the sponsor and lead underwriter in an IPO in China are the same securities company); (b) CSRC review the application; (c) syndicating and structuring the offering by the lead underwriter(s); (d) initial price inquiry by the lead underwriter(s); (e) bookbuilding, pricing and allocation of shares by the lead underwriter(s); and (f) listing of the IPO shares and ongoing sponsor supervision.

Among the steps above, the CSRC's review and approval of the IPO application is the most cumbersome and time-consuming one, whose process could take from six months to two years. Unlike jurisdictions like the United States and United Kingdom, the Securities Law and the rules adopted by the CSRC requires the regulatory authority to conduct a paternalistic substantive review of IPO applications (including the public disclosure documents such as the prospectus) to judge whether a company is qualified for the IPO with relatively subjective and vague standards (e.g., profitability, stability of business model). This approach is often referred to as "approval-based system," which has been the subject of criticism due to its lack of efficiency and market distortion effect, as in certain circumstances, the CSRC used its IPO approval power to balance the capital supply and demand in the stock market and the performance of stock market.

To address the negative effects of the IPO approval system, in November 2013, the CSRC issued a set of new policies[1] to introduce a more market-oriented mechanism for IPOs, paving the way for the migration of China's IPO application review approach from an approval-based system to a registration-based system, which will resemble the securities registration system of the United States, with the onus being on the issuer to make full disclosure, rather than on the regulator to conduct substantive review of application materials. It is expected that the registration-based system will be more explicitly embodied in the upcoming amendment to the Securities Law. Towards this end, in December of 2015, the Standing Committee of the NPC adopted a decision[2] that authorizes the State Council to, during a period of two years commencing from March 1, 2016, adjust the relevant provisions in the Securities Law to allow for the implementation of a registration-based system for IPOs on the Shanghai and Shenzhen Stock Exchanges. The details of such adjustments

---

1 Opinions on Furthering the Reform of New Shares Issuance Regime, issued by the CSRC on November 30, 2013.

2 Decision of the Standing Committee of the National People's Congress on Authorizing the State Council to Adjust the Relevant Applicable Provisions of the Securities Law of the People's Republic of China in the Implementation of Stock Issuance Registration System Reform, adopted by the Standing Committee of the NPC on December 27, 2015.

would be drafted by the State Council and be filed with the Standing Committee.

Comparatively, one of the prime examples of the registration-based system in respect of IPO reviews is embodied in the Securities Act of the United States. The Securities Act was formulated and promulgated by President Roosevelt in the wake of the 1929 stock market crash and the subsequent Great Depression. It aims to maintain a balance between protecting public investors and assisting companies to raise money through the capital markets at a relatively low cost. During the process of drafting the Securities Act, the idea of controlling securities issuances or conducting substantive reviews of securities issuance by the federal government was abandoned; instead, a disclosure scheme was adopted as the Securities Act's core concept and guiding thought. The Securities Act attempts to achieve the above mentioned policy goals mainly through the following: (a) mandatory and full disclosure of the issuers' securities offerings and related transaction terms in the registration statement (the main content of which is the prospectus), (b) review of disclosures rather than substantive review by the Securities and Exchange Commission during the "waiting period," only after which securities issuance by issuers are allowed to commence, (c) delivery of a prospectus to investors prior to the issuances of securities, and (d) requiring issuers and other relevant parties, including the underwriters, to bear civil liability for untrue statements of material facts or omissions of material facts.

3. Foreign access to China's securities sector

(1) Foreign-Invested securities firms

In June 2002, the CSRC adopted the Rules on the Establishment of Foreign-invested Securities Companies, which was subsequently amended in 2007 and 2012, respectively. In the latest amendment in 2012, foreign investors will be allowed to hold up to 49% of the equity interests in a foreign-invested securities firm, which is an increase over the 33% foreign ownership limit committed by the Chinese government upon its WTO accession.[1] According to Article 5 of these rules, a foreign-invested securities firm may engage in the following securities businesses: (i) underwriting and sponsorship of stock and bond offerings; (ii) brokerage of shares quoted in foreign exchange; (iii) brokerage and proprietary trading of bonds; and (iv) other businesses as approved by the CSRC.

(2) Foreign-invested funds companies

The primary CSRC regulation governing foreign-invested mutual funds companies is the Administrative Measures on the Securities Investment Fund Management Companies, initially issued in 2004 and subsequently amended in 2012. While no specific foreign ownership percentage is provided in these measures, Article 10 of this regulation provides that a foreign investor may, directly or indirectly, own up to the percentage of interest in a foreign-invested

---

1 As an exception to the foreign-ownership restriction, under the Closer Economic Partnership Arrangement between the central government of the PRC and the government of Hong Kong Special Administrative Region, a Hong Kong-funded securities companies may own up to 51% of equity interest in foreign-invested securities firms on the mainland of China.

mutual funds company as prescribed in China's related international treaty commitments (under China's WTO commitments, the foreign ownership cap for fund management companies is 49%). In addition, a foreign investor in a foreign-invested mutual funds company must satisfy the following qualification requirements: (i) it is a legally existing financial institution with financial assets management experience established under the laws of the country or region where it is located; its finance is robust; it has a good credit standing, and it has not received any punishment by any regulatory authority or judicial authority in the past three years; (ii) the country or region where it is located has sound securities laws and regulatory rules, and the securities regulatory authority of the country or region has entered into a memorandum of understanding on securities supervision cooperation and maintained an effective supervision cooperation relationship with the CSRC or any other institution recognized by the CSRC; (iii) its paid-up capital is not less than RMB300 million in convertible currencies; and (iv) other conditions prescribed by the CSRC.

In addition to the mutual fund business, starting from June 30, 2016, foreign hedge funds have been allowed to set up private fund management companies in the forms of both wholly foreign-owned enterprises and Sino-foreign joint ventures. The new policy, as embodied in an official Q&A released by the Asset Management Association of China ("AMAC")[1], requires an applicant to satisfy the following conditions to be eligible to register with the AMAC as a private securities fund manager: (i) it is a company incorporated in the PRC; (ii) its foreign shareholder and (if applicable) foreign actual controller are both financial institutions approved or licensed by the financial regulator(s) in its home country/region, and the securities supervisory body in its home country/region has entered into securities supervision cooperation memorandum with the CSRC or other organizations recognized by the CSRC; and (iii) neither it nor its foreign shareholder or (if applicable) its foreign actual controller has been subject to any material penalty by their respective supervisory or judicial authorities in the past three years. AMAC-registered fund managers of foreign-invested private securities may only operate domestically: they may only raise funds within the PRC, provide asset management services to domestic investors, invest in domestic markets, and, unless otherwise permitted by the CSRC, the fund manager must make investment decisions independently, and not to place orders through an offshore entity or system.

Insurance laws

1. Overview of the PRC insurance law

China's first insurance law, the Insurance Law of the People's Republic of China (the "Insurance Law") was promulgated by the Standing Committee of the NPC in 1995. This law established a legal foundation for the regulated and rapid development of the insurance industry in China. The 1995 Insurance Law was subsequently amended by the Standing Committee of the NPC in 2002

---

1   The 10th Q&As of AMAC on Private Investment Fund Registration dated June, 30, 2016. These Q&As were endorsed by the CSRC at its press conference held on the same day.

and 2009, respectively.

The principal contents of the Insurance Law, as amended in 2009, include the following:

- Licensing of insurance companies and insurance intermediaries, such as agencies and brokerages. It established requirements for minimum registered capital levels, form of organization, qualification of senior management and adequacy of the information systems for insurance companies and insurance agencies and brokerages.
- Separation of property and casualty insurance businesses and life insurance businesses. The Insurance Law classified insurance between property, casualty, liability and credit insurance businesses on the one hand, and life, accident and health insurance businesses on the other, and prohibited insurance companies from engaging in either types of businesses. In the 2002 amendment to the Insurance Law, however, property and casualty insurance companies were allowed to offer accidental injury insurance and short-term health insurance products.
- Regulation of market conduct by participants. The Insurance Law prohibits fraudulent and other unlawful conduct by insurance companies, agencies and brokerages.
- Substantive regulation of insurance products. The Insurance Law gives the China Insurance Regulatory Commission ("CIRC"), the primary insurance regulators of the PRC, the authority to review and supervise the policy terms and premium rates for certain insurance products.
- Financial condition and performance of insurance companies. The Insurance Law establishes reserve and solvency standards for insurance companies, imposes restrictions on investment powers and established mandatory reinsurance requirements, and put in place a reporting regime to facilitate monitoring by insurance regulators.

2. The roles of CIRC

CIRC was established in November 1998 as an institution directly under the State Council that performs administrative management functions authorized by the State Council and imposes uniform supervisory administration over the insurance market in accordance with the laws and regulations. CIRC has extensive authority to supervise insurance companies and insurance intermediaries operating in the PRC, including the power to:

- promulgate regulations applicable to the Chinese insurance industry;
- investigate insurance companies and insurance intermediaries;
- establish insurance fund investment regulations;
- approve policy terms and premium rates for certain insurance products;
- set the standards for measuring the financial soundness of insurance companies and insurance intermediaries;
- require insurance companies and insurance intermediaries to submit reports concerning their business operations and condition of assets;
- order the suspension of all or part of an insurance company or an insurance intermediary's business.

3. Foreign access to China's insurance sector

Under the Administrative Regulations on Foreign-Invested Insurance Companies promulgated by the State Council in 2001 and the Implementing Measures on the Administrative Regulations on Foreign-Invested Insurance Companies promulgated by the CIRC and entering into force in 2004, foreign insurance companies may, subject to the CIRC's approval, establish foreign-invested insurance companies within the PRC in the form of joint ventures, wholly foreign-owned enterprises or branches. Under China's WTO commitments, foreign ownership in life insurance companies is capped at 50%.

Foreign insurance companies applying for the establishment of a foreign-invested insurance company must meet the following requirements:

- having been engaged in the insurance business for at least 30 years;
- having a representative office in the PRC for at least 2 years;
- having total assets of USD$5 billion or more as of the end of the year immediately prior to its application;
- being subject to effective insurance regulation by the relevant authorities in their home countries or regions which possess a comprehensive insurance regulatory system;
- meeting the solvency margin requirements in their home countries or regions;
- having received approvals from the regulatory authorities in their home countries or regions of their applications;
- other prudent requirements by the CIRC.

Joint venture insurance companies and wholly foreign-owned insurance companies with the minimum registered capital of RMB200 million must increase their registered capital by at least RMB20 million for each branch they apply to set up, for the first time in each province, autonomous region or directly-administered municipality other than their place of business registration. Joint venture insurance companies and wholly foreign-owned insurance companies with the registered capital of at least RMB500 million are not required to increase their registered capital for establishing branches, as long as they meet the solvency margin requirement.

SELF QUIZ: Indicate whether each of the following statements is true or false.

9. China's central bank is Bank of China.

10. China's interbank lending and bond markets are supervised by the CBRC.

11. For a foreign financial institution to become a controlling shareholder of a foreign-invested bank in China, it must itself be a commercial bank and have established a representative office in China for at least two years

12. The term "securities" as referred to in the PRC Securities Law only encompasses stock and bonds.

13. The primary regulator of the securities sector in China is the People's Bank of China.

14. In a registration-based IPO system, the public offering and listing does not require any approval from the securities regulator.

15. The PRC Insurance Law prohibits insurance companies from engaging in both property and casualty insurance business as well as life insurance business at the same time.

16. Foreign insurance company can establish joint ventures, wholly-owned subsidiaries and branches in China

Part 3   Telecommunications Law

Overview

The telecommunications services market has traditionally been highly monopolized and been largely off limits to foreign investors. Before China's accession into the WTO, China Telecom was the predominant player on the market. Currently, there are three primary basic telecom operators in the PRC (namely, China Telecom, China Unicom and China Mobile) and a large number of value-added telecom operators nationwide.

In September 2000, the State Council issued the Telecommunications Regulations of the PRC (the "Telecom Regulations"), which address, among others, various matters concerning the telecom infrastructure, standards for operators, foreign investment in the telecom sector and security issues. Under the Telecom Regulations, the term "telecommunication" is defined as the activity of using wired or wireless electromagnetic or optoelectronic systems to transmit or receive voice, text, data, images or any other form of information. Also, as a basic requirement in respect of telecommunication services providers, Article 5 of the Telecom Regulations requires that all telecommunications business operators must provide rapid, accurate, secure, convenient and reasonably-priced telecommunications services to telecommunications subscribers.

Basic telecom and value-added telecom

The Telecom Regulations categorize all telecommunications services in the PRC as basic telecommunications services and value-added telecommunications services, and set out extensive guidelines on various aspects of telecommunications operations in the PRC. Basic telecommunications services refer to those services that provide basic public network facilities, public data transmission and basic voice communication service.[1] Value-added telecommunications services refer to information services via public communication networks

---

1   Examples of basic telecommunications services include domestic and international telephone service, mobile phone and data service, satellite telecom service, Internet and other public data transmission services.

(such as fixed networks, mobile networks and the Internet).[1]

According to the Telecommunications Regulations, an operator of basic telecommunications services is required to apply to the Ministry of Industry and Information Technology (the "MIIT") to obtain a basic telecommunication service operation permit, which is issued by means of public tenders. The operation of a basic telecommunication service must meet a few requirements set out in the Telecom Regulations, among which the one that affects foreign participation most is that is must be a lawfully established PRC company exclusively dedicated to the basic telecommunication service and at least 51% of its equity interest must be owned by the State.

A value-added telecommunication service provider in the PRC must obtain an operating license from the MIIT or its provincial-level counterparts as well. Although the Telecom Regulations do not explicitly require a value-added telecommunication service provider to be majority owned by the State, significant restrictions on foreign participation remain. According to the Measures on Administration of Foreign-Invested Telecommunications Enterprises promulgated by the State Council in December 2001 and amended in 2008 and 2016, respectively, the ultimate foreign equity ownership in a value-added telecommunications service provider must not exceed 50%. Moreover, for a foreign investor to acquire any equity interest in a value-added telecommunications business in China, it must demonstrate a good track record and experience in operating value-added telecommunications services. Foreign investors that meet these requirements must obtain approvals from the MIIT and the Ministry of Commerce or their authorized local branches, and the relevant approval application process usually takes six to nine months.

On June 19, 2015, the MIIT issued a new policy, Opinions on Lifting Restrictions on the Foreign Equity Ratio for Online Data Processing and Transaction Processing Business ("Circular No. 196"), which allows foreign investors to hold up to 100% equity interest in e-commerce operations nationwide in China. Under Circular No. 196, MIIT authorized telecommunications administrations at provincial levels to implement the new policy, review foreign investors' applications and issue the relevant qualification/operation licenses to foreign-invested e-commerce companies. Apart from the relaxation on the equity ratio of a foreign-invested enterprise engaged in e-commerce, other licensing requirements and corresponding examination and approval procedures for establishing an e-commerce foreign-invested enterprise are still subject to the Measures on Administration of Foreign-Invested Telecommunications Enterprises.

SELF QUIZ: Indicate whether each of the following statements is true or false:

17. China's telecommunications sector is monopolized by China Telecom.

18. A foreign telecommunications operator can establish a wholly-owned basic telecommunications company in China.

---

1   Examples of value-added telecommunications services include electronic mail, voice mail, online information and database, electronic data interchange, code and protocol conversion, data processing, Internet content provision and Internet service provision services.

19. The primary regulator of China's telecommunications industry is the Ministry of Industry and Information Technology.

Questions

1. Please identify the mode of supply under each of the following services as GATS classified:
(1) A Chinese traveler buys an electronic plane ticket from the website of United Airlines (an airline company of the US);
(2) The Shanghai Pudong International Airport leases its airport space for an airplane of United Airlines to taxi and take on passengers;
(3) To facilitate its operations in China, United Airlines opens a representative office in Shanghai, China;
(4) The Chinese traveler, after arriving in the US, purchases luxury goods at stores in the US;
(5) The Chinese traveler is a singer and performed at a concert in a theater in the US.
2. If Country A issues a regulation to the effect that only banks headquartered in English-speaking countries may open up to two branches in Country A, assuming there is no such qualification in Country A's Schedule of Commitments in its accession into the WTO, what rules of GATS has Country A violated by issuing this regulation?
3. Please explain the difference between basic telecommunications and value-added telecommunications under the Chinese law and provide examples of them, respectively.

Suggested Further Readings

Zhenhua Zhou, *The Development of Service Economy: A General Trend of the Changing Economy in China*, Springer Singapore, 2015.

Wei Wang, *China's Banking Law and the National Treatment of Foreign-Funded Banks*, Ashgate Publishing, Ltd., 2013.

Yuan Dasong, *Financial Law*, University of International Business and Economics Press, 2012.

Lou Yaoxiong, *Telecommunication Law*, University of International Business and Economics Press, 2010.

WTO Secretariat, *A Handbook on the GATS Agreement*, Cambridge University Press, 2005.

WTO Secretariat, *Guide to the GATS — An Overview of Issues for Further Liberalization*, Kluwer Law International, 2001.

Chapter 8

Foreign Investment Law

This chapter focuses on the legal framework for inbound and outbound investment in China. It has six parts:

Part 1 introduces the international and national investment law;

Part 2 focuses on the inbound investment approval procedures;

Part 3 discusses three key issues concerning operating foreign invested enterprises in China;

Part 4 analyzes how foreign capital exits China;

Part 5 explores legal framework for Chinese outbound investment;

Part 6 concentrates on the reform of foreign investment law in China

Learning Objectives

By the end of this chapter you should:

- Understand the legal framework for inbound and outbound investment at the multilateral, bilateral and national level;
- Outline the Chinese inbound investment approval/filing procedures;
- Be familiar with how foreign direct investment operates and exits China;
- Know the reform of investment law in China.

■ Key Terms

Anti-monopoly Review	National Security Review
Concentration of business operators	Nationalization
Enterprise approval	Negative list of non-conforming measures
Expropriation	Pre-establishment national treatment
Foreign Direct Investment	Project approval
Foreign Investment Industry Guidance Catalogue	Record Filing

Part 1   Introduction

Foreign investment can be divided into two kinds: direct investment and indirect investment.

• Foreign Direct Investment (FDI)

FDI is defined as cross-border investment by a resident entity (eg., individual or enterprise) in one economy with the objective to obtain a lasting interest in a resident enterprise in another economy. The resident entity is the so-called direct investor. The lasting interest implies the existence of a long-term relationship between the direct investor and the enterprise and a significant degree of influence by the direct investor on the management of the enterprise.

• Foreign Indirect Investment (FII)

FII is also called portfolio investment. It is an investment made by a resident entity (eg., individual or enterprise) in one economy in securities market in another economy. Foreign indirect investment aims to obtain financial gain only and does not create a lasting interest in or effective management control over an invested enterprise.

This chapter focuses on the legal framework of FDI. Laws for FII are discussed in the Trade in Service Chapter. No worldwide multilateral agreement on FDI exists. Investment issues are covered only to a limited extent by the WTO agreements, in particular TRIMS, GATS and SCM. Besides WTO, the global investment law regime is mainly constituted by more than 2600 bilateral investment treaties (BIT). Chinese investment law is largely shaped by the global investment law regime.

WTO Agreement

1. TRIMs

The WTO Agreement on Trade-Related Investment Measures (TRIMs) is not a comprehensive investment agreement. It applies to investment measures that have trade-restrictive and distorting effects on trade in goods only. It does not apply to services. The term "trade-related investment measures" is not defined in the TRIMs. However, TRIMs is annexed by an Illustrative List of measures that is inconsistent with Article 3 (national treatment) or Article 11 (quantitative restrictions) of GATT 1994. Examples of the measures include:

- Local content requirement: requires the purchase or use by an enterprise of products of domestic origin or domestic source;
- Trade balancing requirement: relates a producer's imports to its exports, to use of locally sourced materials, or to foreign exchange earnings. For example, a measure is precluded by TRIMs if it limits the purchase or use of imported products by an enterprise to an amount related to the volume or value of local products that it exports.

When accessing the WTO, China promised to eliminate a range of restrictions on foreign investment under TRIMs, regardless of whether they are contained in national or local legislation. To fulfill this promise, China revised accordingly the Law for Chinese and Foreign Equity Joint Venture, Law for Chinese and Foreign Contractual Joint Venture, Law for Wholly Foreign Owned Enterprises, etc.

2. GATS

Under the WTO General Agreements on Trade in Services (GATS), the third mode of service, "commercial presence" originates from FDI. For example, if a foreign bank or an insurance company sets up a branch or subsidiary in a foreign country, this commercial presence can be regarded as both service and foreign direct investment. If a WTO member promises to open a certain service sector to foreign service providers using the mode of "commercial presence", this implies that the foreign service providers will be able to make the investment necessary to enjoy the benefits of such commercial presence. Therefore, those service providers, as foreign investors, should also enjoy most-favored-nation treatment and national treatment.

3. SCM Agreement

The WTO Agreement on Subsidies and Countervailing Measures (SCM Agreement) also affects investment, because it prohibits all but the least developed WTO members from using most performance requirements, particularly subsidies conditioned on the use of domestic rather than imported materials. In addition, the SCM Agreement prohibits certain other investment incentives, such as tax benefits provided only to certain sectors (except those generally available to industry at large).

BITs

A bilateral treaty on reciprocal promotion and protection of investments (BIT) is an agreement establishing the terms and conditions for investment by nationals and entities of one state in another state. Generally BITs protect both direct and indirect investment, such as assets, shares, receivables, intellectual property, rights and licenses. Most BITs grant investments made by an investor of one contracting state in the territory of the other the following treatments: fair and equitable treatment, full protection and security, most-favored-nation treatment, national treatment, protection from expropriation and nationalization, free transfer of funds, and investment dispute resolution mechanism. China signed its first BIT with Sweden in 1982, and as of June, 2017, China has 104 effective BITs. This makes China the top two state (only after Germany) in the world with the most complex networks of BITs. BITs can not only attract foreign investment to China but also protect Chinese outbound investment. The latter function of the BITs becomes more and more important, because China has expanded its strategy from focusing on foreign inbound investment to promoting Chinese outbound capital. Consequently, in addition to the world's largest recipient of FDI, China is also becoming a major investor, recently reaching the third place globally.[1]

Chinese investment law

Chinese investment law can be divided into two categories: law for inbound foreign investment and law for outbound Chinese investment. Currently, law for inbound foreign investment is more comprehensive than that for outbound Chinese investment, which is still under development. While the special regulations for foreign investment still exist, the trend is to gradually remove those special regulations (including both discriminative and favorable treatment) for foreign investment in the future.

> **SELF QUIZ: Indicate whether each of the following statements is true or false.**
> 1. There is no universal multilateral investment agreement.
> 2. WTO agreements regulate most of the investment activities in the world.
> 3. Under GATS, commercial presence is regarded as FDI.
> 4. SCM Agreement also has influence on investment activities due to its prohibition in subsidies and tax benefits.
> 5. Chinese outbound investment law is more comprehensive than the inbound one.

Part 2   Invest in China

Foreign Investment Industry Guidance Catalogue

The market access for foreign investment in China is regulated on an industry by industry basis according to the Foreign Investment Industry Guidance Catalogue (hereinafter "Catalogue for Foreign Investment"). This Catalogue was jointly published by the Ministry of Commerce (hereinafter "MOFCOM") and the National Development and Reform Commission (hereinafter

---

1   United Nations Conference on Trade and Development, World Investment Report 2015: *Reforming International Investment Governance* (United Nations, 2015), 5, 8.

"NDRC") in 1997 and has been amended regularly since then.[1] It classifies industries into three categories: "encouraged", "restricted", and "prohibited". Industries in the encouraged category are more likely to receive favorable tax treatment and may be eligible for various forms of financial subsidy. Foreign investment in the "encouraged" industries may also be subject to less stringent government review in the approval procedure. In contrast, where an industrial sector is restricted, foreign investment is usually limited to a minority shareholding up to 49% in a joint venture with a Chinese partner. Foreign investment in "restricted" industries is often subject to stricter government review and more burdensome application requirements. Industrial sectors that are prohibited are not open to any form of foreign investment at all.

Notably, industries not expressly listed in the Catalogue are not fully open to foreign investment. For example, the 2015 Catalogue for Foreign Investment clearly indicates that, besides the Catalogue, foreign investment is also restricted or prohibited in industries according to other national laws and regulations.[2] Moreover, the encouraged category also includes restrictions on and prohibitions against foreign investment.[3] For example, the accounting and auditing service are in the encouraged category but followed by a restriction: the chief partner shall have Chinese nationality.[4]

Foreign investment approval

Only after obtaining Chinese government approval, foreign investors may invest in any non-prohibited industries under the Catalogue for Foreign Investment. Applications for government approvals will be undertaken by the foreign investors if the foreign-invested enterprise will be a wholly foreign owned enterprise, and by the Chinese partner if the enterprise will be a joint venture.

Generally, an inbound foreign investment should go through seven steps of governmental approvals:

Step 1: Anti-Monopoly Review by MOFCOM, if applicable;

Step 2: National Security Review by MOFCOM and a Ministerial Panel, if applicable;

Step 3: Pre-Approving Name and Obtaining Local Site-related Opinion Letters by State Administration of Industry and Commerce (hereinafter "SAIC"), Land and Resources Department, Environmental Protection Department, and etc.;

Step 4: Project Approval by NDRC or its local agencies or State Council;

---

1   China promulgated the Foreign Investment Industry Guidance Catalogue in 1995, and amended in 1997, 2002, 2004, 2007, 2011, and 2015. In the 2015 Catalogue for Foreign Investment, there are 423 articles in total, including 349 articles for encouraged industries, 38 articles for restricted industries, and 36 articles regarding prohibited industries.

2   Article 14 of the restricted category and Article 12 of the prohibited category of the 2015 Catalogue for Foreign Investment.

3   See the encourage category of the 1995, 2002, 2004, 2007, 2011 and 2015 Catalogue.

4   Article 318 of the encouraged category of the 2015 Catalogue for Foreign Investment.

Step 5: Enterprise Approval by MOFCOM or local Commerce Department;

Step 6: Regulatory Approval by relevant industry regulator, if applicable;

Step 7: Enterprise Registration with Administration for Industry and Commerce.

1. Anti-monopoly review

According to Article 21 of Chinese Anti-Monopoly Law, if concentration of business operators reaches the threshold of declaration stipulated by the State Council, a declaration must be lodged in advance with the Anti-Monopoly Authority under the State Council, or otherwise the concentration shall not be implemented. The Anti-Monopoly Authority refers to the "State Council's Anti-Monopoly Commission". This Commission is responsible for organizing, coordinating, and providing guidance for implementing the Anti-Monopoly Law. The Standing Office of the State Council's Anti-Monopoly Commission is in the Anti-Monopoly Bureau of the MOFCOM.

A concentration refers to the following circumstances:

- The merger of business operators;
- Acquiring control over other business operators by virtue of acquiring their equities or assets;
- Acquiring control over other business operators or possibility of exercising decisive influence on other business operators by virtue of contract or any other means.

Where a concentration is under any of the following circumstances, the anti-monopoly review may be exempted:

- One business operator who is a party to the concentration has the power to exercise more than half the voting rights of every other business operator, whether of the equity or the assets;
- One business operator who is not a party to the concentration has the power to exercise more than half the voting rights of every business operator concerned, whether of the equity or the assets.

According to Article 27 of the Anti-Monopoly Law, when determining whether the concentration of business operators exists, the Anti-Monopoly Authority should consider the following elements:

- The market share of the business operators involved in the relevant market and the controlling power thereof over that market;
- The degree of market concentration in the relevant market;
- The influence of the concentration of business operators on the market access and technological progress;
- The influence of the concentration of business operators on the consumers and other business operators;
- The influence of the concentration of business operators on the national economic development;
- Other elements that may have an effect on the market competition and shall be taken into

account as regarded by the Anti-Monopoly Authority under the State Council.

Where a concentration has or may have effect of eliminating or restricting competition, the Anti-Monopoly Authority shall make a decision to prohibit the concentration. However, if the business operators concerned can prove that the concentration will bring more positive impact than negative impact on competition, or the concentration is pursuant to public interests, the Anti-Monopoly Authority may decide not to prohibit the concentration. The whole process of review may take at least 180 calendar days.

2. National security review

Foreign investment that involves mergers and acquisitions of Chinese domestic enterprises will be subject to national security review procedures if the foreign investor would obtain actual control of a domestic enterprise in the following sectors as a result of the transaction:

- Military and military support enterprises;
- Enterprises in the vicinity of key and/or sensitive military facilities;
- Other entities associated with national defense and security; and
- Domestic enterprises engaged in sectors that "relate to national security," including key technologies, major equipment manufacturing industries, important agricultural products, energy and resources, infrastructure, and transportation services.

The MOFCOM or local commerce authorities can initiate to request a foreign investor to submit a national security filing or a foreign investor may voluntarily file with MOFCOM if such investor believes that a transaction is subject to national security review. The MOFCOM or local commerce authorities should forward the filing to the Ministerial Panel, an interagency panel consisting of representatives from MOFCOM, NDRC, and other departments for final decision. The total review procedure may take at least 90 working days.

3. Pre-approving name and obtaining local site-related opinion letters

After undertaking anti-monopoly review and security review or during the process of such reviews, an applicant must register the name of the foreign-invested enterprise it intends to form with the State Administration of Industry and Commerce or with an authorized local Administration of Industry and Commerce. Pre-approval is normally obtained on the same day the application is made.

An applicant will also need to obtain multiple written opinions or replies related to its used of land from various government authorities and these documents are required by the NDRC.

4. Project approval by the NDRC or its local branches

(1) Project approval

The NDRC or its local branches takes charge of project approval. "Project" refers to investments in fixed assets, manufacturing, or specific energy or resource sectors in the 2014 Catalogue of Investment Projects Subject to Government Verification and Approval.[1] The Catalogue of Investment Projects Subject to Government Verification and Approval was first published in 2004 and serves as the pillar document establishing the NDRC approval regime for foreign investment. Investment projects not listed in the Catalogue of Investment Project Subject to Government Verification and Approval only require investors to make a filling for records with NDRC or its local branches.

First, projects subject to NDRC approvals exist in 10 major sectors, including agriculture and water conservation, energy, transportation, the information industry, raw materials, machinery manufacturing, the light industry, new technology, high technology, urban construction, and social undertakings.[2]

Second, (1) the project whose total investment (including capital increase) is at least US$ 1 billion and belongs to the encouraged category in the Catalogue for Foreign Investment, and (2) the project whose total investment (including capital increase) is at least US$ 100 million and belong to the restrictive category (excluding real estate) in the Catalogue for Foreign Investment are subject to the approval of the State Council. For such projects, the NDRC shall, upon review, report to the State Council for approval.

Real estate project that is in the restrictive category of the Catalogue for Foreign Investment and other project in the restrictive category whose total capital (including capital increase) is less than US$ 100 million are subject to the approval of the relevant provincial government.

(2) Approval procedure

Where to submit the application materials?

If a project is subject to the approval of the NDRC and the State Council, the project applicant shall submit the project application report to the provincial-level Development and Reform Commission of the place in which the project is to be located for initial approval and examination before being forwarded to the NDRC for the final approval.

What is the time schedule for NDRC to approve a project?

The NDRC has a basic 30-day time schedule to ratify or reject a foreign investment project. Foreign investors can plan their business establishment in China based on the following pre-determined statutory timetable.

- If the NDRC needs to seek opinions from the State Council department in charge of a certain industry, this department shall, issue a written opinion to the National Development and Reform Commission within *seven working days* after receiving relevant application materials.
- The NDRC shall appoint a qualified consultancy institution to carry out an assessment of the key issues within *five working days* of the date of acceptance of a project application report.

---

1 Circular of the State Council on Releasing the Investment Project Catalogue Approved by the Government (2014 Version), Guo Fa [2014] No. 53.

2 A detailed list can be found in the 2014 Government Investment Project Catalogue.

The appointed consultancy institution shall issue an assessment report to the NDRC within the stipulated time period.

- The NDRC shall either finish verifying the application within *20 working days* after accepting such application, or submit its approval opinion to the State Council within the same period. If the approval cannot be completed within that period, a *10 working day extension* may be granted with the approval of the responsible person at the NDRC, and the applicant shall be notified of the reason for the extension. This time limit does not include the time taken by the consultancy institution.

(3) Approval criteria and effectiveness

The criteria for approval are:

- The project complies with the relevant State laws and regulations, and the provisions of the Catalogue for Foreign Investment and the Guiding Foreign Investment in the Dominant Industries of the Central and Western Regions Catalogue;
- The project complies with the requirements of medium- and long-term plan for national economic and social development, industry plans and policies for the adjustment of industrial structure;
- The project complies with the public interest and the relevant State provisions on anti-monopoly;
- The project complies with the requirements of land use planning, overall urban planning and environmental protection policies;
- The project complies with the requirements of the State standards on technology and techniques; and
- The project complies with the State provisions on administration of capital accounts and foreign debt.

If NDRC decides to reject the application, it must issue a written decision and notify the applicant. The decision should provide the reasons and inform the applicant its rights to apply for an administrative review or bring administrative litigation.

(4) Amendment and re-approval

In any of the following circumstances, an application for amendment to the original application materials shall be made to the NDRC:

- a change in the place of establishment;
- a change in an investor or equity;
- a change in the main establishment particulars or main products;
- the total investment exceeds the investment amount originally verified and approved by 20% or more;
- other circumstances in which amendment is required by the relevant laws and regulations or industrial policies.

The re-approval procedure shall be handled according to the above procedure.

5. Enterprise approval by MOFCOM or local commerce departments

(1) Enterprise approval

MOFCOM and local commerce departments are in charge of examining and approving the formation of foreign invested enterprises. Three forms of foreign invested enterprises are subject to the approval of commerce departments: equity joint venture, contractual joint venture, and wholly foreign owned enterprise.

Local commerce departments are in charge of approving the following types of foreign invested enterprises, and the rest are subject to the approval of the MOFCOM:

- The formation and change of foreign invested enterprises with a total investment of US$ 1 billion or less in the encouraged category or US$ 100 million or less in the restricted category of the Catalogue for Foreign Investment;
- The formation and change of foreign invested enterprises in the real estate industry whose investment is less than 100 million;
- The formation and change of foreign invested enterprises whose investment is less than 1 billion, and according to the Catalogue for Foreign Investment the FIE's major shareholders should be Chinese parties in the encouraged category.
- The formation and change of foreign-funded investment companies[1] with a registered capital of less than US$ 300 million and foreign-funded startup investment enterprises[2] or foreign-funded startup investment management enterprises[3] with a total capital of less than US$ 300 million.

(2) Approval procedure

Commerce Department will review the application materials for completeness and to ensure the credibility of the investors and legitimacy of the foreign investment. It will then either issue a foreign-invested enterprise certificate to approve the establishment of the foreign invested enterprises, or specify its reasons for disapproval in writing. According to the applicable

---

1 "Foreign-funded investment companies" refers to a wholly foreign-owned enterprise or an equity joint venture that conducts direct investment. See Regulations of Foreign Funded Investment Companies issued by MOFCOM on Nov. 17, 2004.

2 The term "startup investment enterprise" refers to any enterprise organization mainly engaging in startup investment activities. "Startup investment" means the investment mode that any stock right is invested into a startup enterprise for expectation of profits of capital increment by way of stock right transfer after the invested startup enterprise becomes mature or relatively mature. "Startup enterprise" refers to any growing enterprise registered and established in China and is during the course of establishing or re-establishing, excluding those enterprises that have listed in the open market.

3 "Startup investment management enterprises" are entrusted by a startup investment enterprise to manage the latter's capital, find investment opportunity, negotiate investment deals, or represent the latter to make investment, as well as provide relevant consultations.

regulations, the Commerce Department's review may take up to 45 days for a contractual joint venture and 90 days for an equity joint venture or wholly foreign owned enterprise.[1] In practice, 20 business days is usually sufficient.

(3) Approval criteria and effectiveness

Approval will not be granted if the relevant Commerce Department determines that the project does any of the following:

- Damage China's sovereignty or the social public interest;
- Jeopardize state security;
- Violate the laws of China;
- Fail to comply with the requirements of the development of China's national economy;
- Cause environmental pollution;
- (For equity joint ventures) include obvious unfairness in the concluded agreement, contract, or articles of association, thereby harming the rights and interests of a party to the joint venture.

(4) Amendment and re-approval

Changes of foreign-funded enterprises formed upon the approval of the Ministry of Commerce, the former Ministry of Foreign Trade and Economic Cooperation or the relevant departments under the State Council (except when a single increase of capital reaches or exceeds US$ 1 billion in the encouraged category or US$ 100 million in the restricted category of the Catalogue for Foreign Investment) shall be subject to the examination, approval and management of the local commerce department.

According to Chinese law, foreign invested projects should be submitted to NDRC or its local branches for project review, and the contract and articles of association should be submitted to MOFCOM or its local branches prior to registration with State Administration for Industry and Commerce. The following chart shows which level of government approvals should be obtained.

---

1 Article 7 of Detailed Implementing Rules for the Sino-Foreign Cooperative Joint Venture Enterprise Law of the People's Republic of China (Ministry of Foreign Trade and Economic Cooperation, No. 6, 1995); Article 11 of Detailed Implementing Rules for the Wholly Foreign-Owned Enterprise Law of the People's Republic of China (State Council, Order No. 301, 2001); and Article 8 of Implementing Regulations for Sino-Foreign Equity Joint Venture Enterprise Law of the People's Republic of China (State Council, Order No. 311, 2001).

Table 1: Approval Requirements for Foreign Invested Projects

Foreign investment industry guidance catalogue	Investment amount (including capital increase)	NDRC	MOFCOM
Encouraged	Less than US$ 1 billion	Local Branches of NDRC	Local Commerce Department
	US$ 1 to 2 billion	NDRC	MOFCOM
	More than US$ 2 billion	State Council	MOFCOM
Restricted	Less than US$ 100 million	Local Branches of NDRC	Local Commerce Department
	US$ 100 million to 2 billion	NDRC	MOFCOM
	More than US$ 2 billion	State Council	MOFCOM

6. License of the industry regulator (if applicable)

If a foreign investor would like to enter a certain restricted industry in Foreign Investment Industry Guidance Catalogue, licenses/permits from the industry regulator must be obtained. For example, approval from the State Food and Drug Administration (SFDA) or its local branches is needed if an investment involves pharmaceutical production. Permit from the Financial Supervision Authority is needed if the investment is made in financial industries. Permit from the General Administration of Press and Publication is needed if the investment is concerning news press.

Industry permits can be obtained either before or after foreign invested enterprises have registered with the Administration of Industry and Commerce and received their business license. If the industry permits are obtained after the enterprises have received their general business license, the enterprises must apply to the Administration of Industry and Commerce to update their business scope.

7. Enterprise registration with administration for industry and commerce

Within 30 days of receiving the foreign invested enterprise certificate from the Commerce Department, the applicant must register the enterprise with Administration for Industry and Commerce. SAIC takes charge of registration of foreign invested enterprises. It can authorize qualified local Administration for Industry and Commerce as the registration authority.[1] The "business license" sets forth the foreign invested enterprises' business scope, which means

---

1 A local Administration for Industry and Commerce that has at least 5 well-trained staffs, administer at least 100 foreign invested enterprises in its jurisdiction, and is equipped with sufficient office facilities can apply for SAIC for authorization.

the range of business activities in which the enterprise is authorized to engage. The enterprise should not undertake business activities outside of its business cope without first obtaining an amendment to that scope through Administration for Industry and Commerce.

If a foreign investor plans to establish a representative office or a foreign-invested partnership enterprise in China, approval from the Development and Reform Commission or commercial department is not required. The foreign investors only need to finish the registration procedure through the local Administration of Industry and Commerce. However, businesses in certain industry will need to comply with other specific regulations and foreign investors should obtain permits from relevant industry regulators before registering with the Administration of Industry and Commerce.

Before October 1, 2015, foreign investors need to apply to the Quality and Technical Supervision Department for an "Organization Code Certificate" and apply to state and local tax bureaus for an "Certificate of Tax Registration". A "Three-in-One" reform was implemented on October 1, 2015, which integrated the Organization Code Certificate and the Certificate of Taxation Registration into the business license. Therefore, foreign investors can apply to the SAIC for a business license that contains information of "Organization Code Certificate" and "Certificate of Tax Registration". The business license provides a unique "Social Credit Code" to every enterprise.

8. Other administrative registrations

After obtaining a business license from the Administration of Industry and Commerce, a foreign invested enterprise must obtain and file certain other administrative registrations. These include:

- A permit to make company seals from the Local Public Security Bureau;
- A permit for foreign currency accounts and a permit for RMB principal accounts;
- Registration with the Import and Export Consignees associated with Customs, and etc.

9. General approval and registration procedures flow chart

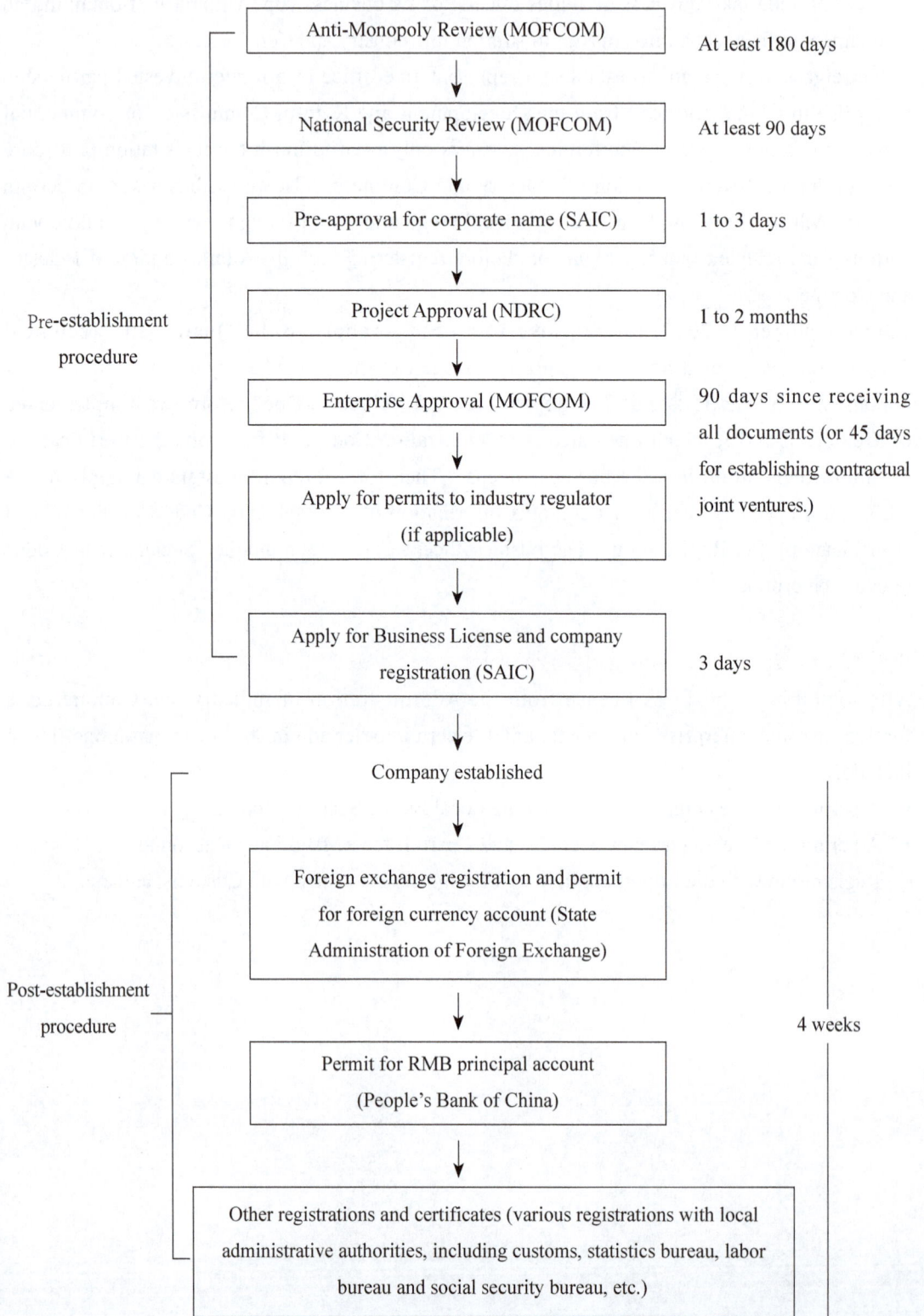

Anti-Monopoly Review (MOFCOM)	At least 180 days
↓	
National Security Review (MOFCOM)	At least 90 days
↓	
Pre-approval for corporate name (SAIC)	1 to 3 days
↓	
Project Approval (NDRC)	1 to 2 months
↓	
Enterprise Approval (MOFCOM)	90 days since receiving all documents (or 45 days for establishing contractual joint ventures.)
↓	
Apply for permits to industry regulator (if applicable)	
↓	
Apply for Business License and company registration (SAIC)	3 days

Pre-establishment procedure

↓

Company established

↓

Foreign exchange registration and permit for foreign currency account (State Administration of Foreign Exchange)	
↓	
Permit for RMB principal account (People's Bank of China)	4 weeks
↓	
Other registrations and certificates (various registrations with local administrative authorities, including customs, statistics bureau, labor bureau and social security bureau, etc.)	

Post-establishment procedure

> **CASE EXAMPLE:** *Mr. Zhengxin Zheng v. Hen Fa Co. Ltd and et al*[1]

Facts: Mr. Jinqiang Chen owned 70% share of the Hong Kong Heng Fa Co. Ltd, which holds 90% share of Long Yan Heng Fa Co. Ltd (a foreign invested enterprise). Mr. Chen is the legal representative of Long Yan Heng Fa Co. Ltd. On January 4, 2006, Mr. Zhengxin Zheng and Mr. Chen signed an equity transfer agreement to transfer all the equity of Long Yan Heng Fa Co. Ltd to Mr. Zheng at the price of RMB 110 million. After signing this agreement, Mr. Chen appointed Mr. Zheng as the general manager of Long Yan Heng Fa Co. Ltd through the board of the company. Mr. Zheng has managed the company for almost two years. Meanwhile, according to the agreement, Mr. Zheng paid RMB 55.7 million for the equity transferring. During this period, Mr. Zheng asked Mr. Chen several times to apply for the governmental approval procedure of equity transferring. However, Mr. Chen shirked the request with various excuses. Therefore, Mr. Zheng requested the court to order Hong Kong Heng Fa Co. Ltd and Long Yan Heng Fa Co. Ltd to jointly apply for the governmental approval procedure.

China Supreme People's Court held that: This case has two issues.

First, whether the equity transfer agreement between Mr. Chen and Mr. Zheng has been established. How to determine its validity?

The equity transfer agreement demonstrates that Mr. Chen intends to transfer his shares of Long Yan Heng Fa Co. Ltd and Mr. Zheng agrees to accept these shares. Although Hong Kong Heng Fa Co. Ltd is a shareholder of Long Yan Heng Fa Co. Ltd. and Mr. Chen is one of the shareholders of Hong Kong Heng Fa Co. Ltd, Mr. Chen is not a shareholder of Long Yan Heng Fa Co. Ltd. Therefore, he has no authority to sign the agreement to transfer the equity of Long Yan Heng Fa Co. Ltd directly. Although this equity transfer agreement has all the essential elements of a contract and has been concluded between Mr. Chen and Mr. Zheng, this agreement is not a contract to transfer the shares of Long Yan Heng Fa Co. Ltd. Therefore, its validity will not be affected by the governmental approval.

While the equity transfer agreement has not directly changed the equity holding in Long Yan Heng Fa Co. Ltd, it reveals the true intention of Mr. Zheng and Mr. Chen. In addition, because Mr. Chen is the chairman of the board and the controlling shareholder of Hong Kong Heng Fa Co. Ltd, as well as the chairman of the board of Long Yan Heng Fa Co. Ltd, Mr. Zheng reasonably believes that he can get 100% equity of Long Yan Heng Fa Co. Ltd if Mr. Chen kept his words and cooperated actively. Therefore, the equity transfer agreement should be determined as valid because it does not violate Chinese laws and regulations.

Second, whether the court should order Hong Kong Heng Fa Co. Ltd and Long Yan Heng Fa Co. Ltd to apply for the governmental approval procedure of equity transfer.

Since this equity transfer agreement is not a valid contract transferring the equity of Hong Kong Long Yan Heng Fa Co. Ltd, the court cannot support Mr. Zheng's request to order Hong Kong Heng Fa Co. Ltd and Long Yan Heng Fa Co. Ltd to apply for the governmental approval

---

[1] 2013 Min Si Zhong Zi No. 30 of the Supreme People's Court.

procedure. However, the equity transfer agreement is a valid contract demonstrating Mr. Chen and Mr. Zheng's intention, so it should be final and binding upon both parties. Both parties shall fulfill obligations according to the agreement; otherwise they shall bear corresponding liability for breaching the agreement.

If Mr. Chen continued refusing to apply for the governmental approval procedure to transfer the equity of Hong Kong Long Yan Heng Fa Co. Ltd to Mr. Zheng, and if Mr. Chen did not bear any legal liability for his non-performance, the contract would have improperly lost its binding force. Although Mr. Zheng cannot get support from a people's court about his claim of applying the governmental procedure for equity transfer, his request demonstrates that he hopes Mr. Chen to perform the contractual obligations. If the performance of the contract cannot be continued, Mr. Zheng can bring another lawsuit, asking to terminate the contract, compensate his loss, and provide corresponding judicial remedies.

Take-away points:

- The dispute of this case comes from the equity transfer agreement signed by Mr. Chen and Mr. Zheng. Mr. Chen is not a shareholder of Long Yan Heng Fa Co. Ltd, and he is only one of the shareholders of Hong Kong Heng Fa Co. Ltd that holds majority of shares of Long Yan Heng Fa Co. Ltd. Therefore, the court cannot order Hong Kong Heng Fa Co. Ltd and Long Yan Heng Fa Co. Ltd to apply for the governmental approval procedure of equity transfer according to the equity transfer agreement. However, although the equity transfer agreement did not get governmental approval, it is still valid between Mr. Chen and Mr. Zheng because it demonstrates the two parties' true intention.

- The contract to establish or transform a foreign invested enterprise should become valid upon approval by relevant governmental agencies. Its validity starts from the day of approval. A people's court assumes the unapproved contract invalid.

- If the equity transferor and the foreign invested enterprise do not fulfill the application obligation after concluding the equity transfer agreement, and if they fail to fulfill the application obligation within a reasonable period after the transferee's request, the people's court shall support the transferee's claim to terminate the contract, return the money paid and compensate the loss causing by the transferor's failing to fulfill the application obligation.

SELF QUIZ: Indicate whether each of the following statements is true or false.

6. Foreign investors need refer to the Catalogue for Foreign Investment to determine whether their invested industry is encouraged, restricted, or prohibited.

7. The Anti-monopoly review may be exempted, if one business operator who is a party to the concentration has the power to exercise more than 30% of the voting rights of every other business operator, whether of the equity or the assets.

8. If a foreign investor would obtain actual control of a Chinese military support enterprise,

this merger or acquisition transaction should be submitted to national security review.

9. All foreign investment projects need to be approved by NDRC or its local branch.

10. If the total investment exceeds the investment amount originally verified and approved by 50% or more, the investor should seek project re-approval at the local branch of the NDRC.

11. The NDRC and its local branches take charge of examining and approving the formation of foreign invested enterprises.

12. Every foreign investor should get a license from an industry regulator before investing in China.

13. Business license is granted by MOFCOM or its local branches.

Compared with the US

Different from China, the market access of foreign investment in the US is subject to fewer governmental approvals. The US approval process for inbound FDI includes anti-monopoly review, national security review, industry regulatory approvals, enterprise registration, site-related and environmental approvals, and approvals related to strategic investments in publicly traded companies.

1. Anti-monopoly review

The US anti-monopoly review agencies are the Antitrust Division of the Department of Justice (hereinafter "DOJ") and the US Federal Trade Commission (hereinafter "FTC"). They may review any acquisition to determine whether"the effect of such acquisition may be substantially to lessen competition, or to tend to create a monopoly"in"any line of commerce or in any activity affecting commerce"in the US.[1] If the reviewing agency determines that the acquisition is likely to result in a substantial lessening of competition, it will seek either to block the transaction or to remedy its concerns through a negotiated settlement (a "consent decree") with the parties. For example, the parties may agree to divest particular assets or a line of business to a buyer approved by the agency in order to preserve the competition that the agency has determined will be lost if the transaction is permitted to proceed as originally structured.

2. National security review

The Committee on Foreign Investment in the US (hereinafter "CFIUS") has jurisdiction to review a merger, acquisition, or takeover that could result in foreign control over a US business and that would threaten to impair US national security. If a proposed inbound foreign investment is a "greenfield" investment and does not entail acquisition of an existing US business, or if it would not result in the foreign investor acquiring "control" (broadly defined) of an existing US business,

---

1   Clayton Act § 7, 15 U.S.C. § 18.

then CFIUS does not have jurisdiction over the transaction.CFIUS can start a review at its own initiative or by parties' application. Once CFIUS finishes the review, it will send a formal report to the US president. The president may prohibit any transaction where credible evidence shows that the foreign interest exercising control might take action that threatens to impair the national security, and other laws or measures are insufficient to protect the national security. Although the vast majority of foreign investments are not subject to CFIUS review, Chinese transactions often receive greater scrutiny than transactions by other foreign investors.

CASE EXAMPLE: *Ralls Corporation v. Committee* **on Foreign Investment**[1]

Facts: US Ralls Corporation is a subsidiary of Chinese company Sany. Ralls intended to purchase four limited liability companies previously formed to develop wind farms in north-central Oregon. The acquisitions were denied by the CFIUS and President Obama for threatening national security in 2012. Sany and Ralls Corporation brought the case to court, alleging a constitutional due process claim against CFIUS and the President. Failing in the district court, Sany and Ralls Corporation appealed to the US Court of Appeals for the District of Columbia.

The court held that: Ralls Corporation was denied due process since CFIUS never advised it the nature of the concern with the acquisitions, nor the evidence considered in making the determination, and CFIUS also did not provide Ralls an opportunity to rebut the evidence. The case was remanded to the district court with instructions that Ralls be provided the requisite process to access to the unclassified evidence on which the President relied and an opportunity to respond thereto.

Take-away points: This case is a landmark success for Chinese companies that want to invest in the US. However, the judgment only touches on the due process of CFIUS's review, which is an important but narrow aspect in the whole investment review process. Comparatively, a BIT can better help Chinese investment and investors to receive fair treatment in the US market.

---

3. Industry regulator approvals

In the US, there is no general project approval requirement such as that required by the NDRC in China. US industry regulator approvals are required only in certain industries and are not usually tied to national industrial policies. For example, the food, pharmaceutical, and medical device industries, the automobile industry and many others do not require foreign investors to obtain industry regulator approvals prior to investing in the US. In contrast, telecommunications industry, the renewable energy industry, and the banking industry are examples where industry regulator approvals are required.

---

1   Ralls Corporation v. Committee on Foreign Investment, 758 F. 3d 296, 302 (2014).

Employment

Foreign invested enterprises and purely domestic companies are in general subject to the same Chinese legal regime for employment matters. In China, the legal regime for employment matters includes Chinese Labor Law, Chinese Labor Contract Law, and the Regulations of Implementation on Chinese Labor Contract Law. There are also local regulations issued by provincial, municipal, and other lower level government authorities that are only applicable to the relevant local regions. These local regulations and the practices of local labor authorities may vary greatly from one region to another. The following summarizes the most important features of Chinese legal regime for employment matters.

1. Employment contract

An employer is required to enter into a written labor contract with employees within one month from the date of commencement of employment. Failure to comply with this provision results in a penalty imposed on an employer who shall pay to the employee twice the amount of the agreed remuneration as salary. Oral employment contract can only be used for hiring part-time employees.

An employment contract may have a fixed term, an indefinite term or a term determined on a particular assignment basis. If an employee has performed two consecutive fixed term contracts, the employer shall offer an indefinite term contract for any renewal of the employment.

2. Minimum wage

Local labor authorities formulate systems of guaranteed minimum wages and salaries for workers working within their jurisdiction. This system varies region by region. The payable wages and salaries (exclusive of any overtime pay, social insurance/housing fund contributions borne by the employee, or any allowance for middle/night shifts, high/low temperature etc.) shall be in no case lower than the local minimum wage and salary standards if the workers have provided "normal work" pursuant to their labor contracts. Employers are also obligated to have their employees enrolled in the applicable social insurance schemes provided by the local labor authorities.

3. Termination of employment contract

An employment contract can be terminated by parties based upon mutual consent, or by employee or employer's initiative. However, any termination should follow laws and regulations.

An employer and an employee may terminate an employment contract by mutual consent.

An employee may unilaterally:

- terminate an employment contract without cause as long as he/she gives a 30-day prior written notice to the employer (in case such employee is in probationary period, such prior notice period is 3 days); or
- immediately terminate his/her employment contract without any prior notice under statutory circumstances, such as when the employer fails to provide labor protection or work conditions as stipulated in the contract; fails to pay the employee in full and on time; or impairs employee's rights and interests by setting working rules inconsistent with law and regulations.

In China, an employer cannot terminate the employment contract with its employee simply by giving notice in advance. Instead, the employer can only terminate an employment contract if one of the circumstances specified under Chinese Labor Contract Law occurs.

An employer can terminate an employment contract without prior notice only when:

- It is proved that the employee does not meet the recruitment conditions during the probation period;
- The employee seriously violates the rules and procedures set up by the employer;
- The employee causes any severe damage to the employer because he/she seriously neglects his/her duties or seeks private benefits;
- The employee simultaneously enters an employment relationship with other employers and thus seriously affects his/her completion of the tasks of the employer, or the employee refuses to make the ratification after his/her employer points out the problem;
- The employment is invalidly formed because of fraud or coercion;
- The employee is under investigation for criminal offense according to law.

An employer may terminate an employment contract if it notifies the employee in writing 30 days in advance or after it pays the employee an amount equal to one month's wages, if:

- The employee is sick or is injured for a non-work-related reason and cannot resume his/her original position after the expiration of the proscribed time period for medical treatment, nor can he/she assume any other position arranged by the employer;
- The employee is incompetent for his/her position or is still so after receiving training or changing to a different position;
- The objective situation, on which the conclusion of the employment contract is based, has changed considerably, so that the contract is unable to be performed and no agreement on changing the contents of the contract is reached after negotiations between the employer and the employee.

If it is necessary for an employer to lay off 20 or more employees, or if it is necessary to lay off less than 20 employees but the layoff accounts for 10% of the total number of the employees for reasons such as serious financial difficulties or technological renovation, the employer needs to inform the labor union, all its employees, and the local labor authority 30 days in advance.

4. Employment of foreigners

Employers who plan to hire a foreigner to work in China must obtain an employment permission certificate for the intended foreign employee from a local labor bureau. Then the foreign employee must apply for a work visa at his/her local Chinese consulate. After entering China, the employee must obtain a work permit and a residence card prior to commencing employment.

Taxation

Foreign-invested enterprises and purely domestic enterprises are subject to the same tax system. Currently China has 19 tax categories, i.e. enterprise income tax, individual income tax, business tax, value-added tax, customs duty, and etc. Most taxes are collected by the State Administration of Taxation and its local branches, except that customs duty is collected by the Customs.[1] Not every taxpayer has to pay all the 19 categories. Only if a taxpayer has the taxable activities specified by the tax laws, it is required to pay relevant taxes. Generally, the enterprises with relevant larger scale and wider business scope may be involved with about 10 tax categories, while most of the enterprises only pay 6 to 8 tax categories. The following are the most common tax categories for foreign-invested enterprises.

1. Enterprise income tax

All enterprises and other income receiving organizations (excluding Sole proprietorship enterprises and partnership enterprises) within China shall pay the enterprise income tax The enterprises are classified into resident and non-resident enterprises.

- A resident enterprise refers to an enterprise that is legally established in accordance with Chinese law, or an enterprise that is legally established in a foreign country or region whose actual administration institution is in China. The actual administration institution refers to the institution that actually and comprehensively manages and controls the production and operation, staff, account, property and other aspects of the enterprises. A resident enterprise should pay enterprise income taxes for their income sourced within and outside of China.

- A non-resident enterprise refers to an enterprise that is legally established in a foreign country or region whose actual administration institution is outside China.This enterprise may or may not have an establishment but it derives China-sourced income. A non-resident enterprise that has an establishment or place in China pays enterprise income tax on income which is derived from sources in China, as well as on income which, although derived from sources outside China, is effectively connected with such establishment. If a non-resident enterprise has no establishment in China, or has an establishment in China but has derived income not effectively connected with such establishment, it pays enterprise income tax only on income derived from sources inside China.

---

1   The import value-added tax and import consumption tax are to be withheld by the customs.

The taxable income is the balance derived from the total income of an enterprise in each tax year after the deduction of tax-free income, tax-exempt income, other deductible items as well as the permitted carry-forward loss of previous year(s). The enterprise income tax rate varies between resident and non-resident enterprises.

- A resident enterprise is subject to enterprise income tax at a rate of 25% on its worldwide income.
- A non-resident enterprise having an establishment in China is subject to enterprise income tax at a rate of 25% on its China-sourced income received by the establishment as well as its non-China-sourced income actually connected with the establishment.
- Where a non-resident enterprise does not set up an institution or establishment in China, or it does set up an institution or establishment but there is no actual relationship between the income and such institution or establishment, the non-resident enterprise should pay enterprise income tax at a rate of 10% in relation to the China originated income, which should be subject to tax withholding with the payer as the withholding agent.
- Under certain tax treaties between China and other countries and/or regions, non-resident enterprise may enjoy more preferential tax treatment depending on the provisions of such treaties.

Various enterprise income tax incentives are provided in the Enterprise Income Tax Law. Preferential treatment is generally granted to industries and projects whose development is supported and encouraged by the State, for example:

- Qualified high-new technology enterprises enjoy a 15% preferential tax rate nationwide.
- Venture capital investment enterprises enjoy a bonus deduction equal to70% of the investment made to qualified medium and small sized high-tech enterprises, upon reaching two years of ownership.
- Income earned from projects of agriculture, forestry, animal husbandry and fishery sectors, software and integrated circuit industry, major infrastructure projects, certain environmental protection projects, and certain transfers of technology may be exempted from tax or with reduced tax rate.

2. Individual income tax

The individual income tax is imposed on the taxable income derived by individuals (including 11 taxable items, such as the income from wages and salaries earned by individuals, the income from production and operation derived by individual industrial and commercial households).

- Generally, an individual who has a domicile in the territory of China or who has no domicile but has stayed in the territory of China for one year or more should pay individual income tax for his/her incomes originated in and/or outside the territory of China.
- An individual who has no domicile and does not stay in the territory of China or who has no domicile but has stayed in the territory of China for less than one year should pay individual income tax for his/her incomes originated in the territory of China.

The individual income tax has a progressive tax rate ranging from 3% up to 45%. A foreign invested enterprise generally serves as a withholding agent for its employees, and withholds and pays individual income taxes on their behalf each month.

3. Business tax

The business tax is imposed on the entity and individual engaged in providing taxable services, transferring intangible assets or selling immovable property within China. The taxable services cover 7 tax items, such as transportation industry, building industry, and finance and insurance industry. The business tax payable shall be calculated on the basis of the business turnover, which is the amount of transfer or sales volume in respect of the taxable services or taxable activities at the statutory tax rate.

- The tax rate applicable to entertainment industry is 20%, except that the tax rate applicable to the billiards clubs and bowling halls in such industry is 5%;
- The tax rate applicable to all the other tax items is 3% or 5%.

4. Value-added tax

The value-added tax (hereinafter "VAT") is imposed on the entity and individual engaged in importing goods, marketing goods, providing processing and replacements services in China. The VAT taxpayer is classified into the general taxpayer and the small-scale taxpayer. The threshold for qualifying general VAT taxpayers is the annual sales of above CNY 0.5 million for manufacturing enterprises and of above CNY 0.8 million for trading enterprises.

- As for the general taxpayer, the VAT is imposed on the increment value of its sale (or import) of goods or provision of processing, repair and/or replacements services, the basic tax rate is 17%, the lower tax rate is 13%, and the tax rate for export goods is 0.
- As for the small-scale taxpayer, a simplified system of computation of tax payable is applied, and the rate is 3%.

China is currently in a nationwide conversion from business tax to VAT, with a pilot program applying to transportation, modern service and other industries in several locations. This is the first step in an overall plan to replace business tax with VAT across the whole services sector in China. The goal of the pilot program is to:

- Avoid double taxation. Business tax is an inefficient turnover tax, which in effect taxes each stage of a supply chain, irrespective of the profit or "value added" by each business in that supply chain. By contrast, the VAT is a tax collected by business, but effectively only born by the end consumer.
- Foster the development of service industry. Currently, the VAT is applicable to the secondary industry except construction, and the business tax applies to the tertiary industry. Therefore, most of service providers are subject to business tax. This impedes the development of service, because business tax is levied upon the whole business turnover and does not permit deduction.

Levying VAT is simpler and more transparent compared to business tax. The dual system of business tax and VAT creates complicacies in practice. Modern business often combines the sale of goods and services. It is increasingly difficult to divide goods and services, and consequently the division between business tax and VAT becomes blurred.

5. Customs duty

Customs duty is imposed on the goods and articles imported into or exported out of China's territory. Customs duty is payable according to a tariff schedule. With free trade agreements, goods traded between China and the FTA signatory countries qualify for lower customs duty rates.

Foreign exchange

China implements a unitary and well-managed floating exchange rate system based on market supply and demand for the exchange rates of Renminbi (RMB). The regulatory authority is the People's Bank of China, China's State Administration of Foreign Exchange and its local branches. Under Chinese law, foreign currency transactions are divided into current account transactions and capital account transactions. The payment in and transfer of foreign exchange for current international transactions will not be subject to the government control or restriction. But the capital account transactions still need government approval.

- "Current account" refers to international balance of payment involving goods, services, profits as well as other items of transactions taking place frequently. For example, payments and receipts from international trade and international labor service; unitary payment, such as the repatriation of dividends by foreign invested enterprise, or repatriation of tax salary and other lawful income by employees of foreign invested enterprises; payments of interests on foreign loans (but not the repayment of principal) . The receipt of foreign exchange under current account may be retained or sold to financial institutions.
- Capital account transactions refer to transactions aiming to create capital (e.g. equity or securities investment, loans, derivative deals, guarantees benefiting a foreign entity, etc.). Foreign exchange controls over the capital account mainly include the following:
  a. All foreign exchange in the capital account and the fund for settlement must be used in accordance with designated purposes approved by the relevant authorities.
  b. Overseas entities and individuals that invest in China or engage in the issuance and transaction of securities or derivatives must register with the China's State Administration of Foreign Exchange.
  c. The provision of outbound guarantees is subject to approval by the China's State Administration of Foreign Exchange. Outbound guarantees must be registered with the China's State Administration of Foreign Exchange at the time the guarantee contract is signed. Financial institutions in the banking industry can directly offer foreign commercial loans within their approved business scope, but other domestic institutions that offer foreign commercial loans must be approved by the China's State Administration of Foreign Exchange.

Repatriation of dividends and funds

Foreign shareholders of a foreign invested enterprise can repatriate their dividends or the funds they receive upon the expiration or early termination of the operational term of the enterprise. Dividends and funds can be exchanged for foreign currencies and remitted abroad in accordance with foreign exchange control regulations.

The wages, salaries or other legitimate income earned by a foreign employee in a foreign invested enterprise, after payment of the individual income tax, may be remitted abroad in accordance with foreign exchange control regulations.

Nationalization and expropriation

Nationalization is the act of bringing an industry or assets under governmental control or ownership.[1] Expropriation is a governmental taking or modification of an individual property rights.[2] "Indirect expropriation" refers to measures having similar effects as direct expropriation. A case-by-case analysis should be adopted and the following four factors may be considered when determining whether a measure is indirect expropriation.

- The extent that this measure has impacted the economic value of the investment. Notably, a measure that has negative economic impact upon the investment may not necessarily be indirect expropriation.
- The extent that this measure is applied in a discriminate way against an foreign investor or investment.
- The extent that the measure interferes with the investor's clear and reasonable investment expectation.
- Whether this measure is adopted for public interests, and whether the measure is appropriate to achieve its goal.

However, a restrictive measure is not indirect expropriation if it is to protect public welfare such as environment, public security and health, and is applied in a non-discriminative method.

Chinese law and the BITs concluded by China generally forbid directly or indirectly nationalize or expropriate investment or profits of foreign investors except for a public purpose, pursuing to applicable domestic laws and legal procedures, carrying out in a non-discriminatory and non-arbitrary manner, and providing compensation. Compensation to foreign investors shall be calculated based on the fair market value right before expropriation or before expropriation is publicly announced, whichever is earlier; the compensation shall not be delayed and shall include

---

1   Page1123 of *Black Law Dictionary*, ninth edition.

2   Page662 of *Black Law Dictionary*, ninth edition.

interests calculated by the prevailing market rate from the date of expropriation to the date of payment, and the compensation can be freely transferred overseas.

> ## CASE EXAMPLE: *Tza Yap Shum v. Republic of Peru*[1]
>
> **Facts:** Tza Yap Shum, a Chinese national resident in Hong Kong, was the shareholder of TSG Peru SAC (TSG), a Peruvian company involved in the purchase and exportation of fishmeal. Mr. Tza alleged that the Peruvian Tax Administration's audit determinations and interim measures constituted an unjustified indirect expropriation of his investment, in violation of the China-Peru BIT. Peru asserted three main objections to the tribunal's jurisdiction. First, Mr. Tza did not qualify as an investor under the China-Peru BIT because he was a resident of Hong Kong. Second, Mr. Tza's investment was not protected because it was held indirectly through investments in the British Virgin Islands. Third, the International Center for Settlement of Investment Disputes (ICSID) tribunal had no jurisdiction to determine whether an expropriation had actually occurred in violation of the treaty.
>
> **ICSID ruled that:** The Tribunal has jurisdiction and competence to try the expropriation dispute filed by Tza Yap Shum under the China-Peru BIT and Peru's imposition of interim measures constituted an indirect expropriation of Tza's investment.
>
> - Residency: The tribunal concludes that nationality was a question of domestic law and, under Chinese law, Hong Kong residents of Chinese descent and born in Chinese territories are Chinese nationals.
> - Indirect investments: Peru argued that Mr. Tza failed to make a covered investment in Peru because Mr. Tza made his investment through a shell company established in the British Virgin Islands. The tribunal concluded that such a structure was permitted under the China-Peru BIT.
> - Jurisdiction over the issue of expropriation: The tribunal concluded that words "involving the amount of compensation for expropriation" includes not only the determination of the amount but also any issues normally inherent to an expropriation, including whether the property was expropriated in accordance with the BIT.
>
> **Take-away points:**
>
> This is the first ICSID decision involving claims under a Chinese BIT. This decision demonstrates that the ICSID Tribunal may interpret a BIT provision in the manner that was most likely to attract foreign investors. Therefore, the Tribunal did not draw implications from China's reservation to the ICSID Convention, which restricted China's consent to arbitration to compensation disputes. In addition, although the China-Peru BIT does not expressly protect "indirect" investment, the Tribunal still held that the Peru-China BIT did cover Mr. Tza's indirect investment because the treaty's definition of "investor" contains no relevant restrictions, the broad

---

1   Tza Yap Shum v. Republic of Peru, ICSID Case No. ARB/07/6.

and non-exclusive definition of "investment" is intended to protect any kind of investment, and Peruvian law does not prohibit indirect investments. It is noteworthy that in 2009 China and Peru signed a free trade agreement that includes an investment chapter providing for ICSID arbitration of "any dispute," and expressly protects indirect investments.

Part 5　Chinese Outbound Investment

China's Belt and Road Initiative strongly encourages domestic companies to invest overseas. The key drivers for Chinese outbound investment are more market share, better technology, advanced human resources from the hosting countries, access to foreign capital, and access to raw materials due to the limited natural resource and overcapacity of production power in China.The main government approval procedure for Chinese outbound investment is as follows.

Approval authorities

According to the 2014 version of Catalogue of Investment Projects that require government verification, Chinese investors who plan to invest overseas generally need to seek approvals from the NDRC, the MOFCOM and the State Administration of Foreign Exchange.

- The investment project should be approved by or filed a record with the NDRC or its local branches.
- The investment agreements and the overseas target company should be approved by or filed a record with the MOFCOM or its local branches.
- Chinese investors must register with the State Administration of Foreign Exchange in order to remit out of China the funds required for the investment.

Approval procedures

1. Ordinary projects

Ordinary projects only require "record filing" with the NDRC and MOFCOM. The two authorities will not look at the substance of the documents. They will accept a filing if the documents are complete and the form of the documents meet the statutory requirements.

- The record filing is required to be made to the NDRC at the central level if (a) a project is invested by a state-owned enterprise administered by the central government, or (b) a project is invested by a local enterprise and the amount of investment is US$ 300 million or more.
- A state-owned enterprise administered by the central government must file with MOFCOM at the central level, and other enterprises at the provincial level.

2. Sensitive projects

NDRC approval will be required if

- The Chinese party's investment amount is US$ 1 billion or more;
- The project involves a sensitive country or industry.

For MOFCOM, verification is only required for projects involving sensitive countries or industries. Chinese law for outbound investment does not explicitly define "sensitive country or industry". Generally, sensitive countries may include countries that have not established formal diplomatic relations with China, are subject to international sanctions, or are at war or in a state of political upheaval. Sensitive industries may include telecommunications, media, land development, power grid and cross-border exploration of water resources.

Self Quiz: Indicate whether each of the following statements is true or false.

14. China's State Administration of Foreign Exchange reviews all foreign currency transactions involving the purchase or sale of RMB.

15. Foreign shareholders can freely repatriate their dividends that they receive from their investment out of China according to law.

16. VIE is used to avoid the foreign exchange control and other governmental reviews in China.

17. Nationalization or expropriation should be done for public interests.

18. The authorities to approve Chinese outbound investment are the NDRC, the MOFCOM and the National Administration of Industry and Commerce.

19. Record filing is applied to all Chinese outbound investment.

Part 6　Reform of Foreign Investment Law in China

China became the second largest economy in the world in 2010. In the past three decades, the success of China's economy largely came from its export-oriented feature, mostly trade in goods. However, the driving force for world economy has gradually shifted from trade in goods to investment and trade in services.[1] Since 2010, the export-oriented economy increasingly cannot sustain China's long-term development. The growth of China's GDP has tapered. Chinese foreign business and economic laws used to center on trade in goods. A rapid and profound

---

1 *Emerging Economies Arrested Development*, The Economist, 9 (4 October 2014) (indicating "measured in value-added terms…the importance of goods trade tumbled, from 71% of world exports in 1980 to just 57% in 2008, because of the increasing weight of services in the production of traded goods. Much of the value of an iPhone, for example, derives from the original design and engineering of the product rather than from its components and assembly."). See also generally Jeremy Rifkin, *The Third Industrial Revolution: How Lateral Power is Transforming Energy, the Economy, and the World* (Palgrave Macmillan) (2011).

breakthrough needs to be made to remove restrictions on investment and trade in services. In this context, China established the free trade zones (hereinafter "FTZ") such as China (Shanghai) Pilot Free Trade Zone, the China (Fujian) Pilot Free Trade Zone, the China (Guangdong) Pilot Free Trade Zone, and the China (Tianjin) Pilot Free Trade Zone since 2013.[1] These "FTZs" shoulder the historic mission as testing grounds to restructure the trade and investment legal system in China.

Moreover, the MOFCOM has also begun to draft a Foreign Investment Law of the People's Republic of China. When it comes into force, the regime created under the new law will supersede entirely the current structure for the regulation of foreign investment in China.

Reform of foreign investment law in China's FTZs

Free trade zones (FTZ) are a type of special economic zones broadly defined as "demarcated geographic areas contained within a country's national boundaries where the rules of business are different from those that prevail in the national territory."[2]

1. Inbound investment

The reform of legal framework for inbound investment in China's FTZs is from three aspects:

- the investment management model;
- the registration system;
- the handling mechanism and the supervision system.

(1) First, investment management model: pre-establishment national treatment with a negative list of non-conforming measures

China's FTZs are pioneers to provide foreign investors with pre-establishment national treatment and special management measures on foreign investment market access (the so-called "negative list of non-conforming measures".

- Pre-establishment national treatment: According to the documents of United Nations Conference on Trade and Development, national treatment can be divided into pre-establishment national treatment and post-establishment national treatment based on the

---

1 On 3 July 2013, the Standing Committee of the National People's Congress in China approved the Framework Plan of China (Shanghai) Pilot Free Trade Zone (hereinafter "Shanghai FTZ"). The Shanghai FTZ was officially established on September 29, 2013. On Dec. 26, 2014, the Standing Committee of the National People's Congress decided to establish the China (Fujian) Free Trade Zone, the China (Guangdong) Free Trade Zone, and the China (Tianjin) Free Trade Zone. This decision will become effective on March 1, 2015. The Shanghai FTZ is 120.72 km^2, the Fujian FTZ is 118.04 km^2, the Guangdong FTZ is 116.2 km^2, and the Tianjin FTZ is 119.9 km^2. See Decision of the 12th Session of the 12th Meeting of the Standing Committee of the National People's Congress on 28 December 2014.

2 Thomas Farole, *Special Economic Zones in Africa: Comparing Performance and Learning from Global Experiences* (World Bank, 2011) 1, 23.

application of national treatment in different stages. The pre-establishment national treatment means the treatment is provided for foreign investors and their investment during the stages of establishment, acquisition and expansion of enterprises, which should not be less than the treatment provided for domestic investors and their investment in like circumstances.

- Negative List of non-conforming measures: Compared with the positive list, the negative list approach is more liberalized, where industries are principally open except for certain exceptions. Any industries that are not included in the list should be fully open to foreign investors, who can automatically receive no less favorable treatment than domestic investors do in like circumstances. Non-confirming measures are the "exceptions" to such liberalization approach. High-standard BITs generally contain a negative list of non-confirming measures. Different from the Catalogue for Foreign investment, the FTZ negative list provides that, for industries that are not stated in the "negative list", foreign and domestic investors will receive the same treatment, by going through filing procedures instead of approving requirements (with the exception of areas specifically defined by the State Council).

The Shanghai FTZ unprecedentedly adopted a Special Administrative Measures (Negative List) on Foreign Investment Access to the Shanghai FTZ in 2013 (the 2013 Shanghai FTZ Negative List).[1] On April 20, 2015, China released the national Special Administrative Measures (Negative List) on Foreign Investment Access to China FTZs (the 2015 FTZ Negative List) as a uniform negative list for the four FTZs. The 2015 FTZ Negative List provides wider market access for foreign investors compared with the 2015 Catalogue for Foreign Investment.[2] It also significantly differs from the Catalogue for Foreign Investment, because all industries not listed are automatically open except for reasons such as protecting national security, public order and culture, financial prudence, government procurement and subsidy, and taxation.[3]

Notably on March 3, 2016, the China NDRC and the MOFCOM jointly issued a trial market-entry negative list (the 2016 Trial Negative List).[4] This List was piloted in Shanghai, Tianjin, Fujian Province, and Guangdong Province.[5] The 2016 Trial Negative List does not provide more market access to foreign investors. It mainly consolidates non-conforming measures adopted by various laws, regulations, rules and polices issued by the central government and applys these

---

1 Special Administrative Measures (Negative List) on Foreign Investment Access to the Shanghai FTZ.

2 Special Administrative Measures (Negative List) on Foreign Investment Access to China Free Trade Zones'.

3 Eg., article 3 of the 2015 FTZ Negative List.

4 The 2016 Trial Negative List was issued in accordance with the China State Council's Opinion on the Implementation of the Negative List Market-Entry System (Opinion) on October 2, 2015. A Chinese version is available at http://www.fdi.gov.cn.

5 The 2016 Trial Negative List also applies to the four FTZs in the four provinces and municipalities, which means foreign investors in the FTZs are subject to both the 2016 Trial Negative List and the 2015 FTZ Negative List.

measures to both domestic and foreign investors on an equal footing.[1] It aims to facilitate Chinese central government to streamline regulation on investment and roll out a nationwide market access negative list in 2018.

As a conclusion, from the 2013 Shanghai FTZ Negative List, the 2015 FTZ Negative List to the 2016 Trial Negative List, China moves towards adopting a nationwide negative list of non-conforming measures.

(2) Second, the system of registration and handling

China's FTZ adopts the one-window handling mechanism for registration of foreign invested enterprises. One-stop Acceptance Window Mechanism refers to a working mechanism in which the approval (filing) of foreign investment projects and the establishment (alteration) of enterprises can be handled by "one application form in one service window." In the past, an applicant needs to send enterprise establishment applications to different government agencies. Now the Administration for Industry and Commerce shall accept applications and deliver the decision result in a unified way to the applicant. This mechanism has been accepted by the Central Government and has been implemented nationwide as the "Three-in-One" system since 2015.[2] This system combines the old business license, the organization code certificate and the tax registration certificate into an integrated business license with one social credit code. Now, companies do not need to submit similar sets of documents to Administration of Industry and Commerce, the Administration of Quality and Technology and the Tax Bureau. Instead, they just submit one set of documents to the Administration of Industry and Commerce and can receive the integrated business license in three days.

---

1 The 2016 Trial Negative List includes 96 prohibited items in 17 sectors and 232 restricted items in 22 sectors. These items are from: (1) investment projects requiring administrative approvals as set out in the Consolidated List of Administrative Approval Items by Departments Under the State Council (included in the list as restricted items); (2) project categories designated for elimination or closed for new investment under the Catalogue for Guiding Industry Restructuring (2011 version), which make up 46 of the 96 prohibited items; (3) projects requiring approvals from the relevant development and reform departments under the Catalogue of Investment Projects Subject to Government Verification and Approval (2014 version) (included in the list as restricted items); and (4) projects restricted or prohibited under other national laws, administrative regulations, and State Council decisions. 12 of the 328 total items are (or include sub-items that are) entirely new and were not restricted or prohibited under previous laws and regulations. These new items include an approval requirement for collaborations between domestic media and foreign news agencies, and a content censorship requirement for gaming and entertainment equipment.

2 Advice regarding Promoting the "Three-In-One" Registration System Reform, issued by the Office of the State Council at June 3 2015, Guo Fa Bang [2015] No. 50.
Circular Regarding Well Handle the "Three-In-One" Relating Works, issued by the State Administration for Industry and Commerce and the State Administration of Taxation on September 10 2015, Gong Shang Qi Zhu Zi [2015] No. 147.

Figure 1: One-stop Acceptance Window Mechanism[1]

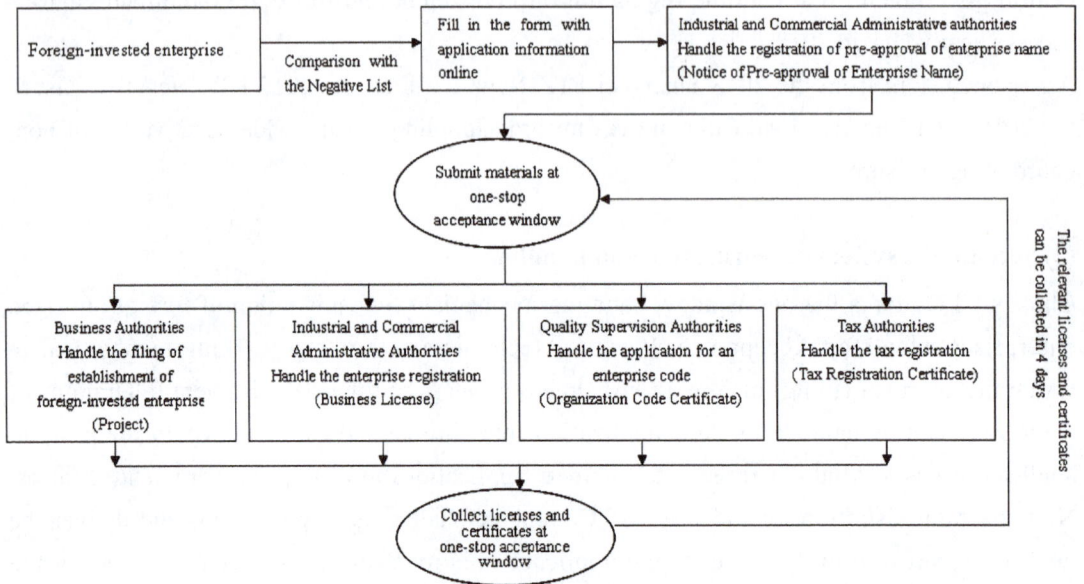

Foreign-invested enterprise → Comparison with the Negative List → Fill in the form with application information online → Industrial and Commercial Administrative authorities Handle the registration of pre-approval of enterprise name (Notice of Pre-approval of Enterprise Name)

Submit materials at one-stop acceptance window

- Business Authorities Handle the filing of establishment of foreign-invested enterprise (Project)
- Industrial and Commercial Administrative Authorities Handle the enterprise registration (Business License)
- Quality Supervision Authorities Handle the application for an enterprise code (Organization Code Certificate)
- Tax Authorities Handle the tax registration (Tax Registration Certificate)

Collect licenses and certificates at one-stop acceptance window

The relevant licenses and certificates can be collected in 4 days

(3) Third, governmental supervision focusing on mid-event control and subsequent supervision

In China's FTZ, the supervision system has shifted from emphasizing ex-ante approval to mid-event control and subsequent supervision. The system of Mid-event Control and Subsequent Supervision is constituted by:

- National security review;
- Anti-monopoly review;
- Publication of corporate annual reports;
- Credit management;
- Integrated enforcement of law system;
- System of sharing supervision information between governmental agencies.

2. Outbound investment

Compared with other parts of China, FTZs adopt a "one-stop filing" and highly efficient filing system for outbound investment. For example, if a company established or an eligible individual employed in the Shanghai FTZ plans to invest abroad, the investor should submit all required filing application documents to the Shanghai FTZ Board. The Board should issue the applicant investor a "certificate of outbound investment" or "investment project filing opinion" within five working days after receiving the application documents. After obtaining the Certificate or Opinion, the investor may apply for foreign exchange settlement and converting RMB into

---

1 A foreign invested enterprise may need to go through anti-monopoly review and national security review, if applicable.

foreign currency for offshore investments.

Case study: Hony Capital

Hony Capital is a Chinese private equity firm that invested in PPTV, a Chinese video streaming services provider by incorporating a fund management company (serving as the general partner of the fund) and a fund company in the Shanghai FTZ. The fund company was used as the investment entity to make the outbound investment. It took Hony Capital only five days to complete the filing with the Shanghai FTZ Board. Hony Capital also filed a subsequent transaction for the acquisition of US-based STX Filmworks, Inc. in the FTZ. The filing system only took four days to complete. This is more efficient than outside of the FTZ.

Take-away points: The Chinese outbound investment management system is under the transition from an approval-based system to a filing-based system. The "one-stop" filing system established by the Shanghai FTZ Board is much more efficient and transparent than the systems established by the MOFCOM and NDRC outside of the FTZ.

Draft Foreign Investment Law published by the MOFCOM

In January 2015, the MOFCOM published the first draft of Foreign Investment Law for public comments. The draft significantly changes the regime governing foreign investment in China that has been in place since the early 2000. The existing foreign investment laws that apply to foreign-invested enterprises (that is, the Wholly Foreign-owned Enterprise Law, the Sino-Foreign Equity Joint Venture Enterprise Law and the Sino-Foreign Cooperative Joint Venture Enterprise Law) will be repealed and replaced with a unified law regulating foreign investment into China. The draft intends to facilitate and protect investments with a view to creating a stable, transparent and predictable investment environment.

This draft has four major features:

- The scope of "foreign investors" and "foreign investment" will be expanded. For example, any domestic entity controlled by a foreign entity (such as variable interest entity) will be classified as a foreign investor and its investment will be subject to the foreign investment restrictions set out in the negative list.

- A negative list of non-conforming measure will replace the Catalogue for Foreign Investment. Foreign investors will no longer be subject to a different regulatory regime from domestic Chinese investors. Instead, foreign investors will enjoy national treatment except in certain industrial sectors that are specified on a negative list.

- The model for government to manage foreign investment will shift from requiring foreign invested enterprises to obtain prior approval from various governmental authorities, to a model of "limited licensing plus comprehensive reporting."

- The scope of the national security review procedure for foreign investments will be expanded and decisions will explicitly receive immunity from judicial or administrative review.

Questions:

1. Please read the following case, do independent research and make comments on (1) the extraterritorial jurisdiction of MOFCOM on overseas acquisition and (2) the review standard for the "operator concentration."

Case Analysis: Inbev Acquisition of Anheuser-Busch

Fact: In July 14, 2008, Inbev, the largest brewer in the world, purchased the brewer magnate Anheuser-Busch (AB) at the price of US$ 52 billion, and consequently has accomplished the biggest acquisition in the brewery industry in the world up till now. This acquisition has tremendous influence in China because it has significantly increased concentration in the brewery industry. Inbev is in a monopoly position in Chinese market. Although this acquisition was between two overseas enterprises, it involved the business of both enterprises in China and their turnover in 2007 were 5.764 billion and 4.49 billion respectively, which has reached the threshold of the Regulation of Criteria for Notification concerning Operator Concentration issued by the State Council. According to the Anti-Monopoly Law, both parties notified MOFCOM before finishing the acquisition.

MOFCOM Decision: According to Article 27 of the Anti-Monopoly Law, MOFCOM reviewed the acquisition and held several seminars, forums and hearings, surveying opinions and suggestions from the relevant departments in charge, local governments, trade associations, competitors in the same industry and the upstream and downstream enterprises. The result of the review indicated that the acquisition would not exclude and restrict competition in Chinese brewery industry in terms of the regional market, product market and competition pattern. Therefore, MOFCOM decided not to ban the acquisition. But in view of the tremendous scale of the acquisition, the significant market shares of the new enterprise from the acquisition and the obvious enhancement of its competitive strength, in order to reduce adverse effects the acquisition may have on the future market competition in Chinese brewery industry, MOFCOM decided to set four limits on this acquisition.

- InBev is not allowed to increase AB's 27% stake in the Tsingtao Brewery Group;
- If there is any change in InBev's shareholders or shareholders of InBev's shareholders, the company must report it in a timely manner to MOFCOM;
- InBev may not increase its 28.56% stake in Zhujiang Brewery Group; and
- InBev should not seek a stake in either China Resources Breweries Co. or Beijing Yanjing Brewery Co.

InBev agreed with the four limits and on July 13, 2008 acquired all AB shares at US$ 70 per share. This was the first operator concentration case that had been approved and published by MOFCOM after the Anti-Monopoly Law came into effect. This acquisition was also the first time for parties to comply with the acquisition limits set by MOFCOM on the basis of the Anti-Monopoly Law.

2. Compare the pre-establishment national treatment between China and the US for FDI and indicate their differences.

Suggested Further Readings

Jie Huang, *Challenges and Solutions for the China-US BIT Negotiations: Insights from the Recent Development of FTZs in China*, 18 Journal of International Economic Law 307, 2015.

Serena Y. Shi, *Dragon's House of Cards: Perils of Investing in Variable Interest Entities Domiciled in the People's Republic of China and Listed in the United States*, 37 Fordham International Law Journal 1265, 2014.

Margie-Lys Jaime, *Relying upon Parties' Interpretation in Treaty-Based Investor-State Dispute Settlement: Filling the Gaps in International Investment Agreements*, 46 Georgetown Journal of International Law 261, 2014.

Guiguo Wang, Essay in Honor of W. Michael Reisman: *Trade, Investment and Dispute Settlement: China's Practice in International Investment Law: From Participation to Leadership in the World Economy*, 34 Yale J. Int'l L. 575, 2009.

Lutz-Christian Wolff, *China's Private International Investment Law: One-way Street into PRC Law*, 56 American Journal of Comparative Law 1039, 2008.

OECD, OECD Benchmark Definition of Foreign Direct Investment (fourth edition 2008).

Jordan Brandt, *Comparing Foreign Investment in China, Post-WTO Accession, with Foreign Investment in the United States, Post 9/11*, 16 Pacific Rim Law & Policy Journal 285, 2007.

Chapter 9

Intellectual Property

Intellectual property is a relatively new legal field, yet it has become a significant form of personal property. This chapter aims to introduce the basic structure and key knowledge of intellectual property protection system from both China and international perspectives. It is laid out in three parts.

part 1   examines the copyright system.

part 2   introduces the patent system.

part 3   discusses the trademark and unfair competition theory.

▪ Learning Objectives

By the end of this chapter you should:

- Identify three pillars constituting the intellectual property legal framework.
- Understand the protection and balancing of owner and public interests as structured by the intellectual property policy.
- Learn the basic theories and key concepts of Chinese copyright, patent and trademark laws.
- Be aware of the evident differences between the intellectual property laws of China and other major jurisdictions as well as the internationalization of domestic legislations.

■ Key Terms

Confusion	Neighboring rights
Copyright	Novelty
Disclosure	Originality
Distinctiveness	Passing off
Economic rights	Patent
Fair use	Trademark
Invention	Utility model
Inventive step	Well-known mark
Moral rights	Work of authorship

Part 1   Copyright

At least as it was originally architected, copyright encourages the creation, and promotes the protection of literary and artistic works. Whether or not copyright, as currently configured, has achieved those conceived purposes is interestingly arguable. As technologies advance, copyright protection continues to extend to industry-oriented products which seem more naturally suitable to be protected by patent or industrial design laws.

In China, copyright is principally protected under the Copyright Law of the People's Republic of China (hereinafter "Chinese Copyright Law"), which was adopted on September 7, 1990 and amended in 2001 and 2010. As this Chapter of the book is being written, the Chinese Copyright Law is undergoing another challenging amendment. A number of other legal instruments have also played important roles in supplementing the copyright protection in China.[1] Some of them may eventually merge into the Chinese Copyright Law as being amended in one way or another.

Internationally, copyright protection is mainly coordinated by the Berne Convention for the Protection of Literary and Artistic Works (hereinafter "Berne Conventions")[2] and also by the

---

1 These legal instruments in respect of copyright include: Implementing Regulations of the Copyright Law of the People's Republic of China (the "Copyright Law Implementing Regulations"), Regulations on the Protection of the Right of Communication Through Information Network, Regulations on the Collective Administration of Copyright, Regulations on the Protection of Computer Software, Provisions on the Implementation of the International Copyright Treaties, Interim Measures for Payment of Remuneration by Radio and Television Stations for Broadcasting Sound Recordings and Regulations on the Protection of Layout Design of Integrated Circuits.

2 The Berne Convention was first signed and accepted in Berne, Switzerland, on September 9, 1886. The convention has currently 168 signatory parties and China joined on October 15, 1992.

Agreement on Trade Related Aspects of Intellectual Property Rights (the "TRIPS").[1]

What does copyright protect?

Copyright law protects works of authorship from being copied only, nothing else. Different than patent and trademark regimes, where infringement may be found even if a defendant independently makes his own creation, copyright is not infringed as long as an act of copying does not exist.

1. What is a work?

A work is eligible for copyright protection if it originates from the author and can be fixed in some form. In the US the fixation is a requirement for the attachment of copyright. Subject matter of copyright has in the past decades gone far beyond what copyright has originally been reserved for works of authors. While traditionally the meaning of the term "author" has been so broad that it includes composers, artists, photographers, sculptors and even architects, contemporary copyright law further extends protection akin to copyright to performers, record producers and broadcasters although the rights so conferred are not connected with the work's actual author.

Categorization of works is an important objective of copyright law because variable proprietary rights may be vested in owners of different categories of works, sometimes with different duration of protection. For most countries, including China, works categorized by respective copyright laws are not meant to be exclusive. Works falling out of the categories enumerated in sections 2 and 3 below can still be copyright-protected as long as they meet the conditions of protection prescribed by copyright laws.

2. Categories of protected works

In a more traditional sense, works that are copyrightable generally include works of literature, art and science, as further illustrated below and mainly based on the Chinese Copyright Law.

(1) Literary works

Literary works are all in writings, but broader than works of literature, whose languages generally emphasize on literariness, as opposed to ordinary languages. This means that as long as originality requirement is met, any organization of words (such as instruction manuals) or alphanumeric (such as computer programs) may be considered literary works.

(2) Oral works

An oral work is different from performance of a work orally in that oral work only comes into being as it is orally presented. Chinese Copyright Law explicitly protects oral works even though

---

1 TRIPS was negotiated at the end of the Uruguay Round of the General Agreement on Tariffs and Trade (GATT) in 1994 and accepted as an annex to the Agreement establishing the World Trade Organization.

without fixation on a tangible media such works cannot be effectively protected. The interesting question, however, is that whether an oral work, once fixed, remains an oral work or becomes a literary or other work. The United States Copyright Act of 1976[1] (the "US Copyright Act" or "Act"), on the other hand, excludes oral works from protection.

(3) Artistic works: musical, dramatic, *quyi*, choreographic and acrobatic works

    a Musical works can be songs or music, with or without lyrics. The lyrics alone are not considered musical works, yet they may be independently protected as literary works if they acquire originality.

    b Dramatic works such as Chinese traditional operas, plays and dramas are normally performed on stage, from which audience is presented with storylines. However, it is not the complete dramatic arrangement as it is perceived, which usually involves multitudinous efforts from scriptwriters, directors, actors/actresses, lighting designers, stage designers and dressers, which would be given copyright protection. Rather, under both domestic and international laws, copyright protection for dramatic works is reserved only for the works to be performed. In general, such works are manifested by the script composed of dialogue, narration and words, among other things.

    c *Quyi* works are specific to China. These Chinese traditional arts include *xiangsheng* (cross talk), *kuaishu* (clapper talk), *dagu* (ballad singing with drum accompaniment) and *pingshu* (story-telling based on classical novels).

    d Choreographic works are similar to dramatic works in that copyright extends to the structuring of the body movements, gestures and facial expression (as opposed to performance on the stage), but the two works are also different in that choreography is not required to tell a live story.

    e Works of acrobatic art are rarely the subject matter of copyright in most countries' laws, with the Chinese Copyright Law being the only notable exception. To be copyrighted, an acrobatic work must show its artistic merit.

(4) Artistic works: works of fine arts, applied art and architecture, and photographic works

    a Works of fine arts such as paintings and sculptures, must impart aesthetic effect to be copyrightable. However, the standard, quality or value of the aesthetic effect of a work of fine arts shouldn't become a factor in determining whether it should be copyrighted or not, because all that copyright requires is minimal creation. Calligraphy is explicitly categorized as work of fine arts under the Chinese Copyright Law. It is worth noting though, that a calligraphic work may at the same time qualify as literary work.

    b Works of applied art, though protected under the Berne Convention, grouped with industrial designs, are NOT a class of works of authorship under the current Chinese

---

1   Title 17 of the United States Code (i.e. 17 U.S.C.)

Copyright Law. Even if works of applied art are officially recognized for copyright protection, they must first impart aesthetic effect.

c Work of architecture are another category of works that need to communicate aesthetic messages before they can be protected by copyright. The current Chinese Copyright Law only sees the actual buildings or structures as works of architecture, but it's possible that scope of such work would be expanded to include the plans, drawings, sketches and models of the buildings or structures.

d Photographic works, whether amateur or professional, should be extended copyright as long as they have constituted certain degree of artistic expression. Simple shots such as head shots, snapshots and duplicating shots are less likely to be copyrightable.

(5) Graphic works

Graphic works normally include drawings of engineering designs and products designs, maps and sketches. Neither the technological proposition depicted in an engineering or product design, however advanced or backward, nor the project or product based thereupon, however fanciful or inferior, should facilitate or inhibit the copyrightability of the work.

(6) Model works

Model works, also known as three-dimensional works[1], scale the objects for the purpose of exhibition, examination or observation of the same. The model of a work of architecture may be protected under the category of model work.

3. Special categories of works

As mentioned earlier, as technology develops, many new types of works have been granted legal protection under the generalized regime of copyright. The following categories of works are such that while they may not be necessarily protected under "copyright" as is, whatever rights prescribed for a particular class of works are similar or related to copyright.

(1) Computer software

Computer software, or computer programs[2], are mainly dealt with by the Regulations on the Protection of Computer Software. They have been effectively treated as literary works, and source code and object code are protected as one computer program.

---

1 It is likely that the Chinese Copyright Law, upon the passage of the ongoing amendment, will use the term three-dimensional works to replace model works.

2 Computer software is the term used under current Chinese law and may be replaced by the term computer programs in the new amendment of the Chinese Copyright Law.

(2) Layout design of integrated circuits

Layout design of integrated circuits, also known as "mask works" (in the US) or "topographies," are not addressed in the Chinese Copyright Law.[1] What the designers of layout designs own is not copyright, but rather, literarily, the "layout design proprietary right". On top of the general originality and minimum creativity requirements, to be protected a layout design must not be a staple or other design familiar to the ordinary designers in the field of semiconductor chip.

(3) Cinematographic works

Cinematographic works and works created by a process analogous to cinematography are called audiovisual works[2] in the US.

The following two special categories of works receive copyright when they meet certain requirement, although in the Chinese Copyright Law they are not enumerated as works of authorship per se.

(4) Derivative works: adaptation, translation, annotation and arrangement of pre-existing works

A derivative work must generally retain the basic expressive elements of the pre-existing work (or underlying work). If the only thing the second work "borrows" from the underlying work is its idea, such second work may come about as an independent new work rather than a derivative. On the other hand, a derivative work should involve creation much more substantial than the originality requirement generally applicable to copyrightable works. Trivial variations from the underlying work do not suffice. The Chinese Copyright Law grants the persons who create derivatives the copyright with respect to such derivatives, but it remains silent as to whether prior approval should be acquired from the copyright owner of the underlying work before one creates a derivative based upon it. What the law really cares is that before derivative is put into use (which should include act of first publication), approval must be acquired from the copyright owner of the underlying work.

(5) Compilations, including databases

Compilations are afforded copyright if the work is the result of original selection or arrangement of materials, which can well be non-work-of-authorship data.

The following four special categories of works are protected with "related right" as opposed to copyright, which will be elaborated in section 1.5, Neighboring Rights, of the Chapter.

---

1 They are separately dealt with by the Regulations on the Protection of Layout Design of Integrated Circuits.

2 The term audiovisual works is being proposed during the ongoing amendment to the Chinese Copyright Law and is likely to be adopted.

- Publications: books and periodicals
- Performance
- Sound recordings (or phonograms)
- Broadcasting: television and radio stations

4. Exclusion

A fundamental of copyright theory is that copyright protection only extends to original expression of an idea, but not the idea itself. However, it is not always easy to make a distinction between ideas and expressions when it comes to judging expressive elements of any given work, particularly in cases where ideas can be expressed intelligibly only in one or a limited number of ways. The idea-expression continuum often needs to be scrutinized to decide what expressive elements constitute original expressions and what should be barred from copyright protection because they are essential ideas.

In the US, the doctrine of merger is a judicial effort to avoid the impermissible protection of idea, in which "courts may withhold protection of matter that is clearly expressive, if that expression is one of the only very limited number of ways of expressing that idea."[1] It often applies to works of science (e.g. computer software) and literature, where an expression is considered to be inextricably merged with an idea. Similar to the proposition of merger, copyright protection also does not extend to scènes à faire, a scene in a book or film, for example, which is customary to or almost obligatory for a genre of its type. Other than inhibition of ideas from copyright protection in the abstract, copyright laws of different countries normally would also identify a few specific articles as non-protectable. The Chinese Copyright Law, for example, is not applicable to, thus explicitly denies protection of, the following:

- Government documents: laws and regulations, resolutions, decisions and orders of state organs, other documents of a legislative, administrative or judicial nature and their official translations
- News on current affairs
- Calendars, numerical tables, forms of general use, and formulas

Conditions of protection

1. Originality

A work is not the work in the sense of copyright law unless it owns originality. Both the English term "originality" and its Chinese equivalent imaginatively carry within themselves the literal meaning of both independent origin and creativity, which have been established by jurisprudence to become the prerequisite to copyrightability. To be copyright protected, a work must:

- originate from one's own efforts (and separate copyrights may therefore exist in independently

---

1 Sheldon W. Halpern, Craig Allen Nard and Kenneth L. Port, *Fundamentals of United States Intellectual Property Law: Copyright, Patent, and Trademark*, p. 10.

created works, even if the works, on close examination, are identical);

- present a certain level of creativity, which means although the creativity does not have to reach the level of fine literature or demonstrate aesthetic value, it must not be too trivial.

CASE EXAMPLE: *Hantao v. Aibang*[1]

Facts: Shanghai Hantao Information Consulting Co., Ltd. ("Hantao") owns and operates www.dianping.com, a review site providing lifestyle information on local dining, leisure and entertainment services and a platform for consumers to post their reviews on individual merchants. www.aibang.com of Aibangjuxin (Beijing) Science & Technology Co., Ltd. ("Aibang") is a vertical search engine. Late 2007, Haotao discovered that www.aibang.com published reviews of thousands of restaurants originally posted by consumers on www.dianping.com. Hantao filed a civil lawsuit against Aibang after the two sides failed to settle the issue.

The trial court ruled that: The introductions of restaurants and users' reviews as a whole constituted a compilation, thus Aibang infringed Hantao's copyright. On appeal, the Beijing First High Court found that users' descriptions of restaurants with very simple languages were not the intellectual result protected by the Chinese Copyright Law, and such descriptions were no more than the common expression of restaurants' features, thus lacking originality. The court further found that even the more detailed reviews may not have necessarily constituted the works recognized by the Chinese Copyright Law because the main purpose of such review languages were to describe objective facts and deliver information, and because the ways of expressing such objective facts or opinions were very limited, to grant them copyright protection was to monopolize the relevant facts or opinions. Last the court determined that listing the users' reviews in the order of posting time was just a normal way of arrangement without showing any creativity or selection of the contents of the reviews by www.dianping.com, so the introductions of restaurants and the users' reviews as a whole didn't constitute a work of compilation.

Take-away point: The simple languages used to describe certain facts or ideas, especially where such facts or ideas are difficult to describe without using such simple languages, do not present originality so they don't constitute the works protected by the Chinese Copyright Law. Listing of consumers' messages on an online platform in the order of their posting time without selection of the content of such messages does not create a compilation work.

---

2. Reproducibility (v. Fixation)

The Copyright Law Implementing Regulations provide that a work must be an intellectual creation "capable of being reproduced in a tangible form". Other than the "reproductability" or "capability of being reproduced", there is no other notable formal requirement of copyrightability such as publication, notice or registration. By contrast, in the US, fixation is a formal requirement

---

1 Shanghai Hantao Information Consulting Co., Ltd. v. Aibangjuxin (Beijing) Science & Technology Co., Ltd., (2009)Yi Zhong Min Zhong Zi Di 5031 Hao.

of copyright protection. The US Copyright Act provides that, copyright attaches and protection begins, once an "original work of authorship" has been "fixed in any tangible medium of expression" by or under the authority of the author.[1]

Ownership

Surely, copyright as a whole is initially vested in the author simply because copyright emerges from the creation of the work. However, authorship and ownership are two distinct concepts. An author of a work, that is, one who actually committed his labor to the creation of the work, may not always be the owner of the copyright pertaining to such work s/he authored. In addition, copyright is in fact the collection of different "copyrights" or to be exact, copyright interests, each of which may be owned separately or disposed of independently.

1. Divisibility and distribution of copyright interests

Copyright is divisible and may change ownership by law or contract.

- Statutory rights. Copyright consists of or is virtually divided by law into an array of specific rights. These rights will be further articulated in the next section, Owner's Rights, of this Chapter.
- Succession of copyright interests. All or any of the economic rights of the copyright owner may be succeeded by other persons through contractual arrangement or as the legal consequences of certain legal events such as inheritance. Copyright owner may arrange the transfer or license of copyright interests such that the particular rights to be transferred or licensed can be freely selected and termination of such transfer or license for each such particular right can be agreed upon. Change hand of ownership of the original copy of a work, however, does not transfer the ownership of the copyright in that work.

2. Authorship

(1) Natural persons as authors

Only those natural persons (or individuals) who actually undertake the creation of works are authors in the copyright sense. Providers of the organizational work, material conditions or supporting efforts in relation to the creation of a work, on the other hand, are not. Similarly, those who merely contribute ideas which lead to certain works, however brilliant or important such ideas are for the creation of such works, should not be considered authors.

(2) Legal persons or other organizations as authors

Although Chinese copyright regime generally follows the civil-law system, China adopts the US

---

1   Sheldon W. Halpern, Craig Allen Nard and Kenneth L. Port, *Fundamentals of United States Intellectual Property Law: Copyright, Patent, and Trademark*, p. 41. Fixation is being discussed during the current amendment of the Chinese Copyright Law, which, if adopted, will replace the reproductability requirement.

practice with regards to the recognition of legal persons or other organization, such as companies, as a type of authors of certain statutorily defined works.[1] Such works are then called "works of legal person." This is troublesome though, because the Chinese Copyright Law at the same time provides that absent an agreement to the contrary copyright in the "works created in the course of employment", the de facto equivalent of the US term of "works made for hire", belongs to the employees.

3. Authorship/Ownership of special works

(1) Joint works

In general, a work created jointly by two or more authors would be considered a joint work where the co-authors have the contemporaneous intention to make their contribution, at the time of such contribution is made, to the unitary whole of the work. Under the Chinese Copyright Law, a song in which lyrics and music are separately composed by two artists may become a joint work where the contemporaneous intention requirement is met.

The copyright in a joint work shall be owned jointly by all co-authors, each of whom at the same time enjoys any independent copyright that may pertain to the work separable from the joint work and which owes its origin to him or her.

(2) Works made for hire

Contemporary copyright systems, even the civil law systems which traditionally adopt a strong link between the rights (at least initially) and the person of the author, generally realize that employers shall enjoy certain economic rights in connection with works created by their employees if conditions are met. Under the Chinese Copyright Law, works made for hire are known as "works created in the course of employment". A work which may constitute one made for hire must be created i) by the employee during his or her employment with the employer and ii) for the purpose of fulfilling the job assigned to him or her by the employer. As a general rule under the Chinese law, ownership of copyright in the works made for hire can be agreed on by the parties and it is vested in the employees where there exists no agreement or if there is an agreement between the employee and employer but such agreement is ambiguous as to who owns the copyright. There is an exception to the general rule, that is, with respect to drawings of engineering and products designs, maps and computer programs, where such works are created mainly with the material and technical resources of the employer and for which the employer bears responsibility, the copyright is owned by the employer while employee enjoys the right of attribution.

Common law system, such as the US, see works as pure private properties, so persons organizing

---

1 Article 11, para 3 of the Chinese Copyright Law provides that *"where a work is created under the auspices and according to the intention of a legal person or other organization, which bears responsibility for the work, the said legal entity or organization shall be deemed to be the author of the work."*

or even sheer investing financially in the creation of works can become copyright owners (or even authors) in the first place. Based on such canon, the US Copyright Act accords the employers the status of authors for the works made by their employees, which means that employers are the initial owner of copyright and enjoy all the rights associated therewith. Furthermore, although employers and employees may agree that copyright in the works made for hire goes to the employees, authorship shall stay with the employers.

(3) Commissioned works

That who own copyright in commissioned works varies considerably among countries. The Chinese Copyright Law grants it to the commissioned party in the event the parties fail to unequivocally agree upon the ownership of copyright in such works, in which case the commissioning party may use for free the commissioned works within the scope purported by the commissioning. The US Copyright Act does not directly address the ownership issue with respect to copyright in commissioned works. Instead, the Act identifies nine categories of commissioned works which should be considered works made for hire if the parties expressly so agree in writing.[1]

Owner's rights

Copyright is composed of an array of exclusive rights prescribed by law, which are assorted to establish two sets of very distinct types of rights, moral rights and economic rights. Copyright protection is designed such that each of the exclusive rights thereof regulates a particular type of acts. For example, the right to reproduce regulates the acts of reproduction and broadcasting right governs the acts of broadcasting.

1. Moral rights

The protection of the moral rights of an author is based on the view that a creative work is in some way an expression of the author's personality. The moral rights are therefore personal to the author, and cannot be transferred to or inherited by another person. Moral rights are generally recognized in civil law countries and, to a lesser extent, in some common law countries.

(1) The right to publish

The right to publish is the right to decide whether to make a work available to the public, but it should be interpreted to confer to the author also the right to decide on when, where and how he would have his work published. Simplistically put, the right to publish is deemed to have

---

1   17 USC §101 provides that a "work made for hire" is "…*a work specially ordered or commissioned for use as a contribution to a collective work, as a part of a motion picture or other audiovisual work, as a translation, as a supplementary work, as a compilation, as an instructional text, as a test, as answer material for a test, or as an atlas, if the parties expressly agree in a written instrument signed by them that the work shall be considered a work made for hire.*"

been used up thus cannot be reclaimed by the author once he has agreed to the exploitation (by others) of the work by ways such as reproduction, distribution, exhibition, performance or cinematography, dependent on the nature of the work.

(2) The right of attribution

The right of attribution allows the author to claim authorship to the work and decide how he would achieve such claim, for example, in his legal name, pseudonymously or anonymously.

(3) The right to the integrity of the work

The right to the integrity of work prevents a copyrighted work from being distorted or mutilated.

(4) The right to alter

The right to alter, available probably only in China, is considered by many to be redundant because the right to the integrity of work has effectively precluded others from altering the work without the authorization from the author.[1]

(5) The right to follow

The right to follow is not explicitly available under the Chinese law. First created in France and called droit de suite, the right to follow is a right granted to artists or their heirs to receive a fee on the resale of their works of art.[2] The right to follow is apparently a hybrid of moral and economic rights, while presenting more evident moral nature in that such right is clearly bound to the identity and character of a person, i.e. the author, and can therefore never be transferred nor relinquished.

2. Economic rights

The other component of copyright is the economic rights. The purpose of the formulation of the economic rights is to promote the creation and dissemination of works by granting limited monopoly to the right owners over a diversified means of exploitation of the works. In common law systems, works are deemed nothing but authors' properties, so protection is centered on excluding others from pirating their proprietary interest, thus the "copy" right.

(1) The right to reproduce

The right to reproduce is obviously the central piece of the series of the proprietary rights

---

1   It is likely that the right to alter would be denounced and incorporated as a part of the right to integrity of work in the current amendment to the Chinese Copyright Law.

2   The right to follow is being proposed for the amendment to the Chinese Copyright Law and if adopted, would probably entitle the author or his heir or legatee to claim a share of the proceeds gained by the owner of the original of a work of fine arts or photographic work, or the manuscript of a literary or musical work, of the resale of such original or manuscript.

constituting copyright. An act of reproduction, or "copying", can be made in different methods, using different devices, but a "copy" is made of a copyrighted work only when it is solidly fixed on tangible media. Copying can be carried out, in its forms, from plane to plane, from plane to three dimensional, from three dimensional to plane or from three dimensional to three dimensional. In digital world, acts of fixing works on different hardware, uploading them to and from web servers and disseminating the same through network are all considered reproduction of works.

(2) The right to distribute

The right to distribute controls the acts of the provision of the original or the copies of the copyrighted works to the general public. Distribution under the meaning of copyright law takes place and, if without authorization by the copyright owner, constitutes an infringement where i) the original or the copies of the work are "made available" to the public and ii) they are sold, donated or otherwise transferred for the purpose of changing ownership.

Owner's right to distribute is subject to limitation imposed by the first sale doctrine, which is defined differently in different jurisdictions but generally means that the copyright owner of a work shall not interfere with the sale, rental or other act of disposition of the copies of the work one has legally obtained through a proper license from or a distribution made by the owner.

(3) The rental right

In many countries, the rental right is often incorporated into the right to distribute as its sub-right. The Chinese Copyright Law, on the other hand, independently enumerates the rental right, which grants the owners the right to allow (or prohibit) others to use temporarily, on a fee basis, their audiovisual works, computer programs (excluding those that are not the main subject matter of the rental), and work of sound recordings, in its original form or a copy.

The three economic rights explained above, sometimes collectively called the "right of reproduction", have one common function, that is, they regulate the changing of ownership or possession of the tangible media embodying the works.

The next few rights, on the other hand, coordinate the appreciation or the use of the substance of the works by the general public, the tangible media of which do not change hands during the process. These rights are therefore called, in aggregate, the "right of public communication". Needless to say, before any work is communicated to the public, permission should be obtained from the copyright owner or collective rights organization.

(4) The display right

The display right, according to the Chinese Copyright Law, is the right to publicly display the authentic or reproduced work of the fine arts or of a photographic work. The transfer of ownership of the authentic works shall not result in the transfer of the copyright in such works; however, the right to display the authentic works of the fine arts or photographic works rests with the owner of such authentic works. Display by the assignee of an authentic work assigned to him before it is published should not be deemed an infringement of the author's right to publish.

(5) The performing right

The performing right is the right to perform certain types of works (most typically music or songs) in the public, i.e. the "live performance", and to publicly communicate the works or the performance of the works by technical devices, sometimes known as the "mechanical performance". The two types of performances are treated by different rights in different countries. Under current Chinese Copyright Law, the mechanical performance refers to only the act of presenting to the public the performance of the works by machines after such performance are recorded. Other acts of mechanical performance include showing works of fine arts, photographic works, cinematographic works and works created by a process analogous to cinematography. These performances are the subject matter of the performing right in some countries, such as the US. However, they are regulated under the Chinese Copyright Law through a separate and independent proprietary right called the right of showing.[1]

(6) The broadcasting right

The broadcasting right administers three distinct acts of broadcasting: i) to broadcast a work or disseminate it to the public by any wireless means; ii) to communicate the broadcast of a work to the public by wired means or by rebroadcasting; and iii) publicly communicate the broadcast of a work by loudspeaker or any other analogous instrument transmitting signs, sounds or images.

(7) The right of communication through information network

The right of communication through information network was adopted to cope with the dramatic changes to the methods of work dissemination as the result of advancement in the internet technologies. Making the work available to the public through the network, either by wireless or wired means, is the fundamental activity the proprietary right is architected to control, and such activity must be interactive, meaning that any member of the public may access to the work from a place and at a time of their own choice. Peer-to-peer sharing of copyrighted works by individual users has been generally decided as a type of such interactive communication of such works.

The final two proprietary rights under the Chinese Copyright Law, elaborated below, can generally be categorized as the "right to prepare derivative works".

---

1 The right of showing may disappear in Chinese law if the proposal of incorporating it into the performing right is eventually adopted by the newest amendment to the Chinese Copyright Law.

(8) The adaptation right

The adaptation right, as defined in the Chinese Copyright Law, is intended to give the copyright owner the right to exclude others from making adaptation to the work without his approval. However, as discussed above in section 3, the person who creates a work based upon a pre-existing copyrighted work by adaptation does not infringe the copyright in such pre-existing work as long as the derivative work is not published nor otherwise exploited. This is because the adaptation right inherently governs not only the act of adaptation but also acts of exploiting such adapted work following the adaptation, such as publishing, distribution and performance.

(9) The translation right

The translation right is the right to change the language in which the work is written into another language.

The economic rights enumerated, like those above, in copyright legislations shouldn't be considered exhaustive. The Chinese Copyright Law, for example, concludes the enumeration with a "catch-all" provision that covers "other rights to be enjoyed by copyright owners."

Neighboring rights

Neighboring rights, or related rights, is a term used in contrast with author's rights. In the civil-law system, "copyright" only protects works of authorship, which would qualify as such only when the works meet the originality requirement, and a work is not considered original if it does not reflect the author's personality or intelligence. Related rights were invented to "protect the legal interests of certain persons and legal entities who contribute to making works available to the public; or who produce subject matter which, while not qualifying as works under the copyright systems…, contain sufficient creativity or technical and organizational skill to justify recognition of a copyright-like property right."[1] In English or US law, on the other hands, authors' rights and related rights are both copyrights.

There is no universal definition of related rights, which vary much more widely in scope between different countries than authors' rights. In contemporary world, related rights have been expanded to include those that protect subject matters which are not in any way related to any works and whose owners are not even disseminators of the works, and they include, within the European Union, for example, the rights of film producers and database creators. The rights of performers, phonogram producers and broadcasting organizations are traditionally covered, and are internationally protected mainly by the International Convention for the Protection of Performers, Producers of Phonograms and Broadcasting Organizations done at Rome on October 26, 1961 (hereinafter "Rome Convention").

---

1 Understanding Copyright and Related Rights.

1. The publishers' rights

The publishers' rights protect the proprietary interests of publishers with respect to the typographical designs presented in their publications. Under the Chinese Copyright Law, publishers are granted the rights to authorize others to use the typographical designs of the book or periodical they publish.

2. The performers' rights

The performers' rights protect the proprietary interests of performers with respect to their performances. Under the Chinese Copyright Law, performers are given the rights to prevent or authorize the fixation (recording) of their performance, the broadcasting or communicating to the public of their live performances and the making available to the public of their performances through information network, and the right to prevent or authorize reproduction and distribution of recordings of their performances under certain circumstances. In addition, as laws of many other countries, the Chinese Copyright Law grants performers two moral rights, i.e. the right of attribution and right to prevent the image inherent in his performance from being distorted.

Performing a copyrighted work absent the fair-use scenarios can be an infringement unless the performer has first obtained permission from the copyright owner to make such performance. At the same time, a performer may only exercise the performer's rights vested in him but he is not entitled to authorize others to use the proprietary rights in the work of authorship based upon which his performance is made.

3. The rights of producers of phonograms

The rights of producers of phonograms protect the proprietary interests of the producers of phonograms with respect to phonograms (or sound recordings as they are called in the US) they produce, the recording of sounds of performance and any other sounds. The producers are provided the rights to authorize or prohibit the reproduction, distribution, rental and the making available to the public of the phonograms (and the copies thereof) they produce.

4. The rights of broadcasting organizations

The rights of broadcasting organizations protect the proprietary interests of radio stations and television stations with respect to the signals of their broadcasts. It is not the broadcast "programs" that are protected by the rights of broadcasting organizations, which, when copyright protectable, are protected as other subject matters available under copyright laws, often the audiovisual works or phonograms. The broadcasting organizations are afforded the right to authorize or prohibit re-broadcasting, fixation (recording) and reproduction of their broadcasts.

Limitation on rights

The owners' rights to exclude unauthorized exploitation of copyrighted works, as conferred by the copyright law, are not and shall not be absolute. Otherwise the ultimate purpose of the law to promote the dissemination of works would be seriously compromised or become too costly to achieve. The Berne Convention recognizes at the international level the needs and practices of national legislators to impose certain limitations on these exclusive rights. Article 9(2) allows the countries of the Union to provide for free "reproduction of such [literary and artistic] works in special cases, provided that such reproduction does not conflict with normal exploitation of the work and do not unreasonably prejudice the legitimate interests of the author." TRIPS and the WIPO Copyright Treaty (hereinafter "WCT") reaffirmed the afore-mentioned Berne three-step-test for conditioning the imposition of limitations but expanded the allowance of establishing limitations or exceptions to all proprietary rights (as opposed to just the reproduction rights).

Limitations of or exceptions to exclusive rights are set out in different mechanisms among different jurisdictions.

The US Copyright Act makes a legislative distinction between "fair use," use without either authorization or compensation, and "statutory license" that requires remuneration but not authorization, and a guidance is given by the Act on how to determine whether a particular use of copyrighted works would constitute a fair use.

The Chinese Copyright Law prescribes an enumerated set of limitation on rights and several scenarios equivalent to statutory license. For the purpose of this Chapter, the terms "fair use" and "statutory license" are used to distinguish the two different types of limitations on rights under the Chinese Copyright Law, each of which is reviewed below.

1. Fair use: free use

Fair use generally means that others may use, for free, certain works of authorship without the permission from the right owners in accordance with and under certain specific circumstances prescribed by law. In China, fair use of a work is sustained if in such use the name of the author and the title and source of the work are mentioned and the other rights enjoyed by the copyright owner are not prejudiced. The following paragraphs explain the free use scenarios explicitly prescribed by the Chinese Copyright Law and other relevant regulations.

(1) Personal use

Reproduction of fragments of a copyrighted work which has been published for the purpose of personal study and research is considered fair use. Personal appreciation is also a ground for claiming fair use under the Chinese Copyright Law but it is likely to be repealed as a response to the extravagant unauthorized downloads of copyrighted works, particularly music, made available by new technologies.

(2) Appropriate quotation

Quotation of published and copyrighted works is often necessary or even unavoidable in writing an introduction or a commentary on such works or in describing certain issue, but normally only when the quotation is limited to a certain length and level of significance could it be "appropriate," and thus a fair use.

(3) News reporting

Unavoidable inclusion or quotation of a published work in the media, such as in a newspaper, periodical, radio and television programs, for the purpose of reporting current events, is fair use.

(4) Articles on current topics

It is an act of fair use to publish or broadcast by the media of an article published by another media on current political, economic or religious topics, except where the author declares that such publishing or broadcasting is not permitted.

(5) Public speech

A speech delivered at a public gathering may be published or broadcast by the media, except where the author declares that such publishing or broadcasting is not permitted.

(6) Use in classroom teaching and research

It is not an infringement to translate or reproduce in a small quantity copies of a published work for use by teachers in classroom teaching or scientific researchers in scientific research, provided that the translation or the reproduction is not published for distribution.

(7) Use in duties by governments

Use of a published work by a State organ to a justifiable extent for the purpose of fulfilling its official duties, such as circulating a copyrighted photo of a criminal suspect associated with the wanted posters, is clearly a fair use.

(8) Reproduction and dissemination in archiving

Reproduction of a work in its collections by a library, archive, memorial hall, museum, art gallery, etc. for the purpose of display, or preservation of a copy, of the work, is prescribed to be legal. Such archiving organization may also make available to their service recipients, through information network, on it premises a legitimately published digital work in their collection and any work lawfully reproduced in a digital form for the purpose of display or preservation of the edition of the work, without the permission from, and without payment of the remuneration to, the copyright owner.

(9) Free performance

For a performance to constitute a fair use, it must be a gratuitous live performance of a published work, for which no fees are charged to the public and no payments are made to the performers.

(10) Reproduction of outdoor artistic works

People are allowed to make copying, drawing, photographing or video-recording of a work of art put up or displayed in an outdoor public place.

(11) Preparation of works in minority languages

Translation of a published work of a Chinese person, either natural or legal person or other organization, from Han language into minority nationality languages for publication and distribution in the country is a fair use.

(12) Preparation of braille

Transliteration of a published work into braille for publication is also a fair use.

(13) Computer program/software

Fair use scenarios in relation with computer software are provided for in the Regulations on the Protection of Computer Software. In brief, the owners of lawful copies of software are not considered infringing the software copyrights where they i) install and store the software in information processing devices, ii) make backup copies against damages, and iii) make necessary alterations to or improve functions or performance of the software for the purpose of applying the software to actual computing environment, provided that such altered software shall not be provided to any third party. Furthermore, anyone may freely use without permission from the copyright owner the computer software through, for example, installation, display, transmittance or storing, for the purpose of studying or researching the concepts and principles associated with the software design.

2. Statutory license: remuneration required

The other subset of limitations on owner's proprietary rights is the statutory or compulsory license, which allows the use of works in certain circumstances for a royalty, but without necessity to get permission from their owners. In exploiting the statutory licenses, users are also required to respect the attribution rights of authors and indicate the sources of the works. The statutory licenses made available by the Chinese Copyright Law are illustrated below.

(1) Reprinting of literary works among newspaper and periodicals

Literary works which have been published on a newspaper or periodical may be reposted or republished as excerpts or materials by another newspaper or periodical, except where a statement is made prominently on the newspaper or periodical that no reposting or republishing is allowed.

(2) Production of phonograms

Phonogram producers are allowed to create their own phonograms of musical works of which a lawful phonogram has already been made (without the permission from the copyright owner of such musical works). This statutory license doesn't render the unauthorized copying of the lawful phonogram first produced legal.

(3) Broadcasting of works and phonograms

A radio station or television station may broadcast the published works and the phonograms created by other persons without the permission of the copyright owners of, respectively, such works and the musical works based on which such phonograms were created.

(4) Compilation of textbooks

For the purpose of compiling textbooks for the compulsory education, short literary works and musical works, and single pieces of work of the fine arts and photographic works which have been published may, without permission from the copyright owner, be compiled in such textbooks.

(5) Preparation of course packs for dissemination through network

The concept of statutory license in relation to the textbook compilation had been adopted in online education by the Regulations on the Protection of the Right of Communication through Information Network which took effect in 2006. According to the regulations, extracts of published works, short literary works and musical works, and single pieces of works of fine art and photographic works may be used for preparing course packs, which can further be made available through information network to the registered students by the persons who prepared the course packs or the distant educational establishments which have lawfully obtained such course packs.

(6) Works in relation to poverty alleviation and works meeting fundamental cultural demands made available to rural areas by information network.

Enforcement and remedies to copyright infringement

If copyright owners or other interested parties (including qualified licensees) believe their copyright have been infringed upon, they can select civil, administrative or criminal remedies according to the situation of each case.

1. Civil remedies

(1) Cessation of infringement

Cessation of infringement, equivalent to injunction issued by courts in Western jurisdictions, orders infringer to stop his or her infringement. Preliminary injunction, a provisional measure, is also available for copyright holder through application to a court prior to the filing of a civil action in the case such holder can present evidence to prove that another person is committing, or is about to commit, an infringement upon his or her right, which, unless prevented promptly, is likely to cause irreparable harm to his or her legitimate rights and interests.

(2) Damages

a. Damages are awarded to copyright holders' whose economic rights have been found infringed by the defendants, but they will not be granted to the holders if the infringers do not know or have the reasonable grounds to know about the infringement.

b. Damages awarded shall compensate for the actual losses suffered by the right holder, or where the actual losses are difficult to calculate, can be commensurate with the amount of the unlawful gains of the infringer. Where neither the actual losses of the right holder nor the unlawful gains of the infringer can be determined, the court shall decide on the amount of the damages not more than CNY500,000, the limit of the statutory damages.[1]

c. The damages shall be of compensatory rather than punitive nature.[2] In the US, the Copyright Act is also silent with respect to punitive damages but there have been courts' decisions in the recent years which indicated that punitive damages might be recoverable under certain circumstances.

d. The damages or the economic compensation for the injured right holder shall include the reasonable expenses that the right holder has paid for putting a stop to the infringing activities, including attorney fees.

(3) Other civil remedies

When trying a case where the copyright or a right related to it is infringed upon, the court may rule to confiscate the unlawful gains, the unlawfully reproduced articles and the money and materials of value used for carrying out the illegal activities.

2. Administrative remedies

(1) Enforcement agencies

The National Copyright Administration and its local counterparts are the primary government organs charged with the responsibilities to regulate the copyright related matters, including enforcing against infringements. Other more important agencies which may be involved in the anti-piracy and other enforcement efforts include the Ministry of Culture, State Administration of Press, Publication, Radio, Film and Television, Ministry of Public Security (hereinafter "MPS") and General Administration of Customs (hereinafter "GAC") and their respective local counterparts.

---

1   The ceiling of the statutory damages is likely to be increased to CNY1,000,000 in the ongoing amendment to the Chinese Copyright Law.

2   The ongoing amendment to the Chinese Copyright Law proposes the addition of punitive damages (of up to three times the assessed damages) for the cases involving repeat and willful infringement of copyright or related rights.

(2) Administrative relief

Where public rights and interests are impaired by infringing activities, the competent copyright office may issue order to discontinue such activities, forfeit the unlawful gains, confiscate or destruct the unlawfully reproduced articles, and may also impose a fine; where the circumstances are serious, the said office may, in addition, confiscate the materials, tools and equipment, the main purpose of which is to make the unlawfully reproduced articles.

3. Criminal procedures

Under the Criminal Law of the People's Republic of China, as amended on August 25, 2011 (hereinafter "Criminal Law"), certain acts of for-profit copyright or related right infringement, including in particular the unauthorized reproduction and distribution of literary or musical work, cinematographic work, television program, video work[1], computer software, phonograms or other work, may trigger criminal investigation against and prosecution of the infringers, who, if found guilty, may be sentenced to imprisonment of up to seven years or criminal detention, and/or be adjudicated to pay a criminal fine, depending on the amount of illegal gains, the amount of illegal turnover and the seriousness of other circumstances of the crime. In the case of sale of illegally reproduced articles, the maximum term of imprisonment is three years.

SELF QUIZ: Indicate whether each of the following statements is true or false.

1. M infringes F's copyright if his work is identical to that of F.

2. Lyrics of a song cannot be copyright protected.

3. Copyright protects the expression of an idea, not the idea itself.

4. Moral rights cannot be sold or transferred although they can be waived.

5. Copyrights are always owned by the authors.

6. There is no formal requirement for copyright protection in the US.

7. If a literary work has been registered with the competent copyright authority, it must own originality.

8. As long as a work is the result of the original endeavor of an author, it is copyrightable.

9. Under Chinese law, all works created by employees during their employment with their company are considered works made for hire.

10. When you ask another person to create a work for you, the first copyright owner of such work is you, unless the two of you otherwise agree to the contrary in writing.

11. If a singer performs without authorization the song of a composer after such song has been performed by a first singer with the consent of the composer, the second signer has infringed the composer's right to publish the song.

---

1 Video work, as it appears in the Criminal Law, needs to be removed in the future to correspond to the abandonment of such concept and term in the 2001's amendment to the Chinese Copyright Law.

Part 2　Patent

Introduction

By granting the patentees for a period of time the rights to exclude others from exercising their inventions, the patent system aims to stimulate technology advancement. However, the exclusive rights are procured for a price—the full disclosure of the technology to the public, so that people may understand, exploit (with proper licenses) and build their own technologies on the technologies disclosed through the patents.

1. Patent system: a rival trade-off between inventor and others

What the patent system has formulated is essentially a rival trade-off between inventors and the public. The trade-off, from the perspective of the inventor, or other stakeholders, of a particular invention, is a mental process wherein the inventor tries to assess the benefits and costs of patenting (and thus disclosing) the invention and seeks to figure out the most proper patenting strategies if s/he so elects. Some companies may choose to avoid patenting of some of their technologies, probably forever; for example, Coca-Cola's natural flavoring recipe, Google's search algorithm PageRank and the mechanics of the *New York Times* Best Seller List are among the most widely discussed proprietary assets kept as trade secrets by their respective owners. Other companies may be able to orchestrate their intellectual property protection strategies in light of their overall business purpose such that only selected technologies or the composition(s) thereof are patented, at the most proper time too.

2. Patenting: an absolute monopolistic approach

Patent is arguably the strongest intellectual property protection made available by laws. The exclusive right conferred by patent is nearly absolute. Save for certain subtly defined exceptions, one may infringe upon a patent even if s/he simply exploits a technology s/he independently develops if such technology is the same as what the patent claims. He or she would not be exempted from the infringement charge even if he or she did not know either the patent or the person who first developed the technology leading to such patent. Absolute monopoly of patent features a sharp contrast with copyright protection, whereby an author who by chance creates a work identical to another earlier work will not infringe the copyright associated with such earlier work.

3. Fundamentals of the patent system

So, what is a patent? Indeed, patent is an arcane term of art and what it implies is even more arcane. However, intuitively a patent is no more than the allowance document or its printout the patent office issues to the applicant of the patent application for his invention, literally. Where the defendant's product is alleged to be infringing a patent of the plaintiff, it is not the plaintiff's own product, nor the notes he made and kept during his inventing process, but rather the patent "claims" as issued to him or her by the government which the court will look into in determining whether infringement exists. The patent system is as sophisticated as how it can be taken advantage of by both the patentees and infringers, but below are a few pillar principles on which (international) patent system is built.

(1) Written application

Unlike copyright, which comes about as soon as the work is fixed on a tangible media, an invention will not be automatically protected. The inventor must, by himself or with the assistance of a professional patent agent, file with a national patent office or a regional patent authority such as the European Patent Office, a patent application which is generally comprised of a series of complex technical and legal documents describing the invention and claiming the rights sought to be protected.

(2) First-to-file

First-to-file (hereinafter "FTF") is a legal principle according to which patent for an invention is granted to the first person who files a patent application for the protection of the invention. The FTF system is now adopted by all countries, including the United States (where it is called the first-inventor-to file, or FITF) which before the enactment of the America Invents Act on March 16, 2013 remained the only country that used the first-to-invent (FTI) system.

(3) Priority

Patent application generally remains a territorial practice, subject to the national patent legislation of each jurisdiction in which patent protection is requested. The territorial limitation makes it cumbersome for businesses seeking international patent protection. To tackle the issue, the doctrine of right of priority was developed, first by the Paris Convention for the Protection of Industrial Property of 1883 (hereinafter "Paris Convention")[1] and then endorsed (or "derived")

1　See article 4, the Paris Convention.

by the TRIPS, to allow the applicant to file a subsequent patent application in another jurisdiction for the same invention claiming as the effective date of such subsequent application the date of his or her first filing. Under the Patent Law of the People's Republic of China, adopted on March 12, 1984 and last amended on December 27, 2008 (the "Chinese Patent Law"), the validity of the priority right lasts for 12 months for invention and utility model patent application and 6 months for design patent application, commencing from the date of first application.[1]

(4) One invention, one patent

It's a universal principle that one patent application should be limited to one invention or creation. That means, while a patent application may disclose multiple inventions, it can only claim protection for one invention.

What is protected?

Patent laws protect inventions, for sure, but what else? How is invention defined? What is the institutional structure of patent protection? National legislations answer these questions quite differently. Most industrial countries nowadays adopt an independent law to protect designs, whether or not they call the right "patent", with the major exception of the US, where design is protected by the US patent law.[2] The protection of designs will be discussed in more details in a later section of Part 2, titled "Design."

Countries are divided as to whether a separate kind of patent right is granted to utility models, sometimes known as "petty inventions". The US is one of many countries which do not recognize or protect utility models. Among those countries which explicitly protect utility models, some (such as Germany and Japan) regulate them through a specific utility model patent law.

1. Invention-creations: inventions, utility models and designs

The Chinese Patent Law, in its very first article, proclaims that it encourages and promotes "invention-creation," as opposed to only "invention" generally referred to in other countries' patent laws. This is because under the Chinese system, inventions, utility model and designs are all protected under this one piece of legislation. However, only the invention-creations that fall into the following definitions stipulated by the Chinese Patent Law will be granted with patents:

- Inventions mean new technical solutions proposed for a product, a process or the improvement thereof.
- Utility models mean new technical solutions proposed for the shape and structure of a product, or the combination thereof, which are fit for practical use.
- Designs mean, with respect to a product, new designs of the shape, pattern, or the combination

---

1 See article. 29, the Chinese Patent Law.

2 Title 35 of the United States Code (i.e. 35 U.S.C.)

thereof, or the combination of the color with shape and pattern, which are rich in an aesthetic appeal and are fit for industrial application.

The US patent law allows and governs three categories of patents, utility patent (equivalent to the Chinese invention patent), design patent and plant patent, none of which is defined. The law does specify four types of patentable subject matters, that is, inventions or discoveries of "any new and useful process, machine, manufacture, or composition of matter, or any new and useful improvement thereof"[1], but the terms used are very expansive. Such positive and expansive listing of the four types of subject matters has left courts with almost unlimited power to judge the patentability of the individual inventions and hence have unavoidably caused continuous debate and resulted in inconsistency over the topic.

2. Invention-creations barred

Unlike the US, many nations (including most of the European countries) run a negative and more precise list of unpatentable subject matters in their patent laws, thus more effectively lessen the ambiguity of patentability. Under the Chinese Patent Law, the following matters are explicitly barred from being patented:

- Scientific discoveries
- Rules and methods for intellectual activities
- Methods for the diagnosis or treatment of diseases
- Animal and plant varieties, excluding the methods for producing the same
- Substances obtained by means of nuclear transformation
- Designs, with respect to two-dimensional printed matters, of patterns, colors or the combination thereof, which mainly serve as indicators

On top of the negative list, the Chinese Patent Law also includes a catch-all provision which generally denies patent grants to invention-creations in violation of laws, social ethics or public interests.

Patentability: invention, utility model

Where a claimed invention or utility model fits within the statutorily defined subject matters, it can be patented if it is new (or novel), involves inventive step and possesses practical use. For the purpose of convenience, invention and utility model may be in some occasions collectively referred to as "invention" in the following text.

1. Novelty

Patentability examination first looks at "new v. old", rather than "superior v. inferior" or "original v. copy". A patented machine does not have to function "better" than the previous versions but the

---

1 See § 101, 35 U.S.C.

technical solution it presents must be relatively new when compared with what is known in the art, or the prior art, as of the filing date.

(1) Existing technology: prior art

In most patent systems, including that of China, prior art refers to the collection of all information that has, at the date of filing of the claim or the priority date (as the case may be), been made "available to the public" anywhere in the world, and in any form, such as public use, sale or publication of all kinds, including of course issued patents and published patent applications.[1]

- Whether or not the public actually get to know about the information is not relevant.
- Private and secret information, whether based on express or implied confidentiality obligation, isolated private uses, idle gossip or experimental uses usually will not constitute prior art nor anticipate a claim.
- In order for a prior art reference to anticipate a claimed invention, it is generally expected to disclose sufficient information so as to enable a person skilled in the art to implement the subject matter so disclosed.

(2) Grace period

Certain countries, such as China and the US, offer the applicant a grace period during which s/he may disclose his or her invention before filing an application with the patent office without losing novelty. The grace period under the US patent law is one year[2], while in China it is six months and is only applicable to the claimed invention disclosed in the following circumstances:

- exhibited for the first time at an international exhibition sponsored or recognized by the Chinese Government;
- published for the first time at a specified academic or technological conference; and
- contents thereof divulged by others without the consent of the applicant.

In other countries, including the European countries, there is no grace period to the novelty. Therefore, where an invention is made available to the public, regardless of place, before the filing date or the priority date, it becomes unpatentable.

2. Inventive step: non-obviousness

Novelty test examines whether the claimed invention differs from one single prior art reference, which is relatively easy to pass because in inventing and patenting practice any inventor or applicant would presumably try his or her utmost to differentiate his or her invention with the prior art. It is the requirement of inventive step, a term used in Europe and China, or non-obviousness, used in the US, that generally takes up most of the patentability debates during either patent application or invalidation proceedings, or both.

---

1 See article 22, para.2 and 5, the Chinese Patent Law, § 102, 35 U.S.C. and Article 54(2), European Patent Convention (the "EPC").

2 § 102(b)(1), 35 U.S.C.

The law of inventive step asks whether a claimed invention possesses inventive ingenuity that substantially distances itself from the state of the art, or it is a simple assembly of different elements picked up from multiple prior art references which can be achieved without extra effort by a person of ordinary skill in the art. In the words of the Chinese Patent Law, in order to satisfy the inventive step requirement, an invention must possess "prominent substantive features" and "remarkable advancements", and a utility model must indicate "substantive features" and "advancements". Substantive features mean the composition (or limitations) of the technical solution claimed is substantively different than that of the prior art, while advancements care for the technological and social effect the solution has brought about.

Whether an invention is obvious or does not involve inventive step is a difficult question of law which can only be answered by evaluating some underlying factual considerations. The test, therefore, is objective and is discussed below.

- China test on inventive step. The State Intellectual Property Office (hereinafter "SIPO") adopts a three-prong approach which is substantially similar to the EPO "problem-solution approach", and it consists in:

    a. identifying the closest prior art, the most relevant prior art;

    b. determining the objective technical problem, that is, determining, in the view of the closest prior art, the technical problem which the claimed invention addresses and successfully solves; and

    c. examining whether or not the claimed solution to the objective technical problem is obvious for the skilled person in view of the state of the art in general.

- US test on non-obviousness. In the US, the inquiries most likely to be made by courts when determining obviousness came from the Supreme Court's decision in *Graham v. John Deere Co.*[1]. These inquiries, also known as the "Graham factors", look at the following:

    a. the scope and content of the prior art;

    b. the level of ordinary skill in the art;

    c. the differences between the claimed invention and the prior art; and

    d. objective evidence of non-obviousness.

In addition, the court illustrated the following factors that show "objective evidence of non-obviousness", most commonly known as the "secondary considerations":

    a. commercial success;

    b. long-felt but unsolved needs;

    c. failure of others.

- Person of ordinary skill in the art, or POSITA, is a hypothetical person proposed primarily for the purpose of harmonizing the standards applied in the evaluation of inventive step. Such person is imagined to possess the normal skill and knowledge in the technical field of the invention existing as of the application date. He should have access to the prior art

---

1   383 US 1 (1966)

and the ability to apply the normal experiment measures but he should not be a genius. The level of ordinary skill in the art and whether the prior art as a whole would provide guidance or suggestion as to the combination of the closest prior art with other prior art references such that a POSITA would be motivated to conceive the claimed invention are two abstract concepts whose connotations will largely affect the likelihood of the acquisition of the inventive step in the invention.

3. Practical use: utility

An invention must be useful to be patentable. Similar in essence to other important jurisdictions, including the Europe where the requirement is called "industrial applicability" and the US which adopts the doctrine of "utility", the Chinese Patent Law requires that the invention or utility model "can be used for production or utilized, and may produce positive results."

- Capability of being used for production or utilized. An invention should be capable of being applied in real industries, as opposed to in theory or concept. Actual use is not required, and as long as a person of skill in the art is able to discern from what is disclosed in the specification of the patent application that the invention can be used for production or utilized, it suffices.
- Possibility of producing positive results. An invention needs not be fully operational or all-around positive because every new technology can only start somewhere. It, however, when used, must achieve certain beneficial results, whether they be technological, economic or societal.

In reality, very few applications will be turned down and very few patents will be invalidated for failing to satisfy the practical use requirement, but the doctrine has the critical value of preventing the patenting of implausible or fanciful invention which is against the true purpose of patent system.

4. Disclosure

The cornerstone of patent system is the disclosure of invention to the society in exchange for the exclusive rights. Several concepts, called different terms in different jurisdictions but largely having the same implications, have been developed to determine whether the specification of a patent or patent application is considered to have disclosed the invention in the legal sense. Each of these concepts is examined below.

(1) Enablement or sufficiency of disclosure.

A patent applicant must describe how to make and use the invention with sufficient clarity, precision and detail to enable a person skilled in the relevant art to make and use it without undue experiment. Article 26 of the Chinese Patent Law, in its paragraph 3, provides that the specification (including the drawings therein) of a patent application shall contain "a clear and comprehensive description of the invention or utility model which shall enable a person skill in the relevant art to carry it out." "Clarity" means the specification should, in accurate and unequivocal description, identify the technical problem the invention or utility model seeks to solve and specify the technical solution it applies to solve such technical problem. "Enabling" means that a person of skill in the art is able to implement the technical solution disclosed in the specification to solve the technical problem described therein and realize the expected results without further creative labor. Once an application is filed at the patent office and given an application date, the specification cannot be modified to the extent of its enabling content.

(2) Best mode

The specification must detail the preferred mode contemplated by the inventor to be one that would best practice the invention or utility model.

(3) Written description

To fulfill the written description requirement, a term used in the US patent system, the patent specification must clearly allow persons of skill in the art to recognize that the inventor invented what is claimed. The central issue of written description lies in whether the patent claims are adequately supported by the written description of the inventions set forth in the specifications of the patent.

(4) Definiteness of claims

Patent claims define the scope of a patentee's rights. Therefore, patent claims are required to be "definite" and point out and distinctly claim the technical solution which the applicant regards as his or her invention.

Invalidity

During its term, a patent is presumed valid until it is invalidated. Invalidation request can be made by anybody but most often it is taken up by the alleged infringer as the most thorough defense against a patent infringement claim. In most countries, the US as an example, competent courts hear and judge on both invalidation and infringement issues, while in some but very few other jurisdictions such as Germany, Japan and China, invalidation is independently processed by one authority (a special patent court, in the case of Germany, or an administrative organ, such as SIPO in China) and infringement by another (i.e. a trial court). Crucial topics about invalidity are outlined below.

1. Grounds for invalidation

Failures to meet the various patentability requirements, violations of statutory bars and procedural restrictions on the patenting of invention-creations, or inconsistencies of subject matters with the definitions of invention-creations can all become the grounds to assert invalidation claim against an issued patent.

2. Amendment to patent documents during invalidation

Many countries allow amendment to the claims of patents after they issue. Under the Chinese Patent Law, the patentee of an invention or utility model patent subject to an invalidation proceeding may modify the claims of such patent but such modification should not enlarge the scope of patent protection as originally granted and must not exceed what has been disclosed in the patent specification.

3. Consequences of invalidation

Any patent right that has been declared invalid shall be deemed to be non-existent ab initio. Where only part of the claims of a patent is declared invalid, the other claims remain valid.

Ownership and assignment

1. Ownership v. inventorship

Patent laws generally make a distinction between ownership and inventorship. The proprietary rights in an invention initially vest in the person who invents the subject matter claimed, but such rights may be transferred. Ownership, on the other hand, rests with whoever owns the legal title to the invention, either by law or through contract, but regardless of who actually made the invention.

2. Co-owners: joint invention

Where an invention-creation is attributed to two or more inventors, the proprietary rights pertaining to it belong to all the inventors, unless otherwise agreed upon.

3. Employment invention-creation

All inventions can only be the direct products of human being. However, when an inventing person is employed by a company, the question as to who owns the proprietary rights in the invention becomes a complex question which national laws have to address. The Chinese Patent Law tries to solve the question by limiting the "employment invention-creations" to certain circumstances discussed below, hoping that the ownership of the invention-creations made by a person employed by his or her company can be discerned accordingly.

(1) Executing (by the employee) of the tasks set by the employer

If the invention is the result of an employee's fulfillment of his or her jobs within the scope of employment, such invention should belong to the company. According to Article 12, paragraph 1, of the Implementing Rules of the Patent Law of the People's Republic of China as amended in 2010 (the "Patent Law Implementing Rules"), an invention-creation considered the product of the execution of tasks set by the employer is one that is accomplished:

- in the course of performing his or her own duty;
- in the execution of any task, other than his or her own duty, which was delegated by the

employer;

- within one year after the termination of employment relation with, and where it relates to his or her own duty or the other task assigned to him or her by, the employer to which he previously served.

(2) Primarily utilizing the material and technical conditions of the employer

A person may during his employment with a company invent something totally unrelated to his or her job responsibility or assignment but such invention is attributed, at least to some extent, the use of the company's resources. Material and technical conditions are said to include employer's funds, equipment, components, raw materials or technical materials which are not disclosed to the public. Some argue that the technical conditions should be given more weight than material conditions in their attribution to the invention, because the material aspects of the company resources, which can be compensated by pecuniary means, are usually not essential to the inventing activities whereas the technical conditions are. It's also necessary to emphasize that to constitute "primary utilization" the conditions used by the employee-inventor must be indispensable or irreplaceable in achievement of the invention.

4. Commissioned invention-creation

With regard to an invention-creation accomplished by a person commissioned by another, the relevant proprietary rights should go to the person so commissioned, unless the two parties have reached a different solution.

5. Assignment

The substance and effect of the proprietary rights transforms as the patent application proceeds, and the transfer or assignment of such proprietary rights is dealt with differently at different stages of the acquisition of ownership of the rights. Although the Chinese Patent Law merely provides that it is the "inventor or designer" who has the "right to apply for a patent", such right to apply for patent can in fact be freely transferred before any application is filed. On the contrary, assignment of the proprietary rights after the application is filed, known as the "right in patent application", should be recorded with the patent office at SIPO before it would become valid. Only after a patent issues does the patentee or the subsequent assignee start to own the patent right and the assignment of such patent right should of course be made in written form and will not become effective until it's been filed with the patent office. Assignment of both the right in patent application and the patent right will be published by the patent office.

Owner's rights and limitations

1. Right to exclude

Essentially, a patent confers the right to exclude, rather than the right to practice. For example, where a later patented invention L is an improvement over an earlier invention E that is still within the term of its own patent grant, the patent holder of L may not legally make his own L if in doing so he must exploit E, unless a license is given by the patentee of E, which however he may deny.

- Term of right to exclude. The term of an invention patent is 20 years, and for utility and design patens, each 10 years, all starting from the date of the application to which each pertains. Patent term terminates before it expires in the event that the patentee fails to pay up the maintenance fee or abandons his patent right by a written statement.
- Only commercial exploitation excluded. The societal aspect of the patent system has led to the common policy that only the activities with commercial purposes are the targets the patentee may seek to stop. Personal and other non-commercial exploitation of a patent without the permission of the patentee is usually not an infringement.

2. Acts of patent exploitation excluded

Article 11 of the Chinese Patent Law prohibits one from "making, using, offering for sale, selling and importing" of patented products without first getting a permission from the patent owner. Such exhaustive listing of acts of patent exploitation in fact limits the patentee's rights to the extent that the practice of any acts other than the five acts specified in the law will not constitute a "direct infringement" of the patent rights. Furthermore, different types of patents carry different protection. With respect to the product patent or claim (known as "apparatus claim" in the US), the patentee can prevent the unauthorized acts of making, using, offering for sale, selling and importing that product. Where the subject matter of the patent is a process, the only type of exploitation the patentee may control is the act of using the process, provided however that the products directly obtained through the unauthorized use of such patented process should also be barred from being used, offered for sale, sold or imported.

The five individual acts of patent exploitation are examined as follow:

(1) Making

Making is the most important exclusive right of patent grant, without practice of which other acts of patent exploitation would simply not exist. Any use, offer for sale, sale or import of the products made under a proper license from the patentee will not infringe the patent right. The protection with respect to making of patented product is considered absolute in that as long as someone has made the patented products without the consent of the patentee, s/he would be held infringing the patent, regardless of whether s/he willfully did that or whether s/he was aware of the existence of the patent or the patent application.

(2) Using

Use of the patented products without permission from the patentee is an act of infringement independent of who first makes such infringing products. There is a major exception under the

Chinese Patent Law where use of a design, even without the consent of the patentee, is allowed. This is because designs are, arguably, used in the most cases for the purpose of appreciation instead of commercial application.

(3) Offering for sale

Acts of offering for sale typically include advertising, window displaying and exhibition. The purpose of prohibiting unauthorized offering for sale is to deter illegal transaction involving patent infringement as early as possible. However it's sometimes difficult, for example in the case of advertising, to prove that what are being offered indeed involve patent at issue.

(4) Selling

No country really defines what a sale is and at which point of a sale process the act of sale of unauthorized patented product should be considered for a patent infringement test. Another difficulty in determining the legality of an act of selling lies with the case where what is sold is not the patented product but rather another product containing a patented product. The Supreme People's Court has made it clear that the act of manufacturing other products using as their components the patented products should be deemed as the act of using the patent under the Article 11 of the Chinese Patent Law, whereas the act of selling such other products should be determined to be the act of selling.

(5) Importing

The Chinese Patent Law prohibits import of patented products without the permission of the patentee if such imported products are not made outside China by or with the consent of same patentee.

3. Commercial license

Because patents are exclusionary rights, their individual value as well as the overall purpose of the patent system would be undermined if they are not adequately practiced. This is particularly true where the patent owners themselves are not capable or otherwise unwilling to exploit the patents yet have decided not to give up their titles. Commercial licensing addresses this problem. By allowing another to practice his or her patents, a patentee/licensor compromises part of his or her exclusive right in exchange for monetary compensation, while the licensee obtains the authority to practice the licensed patent in a legitimate way.

(1) Scope of license

Under the patent licensing practice, the licensor and licensee can negotiate on the scope of the license along with other terms and conditions. The scope of a license can be full-blown that it covers all territories and the remaining term the licensed patent imparts, and that the licensee is given the right to practice all acts of exclusive right reserved for the licensor. Yet, the licensor may also allow for only a portion of the said territory for only a certain period of the patent term, and limit the licensee's exploitation practices to only selected kinds of, or specially defined, acts.

(2) Exclusivity of license

Depending on the extent a license would exclude the rights of exploitation of the subject matter patent by persons other than the licensee, there are three types of licenses, namely, exclusive, sole and non-exclusive. An exclusive license excludes everyone (including the licensor) from exploiting the patent. The licensor of a sole license reserves the right to practice the patent himself or herself if s/he wants to. A non-exclusive license, being least valuable for the licensee, does not forbid the licensor to use the licensed patent by himself or herself or license it to any other persons.

4. Limitation to right to exclude

(1) Exemption of patent infringing liabilities

The following scenarios are typically infringements of patent rights, but for social reasons the Chinese Patent Law has exempted the liabilities of the "infringing" persons while at the same time requires them to compensate the patentees.

- Exploitation of invention patent owned by state-owned enterprise and institution. Competent authorities, upon the approval of the State Council, may promote the application of the invention in a defined scope and appoint specified units to exploit the patent if the invention is of great significance to the national or public interests.
- Compulsory licenses. Compulsory licenses, applicable to only invention and utility model patents, are granted by the government either on its own initiative or upon request. The grounds for compulsory licenses include the occurrence of state emergency or other extraordinary affairs, the requirement for public interests, and the acts of right owners constituting laches or monopoly in the exploitation of their patents.

(2) Acts considered non-infringement

Different than the above, the following scenarios are by themselves not considered infringements, thus no compensation will be imposed on them.

- Exhaustion of right after first sale: where, after the sale of a patented product or a product obtained directly by a patented process by the patentee or any entity or individual authorized by the patentee, any other person uses, offers to sell, sells, or imports that product;
- Existing use: where, before the date of filing of the application for patent, any person who has already made the identical product, used the identical process, or made necessary preparations for its making or using, continues to make or use it within the original scope only;
- Visiting foreign vehicles: where any foreign means of transport which temporarily passes through the territory, territorial waters or territorial airspace of China uses the patent concerned, in accordance with any agreement concluded between the country to which the

foreign means of transport belongs and China, or in accordance with any international treaty to which both countries are parties, or on the basis of the principle of reciprocity, for its own needs, in its devices and installations;

- Research and experiment: where any person uses the patent concerned solely for the purposes of scientific research and experimentation; or
- Bolar exemption: where for the purposes of providing information needed for the regulatory examination and approval, any person makes, uses or imports a patented medicine or a patented medical apparatus, and where any person makes or imports the patented medicine or the patented medical apparatus exclusively for such person (who seeks such regulatory examination and approval).

Design

1. Patentability

Design patent essentially protects the ornamental, as in the US, or aesthetic, as in China, aspect of a design. Whether a design can be granted a patent is summarized below:

(1) Novelty

Any design sought to be patented shall not be a prior design, nor has anyone filed before the date of filing of the current application with SIPO an earlier application pertaining to the identical design disclosed in patent documents announced after the date of filing. The prior design means any design known to the public before the date of filing in China or abroad.

(2) Distinct difference

Any design for which patent right may be granted shall significantly differ from prior design or combination of prior design features.

(3) Usefulness

A design must be fit for industrial use, which means that the articles adopting the design should be suitable for mass productions.

(4) Not in conflict with prior lawful rights

Any design for which patent right may be granted must not be in conflict with the lawful right obtained before the date of filing by any other person. Such prior lawful right includes among other things the rights in trademark, copyrighted works, enterprise names, portraits and packaging or get-ups of famous merchandises.

2. Scope of protection

The extent of protection of a design patent is determined by the design of the product as shown in the drawings or photographs filed with the patent office. The brief explanation may be used to interpret the design of the product as shown in such drawings or photographs.

Enforcement and remedies to patent infringement

1. Civil remedies

(1) Cessation of infringement

In the civil procedure related to patent infringement dispute, a court may, as in considering remedies to copyright infringement introduced in Part 1 of this chapter, adjudicate the cessation of infringement as well as the provisional measure to restrain infringement.

(2) Damages

- Courts in patent infringement cases may look to the multiple of patent license royalty to determine the amount of damages in the event that neither the (right holder's) actual losses nor the (infringer's) unlawful gains can be determined. Where all three references have failed to yield an amount of the damages, the court shall, after taking into account the totality of circumstances, assess the proper damages amounting to not more than CNY 1,000,000.
- Despite the fact that there are significant arguments and supports to adopt exemplary damages for patent infringement, the current Chinese Patent Law still advocates that any damages awarded to patent holders shall remain compensatory.
- The damages for the injured patent holder shall include the reasonable expenses that he or she has paid for putting a stop to the infringing activities, including attorney fees.

2. Administrative remedies

(1) Enforcement agencies

SIPO and its local counterparts administer the patent affairs and local SIPOs are obliged to handle patent infringement disputes upon request by patent owners.

(2) Administrative relief

- A patent holder who believes his or her patent has been infringed upon can file a complaint with a competent local SIPO, which may upon investigation and hearing make decision as to whether the alleged infringer has infringed the patent at issue. The decision can be submitted to a court for judicial review if the losing party elects so. The local SIPO may actually order the infringer to cease infringement if it decides that an infringement exists. Such administrativehandling procedure of patent infringement disputes is a unique practice of the China's dual-track IP enforcement system, but the procedure should be suspended if the same dispute is brought before a civil court.
- Patent counterfeiting, which may or may not at the same time infringe a patent, is another type of illegal activity local SIPOs regulate. If patent counterfeiting has been established, the

counterfeited products can be attached or seized, the illegal gains be forfeited, and fine (of up to three times the illegal gains) be concurrently imposed.

3. Criminal procedures

Where patent counterfeiting meets certain statutory thresholds, it may result in criminal prosecution of the offender, who when convicted may be sentenced to imprisonment of not more than three years or criminal detention, and he or she may in addition or separately be sentenced to pay a fine.

SELF QUIZ: Indicate whether each of the following statements is true or false.

16. You may keep your technology in confidence after you patent it.

17. The US is the only country which adopts a first-to-invent patenting system.

18. If you have filed an application for a utility patent in the US, you can always claim the filing date of such US application as the filing date of your Chinese patent application as long as you file such Chinese application within one year of your US filing.

19. The scope of a patent is determined by the specification.

20. Both China and the US, respectively, protect designs with the same piece of legislation they use to protect invention.

21. An invention cannot be patented if there exists a prior art.

22. An invention can be patented if there is not a prior art.

23. Anyone is allowed to petition the patent office to invalidate a patent.

24. In defending an invalidation petition, the patentee may amend the patent claims as s/he wishes.

25. Patent rights belong to inventors.

26. An employee will be entitled to the invention made by him or her which is beyond his or her job responsibility or assignment at the company s/he works for.

27. The proprietary right in a patent application can only be effectively transferred after the transfer agreement has been registered with SIPO.

28. Products directly manufactured through the use of a patented process should be prohibited from being sold if the use of such process is not authorized by the patent owner.

29. Patents can sometimes be practiced without the owners' permissions.

30. A design is patentable if it is novel, possesses significant difference from prior design, and is fit for industrial use.

Introduction

Trademarks have long been labeled intellectual property (most authoritatively defined by the Convention Establishing the World Intellectual Property Organization), but some insist on calling them industrial property, for no trifling reason. In conventional society, only inventions and writings were considered creation of mankind, while trademark was no more than a simple, randomly picked or sometimes ineffectively designed indicia which helped people identify where the products bearing such mark came from. Unlike patent and copyright, which are instantly linked to intellectual activity, trademark is born for commercial purpose.

For the same inherent commercial nature of trademarks, continual exposure of and investment in trademarks often develop their value. Over the history, especially with the rapid development of communication technology and growth of international trade, functions of trademarks have profoundly changed. While trademarks continue to serve their essential function of distinguishing products source and promising quality, they also classify consumers.

Naturally, major developments of trademark law have been by and large the result of the evolution of the functions of trademarks in the commercial world. The study and development of the important legal theories of confusion, protection of well-know marks, likelihood of association and dilution (and anti-dilution) can all be traced back to or linked with the transformation of trademark functions.

1. Trademark and competition

Passing off is a common law tort concept focused primarily on preventing consumer deception, and in the words of the Paris Convention it is considered an act of "such a nature as to create confusion by any means whatever with the establishment, the goods, or the industrial or commercial activities, of a competitor."[1] The tort action of passing off, while being widely applied in claiming loss of goodwill associated with different types of property (name, slogan, image, packaging, touch and feel, etc.), is more commonly known in protecting trademark.

The law of passing off prevents one person from misrepresenting his/her goods or services as being the goods or services of others, and also prevents one person from holding out his or her goods or services as having some association or connection with others when this is not true. In fair competition marketplaces, trademarks can be protected regardless whether they are registered or not. Passing off and trademark law regulate overlapping factual situations, but deal with them in different ways:

---

1   Article 10 bis, the Paris Convention for the Protection of Industrial Property, as amended on September 28, 1979.

(1) Different kinds of rights

Passing off is a common law tort action based on goodwill acquired by use of an unregistered mark. On the contrary, claim against infringement arises from statutory right vested in a registered trademark.

(2) Different level of similarity between parties' goods

In passing off, the goods or services of defendant don't have to be same as those of the plaintiff—they may be allied or even different. In case of an action for trademark infringement, the defendant's use of the alleged mark should be in respect of either the goods or services for which plaintiff's mark is registered or similar goods or services, except in the case of well-known mark.

(3) Burden of proof

In passing off action, identity or similarity of marks is not sufficient, there must also be likelihood of confusion and actual or likely damage. But in case of standard infringement if identical mark is used on identical product no further proof is required.

Civil-law countries apply competition (or anti-unfair competition) law, rather than the doctrine of passing off, to avoid consumer deception. In the US, Section 43a) of the Lanham Act[1], the primary federal trademark statute, codifies the common law passing off. This is because today in highly competitive environment states can no longer effectively regulate the markets without adopting some sort of a "catch-all" mechanism similar to passing off.

2. Registered mark v. unregistered mark

Unregistered trademarks may still be protected, but with many limitations, thus not advisable for most businesses. China does protect unregistered trademarks under certain circumstances, which are set out mainly in the Trademark Law of the People's Republic of China, adopted August 23, 1982 and last amended on August 30, 2013 (hereinafter "Chinese Trademark Law") and Law of the People's Republic of China Against Unfair Competition, adopted September 2, 1993 (hereinafter "Chinese Competition Law"). These provisions include:

(1) Unregistered well-known marks

The protection of unregistered well-known marks will be discussed in the section titled "Well-known Marks", of this chapter.

(2) Prior right

No applicant for trademark application may infringe upon another person's existing prior

---

1   Title 15 of United States Code (i.e. 15 U.S.C.)

rights[1], nor may s/he, by illegitimate means, preemptively register a trademark that is already in use by another person and has certain influence.

(3) Opposition to application for registration by prior business partners

An application for trademark registration will be rejected when the trademark applied for is identical or similar to, in respect of the same or similar goods, another person's trademark that has been used earlier though not yet registered, if the applicant has a contractual or business relationship (such as agency, distributorship or sourcing) or any other relationship with the said person and thereby is well aware of the existence of the said person's prior mark.

(4) Name, packaging and get-up of famous merchandise or trade dress

A business operator shall not harm his or her competitors in market transactions by resorting to any of the following unfair means: using for a commodity without authorization a unique name, packaging or get-up of another's famous merchandise, or using a name, packaging or get-up similar to that of another's famous merchandise, thereby confusing the commodity with that famous merchandise and leading the purchasers to mistake the former for the latter.

CASE EXAMPLE: The Xiaofeiyang Trademark

Fact: In 1999, Inner Mongolia Little Sheep Co., Ltd., a restaurant chain that serves hot pot, applied for registration of its "小肥羊" (meaning "little fat sheep") trademark. The application was rejected on the ground that "such trademark directly represented the content and characteristic of the service" and thus lacked distinctiveness. Little Sheep filed its applications under various classes again for its "小肥羊LITTLE SHEEP+Device" trademark in December 2001, immediately after the taking effect of the second amendment of the Chinese Trademark Law, which in its Article 11 provided that marks "that have acquired distinctive features through use and readily distinguishable may be registered as trademark." The proceedings at the Chinese Trademark Office (the "CTMO") and the Trademark Review and Adjudication Board (the "TRAB") went back and forth due to the multiple oppositions raised by many other companies, which were basically denied. During that period of time, Little Sheep filed various civil lawsuits under the Chinese Competition Law against different companies using "小肥羊" mark in their businesses. Notably, courts in Beijing and Hebei Province granted protection for Little Sheep of "小肥羊LITTLE SHEEP+Device" trademark because the mark had been a unique name of, and closely associated, with the well-known catering service. Eventually Little Sheep's trademark was granted many registrations.

Take-away point: A trademark that has not been registered, even it is inherently non-distinctive,

---

1 Prior rights mean civil rights, other legitimate rights and interests that shall be protected, owned by another as of the day of application of a disputed mark, which may include the copyrights, right in personal name and business name.

can be protected if it has established unique meaning in the marketplace which can distinguish commercial origin of goods or services, and thus can be registered when an application for registration is filed.

Subject matter of protection

Though varied among jurisdictions, traditionally trademarks are generally defined or interpreted to include words, letters, numerals, symbols, devices or the like. However, scope of trademark protection has continuously been expanded, at least in major economies.

1. Categories of marks: trademark, service mark, collective mark, certification mark

Laws of most countries generally protect trademarks, service marks, collective marks and certification marks.

2. Trademarkable signs

Arguably, the most liberal definition of trademarkable signs can be found in Article 15 of the TRIPS, which states that "any sign, or any combination of signs, capable of distinguishing the goods or services of one undertaking from those of other undertakings, shall be capable of constituting a trademark."

(1) Visual trademarks

Below are some traditional trademarks, all of which are visual.

a. Word marks: words, names, letters, numerals

International				China			
iPhone	Marc Jacobs	VW	4711	海尔	李宁	QQ	361°

b. Figurative marks: stylish words, logos, pictures, characters

c. Color marks:

d. Combination of the above

International | **China**

NIKE   **Walmart** :¦:   Save money. Live better. | TSINGTAO   中国银行 BANK OF CHINA

(2) Non-visual trademarks

Non-visual trademarks are by and large considered non-conventional. The protection of non-conventional trademarks remains relatively undeveloped and practices vary from jurisdiction to jurisdiction. Listed below are some representative non-conventional trademarks which have been registered or were attempted to be registered.

a. Sound trademarks

US: Intel(US Reg. NO. 7,533,2744)-"five-tone" sound registered in US, Australia and New Zealand

US: Nokia-default ringtone (US Reg. No. 3,288,274)

China: China Radio International – opening music of CRI's broadcasting (Chinese Reg. No. 14503615)

b. Scent trademarks

US: plumeria scent as a trademark for its sewing thread and embroidery yarn (US Reg. No. 1,639,128, subsequently abandoned).

c. Taste trademarks

A number of attempts to register but no success (yet) has been reported.

d. Touch/texture trademarks

US: "a velvet textured covering on the surface of a bottle of wine", for Khvanchkara of Georgia (U.S. Reg. No. 3,155,702).

e. Motion trademarks

EU: the Lamborghini moving image trademark for car doors opening and turning upward (CTM 1400092).

"Visuality" has also been a requirement under Chinese law for a sign to be registrable as trademark. Such requirement has been eliminated from the 2013 amendment of the Trademark Law, which explicitly added "sounds" to the enumeration of trademarkable signs but remains uncertain as to whether single colors can be protected.[1]

---

1 In Europe, protection of non-conventional trademarks is tested by whether or not a mark can be graphically represented or defined. Sieckmann v. Deutsches Patent- und Markenamt (Case 273/00, 12 December 2002) is a landmark decision of the European Court of Justice (the "ECJ") on graphical representation of non-conventional trademarks. The court confirmed that "Article 2 of the *EU Trademark Directive* does cover signs that cannot be perceived visually, if they can be represented graphically by the means of images, lines or characters, where the representation must be clear, precise, self-contained, easily accessible, intelligible, durable and objective." These are known as the Sieckmann criteria, which, however, have been proved to be difficult to meet.

3. Trade dress

"Trade dress includes the total look of a product and its packaging and even includes the design and shape of the product itself."[1] The architecture of the legal protection of trade dress varies significantly from jurisdiction to jurisdiction and arguably trade dress is the most complicated regime in intellectual property protection. While trade dress does not have to be registered to obtain protection, as general rules,

- trade dress eligible for protection "must be distinctive, either inherently or through secondary meaning, and it must identify the source of the product;"[2]
- trade dress that is functional does not qualify for protection.

A few protected trade dresses are illustrated below:

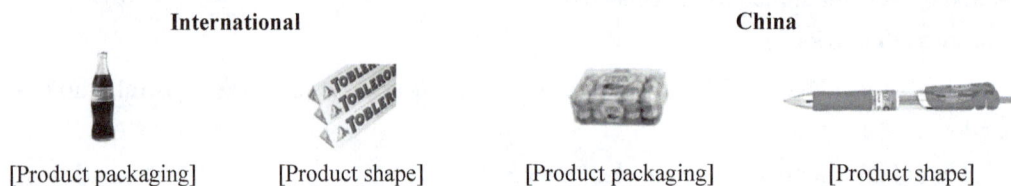

International		China	
[Product packaging]	[Product shape]	[Product packaging]	[Product shape]

Conditions of protection

The Paris Convention allows members to deny registrations or invalidate trademarks under the following four scenarios:

- When they are of such a nature as to infringe rights acquired by third parties in the country where protection is claimed;
- When they are devoid of any distinctive character, or consist exclusively of signs or indications which may serve, in trade, to designate the kind, quality, quantity, intended purpose, value, place of origin, of the goods, or the time of production, or have become customary in the current language or in the *bona fide* and established practices of the trade of the country where protection is claimed;
- When they are contrary to morality or public order and, in particular, of such a nature as to deceive the public. It is understood that a mark may not be considered contrary to public order for the sole reason that it does not conform to a provision of the legislation on marks, except if such provision itself relates to public order;
- When there is violation of Article 10bis (i.e. provision on unfair competition.)"[3]

---

1 McCarthy, Trademarks and Unfair Competition §8:4.

2 Halpern, Nard and Port, *Fundamentals of United States Intellectual Property Law: Copyright, Patent, and Trademark, p. 327*. However, it should be noted that compared with the conventional visual trademarks, which are normally two-dimensional, the distinctiveness requirement of trade dress is much more difficult to meet.

3 Article 6 quinquies, Paris Convention.

1. Absolute bars

Absolute bars, in general, may mean a set of national rules which prohibit or impede the registration or even the use of certain trademarks which fall into the governing of such rules. While some jurisdictions in a way define what absolute bars are, others specify the types of trademarks that should be barred from registration or use. For the purpose of this Chapter, bad faith or malicious registration, while absolutely barred, is discussed separately because it usually involves inter-party contest not easily detectable by the trademark prosecution authorities alone.

According to Article 10 of the Chinese Trademark Law, none of the following signs may be used (and, of course, registered), as trademarks:

- those that are identical or similar to the state name, national flag, national emblem, national anthem, military flag, military emblem, military anthem or medals, etc., of the People's Republic of China and those that are identical to the names or symbols of state central authorities, the specific names of places where central state authorities are located or the names or images of landmark thereof;
- those that are identical or similar to the state name, national flag, national emblem, military flag, etc. of a foreign country, unless approved by the government of the said country;
- those that are identical or similar to the name, flag, emblem, etc. of an inter-governmental international organization, unless with the consent of the said organization or unless doing so would not be likely to confuse the public;
- those that are identical or similar to official signs or hallmarks indicating control or warranty, except where authorized;
- those that are identical or similar to the name or mark of the "Red Cross" or the "Red Crescent";
- those that are of a racial discriminatory nature;
- those that are of a deceptive nature and likely to cause the public to mistake the quality or other feature of a product or its origin; and
- those that harm socialist morality or practices or that have other adverse effects.

Besides, names of administrative districts at or above the county level and commonly-known foreign place names may not be used as trademarks, except where such names have other meanings or are an integral component of a collective mark or certification mark. Trademarks using place names that have already been registered shall remain valid.

2. Distinctiveness

Distinctiveness is arguably the single most important concept in trademark law. It deals with the fundamental issue of whether a mark can distinguish the products or services in respect of which the mark is used. This issue is the foundation of trademark protection theory. Distinctiveness is the foundation of trademark protection theory.

Distinctiveness is a relative proposition. Nothing is always distinctive, or always non-distinctive. The same exact trademark which shows strong distinctiveness on one type of products can be a weak (or weaker) mark for another, or becomes totally devoid of distinctiveness. Strength of a trademark (in association with one same products or services) can also change drastically over time. Therefore, distinctiveness is merely a threshold for protection conferred by law, that is, the precondition for registration, but it is the scope of protection that really matters for traders. The determination of the scope of protection for a particular trademark, however, is focused on the strength of the distinctiveness of such trademark.

In the order of strength or level of distinctiveness, marks are generally categorized into five different types:

(1) Fanciful marks

Fanciful marks are literally "invented" or "coined" words and therefore convey no meaning at all, other than their trademark meaning. The missing of any relation with the product or service on which they are used has made fanciful marks the strongest type of marks. Examples of fanciful marks are:

International			China		
KODAK	ADVIL	YAHOO!	海尔/HAIER	万科/VANKE	国美/GOME
[imaging]	[medicine]	[Internet]	[electric appliance]	[real estate]	[retail]

(2) Arbitrary marks

A mark is arbitrary if it does not describe or is not normally associated with the product or service it identifies or any of its characteristic, ingredient or function, albeit an existing word or symbol. Examples of arbitrary marks are:

International			China		
APPLE	RED BULL	AMAZON	联想	雪花	芒果
[computer]	[soft drinks]	[e-commerce]	[computer]	[beer]	[TV Station]

(3) Suggestive marks

Suggestive marks are marks that indirectly describe the product or service they identify. The consumer must engage in a mental process of his or her own in order to associate the mark with a description of the product or service.[1] Examples of arbitrary marks are:

International			China		
MICROSOFT	ROACH MOTEL	SNUGGLE	福临门	平安	搜狗
[software]	[insect killer]	[fabric]	[food and dairy]	[insurance]	[search engine]

The three types of marks discussed above are all inherently distinctive because consumers will never or are normally unlikely to directly associate the marks with the products or services on or

---

1　Margreth Barrett, *Intellectual Property*.

in connection with which they are used. All inherently distinctive marks can be registered without acquiring secondary meaning, subject to the bars imposed by applicable law in each jurisdiction.

(4) Descriptive marks

By contrast, a descriptive mark is one that readily makes consumers link to the products or services on or with respect of which they are used as soon as they see it. Descriptive marks are not registrable unless or until they have established secondary meaning. Examples of descriptive marks are:

International			China		
NESCAFE	AMERICAN STANDARD	TV GUIDE	五粮液	蒙牛	国航
[coffee]	[sanitary ware]	[magazine]	[alcoholic liquor]	[dairy products]	[airlines]

Secondary meaning of a term or other indicia is relative to the meaning that are commonly known or perceived for such term or indicia. For example, the alphabets HB or alphanumeric 2B are commonly understood as standard grading of pencils; a map of Florida mostly likely will connect people's mind to the US state of Florida; and "McDonald" was once most thought of as a surname. However, use of a descriptive mark for a period of time may create association between the mark and the products or services marketed with it. Once consumers have come to realize that such mark is the indication of the commercial source of the products or services, the secondary meaning of source identifier has been successfully established. Article 11 of the Chinese Trademark Law provides that a trademark that "has acquired distinctiveness through use and is readily distinguishable may be registrable as a trademark."

(5) Generic marks

Generic marks are also non-inherently distinctive. But as opposed to descriptive marks, generic marks will never qualify for trademark protection even if they acquire secondary meaning. This is so because generic marks are words that are the universal identifiers of the products used by all competitors in a nation or a particular industry to describe such products. Generic marks can be generic from inception or they can become generic through use.[1] While some brand owners have managed to avoid their brands from genericizing (e.g. XEROX, BAND-AID) through smart marketing and branding campaign, some others unfortunately lost protection of their originally distinctive marks (e.g. WALKMAN, in Austria, and YO-YO, in the US) because relevant consumers used them as generic. By the same token, owners of other well-known marks such as iPad and GOOGLE have realized that if they didn't adopt some precautionary measures their highly valuable trademarks could become generic.

More examples of generic marks are:

---

1   Halpern, Nard and Port, *Fundamentals of United States Intellectual Property Law: Copyright, Patent, and Trademark.*

International			China		
THERMOS	ASPRIN	BLUETOOTH	优盘	PDA	吉普
[vacuum flask]	[medicine]	[wireless]	[USB flash disk]	[mobile device]	[automobile]

The doctrine of distinctiveness, as they are applied, in both law making and court ruling, can become extremely sophisticated and sometimes brings about divergent opinions. In the area of trade dress, it is particularly so. China law allows registration of distinctive three-dimensional marks, which arguably includes trade dress. However, it is not clear whether trade dress can be inherently distinctive or the distinctiveness of trade dress can only be acquired through use. US courts examined the distinctiveness issue in connection with trade dress. In the famous Two Pesos case[1], the US Supreme Court found that trade dress of restaurants may be inherently distinctive and as long as jury found such inherent distinctiveness the trade dress is protectable without showing that is has acquired secondary meaning. However, in another famous case involving trade dress, the Court ruled that product design, that is the design or the shape of the product itself, may not be inherently distinctive and must acquire secondary meaning to be protected.[2]

3. Use

The US is probably the only country which requires showing of use (or intent-to-use, ITU) when applicants file for trademark registrations. In most other countries ownership of trademark is determined by registration, subject in some jurisdictions to ownership contest made available by law, which will be further discussed below. In all countries to maintain the trademark rights the trademarks must be used in commerce.

So what constitutes a use under the trademark law? Under Chinese law, the use of a trademark shall include the use of the trademark on goods, packages or containers of the goods or in trading documents, and the use of the trademark in advertising, exhibition or any other business activities. In interpreting what kinds of use indeed qualify as trademark use, courts look to particular factual elements, but as a general rule "token" use is not likely to be considered sufficient. Use that can be recognized by trademark law must be in public, for real, and in legal manner.[3] A mere act of transfer or license of a trademark, or a publication of trademark registration information or statement of possession of trademark right, will not suffice.

Well-known marks

1. The well-known mark theory

The needs to protect well-known marks arose as businesses expanded across borders. Because protection of trademarks is territorial, some trademark owners may not be able to register their

---

1   Two Pesos, Inc. v. Taco Cabana, Inc., 505 US 763 (1992)

2   Wal-Mart Stores, Inc. v. Samara Bros., Inc., 529 US 205 (2000)

3   Ba Yan NaoEr He Mu Wine Making Co., Ltd. v. Trademark Review and Adjudication Board, (2009) Yi Zhong Xing Chu Zi Di 936 Hao.

trademarks in some countries fast enough although these trademarks have been so widely known by the relevant public in such countries that they are generally recognized to be the owners of such trademarks. The doctrine of well-known marks was conceived from the outset to protect these unregistered but famous trademarks and the doctrine had since been continually developed through international efforts.

2. Recognition of well-known marks

(1) What constitutes a well-known mark?

While there is no commonly agreed definition of what constitutes a well-known mark, it is in general a trademark which is widely known by relevant sector of the public and which enjoys high reputation in the marketplace. Relevant sector of the public generally includes, but not limited to, consumers, persons involved in the channel of distribution and business circles of the types of goods and/or services on or in respect of which the mark applies.

The facts from which a mark may be inferred well-known (or not) generally include:

- the degree of knowledge or recognition of the mark in the relevant sector of the public;
- the duration, extent and geographical area of any use of the mark;
- the duration, extent and geographical area of any promotion of the mark, including advertising or publicity and the presentation, at fairs or exhibitions, of the goods and/or services to which the mark applies;
- the duration and geographical area of any registrations, and/or any applications for registration, of the mark, to the extent that they reflect use or recognition of the mark;
- the record of successful enforcement of rights in the mark, in particular, the extent to which the mark was recognized as well known by competent authorities; and
- the value associated with the mark.

(2) Venue and procedure for recognition of well-known marks in China

- Recognition through administrative proceedings

  Relevant parties may apply for recognition of their trademarks to be well known during the proceedings at or by China Trademark Office (hereinafter "CTMO") or Trademark Review and Adjudication Board (hereinafter "TRAB"), including the trademark registration examination, the investigation of trademark violation, and the handling of trademark dispute.
- Recognition through judicial proceedings

  Courts may, during the civil proceedings involving trademark disputes, determine whether the trademark at-dispute is well-known or not.

3. Protection of well-known marks

Scope and level of protection of well-known marks has undergone profound development and has expanded to circumstances where protection would not traditionally be available. The following paragraphs summarize such extended protection afforded to well-known marks by the most recently amended Chinese Trademark Law, as well as other relevant law, regulation and judicial interpretation.

(1) Protection of unregistered well-known marks

Application for registration of a trademark, for identical or similar goods, which constitutes a reproduction, an imitation or a translation, likely to cause confusion, of another's well-known trademark not registered in China, shall be refused and use of such trademark shall be prohibited.

(2) Protection of registered well-known marks on dissimilar products

A trademark that constitutes a reproduction, an imitation or a translation of another's well-known trademark registered in China and which is the subject of an application for registration for dissimilar goods or services shall be refused registration, and its use shall be prohibited, if the use of such trademark would mislead the public and possibly prejudice the interests of the registrant of the well-known trademark.

(3) Protection against company names and domain names

Use as the trade name of an enterprise of a well-known trademark, even if it is unregistered, may constitute an act of unfair competition if such use misleads the public. Furthermore, where the defendant's domain name or main part thereof is the copy, imitation, translation or transliteration of a well-known trademark of the plaintiff, the registration or use of such domain name shall be determined an act of infringement or unfair competition.

Ownership and transfer

As indicated above, trademarks are, in the most part, owned by the persons who use or register them. One does not "own" a mark merely because he "creates" or "designs" such mark (e.g. a logo).

1. Ownership contest

(1) Business partners

As discussed in the introduction of Part 2 of this Chapter, Article 15 of the Chinese Trademark Law gives the principle in an agency relation and the business partner of or contracting party to an applicant the right to challenge the application for registration of the mark of such principle, partner or contracting party if such applicant is aware of the existence of such prior mark.

(2) Prior rights: trademark squatting and malicious registration

If a person or entity is able to prove that it possesses certain rights (including but not limited to prior trademark, copyright, design, rights in personal name and portrait, company name, trade name and trade dress) which existed prior to the date when an applicant filed a trademark registration, it may be able to convince the trademark office to refuse the trademark registration application such filed.

Furthermore, laws prohibit trademark squatting because it is bad-faith and sometimes malicious. For example, CTMO shall revoke a registered trademark, either on its initiative or upon request, if it finds that such trademark "is registered by deceitful or other illegitimate means." A malicious registration is one where the defendant knowingly registers someone else's trademark with an intention to profit from potential confusion.

(3) Well-known marks

Well-known marks, if recognized, are likely to defeat a subsequent attempt to register a same or similar trademark. Details about well-known marks have been discussed in the earlier part of this section of the Chapter.

2. Assignment and license of trademarks

(1) Assignment

Most, if not all countries, allow ownership of trademarks change hands from one person to another. The question is whether trademarks can be assigned independent of the goodwill in connection with the marks, after all the basic function of trademarks is to distinguish commercial source. The Paris Convention is unable to answer the evolution of the functions of trademarks, such that "the assignment of a mark is valid only if it takes place at the same time as the transfer of the business or goodwill to which the mark belongs."[1] It is the TRIPS that goes beyond the Paris Convention and affirms that trademarks can be assigned "with or without the transfer of the business to which the trademark belongs."[2]

Under Chinese laws,

- Assignment of a trademark shall be made through an agreement between the assignor and assignee, who shall jointly file an application with the CTMO. But the assignee shall guarantee the quality of the goods on which the registered trademark is used.

- To avoid causing misunderstanding, confusion or other adverse influence, where a registered trademark is assigned, the similar trademarks of such trademark registered for identical goods and the identical or similar trademarks registered for similar goods which are owned by the same registrant shall be assigned therewith.

- Although during the assignment process the actual assignment agreement doesn't need to be filed with the CTMO, the assignment will become effective only after the CTMO approves and publishes such assignment.

The US, on the other hand, is one of the very few jurisdictions which take the position that an assignment of a mark without the associated goodwill (sometimes called an assignment "in

---

1 Article 6 *quater,* Paris Convention.

2 Article 21, the TRIPS.

gross") is deemed invalid.[1]

(2) License

Similar to the situation historically facing trademark assignment, for a time licensing of trademarks, that is, allowing people other than a trademark owner to use the trademark, has brought concern because the license practice may have potentially departed from the basic function of trademarks. As consumers started to care not so much about whether the products came from one single manufacturer as they do about getting products of same or compatible quality, trademark licensing became acceptable. Trademark licensing has been adopted by a vast majority of countries in the world, but to assure the quality of products made by licensees who apply particular trademarks, the licensors of such trademarks are often held liable for the acts of the licensees.

Owner's rights and limitations

Put in a simple way, the owner of a registered trademark has the right to prohibit use without authorization by other persons of any trademark identical or similar to such registered trademark on identical or similar products or services in respect of which the trademark is registered if such use is likely to cause confusion as to the source of the products or services of such other persons. Because the fundamental responsibility of trademarks is to help consumers identify the source of products or services they purchase, whether or not the consumers are so confused or likely to be confused is the core test in examining any trademark infringement dispute. Critical issues influencing the evaluation of the scope (as well as the violation) of the exclusive right in a trademark infringement claim are outlined below.

• **The degree of similarity of marks**

Similarity between an alleged infringing mark and the trademark sought to be protected is a threshold question each judge must answer before he would apply the confusion test, however identifying the similarity between the marks is not always an easy task. In general, marks should be first compared in their entireties and in their settings, followed by the consideration of their dominant portions if the marks are composite, which should be given greater weight. Further, the marks should be observed singly or independent of each other.

• **Distinctiveness and public awareness of the trademark**

The degree of similarity will undoubtedly be affected by the distinctiveness of the trademark at issue and awareness thereof among the relevant public. In fact, the more distinctive a trademark is, the stronger the trademark would become. By the same token, trademarks that are more extensively known of by consumers would naturally receive greater protection.

• **The attentiveness of the relevant public**

Likelihood of confusion in any trademark dispute, though eventually determined a judges, should

---

1   See 15 U.S.C.§1060.

be assessed by and in accordance with only the ordinary attentiveness of the relevant public.

• **The degree of similarity between goods**

Goods are generally considered similar if their function, use, manufacturing department, sale channel and target consumers are the same. To examine the similarity between goods, it's always a practical first step to resort to the International Classification of Goods and Services for the Purposes of the Registration of Marks under the Nice Agreement or its national version.

• **Use of trademark in the course of trade**

Uses recognized under trademark law are interpreted broadly. Use of trademark on or in association with products, packaging or containers, transactional documents, marketing and other business materials or events are all considered use in the course of trade, either by the right owner or infringers. Acts of manufacture or sale of products bearing the registered trademarks and forging, manufacture or sale of labels or other representations containing the same are also treated as norms of trademark use, thus infringement where they are not authorized.

1. Confusion: similarity

As discussed earlier, likelihood of confusion is the central focus of trademark infringement examination. The 2013 amendment of the Chinese Trademark Law officially recognizes and expressly requires the likelihood of confusion analysis.

In the event of use of an identical trademark on identical products or services, the likelihood of confusion is presumed. However, where similar marks are used on identical or similar products, the determination of confusion is often challenging and controversial.

Confusion and similarity are interdependent, because similarity between two marks may not be properly discerned without evaluating the likelihood of confusion the marks would cause. Although laws and practices in respect of the doctrine of confusion vary between countries, and sometimes even between courts of a same country, confusion mostly exists where one of the two following scenarios happens: i) where origin of the products or services of defendant has been or is likely to be mistaken to be the plaintiff; and ii) where an affiliation, sponsorship or association or the like relation has been or is likely to be wrongly perceived of the defendant with the plaintiff.

2. Limitation of exclusive right

(1) Fair use

Fair use, or "trademark fair use," is a defense to trademark infringement claim. It is different from the fair use doctrine in copyright law.

• Descriptive use

Trademark fair use occurs when a descriptive mark is used in good faith for its primary, rather than secondary, meaning, and no consumer confusion is likely to result. The trademark such used is not to distinguish sources of products or service, that is, the use is not a use in the sense of trademark law, rather the trademark is used only to explain or describe what the user offers in trade.

- Nominative use

  Nominative use is closely-related to, and often considered as a type of, trademark fair use. Nominative use occurs when one uses a trademark of another as a reference to describe the other product, as opposed to the user's own product. Nominative use most often happens where a business needs to indicate to his customers that what he offers is either produced by another or a service rendered on such products produced by such other.

(2) Exhaustion of right: parallel import

Most countries do not treat it as an infringement where products bearing a trademark are resold by others in the same country after they were first put on the marketplace by or with the authorization of the trademark owner, because the exclusive right of the trademark owner is deemed to have exhausted as soon as such products left its hands legitimately. Problem arises however where same products are distributed in different countries with different pricing structures set by the trademark owner, which often results in imports without the permission of the trademark owner of the cheaper but legitimate products (i.e. the grey products) from a country for resale in another country where price is set higher.

If the exhaustion of right is considered by the importing jurisdiction to be on international level, then parallel import will be allowed; if on the other hand the right is considered exhaustive only within the country of first sale, then parallel import will be considered illegal. Attitudes towards parallel import vary significantly among jurisdictions.

Although the Chinese Trademark Law does not specify whether parallel imports infringe trademark right, court practices in principle allow the act of parallel imports. In the US, parallel import is prohibited if the trademark owner demonstrates that the imported goods are physically and materially different than the authorized goods sold in the US.

Enforcement and remedies to trademark infringement

1. Civil remedies

(1) Cessation of infringement

As in copyright and patent infringement suits, permanent and preliminary injunction (i.e. cessation of infringement) are available and are commonly sought civil remedies in trademark infringement suits.

(2) Damages

- Amount of damages can be assessed by one of the three measuring references, in the following order: the (right holder's) actual losses, the (infringer's) unlawful gains, and multiple of trademark license royalty. Where the damages cannot be determined after applying all three references, the court shall, after taking into account the totality of circumstances, fix damages amounting to not more than RMB 3,000,000.

- Although the general principle for measuring damages remains compensatory as opposed to punitive, the Chinese Trademark Law explicitly allows exemplary damages in the case the trademark infringement is malicious and where circumstances are serious.
- The damages for the trademark holder shall include the reasonable expenses that he or she has paid for putting a stop to the infringing activities, including attorney fees.
- If a party that sold goods that it did not know to be infringing a trademark is able to prove that it obtained the same lawfully and it identifies the supplier, it shall not be liable for damages.

(3) Other civil remedies

When trying a case where a registered trademark is infringed upon, the court may rule to impose a fine and confiscate the infringing goods, the forged representations of the trademark, and the materials, tools and equipment of value specially used for manufacturing the infringing goods.

2. Administrative remedies

(1) Enforcement agencies

The State Administration of Industry and Commerce (hereinafter "SAIC") and its local counterparts, the Administration of Industry and Commerce (hereinafter "AIC"), are the principal government authorities regulating the market order in relation to trademark, including enforcing against trademark infringements. In addition to the AIC, the most active and efficient trademark enforcement agency is the customs authorities, which in fact oversee the protection of all three main types of intellectual property in connection with the imports and exports of products. The border measures, as it is called by the TRIPS and administered by the customs authorities in China, is discussed under this section because they are most often implemented against trademark infringements.

(2) Administrative relief

- Acting on its initiative or upon request by trademark holder, a local AIC can investigate against the alleged infringing conduct and can order the infringer to cease infringements if it determines that an infringement has taken place. The AIC can also confiscate or destruct the infringing goods and the tools mainly used to manufacture the infringing goods or to forge the representations of the registered trademark. If the unlawful turnover is over CNY 50,000 or above, it may impose a fine of up to five times the illegal turnover.
- A trademark (as well as other IP) holder may apply to the GAC for recording his or her intellectual property rights according to the provisions of the PRC Regulations on the Customs Protection of Intellectual Property Rights. The recordal is not the prerequisite to customs protection as an IP holder can always apply to the customs for their action, yet it is critical because most of the infringements can be effectively identified and measures be initiated by the customs authorities only where the relevant information is recorded within their system.

The customs authorities may, upon the fulfillment by the IP holder of relevant requirements, suspend the release of the suspected infringing goods. The customs authorities shall within thirty days of the suspension determine whether the suspected goods have infringed the rights of the IP holder and where they are unable to make a determination they shall notify the right holder who may then resort to other remedies such as filing a civil action.

3. Criminal procedures

Trademark counterfeiting, sale of commodities bearing counterfeited trademark and illegal manufacture of representations of trademark, sale of the illegally manufactured representations of trademark are the three crimes codified by the Chinese Criminal Law. A convicted person under each of these crimes can be sentenced to imprisonment of up to seven years or criminal detention, and he or she may in addition or separately be sentenced to pay a criminal fine.

SELF QUIZ: Indicate whether each of the following statements is true or false.

31. Passing off is a US legal doctrine often used to protect unregistered trademarks.

32. If you have a registered mark, you have the legal right to take action only against one who uses your mark or a similar mark on the same goods and services.

33. In China a mark has to be visual to be registrable.

34. Trade dress with particular function is not likely to be protected.

35. Marks which indicate the content or nature of goods or services may be rejected for registration.

36. Only registered trademarks can be protected by law.

37. Suggestive marks cannot be registered until they acquire secondary meaning.

38. Descriptive marks will not be protected.

39. Even the most distinctive fanciful marks can become generic and thus not protectable.

40. In China the applicants do not need to show use of marks when they file for trademark registration.

41. Well-known marks are those marks which are widely known by the public and which possess significant reputation.

42. Protection of well-known marks could be extended to cover company names and domain names.

43. Under the US law, the assignee of a trademark transferred independent of the goodwill associated with it would not actually acquire the rights in such trademark.

44. The plaintiff must prove that defendant's use of the alleged mark is likely to cause confusion to if he wants to win a trademark infringement claim.

45. An authorized Mercedes-Benz dealer can freely use the car's famous logo whenever it needs to.

Questions:

1. What can you do with your copyright?
2. Li Jing ("LJ"), owner of the trademark "DP", registered under Class 25 (clothing, footwear, headgear), discovered that Gao Da Shang Co., Ltd. ("GDS") was offering some of its garment products bearing the letters "DP" on both the garments and their packaging. LJ filed a civil action against GDS claiming trademark infringement. DP is (assumed to be) the abbreviation commonly known for Durable Press, a fabric treating technology extensively applied by the industry to resist wrinkle.

   Question A

   Would GDS be found infringing LJ's trademark right?

   Question B

   What defenses could GDS raise to respond to LJ's claim? How could LJ defy each of these defenses raised by GDS?

Suggested Further Readings

Nari Lee, Niklas Bruun & Mingde Li (ed), *Governance of Intellectual Property Rights in China and Europe*, Elgar, 2016.

Joshua Galgano, *Patent Reform Under the American Invents Act: Does China's Success After the 2009 Chinese Patent Reform Predict Similar Success for the U.S. Patent Regime*, 23 Transnational Law & Contemporary Problems 197, 2014.

Sunny Chang, *Combating Trademark Squatting in China: New Developments in Chinese Trademark Law and Suggestions for the Future*, 34 Northwestern Journal of International Law and Business 337, 2014.

Barton Beebe, *Shanzhai, Sumptuary Law, and Intellectual Property Law in Contemporary China*, 47 U.C. Davis Law Review 849, 2014.

Xuan-Thao Nguyen, *China's Apologetic Justice: Lessons for the United States?*, 4 Columbia Journal of Race and Law 97, 2014.

Jayanth S. Swamidass & Paul M. Swamidass, *The Trajectory of China's Trademark Systems Leading up to the New Trademark Law Taking Effect in May 2014*, 96 Journal of the Patent and Trademark Office Society 56, 2014.

Giuseppina D'Agostino, *Challenges to the Patent System*, 25 Intellectual Property Journal 57, 2012.

Wenqi Liu, *Reform of China's Copyright Legislation*, 59 Journal of the Copyright Society of the USA 842, 2012.

Index of Acronym

English Full Name	Acronym	Chinese Translation
A		
Administration for Industry and Commerce	AIC	工商行政管理局
Administrative Regulations on Foreign-Invested Banks of the PRC	FIB Regulations	《中华人民共和国外资银行管理条例》
Agreement on Government Procurement	GPA	《政府采购协定》
Agreement on Subsidies and Countervailing Measures	SCM Agreement	《补贴与反补贴措施协议》
Agreement on Technical Barriers to Trade	TBT Agreement	技术性贸易壁垒协定
Agreement on the Application of Sanitary and Phytosanitary Measures	SPS Agreement	《实施动植物卫生检疫措施协议》
Agreement on Trade-Related Aspects of Intellectual Property Rights	TRIPS	与贸易有关的知识产权协定
Agreement on Trade-Related Investment Measures	TRIMs	与贸易有关的投资措施协定
Air Waybill	AWB	空运单
Amicable Dispute Resolution	ADR	友好争议解决
Anti-Dumping Agreement	AD Agreement	《反倾销协议》
Asset Management Association of China	AMAC	中国证券投资基金业协会
B		
Berne Convention for the Protection of Literary and Artistic Works	Berne Convention	《保护文学及艺术作品伯尔尼公约》
Bilateral Investment Treaties	BIT	双边投资条约
Bill of Lading	B/L	提单
C		
Carriage and Insurance Paid to	CIP	运费和保险费付至
Carriage Paid to	CPT	运费付至
China Banking Regulatory Commission	CBRC	中国银行业监督管理委员会
China Food and Drug Administration	SFDA	国家食品药品监督管理总局
China Insurance Regulatory Commission	CIRC	中国保险业监督管理委员会

China International Economic and Trade Arbitration Commission	CIETAC	中国国际经济贸易仲裁委员会
China Trademark Office	CTMO	中国商标局
Chinese-Foreign Contractual Joint Ventures	CJV	中外合作经营企业
Chinese-Foreign Equity Joint Ventures	EJV	中外合资经营企业
Commercial Banking Law of the PRC	Commercial Banking Law	《中华人民共和国商业银行法》
Committee on Foreign Investment in the US	CFIUS	美国外资投资委员会
Convention for the Unification of Certain Rules for International Carriage by Air	Montreal Convention	《统一国际航空运输某些规则的公约》（"《蒙特利尔公约》"）
Convention for the Unification of Certain Rules Relating to International Carriage by Air	Warsaw Convention	《统一国际航空运输某些规则的公约》（"《华沙公约》"）
Convention of Contracts for the International Carrying of Goods Wholly or Partly by Sea	Rotterdam Rules	《联合国全程或部分海上国际货物运输合同公约》（"《鹿特丹规则》"）
Convention on International Multimodal Transport of Goods	United Nations MT Convention	《联合国国际货物多式联运公约》
Convention on the Settlement of Investment Disputes Between States and Nationals of Other States	Washington Convention	《解决国家与他国国民之间投资争议公约》
Copyright Law of the People's Republic of China	Chinese Copyright Law	《中华人民共和国著作权法》
Cost and Freight	CFR	成本加运费付至
Cost, Insurance and Freight	CIF	成本、保险加运费付至
Countervailing Duties	CVDs	反补贴关税
Criminal Law of the People's Republic of China	Criminal Law	《中华人民共和国刑法》
Customs Union	CU	关税同盟

D

Delivered at Frontier	DAF	边境交货
Delivered at Place	DAP	目的地交货

Delivered at Terminal	DAT	终点站交货
Delivered Duty Paid	DDP	完税后交货
Delivered Duty Unpaid	DDU	未完税交货
Delivered Ex Quay	DEQ	目的港码头交货
Delivered Ex Ship	DES	目的港船上交货
Demand Draft	D/D	票汇
Dispute Settlement Body	DSB	争端解决机构
Documentary Collection	D/C	跟单托收
Documents Against Acceptance	D/A	承兑交单

E

Electronic Data Interchange	EDI	电子数据交换
European Commission	EC	欧盟委员会
European Patent Office	EPO	欧洲专利局
European Union	EU	欧盟
Ex Works	EXW	工厂交货

F

Federal Trade Commission	FTC	联邦贸易委员会
First-Inventor-to-File	FITF	发明人先申请原则
First-to-File	FTF	先申请原则
First-to-Invent	FTI	先发明原则
Foreign Direct Investment	FDI	外国直接投资
Foreign Indirect Investment	FII	外国间接投资
Foreign Invested Entities	FIE	外商投资企业
Free Alongside Ship	FAS	船边交货
Free Carrier	FCA	货交承运人
Free from Particular Average	FPA	平安险
Free on Board	FOB	船上交货
Free Trade Agreements	FTA	自由贸易协定
Free Trade Areas	FTAs	自由贸易区
Free Trade Zones	FTZ	自由贸易试验区

G

General Administration of Customs	GAC	海关总署
General Agreement on Tariffs and Trade	GATT	关税及贸易总协定
General Agreement on Trade in Services	GATS	服务贸易总协定
General Agreements on Trade in Goods	GATG	货物贸易总协定
General Principles of the Civil Law (1986)	General Principle of Civil Law	《民法通则》

H

Hague Conference on Private International Law	HCCH	海牙国际私法协会

I

ICC Rules for Documentary Instruments Dispute Resolution Expertise	DOCDEX Rules	《解决跟单信用证争议专家意见规则》
Implementing Rules of the Patent Law of the People's Republic of China	Patent Law Implementing Rules	《中华人民共和国专利法实施细则》
Individual Industrial and Commercial Households	IICH	个体工商户
Initial Public Offering	IPO	首次公开发行
Insurance Law of the People's Republic of China	Insurance Law	《中华人民共和国保险法》
Intent to Use	ITU	意图使用
Intergovernmental Organizations	IGOs	政府间国际组织
International Air Transportation Association	IATA	国际航空运输协会
International Bank for Reconstruction and Development	IBRD	国际复兴开发银行
International Center for Settlement of Investment Disputes	ICSID	国际投资争端解决中心
International Chamber of Commerce	ICC	国际商会
International Convention for the Unification of Certain Rules of Law Relating to Bills of Lading	Hague Rules	《统一提单的若干法律规定的国际公约》("《海牙规则》")

International Development Association	IDA	国际开发协会
International Finance Corporation	IFC	国际金融公司
International Institute for the Unification of Private Law	UNIDROIT	国际统一私法协会
International Monetary Fund	IMF	国际货币基金组织
International Standard Banking Practice	ISBP	《国际标准银行实务》
Invitation to Treat	ITT	邀约邀请
J		
Japan Commercial Arbitration Association	JCAA	日本商事仲裁协会
L		
Law of the People's Republic of China Against Unfair Competition	Chinese Competition Law	中华人民共和国反不正当竞争法
Letter of Credit	L/C	信用证
Limited Liability Company	LLC	有限责任公司
Limited Liability Partnership	LLP	有限责任合伙
M		
Mail Transfer	M/T	信汇
Ministry of Commerce	MOFCOM	中华人民共和国商务部
Ministry of Foreign Trade and Economic Cooperation	MOFTEC	对外贸易经济合作部
Ministry of Industry and Information Technology	MIIT	工业和信息化部
Ministry of Public Security	MPS	公安部
Mongolian National Arbitration Court	MNAC	蒙古国家仲裁庭
Montreal Additional Protocol Number 4	MAP 4	《蒙特利尔第4号议定书》
Most-Favored-Nation Treatment	MFN	最惠国待遇
Multilateral Investment Guarantee Agency	MIGA	多边投资担保机构
Multimodal Transport Operator	MTO	多式联运经营人
N		
National Development and Reform Commission	NDRC	国家发展和改革委员会

National People's Congress	NPC	全国人民代表大会
Non-Governmental Organizations	NGOs	非政府间国际组织

O

Ocean Marine Cargo Clause of the People's Insurance Company of China	PICC Ocean Marine Cargo Clauses	《中国人民保险公司海洋运输货物保险条款》
Organization for Economic Co-operation and Development	OECD	经济合作与发展组织
Other Duties or Charges	ODCs	其他税费

P

Paris Convention for the Protection of Industrial Property of 1883	Paris Convention	《保护工业产权巴黎公约》
Patent Law of the People's Republic of China	Chinese Patent Law	《中华人民共和国专利法》
Person of Ordinary Skill in the Art	POSITA	所属技术领域的普通技术人员
Preferential Trade Agreement	PTA	特惠贸易协定
Protocol to Amend the Convention for the Unification of Certain Rules relating to International Carriage by Air	Hague Protocol	《统一国际航空运输某些规则的公约》(1955年修订)("《海牙议定书》")
Protocol to Amend the International Convention for the Unification of Certain Rules of Law Relating to Bills of Lading	Visby Rules	《修改统一提单若干法律规定的国际公约议定书》("《维斯比规则》")
Rome Convention for the Protection of Performers, Producers of Phonograms and Broadcasting Organizations	Rome Convention	《保护表演者、音像制品制作者和广播组织罗马公约》

S

Securities Law of the PRC	Securities Law	《中华人民共和国证券法》
Special Drawing Rights	SDRs	特别提款权
Special Purpose Vehicle	SPV	特殊目的公司
State Administration for Industry and Commerce	SAIC	国家工商行政管理总局

State Intellectual Property Office	SIPO	国家知识产权局

T

Tariff-Rate Quota	TRQ	关税税率配额
Telecommunications Regulations of the PRC	Telecom Regulations	《中华人民共和国电信条例》
Telegraphic Transfer	T/T	电汇
The Harmonized Commodity Description and Coding System	HS	《商品名称及编码协调制度》
The Hong Kong and Shanghai Banking Corporation Limited	HSBC	汇丰银行
The People's Bank of China	PBOC	中国人民银行
The United States Department of Justice	DOJ	美国司法部
Trade in Services Agreement	TiSA	《国际服务贸易协定》
Trade Policy Review Body	TPRB	贸易政策审议机构
Trade Policy Review Mechanism	TPRM	《贸易政策审议机制》
Trademark Law of the People's Republic of China	Chinese Trademark Law	《中华人民共和国商标法》
Trademark Review and Adjudication Board	TRAB	商标评审委员会
Trans-Pacific Partnership Agreement	TPP	《跨太平洋伙伴关系协定》
Transatlantic Trade and Investment Partnership	TTIP	《跨大西洋贸易与投资伙伴协议》

U

UNCTAD/ICC Rules for Multimodal Transport Documents	UNCTAD/ICC MT Rules	《联合国贸易和发展会议/国际商会多式联运单证规则》
Understanding on Rules and Procedures Governing the Settlement of Disputes	DSU	《关于争端解决规则与程序的谅解》
Uniform Customs and Practice for Documentary Credits	UCP 600	《跟单信用证统一惯例》(2007年修订)
Uniform Foreign Money Judgments Recognition Act	UFMJRA	《1962承认外国金钱判决统一法》
Uniform Foreign-Country Money Judgments Recognition Act	UFCMJRA	《2005承认外国金钱判决统一法》

Uniform Rules for Collections	URC	《托收统一规则》
United Nations	UN	联合国
United Nations Commission on International Trade Law	UNCITRAL	联合国国际贸易法委员会
United Nations Convention on Contracts for the International Sales of Goods	CISG	《联合国国际货物销售合同公约》
United Nations Convention on the Carriage of Goods by Sea	Hamburg Rules	《联合国海上货物运输公约》（"《汉堡规则》"）
United Nations Convention on the Recognition and Enforcement of Foreign Arbitral Awards 1958	the 1958 New York Convention	《1958年关于承认和执行仲裁裁决的纽约公约》
United States Patent and Trademark Office	USPTO	美国专利商标局
V		
Value Added Tax	VAT	增值税
Variable Interest Entity	VIE	可变利益实体
W		
Wholly-Foreign Owned Enterprise	WFOE	外商独资企业
WIPO Copyright Treaty	WCT	《世界知识产权组织版权条约》
With Particular Average	WPA	水渍险
World Customs Organization	WCO	世界海关组织
World Intellectual Property Organization	WIPO	世界知识产权组织
World Trade Organization	WTO	世界贸易组织

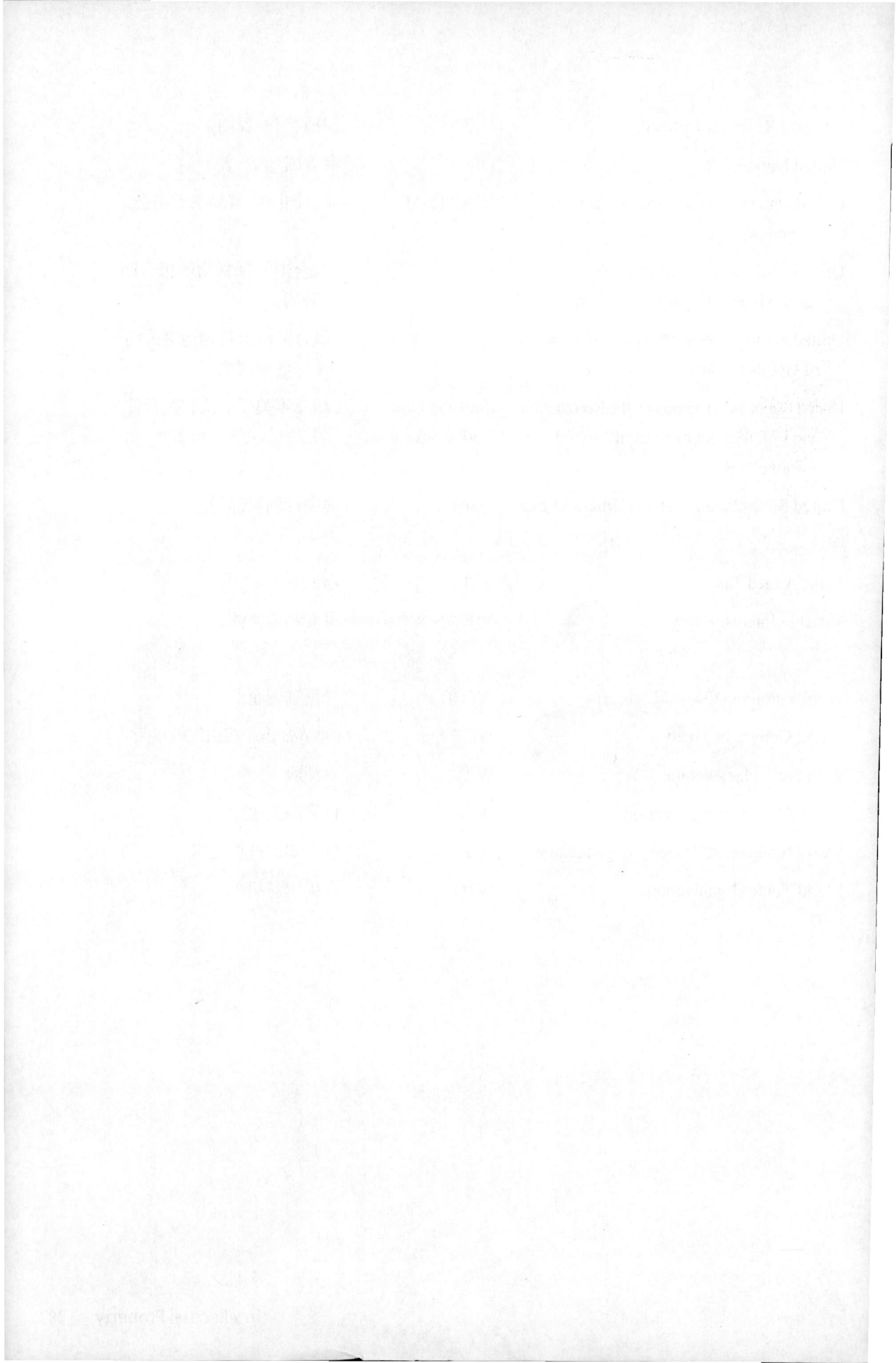